Patricia L. Scharer, Editor

RESPONSIVE LITERACY

A Comprehensive Framework

SCHOLASTIC

Photos ©: cover top left and 33: Jack Hollingsworth/Getty Images. Additional classroom photography by James D. DeCamp.

Pages from *I'll Wait, Mr. Panda* by Steve Antony copyright © 2016 by Steve Antony. Used by permission of Scholastic Inc. and Hodder Children's Books, an imprint of Hachette UK. Pages from *Aaron and Alexander* by Don Brown copyright © 2015 by Don Brown. Used by permission of Roaring Brook Press, an imprint of Macmillan Children's Publishing Group. Pages from *My Loose Tooth* by Gaynell R. Jamison, *Wishy-Washy Sleep* by Joy Cowley, *Butterfly* by Lee Waters, *Wishy-Washy Ice Cream* by Joy Cowley, *Animals Everywhere* by Susan Bennett-Armistead, Ph.D., and *Growing Things* by Susan Bennett-Armistead, Ph.D. copyright © by Hameray Publishing Group. Used by permission of Hameray Publishing Group. "Fountas and Pinnell Systems of Strategic Actions" from *Guided Reading: Responsive Teaching Across the Grades*, Second Edition by Irene C. Fountas and Gay Su Pinnell copyright © 2017 by Irene C. Fountas and Gay Su Pinnell. Used by permission of Heinemann. "Planning Guide for Scaffolding Book Introductions" by Mary D. Fried from *Teaching for Comprehension in Reading*, Grades K–2 by Gay Su Pinnell and Patricia L. Scharer copyright © 2003 by The Ohio State University Literacy Collaborative. Used by permission of Scholastic Inc. Pages from *Zoo Animals*, *Three Little Pigs*, *Growing a Pumpkin*, *Trucks*, *Look at Me!*, *My Backpack*, *Home Sick*, *Be Careful!*, *Cats Are Hunters*, *Mugs Indoors and Outdoors*, *My Brother's Motorcycle*, *Clickety-Clack*, and *Our Favorite Snowman* copyright © The Ohio State University Literacy Collaborative. Used by permission of The Ohio State University Literacy Collaborative. All rights reserved.

Publisher/Content Editor: Lois Bridges
Development Editor: Raymond Coutu
Production Editor: Danny Miller
Editorial Director/Video Editor: Sarah Longhi
Editorial Assistant Manager: Suzanne Akceylan
Cover Designer: Kyle Kirkup
Interior Designer: Maria Lilja

ISBN-13: 978-1-338-24562-2
ISBN-10: 1-338-24562-7

3 4 5 6 7 8 9 10   106   26 25 24 23 22 21

Gay Su Pinnell

The Literacy Collaborative educators dedicate this book to Dr. Gay Su Pinnell. We offer this "found poem" from words we used to describe Gay and her efforts to provide the very best literacy learning possible for all children. She founded Literacy Collaborative at The Ohio State University and is the guiding light of all that we do.

Gay Su Pinnell: A Champion for Children

Quiet, dedicated, hard-working force
Works tirelessly

A Champion for Children

Generous   sharing ideas   giving time
Lifetime of contribution
So we may all make a greater difference in the literate lives of children

A Champion for Children

Helps us understand   that literacy enriches inner lives
Helps us understand   how theory underpins the decisions teachers and coaches make
Helps us understand   that getting the most out of life isn't about how much you keep for yourself but
                      how much you pour into others

A Champion for Children

Provides
        sure foundations for achievement
                space for teachers to communicate and collaborate
                        "just the right words" that clarify and expand our teaching moves

A Champion for Children

Gay Su Pinnell's life work has positively changed the life trajectories of children and teachers around the world.

Patricia L. Scharer

A dynamo of determined dedication, Pat is the hardest worker we know. She is a visionary who has an uncanny ability to make things happen, and is constantly moving Literacy Collaborative forward. Because of her unwavering belief in our project and a commitment to promoting literacy understandings, we have been the recipients of countless opportunities for growth.

From teacher to leader, Pat is an inspiration—an example of the professional we all strive to be. She makes us want to be better coaches and teachers, and makes us believe we can do anything, even when the task seems impossible. She stays alongside us to encourage, support, and forever fight for children and teachers.

Through all of this, Pat remains foremost a passionate teacher whose influence on learners cannot be measured. She empowers children, students, and literacy colleagues to strive for the best through her gentleness, determination, and encouragement. Because of this, her work touches so many. Pat has carried the literate lives of children, teachers, and literacy coaches close to her heart throughout her journey in education. We are most fortunate to have the opportunity to journey with Pat along the way, being forever changed, both personally and professionally. We are so appreciative of her positive, skillful leadership with Literacy Collaborative and her commitment for this important work we do.

Thank you, Pat, for your generous impact on our work and our lives!

—Literacy Collaborative Trainers and Staff
at The Ohio State University

LITERACY COLLABORATIVE

This book is authored by educators who all work within Literacy Collaborative at The Ohio State University. Many provide professional development for teachers and travel to schools across the country supporting coaches implementing comprehensive literacy. Their goals are not only to teach students to read and write but also for those students to become lifelong readers and writers. The authors of these chapters are learners who read widely, discuss deeply, and work very hard to support teachers providing high-quality classroom literacy instruction, individualized according to student needs, using the very best children's literature across the language and literacy framework. For more information about Literacy Collaborative, visit www.lcosu.org or see the appendix.

Authors

JONATHAN BAILEY is a Senior Systems Manager at The Ohio State University. A particular focus of his work with the Literacy Collaborative has been instructional technologies and digital media that trainers and schools can use to better implement the Literacy Collaborative framework.

ROBERT S. DREWRY is a literacy specialist for grades 5–8 at The Joseph Sears School in Kenilworth, Illinois. His dissertation research described the vocabulary selections and explanations intermediate Literacy Collaborative teachers made when planning for Interactive Read-Alouds.

MARY D. FRIED has contributed to the development of three early literacy projects at The Ohio State University: Reading Recovery, Literacy Collaborative, and the school-to-home KEEP BOOK project for over 30 years. Most recently she received, along with three colleagues, the ILA Dina Feitelson Research Award for a study published in *Reading Research Quarterly*.

JUSTINA M. HENRY is a former classroom teacher, Reading Recovery teacher leader, and Literacy Collaborative Trainer. She also served as an associate editor for *The Reading Teacher*, a journal of the International Literacy Association.

DAVID HENSINGER is an instructional coach at Northwood Elementary in Marysville, Ohio. He has worked as a fourth grade teacher, Reading Recovery teacher, building Literacy Collaborative coach, Literacy Collaborative Trainer, and a building principal at Edgewood Elementary.

JASON HILLMAN is an award-winning educator who worked as Executive Director of Literacy Collaborative, Reading Recovery, and KEEP BOOKS before returning to Wyoming to be an elementary principal. He is an expert in Professional Learning Communities and a frequent speaker at conferences and districts across the country.

SHERRY KINZEL is a Literacy Collaborative Trainer at The Ohio State University. Sherry supports teachers, coaches, and administrators in developing their capacity to work collaboratively to create a rich literacy environment and provide best practice in classrooms.

MARSHA LEVERING is the Executive Director of Reading Recovery, Literacy Collaborative, and KEEP BOOKS. She is a former teacher, elementary administrator, and Literacy Collaborative Trainer for primary and intermediate at The Ohio State University.

CAROL A. LYONS is professor emeritus from The Ohio State University, where she worked as a Reading Recovery Trainer and wrote many books and research articles on early literacy, professional development, school change, and brain research.

JENNY McFERIN is a primary Literacy Collaborative Trainer at The Ohio State University. She has worked as a classroom teacher, Reading Recovery teacher, and literacy coach. Jenny enjoys working with children, teachers, and administrators to improve literacy learning.

LYNDA HAMILTON MUDRE is a former Literacy Collaborative Trainer, Reading Recovery teacher, author, reading specialist, and primary grade teacher. Her professional interests include early literacy, literacy coaching, and teacher professional development.

LISA PINKERTON is a Literacy Collaborative and Reading Recovery Trainer at The Ohio State University. She is passionate about the literacy rights of students and is an avid reader; she can often be found putting books in the hands of children and teachers.

GAY SU PINNELL is professor emeritus from The Ohio State University. where she was instrumental in developing Reading Recovery, Literacy Collaborative, and KEEP BOOKS to support early childhood literacy. With coauthor Irene Fountas, she has written many professional books and designed programs that define and promote exemplary literacy instruction.

DENISE ROWE is a District Literacy Collaborative Trainer for Newark City Schools. Her passion for Literacy Collaborative began in 1999 when she was trained as a classroom teacher in Newark. This passion is now being shared with other classroom teachers and coaches.

PATRICIA L. SCHARER is a professor of education at The Ohio State University. She is a Literacy Collaborative Trainer, a Reading Recovery Trainer, and author of many books, book chapters, and research journal articles about early literacy and children's literature.

SHELLY SCHAUB is a Literacy Collaborative and Leveled Literacy Intervention Trainer at The Ohio State University. She has worked as a classroom teacher and literacy coach in urban and suburban districts in the central Ohio area.

WENDY SHEETS is a Literacy Collaborative Trainer at The Ohio State University, where she provides professional development for teachers, literacy coaches, and literacy leadership teams. Her experience includes classroom teaching, coaching, and Reading Recovery training.

CARLA STEELE is a Literacy Collaborative Trainer at The Ohio State University, where she continues to share her passion for literacy teaching and learning. She is Reading Recovery trained and has experience as a classroom teacher, Literacy Collaborative district trainer, and elementary curriculum/assessment director.

BARBARA JOAN WILEY is a former Literacy Collaborative Trainer at The Ohio State University. She feels that the best part of her job was visiting teachers and writing about what she learned.

NIKKI WOODRUFF is a Literacy Collaborative Trainer at The Ohio State University. Her professional experiences include primary classroom teaching and working with struggling readers as a Reading Recovery and Leveled Literacy Intervention teacher.

Contents

ACKNOWLEDGMENTS

Appreciation must first go to the Literacy Collaborative team of trainers at The Ohio State University who, when asked about doing this book, responded enthusiastically by immediately naming the book chapters they would write. Readers will recognize both their enthusiasm and the depth of their knowledge in every chapter. Next comes our fantastic support staff: Diann Guy, Desiree Crownover, Jonathan Bailey, Jeanette Montoney, and Leah Burch. Their talents and support are essential for everything that we do from professional development to writing a book. The beautiful photographs readers will enjoy in this book came from many sources, with special thanks to Jonathan Bailey, James D. DeCamp, and Tammy Dean.

We are so thankful for our wonderful editor, Lois Bridges, who first brought the idea of a book on comprehensive literacy to us. She was much more than an editor on this project, she was a valued partner working right alongside us as the book came to life. Her support, thoughtfulness, and creativity has truly brought a germ of an idea to fruition. The final version of this book would not have been possible without the talents of many other people at Scholastic: Sarah Longhi, Editorial Director; Brian LaRosa, Art Director; Danny Miller, Production Editor; Maria Lilja, Graphic Designer; Suzanne Akceylon, Editorial Coordinator; Shelby Hast, Permissions; Justine Ciovacco, Director of Proofreading; William Turoczy, Production Manager; Pam Parker, Marketing Director; and Megan Bedell, Senior Marketing Manager. This team worked together seamlessly to design and publish an attractive book to support educators implementing comprehensive literacy instruction K–6. We are very thankful for their many talents, kindness, and assistance.

This book was made possible by the efforts of many educators who were willing to share their classrooms with us to learn, to photograph, and to document student learning. We truly appreciate their willingness to work with us in so many ways. Thanks goes to the teachers at New Albany Plain Local Schools: Amanda Coe, Cheree Kirven, Erin Heiing, Missy Mackey, Jen Thompson, Tara McCloud, Linda Derrow, Natalie Weitz, Michelle Kuebler, Kara Kent, Diana Smith, Sara Rex, and Cary Ballard. So many teachers and students were willing to share projects, student work, and classrooms with us: Mary Taylor, Angie Chandler, Amy Harrison, Sandy Monroe, Beth Cummings, Jamie Barrows, Allison Dietsch, Lindsey Rindfuss, Susan Duke, Kristy Staten, Juakita Bowens, Katie Mount, Aprille Hurst, Jennifer Holbrook, Erica Miranda, Amy McCullough, Stephanie Simmons, Abigayle McFerin, and Leslie Gillespie.

The teachers and students at Ohio Avenue Elementary School in Columbus City Schools welcomed us for a photo shoot: Johari Mitchell, Jacqueline Hurwitz, Sonja Johnson, Marisa Cassette, Trina Marion, Jessica Bedra, and Myra Syfax. We also went to Hillview Elementary School in Newark, Ohio, thanks to Denise Rowe, Nick Myers, Amy Cox, Tami Loughman, Stephanie Simmons, Megan Murphy, Kate McLaughlin, Carrie Griffith, and Amber Powers. The teachers and students at Zane Grey Elementary and Intermediate Schools in Zanesville, Ohio, also welcomed us to take photographs: Tara Neptune, Megan Witucky, Mark Stallard, Megan Moore, Whitney Newsom, Sarah Gantzer, Emily Brady, Clay Lawyer, Kathy Stilwell, Ashley Lucas, Heather Ward, Amanda Hitchcock, Kelly Morrison, Beth Hickman, and Alan Higgins.

The chapters in this book are firmly positioned within Dr. Marie Clay's reading and writing processing theory as evidenced in her design of Reading Recovery®, which was further expanded into elementary and middle school classroom teaching by Drs. Gay Su Pinnell and Irene Fountas. Their work has truly made a difference in the lives of teachers and students.

Special thanks goes to our families for their willingness to endure late dinners, missed events, late nights, and deadlines so we could complete this book.

FOREWORD BY GAY SU PINNELL

This book is about school—the place where almost all of us learned some very important lessons about life. We learned to be part of a group and to work together with others; we learned to be kind and friendly. We learned to follow directions and to manage ourselves within a large group in a small room. We learned that you have to share. And we learned that language is powerful. It brings pleasure, excitement, and a way to express what we think. We learned to become literate human beings—and to know that reading, writing, thinking, and talking are an integral and necessary part of life.

The family is, of course, the primary influence on the child. But the writers of this book recognize the profound influence of the school, where children spend six to seven hours, five days a week, ten months of the year in a randomly formed group of 25 to 30 individuals, in a relatively small space, with one leader—you, the teacher. For ten months you are responsible for helping your students to live literate lives. The authors share their theoretical learning and their practical experience in a teacher-to-teacher dialogue that will help you think through your classroom story and extend your own learning.

The chapters in this book are based on the writers' study of research and theoretical material published by other scholars. But these chapters are also based on the years of dedicated practice these educational leaders have spent learning from teachers and honing their craft. The topics range from the very practical aspects of classroom management (after all, 25 to 30 people cannot work together daily in a small space without self-regulation) to the exciting and very rewarding evidence of learning in reading, writing, vocabulary, and scientific inquiry.

No aspect of literacy education is unimportant. The volume addresses handwriting, vocabulary, phonics, the writing process, the use of data, guided reading, shared reading, scaffolding the first reading of a book, shared and interactive writing, writing about reading, and others. The goal of all of the instructional practices described here is joyful independent reading and writing, as well as deep thinking and rewarding talk about students' thinking. The volume emphasizes coherence, the hallmark of effective literacy education.

The examples throughout this book are authentic, drawn from the classrooms of excellent teachers who are continually learning. The final section of the book presents those who are educators as learners, discussing coaching, professional development, and the important role of the principal. Overall, these writers represent a learning community, an example of researchers, authors, and teachers who work together and, in the process, increase their own expertise. And in their daily work, they foster a similar culture in the schools they support.

Welcome to the Comprehensive Literacy Classroom!

Patricia L. Scharer with Carla Steele, Shelly Schaub, and Jonathan Bailey

The six color-coded sections of this book represent the essential components of responsive literacy organized around a comprehensive framework: professional learning, organizing for learning, reading, writing, building blocks of language, and learning community. The colors for each section are then echoed on the edge of the pages so you can find topics easily.

Our goal was to create a reader-friendly book brimming with illustrative photographs, easy-to-navigate charts, and essential understandings to support professional learning and student achievement.

Let's take a closer look now at each section. While there is a logical sequence to this book, you can also study sections one at a time depending on your needs and interests.

Section One: Professional Learning

The first five chapters of this book are labeled as Professional Learning because the content of these chapters reflects core beliefs we share that influence every chapter that follows. We believe in the importance of oral language, the essential role of children's literature, and the connection between teachers' actions and their students' emotional well-being and literate identity. These core beliefs are carefully examined in Section One and then woven throughout the rest of the book.

The design of the book assumes that educators will work together to read the chapters, discuss the impact of new learning in their classrooms, and participate in the suggestions for professional learning at the end of each chapter. Lifelong learning is the goal for all educators affiliated with Literacy Collaborative at The Ohio State University.

We believe that oral language is truly the foundation for comprehensive literacy. In Chapter 1, Gay Su Pinnell challenges the notion that a "quiet classroom is a good classroom" and argues, instead, for intentional instructional decisions that foster discussion and develop a literate environment in the classroom. For example, these two girls are learning about words, making decisions, and creating a rationale for those decisions as they work together to sort the words into categories. The boys are sharing their favorite books. Such small-group activities are found across the literacy block as the room quietly "hums" with literacy discussion and learning. And, in large-group meetings, the voices of students are also heard as the teacher invites discussion during Interactive Read-Aloud or shared reading.

Learners sharing their thinking together

Children's literature is the focus in Chapter 2 as Patricia Scharer helps you think about comprehension via a literary lens that helps foster understanding of texts and an appreciation for the craft of authors and illustrators. The comprehensive literacy classroom must be rich with quality books and opportunities for students to read, discuss, and write about books.

Inviting and organized classroom library

Books We've Shared anchor chart

Both oral language and children's books are found in Chapter 3 as Shelly Schaub introduces you to a range of instructional contexts found in comprehensive literacy classrooms. These are classrooms where students know that their role is to read and write extensively every day and where teachers have established rich opportunities for that to happen. For example, a circular rug is used daily for independent reading, book discussions, and whole-class meetings about reading and writing as described in this chapter.

Environment: areas for large-group, small-group, and individual study

Chapter 4 by Carol A. Lyons and Chapter 5 by Wendy Sheets are important reminders that everything we say and do as teachers can affect a child's emotional health and literate identity. The authors remind us that when students find tasks too difficult, the brain is affected, making learning impossible. Developing a student's identity as a reader and writer is just as important as helping them read increasingly more difficult texts.

Section Two: Organizing for Learning

The chapters in Section Two focus on the classroom environment and routines which make independent learning possible so that the teacher can work with individuals and small groups of students with similar needs. In Chapter 6, Justina Henry, Barbara Joan Wiley, and Shelly Schaub focus on how one teacher established routines in her primary classroom so students knew how to use activities such as their browsing boxes, Writing Center, Listening Center, Reading Center, and Word Study Center to experience authentic reading and writing tasks independently.

Individual browsing boxes for independent reading and Writing Center

Listening Center

ABC/Word Study Center

In Chapter 7, Shelly Schaub and Denise Rowe explain how second-grade students develop stamina to read and write for increasingly long periods of time independently as they transition to Reading Workshop in grades 3 and beyond. Anchor charts are created during whole-class mini-lessons as the students learn how to make good decisions about choosing books from the class library to read during Reading Workshop.

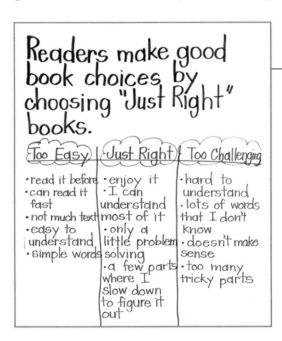

Anchor chart

Whole-group meeting area for reading and writing mini-lessons, Interactive Read-Aloud, and group share

Chapter 8, authored by Sherry Kinzel and Wendy Sheets, offers 30 days of mini-lessons including examples of teacher language to support each lesson and anchor charts. Mini-lesson #1, for example, is about teaching the class how to select and return books to the right bin to keep the classroom library well organized according to genre, topics, and author/illustrator. The instructional content of mini-lessons may last one day or several depending on the students' needs, but all lead to establishing routines supporting independent reading and writing.

Inviting classroom library organized by genres, authors, and topics

Readers choose books based on their interests during independent reading

Readers proofread their response letters so others may easily understand what they have written.

{ Proofreading Your Response Letter }

▸ Reread your letter to be sure it makes sense
▸ Be sure you have responded to what the teacher wrote to you
▸ Check for the date, greeting, body, closing, and signature
▸ Check your spelling, capitalization, and punctuation

Charts with mini-lessons

Independent reading and writing about reading

Section Three: Reading

Chapter 9 by Lisa Pinkerton introduces readers to the daily Interactive Read-Aloud, celebrated in every comprehensive literacy classroom. The chapter emphasizes how to carefully select a book and prepare for this whole-class learning experience, a powerful learning time as students share their thoughts before, during, and after the reading. Later, teachers may choose to use some of these books as mentor texts in writing mini-lessons. You will find an extensive list of recommended books at the back of the book.

Interactive Read-Aloud

The next two chapters in this section focus on ways to support readers' phrasing and fluency. In Chapter 10, Andrea McCarrier writes about supporting fluency during Interactive Read-Aloud, shared reading, guided reading, and independent reading. In Chapter 11, Patricia L. Scharer focuses on shared reading, reminding us that students of all ages can benefit from shared readings of books, poems, charts, and other texts. Both chapters emphasize the importance of fluency relative to comprehension and text interpretation.

Shared Reading

Next, in Chapter 12, Sherry Kinzel writes about the crucial role of data analysis to make instructional decisions. You will learn about Evan as a reader by analyzing his reading records so that the teacher knows exactly what Evan already understands and what he is ready to learn next. Data analysis is also a central part of Nikki Woodruff's Chapter 13 on Guided Reading. Key to this chapter is how teachers can support students' strategic actions, which leads to deeper understanding and higher achievement. Chapter 14 by Mary Fried demonstrates how to think about the book introduction when working with young readers to scaffold their learning and ensure success.

The u-shaped table in the picture below is organized for the day with the first set of guided reading books carefully selected and the notebooks holding running records and other student data gathered daily. Of course, schools must have a well-stocked collection of guided reading books so that teachers can choose that "just right" text for each group.

Environment: small-group meeting area

Meeting students' instructional needs during guided reading

School book room with a variety of genre and text types organized by level and clearly labeled

Section Four: Writing

Chapter 15 by Jenny McFerin and Nikki Woodruff details learning to write through interactive writing. This is a time to slow down the writing process and share the pen with students to work together to create a message and write the message as students contribute what they know about letters, sounds, and words during the writing. In Chapter 16, Sherry Kinzel offers multiple ways to collect assessment information about students as writers to inform instruction decisions. As you'll see in Chapters 17 and 18, such assessment is the basis for teacher decisions during Writing Workshop in the primary grades described by Jenny McFerin and in the intermediate grades written by Wendy Sheets.

You will find similarities across the two chapters in terms of creating mini-lessons, establishing routines for independent writing, conducting student conferences, and sharing. Writing Workshop begins with a mini-lesson on the writer's craft, a convention, or procedure, chosen by the teacher based on the needs of the class. Students then collect their writing materials and work on drafts of their writing while the teacher confers individually or pulls a small group together for some focused instruction. The workshop always ends with several students sharing their writing with the class.

Writing about reading through interactive writing

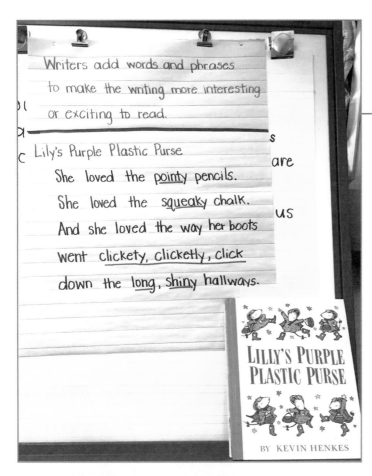

Writers add words and phrases to make the writing more interesting or exciting to read.

Lily's Purple Plastic Purse

She loved the pointy pencils.
She loved the squeaky chalk.
And she loved the way her boots
went clickety, clicketly, click
down the long, shiny hallways.

LILLY'S PURPLE PLASTIC PURSE
BY KEVIN HENKES

Writing mini-lesson anchor charts constructed with students serve as visual mediators for independent learning

Independent writing

Independent writing

Writing conference

Conferring with
readers and writers

Section Five: Building Blocks of Language

Chapter 19 opens Section Five with an overview of phonics and word study by Carla Steele, Patricia Scharer, and Denise Rowe. The authors describe this essential component of the comprehensive literacy classroom in two important ways—1) explicit; and 2) embedded. Both instructional approaches are based on analysis of student data. Explicit word study occurs in large- or small-group settings; embedded word study is found across the framework in contexts such as guided reading, interactive writing, and independent writing.

Whole-group word study

Explicit word study block— phonics, spelling, and vocabulary are also embedded throughout the framework

In Chapter 20, Rob Drewry shares insights into increasing students' vocabularies by "vocabularifying" your classroom and developing word consciousness. Gay Su Pinnell and Lynda Mudre close this section with Chapter 21, discussing the importance of explicitly teaching handwriting so students know how to efficiently and legibly make letters and words to facilitate their writing.

Section Six: A Learning Community: Students, Teachers, Principals, and Families

We close this book with a celebration of learning communities and their role in supporting reading and writing achievement. First, in Chapter 22, we examine how each classroom community can use inquiry to learn about working together to explore a topic through reading and writing. Sherry Kinzel, Wendy Sheets, and Carla Steele offer examples of inquiry into genre, famous people, and other topics that engage student interest. Such studies not only develop stronger classroom communities but also provide important authentic opportunities for reading and writing.

Science inquiry interactive writing

John McCarrier and Gay Su Pinnell explore the school-home connection and the importance of home libraries in Chapter 23. John writes about the KEEP BOOKS he has authored and how he talks about his writing with students during author visits. The children in the picture below are enjoying their KEEP BOOKS at school. The books go home with the children to ensure that they have books to read, enjoy, and learn from with their families.

KEEP BOOKS
for independent
reading

Coaching conversation

Literacy team

In Chapter 24, Marsha Levering explores reflections as a coach, staff developer, and teacher, helping you think about how such collegial reflection can support teacher development and student achievement. Through joint inquiry, teachers and coaches can work together analyzing data and planning lessons to maximize student learning.

The last two chapters, 25 and 26, are written by two principals, David Hensinger and Jason Hillman. Both have important ideas about how to develop a school-wide community which supports comprehensive literacy through shared decision-making, self-evaluation, and celebrations of learning.

Readers will find book lists and helpful documents in the appendix and also online, in addition to instructional videos, at Scholastic.com/RLResources.

Happy reading!

Patricia L. Scharer

SECTION ONE:
PROFESSIONAL LEARNING

Professional videos and downloadables are available at Scholastic.com/RLResources

CHAPTER 1

Oral Language as a Foundation for Literacy Learning

Gay Su Pinnell

> **"**Hug your children by surrounding them with love and language. Talk is the road that leads to reading and changes lives.**"**
>
> **—Adria Klein**

Throughout our lives, oral language is our vehicle for communicating and constructing meaning. It pervades every human activity and is essential for making social connections and forming communities. Adults in a community pass on critical understandings and cultural values to the young, largely through oral language. Oral language is essential for human survival.

Oral language takes many forms. In some settings, language may be elaborate, for example, in storytelling or rich description. In other settings, language may be spare but include nonverbal elements and demonstrations. The gestures we make, for example, while nonverbal, are part of the oral communication system.

Oral language always adjusts itself to the purpose and the setting. Yet, across all of its variations, there is great similarity. All registers (variations) just described and dialects (regional variations) of English are mutually intelligible. And, that is true of many, but not all, other languages students may bring to the school setting. Oral language creates human connections. It is the most powerful human tool. It is how we create our world and, in turn, it shapes us as thinkers and doers.

In this chapter, I briefly describe the language system and the enormous amount of language learning that children bring to the task of becoming literate. They learn much about language before they even begin to connect it with written signs. I'll then examine how oral language is a critical learning support across contexts for learning to read and write.

Oral Language as a System

You can think of language as an integrated set of three huge and complex systems—phonological, syntactic, and semantic (Harris & Hodges, 1995). This is true for all languages.

A Phonological System

The phonological system is the *sound system* of a language. The *phoneme* is the smallest unit of sound that we can identify in a word. In fact, a single *phoneme* or sound may actually have a few different "shadings" of sound, but they are close enough to be categorized as a "sound." The phoneme is the smallest unit that makes a difference in meaning. For example, one phoneme distinguishes between *meat* and *neat* or *made* and *make*. Phonemes may be harder to hear (for example the sound of /n/ in *bend*), or they may be easier to hear (for example the sound of /t/ in *cat*). In any case, several sounds, in sequence within a word, have meaning to the speakers of a language. You may have had the experience of going into an elevator where a group of people are conversing in a language you do not know. The phonemes flow around you like so much "noise," and you pay little attention. If in the midst of it, you hear a term such as *New York*, then suddenly the phonemes are clear and meaningful. Recognition of meaningful strings of phonemes is something that every speaker of a language learns.

Phonemes are very important in the education of young readers and writers. In fact, the process of becoming literate has added value in that it sharpens children's listening and speaking powers. Teachers help children say words slowly and prompt children to make the first connections between spoken words and letters (McCarrier, Pinnell, & Fountas, 2000 and Fountas & Pinnell, 2016). Teachers help children learn how to pronounce the words as accurately as possible. It is not productive to constantly correct children's everyday pronunciation of words; everyone has casual ways of speaking and no one appreciates continual correction. But teachers can easily explain that writers often say words very carefully to help them process the words while reading and spell the words correctly while writing.

When young children say words slowly, they can hear the sequence of sounds and feel the position of tongue, lips, and teeth as they say them. This process then makes it easier to connect sounds to the letters that they can write. The process is complex, because children must not only hear the phonemes but think about how the letters look as well as about the directional movements needed to write them (see Chapter 21: Learning About, From, and Through Handwriting).

Young children acquire the phonology of the language they speak. Many learn the phonology of several languages when they are young and very flexible in the sounds that they can make. So, some fortunate individuals can speak two or more languages and sound almost like native speakers. Many of us in the U.S. learned languages as adults; in this case, it is very difficult to speak the second language without an accent. Why? Because while we may be highly accurate, we have difficulty representing the phonology as natural speakers do automatically.

A Syntactic System

As important as phonology is, we must examine the syntactic and semantic systems to understand the full power of oral language. The *syntactic* system (or syntax of language) refers to the way words are arranged according to rules. Here we do not mean "correct grammar rules," although there is a relationship between syntax and grammar. Rather, it is simply the case that language is very predictable. We do not have an infinite number of ways that words can be strung together in phrases and sentences and still make sense. *To the river* cannot be *river the to*. It can be *river to the* only when surrounded by a grammatically constructed sentence, such as in *We went over the river to the island*.

All speakers learn these rules. If you think about your own learning of a new language, you realize that the hardest part was not just using your dictionary to find individual words. In fact, nouns were probably the easiest words to acquire. But putting words together in sentences with verbs and phrases—*that* was difficult! The interesting thing about your native language is that you learned the rules of syntax through interactions with other speakers; your knowledge is largely unconscious. Sometimes you cannot even say why a sentence should be organized in a certain way—you just know that it should be. This makes it very easy for you to understand and use the system. In oral language, you "parse" or process the sentence into meaningful units without effort.

Just as young children learn the sounds of language, they also learn the underlying rules of language. They rely on their knowledge of syntax as they read their first books; knowledge of language structure is clearly helpful. For example, a text may say something such as *I like peanut butter and jelly*. The first word, *I*, must be recognized by the reader, but she knows that the next word is likely to be a verb (or possibly an adverb followed by a verb, as in "*I really like …*"). She does not know *which* verb; it is still necessary to look at the letters and associate them with sounds. But the predictability is increased; the possibilities are narrowed. After reading *I like*, the readers know that there is a good chance that the next word is a noun (or perhaps a verb made into a noun with *-ing*, such as *running*). Again, the possibilities are narrowed, so the reader's use of sound-to-letter analysis is more efficient. A young reader can think whether a sentence "sounds right," meaning that she can check her reading against her knowledge of the syntactic system of language.

As readers change and grow over time, the demands of text require them to parse ever more complex sentences. The sentences are not just longer. They have embedded phrases and clauses (at higher levels, there are multiple phrases and clauses). And, they depart from the grammar of oral language, so much so that you can usually tell when a person is reading aloud instead of talking. Complex texts have complex syntax. Readers are aided by punctuation, but they must still understand the language patterns (the "rules" of the grammar). Readers build the ability to process complex language gradually over time by reading thousands of books. It helps to "lead" syntactic knowledge with an excellent Interactive Read-Aloud approach; but ultimately, readers must build a sense of written language grammar in their own heads.

> Readers build the ability to process complex language gradually over time by reading thousands of books.

Syntax is also important in writing. Here, children must compose messages, stories, and informational pieces by putting words together in sequence in rule-governed ways. Like reading, writing is much, much more than simply learning to spell some words. No amount of practice on isolated words can build a writer. The young writer must draw on everything she knows about oral language to compose a sentence that is meaningful and to hold it in memory while thinking about the individual words and how to write each of them. It helps the child to have some high-frequency words that she can write without effort. Young writers also need to learn to reread what they have written to recapture the syntax and meaning again.

As writers change and grow over time, you will find their writing becoming more complex in syntax. They need this kind of syntax to express the more complex thinking they are doing. They are aided by the models in the books they have heard read aloud and that they have read—and noticed—for themselves. They may have used a Reader's Notebook to record the language they find most effective. By using some of this language in their own writing, they internalize forms and patterns.

As we think about the resource of a child's knowledge of the syntax of oral language, we realize how important it is to make opportunities for children to expand this knowledge. For a variety of reasons, children may come to school with somewhat limited knowledge of syntax. Sentences may be short and very immature; vocabulary may need development. Oral language is a system that expands through use, so we want to give students ample opportunity to engage in conversation; and there is no better way to expand the syntactic system than reading aloud to children and discussing books (see Chapter 9: Interactive Read-Aloud: The Bedrock of the Literacy Block).

A Semantic System

It is impossible to select the most important system of a language. All languages have phonological, syntactic, and semantic systems. All systems work together to convey meaning. But the semantic system refers directly to the *meanings* or ideas in our heads, and this is the primary purpose of language. Speakers build meaning through experience and interaction. Writers have their ideas, and they map them onto a page by composing messages with acceptable syntactic patterns. The meaning system of a speaker is comprised of everything she understands. For example, think again about the sentence *I like peanut butter and jelly*. A reader who has experienced peanut butter and jelly sandwiches will have less difficulty in predicting the words *and jelly* than one who has never heard of this food item.

Written language represents oral language, so it reflects the same systems. But there are some differences between the syntax and vocabulary used in speech and those used in written language. Because written language is "frozen," it is easier to construct well-organized and complex sentences such as, *"The lake is a frozen bowl of ice," Dad remarked as he entered the cabin door and shook the white flakes off of his jacket*. Words such as *remarked* are infrequent in oral language but more common in the specialized language of books.

All language users have a lexicon, a very large oral vocabulary comprised of words they understand and use. And, as they grow in literacy learning, students continually add to their oral vocabularies but also to their reading and writing vocabularies.

But the semantic system is much more than the lexicon. It refers to the way all systems work together to communicate meaning in the language. The meaning is mapped out by putting meaningful words (understood by the speakers because of the phonemes within words) together in grammatical patterns that other speakers can understand. In the case of reading, children construct the meaning that another person has mapped out this way and, increasingly over time, bring their own interpretations to it. In the case of writing, the student is the one who creates the meaning and maps it out in meaningful words and language patterns.

Nonverbal Communication

Not only do we have the complex phonological, syntactic, and semantic systems, all of these are overlaid by nonverbal signals—gestures, facial expression, intonation, volume, and stress. Have you ever heard someone say, "It's not what she said, it's the way she said it!" That's really true. Much meaning is conveyed by the way we present oral language.

What about written language? There is no nonverbal overlay. Still, sophisticated readers can use the syntactic patterns and the meaning to "hear" that overlay and "see" it in their heads. They are aided by punctuation, but that is only part of their resource. Perhaps this is why you are sometimes disappointed when you see a movie that is based on a favorite book. Your own interpretation of the tone and body language of the characters may have been quite different because you were drawing on your own knowledge of language.

Readers grow in their understanding of the nonverbal cues and tones of language as they hear books read aloud and read them for themselves. Nonverbal cues are integral to the way language is used socially to communicate in many social contexts; the ways people produce and share meanings include these nonverbal signals. Shared reading and readers' theater can be a solid support for helping them to think deeply about the meaning of a written text and reflecting it in the voice. It's important not to accept robotic reading but to teach actively for expressive, fluent reading. Individuals often find themselves called upon to read orally, and some are quite frightened to do so; but the real reason is so they can hear that voice in their head (see Chapter 10).

> Writers develop voice over time so that whether they are writing fiction or nonfiction, they are communicating their passion for a topic.

Writers need this sense of nonverbal cues and tones of language as they work to find "voice" in their writing. It is amazing how some students can write as if they are telling a very interesting story. You can almost hear their voices. Writers develop voice over time so that whether they are writing fiction or nonfiction, they are communicating their passion for a topic.

The Child as a Language Learner

It may seem to be an overwhelming task to learn thousands of sound sequences that make up words and to develop an unconscious awareness of all of the complexities of oral language. Yet, every child, all over the world, at about the same points in time, develops language with no apparent instruction. Many scientists argue that our brains are "hardwired" to develop language, and that is a very good thing.

Children interact with people around them. They acquire words and ways of putting them together to convey meaning. Their first attempts at sentences may sound somewhat abbreviated, for example, *Me go bye-bye* or *Me go Papa*, but their meaning is crystal clear, and they do follow grammatical rules that the child internalized at the time. Similarly, two-year-old Lauren calls out, "Oh Hi Ho" when she sees The Ohio State University's marching band on television. When her mom tells her to "hold my hand," she abruptly says, "Me do it!" And, she clasps her own two hands together. Her understanding of pronouns is not quite correct, but her meaning is clear!

Notice that even in these developing, approximated sentences, words are arranged in rule-governed ways. Adults around children understand these utterances and seldom correct them, although they may expand them in reply—for example:

- *Yes, it's time to go bye-bye. Say bye-bye.*
- *You want to go with Papa? Okay, you can go with Papa.*
- *I know you can hold your own hands, but right now you need to hold my hand!*

Gradually, over time, individuals expand and expand their oral language, always moving in a rule-governed (as they currently understand it) way. Scientists hypothesize that almost every utterance represents a little experiment. The child knows she is understood when someone replies. She is part of a turn-taking, meaningful conversation, and that is inherently pleasurable. It is its own reward.

So what does this tell us about oral language? Below is a summary of some important points that can guide our examination of the developing reader and writer:

1. Oral language is a complex, integrated system with many subsystems—sound, language structure or syntax, and meaning.

2. Writers and readers use their knowledge of the sound system of language and link it with letters and letter clusters.

3. Writers and readers use their knowledge of the syntactic system of language to create and access meaning.

4. Writers and readers use their background knowledge of the world and language to create and understand texts.

5. Language is learned through use and is supported and expanded by interaction with more expert users.

6. Talking about texts is a way to expand oral language to take on the particular characteristics of written language.

7. School offers the opportunity for children to use oral language as a primary resource in becoming literate.

Oral language is even more important for emerging bilingual learners than for the rest of the students we teach. In today's schools, we have a wonderfully diverse mixture of students from different cultures and language groups. All are in the process not only of becoming literate, but also of learning all aspects of English.

Language is learned through interaction. In every setting described in the next section, we need to ensure that these English language learners have maximum opportunity to interact with the teacher and other students orally. They will listen and learn, but they will learn even more as they begin to produce a new language. Their growth will be scaffolded by the English speakers who talk with them. So, for every point in the following section of this chapter, double the effort and the explicitness for English language learners.

Supporting Oral Language Within a Multi-Text Approach

All children bring the richness of oral language to the school situation, but we must remember that they are still rapidly *learning* oral language. An important component of the curriculum is the intentional development of language. We want to support children's language across instructional contexts; and, the many different kinds of texts we use offer huge opportunities to do so. In Figure 1.1, I summarize opportunities for expanding language across five contexts: (1) Interactive Read-Aloud; (2) shared reading; (3) guided reading; (4) Writing Workshop; and (5) phonics and word study. These opportunities are especially critical for English language learners. They need rich language experiences every single day that include both the opportunity to hear and respond to language but also the opportunity to engage and participate in it.

Instructional Context	Brief Description	Opportunities to Expand Language
Interactive Read-Aloud (Chapter 9, this volume)	The teacher selects texts and reads them aloud to students. Includes extensive discussion of the text and may include drawing and writing about it.	• Provides a model of rich and complex language. • Expands knowledge and control of written language structures. • Engages students in using strategic actions and articulating understandings—inferring, synthesizing new information and ideas, and engaging in critical thinking. • Expands vocabulary used in context. • Expands content knowledge that students can bring to other reading. • Builds understandings of the characteristics of genres and gives students experience in using academic language. • Builds understanding of text structure (the way texts "work" and are organized). • Provides models of well-crafted writing that students can "borrow."
Shared Reading (Chapter 11, this volume)	The teacher reads an enlarged text to the students. They can see the print and join in on subsequent readings. Older students may read scripts or poetry in unison.	• Provides a supportive context for students to notice and use the language of texts. • Helps readers internalize new vocabulary and patterns of language syntax. • Enables students to notice and talk about text features—graphics, legends, table of contents, headings, and subheadings. • Expands readers' appreciation for aspects of language such as rhyme and rhythm. • Promotes word solving—letters, sounds, word parts, and high-frequency words. • Draws attention to interesting vocabulary and language that students can use to compose their own texts.

Instructional Context	Brief Description	Opportunities to Expand Language
Guided Reading (Chapters 13 and 14, this volume)	The teacher selects and introduces a text to a small group of readers who are similar in their level of reading development. The teacher supports students' reading of the text in a way that helps them learn and expand a range of effective strategic actions.	• Expands students' ability to use syntax and meaning to read and understand more complex texts. • Supports students' ability to take words apart, noticing meaningful units. • Provides the opportunity to extend meaning through talk, drawing, and writing. • Provides the opportunity to use academic language to talk about texts, including the characteristics of genres. • Provides the opportunity to work with words in a flexible way, noticing meaningful word parts. • Offers examples of ways to expand ideas through written language. • Provides a way for students to experience a great variety of fiction and nonfiction texts and to notice the language across texts.
Writing Workshop (Chapters 17 and 18, this volume)	This whole-class instruction involves students in the writing process from drafting to publishing. The teacher provides a mini-lesson on any aspect of writing, and students engage in independent writing of their own pieces, with the teacher conferring as needed. Mentor texts from Interactive Read-Aloud are used in mini-lessons. The workshop ends with a brief sharing of work and discoveries.	• Presents excellent examples of language through mentor texts. • Provides lessons on what writers do when they construct the language of texts. • Helps students understand genre so that they can use it to compose texts. • Demonstrates aspects of craft, such as the way a writer organizes texts (text structure) or the way ideas are supported by details. • Records language and interesting words on charts so that students can refer to them. • Helps students relate conventions such as spelling and punctuation to the meaning of the language of texts. • Involves students in the construction of text, using language structure, text organization, and vocabulary. • Helps students apply everything that has been learned about the language of texts in other instructional contexts. • Gives students the opportunity to talk about their writing with others—organization, language, word choice. • Provides ways for students to reflect on their writing and say what they have learned.
Phonics and Word Study (Chapter 19, this volume)	The teacher provides a mini-lesson on any principle of how words work; for example, phonological awareness, phonogram patterns, base and root words, affixes, or word meaning. Students engage in a practical application of the principle and then share their discoveries.	• Raises awareness of the sounds in words and the connections between words. • Helps young students see the patterns and connect words. • Helps students see words as interesting and suitable for inquiry. • Reveals the inner workings of words—bases, roots, prefixes, suffixes. • Expands vocabulary through direct teaching of synonyms, antonyms, and homonyms. • Expands vocabulary through teaching of meaningful parts of words. • Helps students apply word-solving principles in flexible ways. • Brings conscious attention to words and their meaningful parts.

FIGURE 1.1

Interactive Read-Aloud

Interactive Read-Aloud is a context in which you read aloud to students an array of specially selected and sequenced fiction and nonfiction texts. Supported by a rich text, students have the opportunity to talk about and write about a variety of topics and stories (see Chapter 9). Through Interactive Read-Aloud, students experience written language read aloud, and they enter into the complex language of texts. In every way except decoding the words, they process the text, understanding the language and engaging in a discussion of the deep meaning. They engage strategic actions:

PHOTO 1.1 Interactive Read-Aloud

- **Inferring** what the writer has implied but not stated.
- **Synthesizing** new information.
- **Predicting** what might happen.
- **Connecting** to other texts.
- **Analyzing** elements of the writer's craft.
- **Critiquing** the message or supporting details.

In the process, of course, they acquire vocabulary, and they do it in the most meaningful way, often using new vocabulary as they talk about texts. The read-aloud texts provide models of well-crafted language that students can use as models for their own writing. They can use academic language to talk about texts—character development, problem and solution, and the quality of illustrations.

Shared Reading

In shared reading, the students read together in unison, using expression to show the meaning of the text. In the process, they can internalize more complex syntax and new vocabulary. The text is enlarged so that all can see and become intimately involved with the print. Older students may have their own copies but read in chorus or parts (see Chapter 11).

PHOTO 1.2 Shared Reading

Through shared reading, students can notice features of texts; at early levels, this means noticing repetitive language and following print layout. At more complex levels, they can notice and talk about text features such as headings and labels or structures such as compare and contrast. Engaging in shared reading is as enjoyable as a sing-along. Children can develop awareness of phonological understandings such as rhyme and rhythm. Also, shared reading promotes word solving because children can attend closely to the print.

Guided Reading

Guided reading is a small-group instructional context in which the teacher convenes a group of students who are alike enough in their reading ability (based on systematic assessment) to teach in a group. The teacher selects the texts (from a leveled set), and introduces it. Then, each student reads the text individually, with occasional teacher prompting. After reading, there is a discussion of the text and the teacher can make very explicit teaching points that address any aspect of reading. One or two minutes of word work is designed to create flexibility in the way students apply word principles including connecting words and taking them apart (see Chapter 13).

Experiencing a new, more complex text every day expands students' ability to use multiple sources of information—letter/sound information, syntax, and meaning—to solving words. In addition, students expand knowledge of syntax and content. In the discussion, they have the experience of using academic language to talk about texts. Guided reading gives them daily experience in the way authors express ideas through written language and so it can contribute to their understanding and their writing.

PHOTO 1.3 Guided Reading

Writing Workshop

Writing Workshop is a dedicated time in the curriculum when students can concentrate on their own writing; nevertheless, it is a highly intentional instructional context (see Chapters 17 and 18). The teacher begins with a mini-lesson on any aspect of the writing process; often, mentor texts from Interactive Read-Aloud are used to illustrate points. Students may be asked to notice how a writer used verbs or made comparisons or showed feelings of characters. This is the ideal time to teach aspects of craft for fiction and nonfiction; and these young students have models to teach them about their own writing.

PHOTO 1.4 Writing Conference

Through Writing Workshop, students learn to relate conventions such as spelling and punctuation to the messages they want to convey. They get involved in constructing the organization of a text; this is the time that they can apply what they are learning in all the other instructional contexts—everything they have learned from the texts they have heard and read.

PHOTO 1.5 Small-group word study

Phonics and Word Study

In every classroom in a comprehensive literacy approach, students have a time in the day when the teacher explicitly explains something about language itself. That means lessons on how words work. You provide a mini-lesson on any principle. It might be letters and sounds, phonogram patterns, prefixes and suffixes, high-frequency words, etc. Words are presented in an interesting way so that students are asked to stretch their minds to notice what they can and puzzle about it. Actually, the parts of words are fascinating, and our job as teachers is to make students inquirers into words. After the mini-lesson, students apply the principle as a game or inquiry experience. Then, they share their discoveries with the class. The emphasis is on noticing patterns and structure. For example, once a young student discovers –*ing,* he's going to notice it as a part of a word or an addition to a word.

Word study expands vocabulary directly by teaching students the meaning of the building blocks of words and by helping them see patterns and connections between words. At advanced levels, they learn about Greek and Latin word roots, a life skill for deriving the meaning of words. Most importantly, it can develop lifelong curiosity about words which is a road to rich vocabulary expansion (see Chapter 19).

Conclusion

If we have to identify one foundation for literacy learning, it must be oral language. Children do not simply "practice" language; they engage in it. They use it to represent their experiences and themselves (Britton, 1970). Young children use language to take on the world, and many use it to begin the process of becoming literate long before schooling. They respond to stories and even pretend to read. They play with words and poetry. When they enter school, oral language is an even more important tool in the process of learning to be a proficient reader and writer. Language is the wind that fills the learning sail and allows the learner to stay on course. As teachers, we recognize that our language has a powerful influence on students. It tells them what we think of them as learners. And when we invite them into conversation, they become active partners in their own learning. Examples of teachers and children talking about written texts and about what it means to be a writer populate this book. As you read, take the opportunity to talk with your colleagues about this powerful process.

> Language is the wind that fills the learning sail and allows the learner to stay on course.

Suggestions for Professional Development

The most powerful way to expand oral language in every area of the curriculum is to engage children in text-based talk around a work of children's literature. Work with colleagues to create book collections that intentionally build language knowledge—you will be teaching comprehension at the same time! Gather a group of grade-level colleagues (or cross-grade-level groups) for the following activity to help teachers prepare for talking with children about books.

1. Plan a core curriculum for Interactive Read-Aloud. Meeting before school starts for the year is helpful, as is having a budget to buy some new texts. With good planning, texts can be shared across three or four teachers. If you have a school librarian, that important person should be involved in the curriculum planning. Of course, the core curriculum does not need to include every book that you and your colleagues read aloud to children. Instead, set a goal of including 20 to 30 books for this first plan.

   Examine each text for its potential in terms of the following:

   - Expanding knowledge of the syntax of written language
   - Developing vocabulary
   - Expanding content knowledge
   - Developing oral language through discussion

2. Place the texts in sequence or group them by genre, content, or style. (You may want to consider doing an author study, because that helps children notice how a particular writer uses language.) Make a brief (half-page) plan for using each text that includes an "opening" for each text (informal plan for the way you will introduce it to your class) and one or two points in the text where you will stop and ask children to "turn and talk" or make brief comments about what they have heard so far. Write one or two goals for post-reading discussion, and plan some writing or drawing exercises to extend the meaning of some of the texts.

3. Organize teachers' schedules so that each teacher can use the group of texts for about a month in the classroom. (Of course, some texts might be so important that everyone will want to have them all year!) Hold a follow-up meeting toward the end of the year to discuss the Interactive Read-Aloud program's results and to plan for next year.

CHAPTER 2

The Literary Path to Becoming a Reader and Writer

Patricia L. Scharer

> *"Hearing family stories, the luxury of dramatic play, reading, and loving books—eventually led me to my writing life and the most wonderful gift in return, readers."*
>
> **—Pam Muñoz Ryan**

When I taught first grade, my students knew that I would start reading to them as soon as they put away their coats and were seated on the carpet in our reading nook after lunch. The appeal of listening to a good book motivated them to move quickly to the carpet in anticipation of a good story. The children were as hungry for the stories as they were for lunch!

Quality children's literature is an absolute requirement for implementing comprehensive literacy instruction. Books will be found in every chapter of this book—from Interactive Read-Aloud to shared reading to mentor texts for writing and inquiry-based units. Children's literature is key to not only learning to read and write but also to truly becoming a reader and a writer. There's a difference between the two! The goals of comprehensive literacy instruction go way beyond teaching children to read and write. Rather, the goals are to develop a lifelong love of reading and writing.

In this chapter, I will explore the ways that thinking about the writer's craft and the techniques of the illustrator can influence the instructional decisions we make during Interactive Read-Aloud, shared reading, and Writing Workshop.

Exploring the Craft of Writers and Illustrators

The authors of *Charlotte Huck's Children's Literature* (Kiefer & Tyson, 2014) argue that although children are not born with literary insights in a conventional sense, their natural responses to books should be valued and encouraged because they are an important start in developing an awareness of the writer's craft. Teachers "need to value children's own interests, interpretations, and judgments. At the same time, they need to help children discover what practiced readers look for in a well written book" (p. 10) through purposeful literary study across genres beginning with the very youngest of readers. Writers use many tools while crafting their work, and it is our job to help students to understand these tools.

Plot

Often, the plot in books for children is told in a sequential, step-by-step manner as the writer describes what happens to the story's characters. For example, the plot may build toward a problem of some kind that is then resolved. The way the writer creates the plot is well worth exploring with young readers because it fosters greater understanding of writing styles and expands comprehension. Laura Joffe Numeroff, for example, employs a cyclical device in *If You Give a Mouse a Cookie*

Literary Elements and Definitions	
Plot	What happens to the characters
Setting	When and where the story takes place
Mood	How the story makes the reader feel
Theme	What the story is really about
Characterization	How the reader understands the characters' thoughts, feelings, and actions
Point of View	Who is telling the story

(1985). The story ends where it began, with the same problem at the end as at the beginning. In other stories, such as *I'll Wait, Mr. Panda* (2016) by Steve Antony, the repeated text "Wait and see. It's a surprise" helps children anticipate changes in the plot, participate in the story, and support their understanding of the story line. The young boy in *Let Me Finish!* (2016) by Minh Lê desperately wants some peace and quiet to read his book but continues to be interrupted. Readers can quickly see the pattern in the story and anticipate how the little boy will be interrupted next. The story's plot should keep the reader's interest throughout the action, challenges, and resolution of the story.

Discussing how writers achieve successful plots helps children understand the artistic devices writers use. Second graders, for example, discussed how Eve Bunting let the reader know that Timothy's Gram in *Sunshine Home* (1994) was joking when she described another resident of the nursing home by saying, "That Charlie Lutz is my destruction…he's a terrible driver. Always bumping me with his wheelchair. He shouldn't be allowed on the road." It was important that the readers did not read this comment literally, as Gram's playful attitude toward Charlie was an important element in the story's plot.

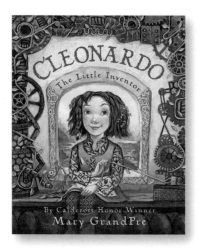

Setting

The setting of a story is often described through both text and illustrations. In the classic text, *Owl Moon* (1987), for example, Jane Yolen's opening text combines with John Schoenherr's watercolor and ink drawings to create a quiet, peaceful nighttime setting as the child and father leave the house to go owling.

Other books like *Cleonardo: The Little Inventor* (2016) by Mary GrandPré create the setting totally through the illustrations, carefully depicting long ago during the time when Leonardo DaVinci lived.

Mood

In Yolen's *Owl Moon*, the writer's and illustrator's use of poetic text and calm shades of blue and evening black contribute to the story's mood as the father and child experience both the search and the discovery of a Great Horned Owl. Similarly, the text of *Granddaddy's Turn: A Journey to the Ballot Box* (2015) by Michael S. Bandy and Eric Stein employs text like "Sometimes when I did my chores, I made so much sweat, it was like I was raining" to express the mood of the grandson as he was working alongside his granddaddy. Watercolor illustrations in deep colors by James Ransome set the mood for the day Granddaddy was denied the chance to vote because he couldn't read.

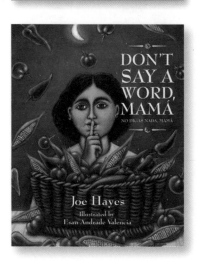

Theme

The theme of a story moves readers beyond a literal understanding to consider something even larger than the plot itself. The theme of variations of the folktale *Little Red Riding Hood* suggests that children should never talk to strangers, while the benefits of working together is the theme in a folktale such as *The Great Big Enormous Turnip*. Other themes common to children's books include growing up, overcoming fears, the importance of being a friend, and the cycle of life. Students discussing *Don't Say a Word, Mamá* (2013) by Joe Hayes may generate multiple themes of keeping a promise, sharing with others, and the importance of loving each other. Discussions identifying themes move readers' understanding beyond the literal meaning of the text and into interpretations of the text by asking, "What is this story really about?"

Characterization

Readers learn about the author's use of characterization by discussing how the text develops the qualities of each character. Teachers can begin exploring characterization by asking questions such as "How do you know that the wolf in this story is bad?" The discussion in response might center on things the wolf says, what the pigs say about the wolf, the size of the words on the page, or the menacing style of illustrations emphasizing the wolf's teeth, drooling jaws, or dangerous size. The changes in and growth of a character are also important to discuss. For example, readers should consider how the character of Miss Keller changes across the story in *An A from Miss Keller* (2015) by Patricia Polacco from a frightening, demanding teacher to a loving, supportive writing teacher.

Point of View

It is important to discuss a story's point of view from both the writer's and illustrator's perspectives. The first-person narrative, used by Jeri Watts in *A Piece of Home* (2016), tells the story of the struggles of a young boy moving to West Virginia from Korea. It's important to note as it emphasizes the feelings and point of view of the boy both in Korea and in the U.S. In *Shake a Leg, Egg!* (2017) by Kurt Cyrus, the mother goose is anxiously awaiting the hatching of her very last egg. The suspense is accentuated by close-ups of the egg surrounded by the rest of the chicks, as well as distance shots of the world awaiting the newborn.

Questions to Explore the Writer's Craft	
Plot	What did you notice about the way the writer told the story? Tell me about the problem in the story. How was the problem fixed?
Setting	Where does this story take place? How do you know?
Mood	How does this story make you feel? What does the author do to make you feel like that? Did your feelings change during the story? If so, how?
Theme	What is this story really about? What did the characters learn in the story? What can we learn from the story?
Characterization	What do you know about the characters in the story? How did you learn about them?
Point of View	Who is telling this story? How do you know?

Questions to Explore the Illustrator's Technique	
Media	How did the artist make the pictures? What materials were used? Why do you think those materials were chosen?
Format	What is special about the shape of this book or the ways the pictures are placed on the page? How do these pictures help readers understand the story?
Use of Color	Why did the artist use certain colors in the pictures?
Mood	How do the colors make you feel?
Point of View	Where are you in the story? In front of the pictures? Above? Up close? Far away? How do the pictures change? Why does this artist do that?

Format

Finally, discussing the style of illustrations and characteristics of each book's format supports young readers' understanding of the book's meaning. Why are there holes and various page sizes in Eric Carle's *The Very Hungry Caterpillar* (1969)? Why do the illustrations and white space change in size in Maurice Sendak's *Where the Wild Things Are* (1963)? Why does *Every Day Birds* (2016) by Amy Ludwig VanDerwater feature the name and paper-cut illustrations of a single bird on each page, yet the poem uses four pages for each stanza? How does the layout of the illustrations with Aaron on the left and Alexander on the right in *Aaron and Alexander: The Most Famous Duel in American History* (2015) by Don Brown support the author's use of compare and contrast in this nonfiction text? All of these questions will help children to study the intentional decisions authors and illustrators make as they create meaning through the marriage of text and pictures.

It is not necessary to use sophisticated, technical language while studying the writer's craft or illustrator's technique with students. Rather, the questions presented in the earlier charts can help them think about complex ideas without complicated language.

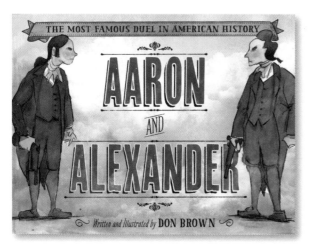

Both boys were orphans, but Aaron joined a large family that included young aunts and uncles, as well as Uncle Timothy's own children that eventually numbered fifteen.
Thirteen-year-old Alexander, on the other hand, was taken in by a generous merchant, while brother James went to live with a carpenter.

Studying Craft: Why Bother?

Decisions about the use of instruction time hinge on the value placed on the activity. If having children read books from their browsing boxes is important, there will be time for independent reading. If reading in small groups is important, there will be time for guided reading and literature discussions. The same is true for studying craft—if it is important, there will be time. Craft can be so easily integrated into interactive reading, shared reading, guided reading, and Writing Workshop. So, what are the values of studying craft—why bother?

We study the writer's craft to

- increase enjoyment
- encourage high-level thinking
- help children see connections across texts
- support personal writing

PHOTO 2.12 Classroom library organized in labeled tubs

Increases Enjoyment

Enjoyment begins with access to quality books in the classroom. Every room should have a well-stocked library with tubs of books organized by genre, author, or topic. Books should be organized in a way that it is easy to find a good book to read and also return the book when the reader has finished. Well-selected books to read aloud may send readers to find other books by the same author or on the same topic. A good book invites readers into the story and builds an appreciation for reading.

Certainly, many of the books the youngest readers find in guided reading lessons are simple, accessible texts. These texts, however, are not without literary merit. Efforts by publishers to provide interesting books for early readers have resulted in quality writing with fascinating characters, suspenseful plots, and illustrations worth exploring. In addition, lists of quality children's trade books are leveled in *Matching Books to Readers* (Fountas & Pinnell, 1999) and *Leveled Books for Readers, Grades 3–6* (Pinnell & Fountas, 2002) to support the acquisition of high-quality children's literature in paperbacks quite suitable for guided reading instruction. The quality of these books provides rich opportunities for readers of all ages to heighten their enjoyment of reading by looking carefully at the techniques used by both the writer and the illustrator.

Encourages Higher-Level Thinking

Inviting children to respond to their reading, valuing their responses, and offering interpretive questions to support further conversation ensures that children will continue to think about their reading in similarly complex ways. The discussion resulting from such instruction not only encourages higher-level thinking but also benefits children as they listen to the comments and questions of the other readers in the group.

Helps Children See Connections Across Texts

Discussing texts encourages children to think deeply as they read so they can talk about other stories that come to mind and how their knowledge of that story connects with the book they are reading. Children who first meet Joy Cowley's Greedy Cat, for example, in *Greedy Cat Is Hungry* (1997) will easily apply what they learned about the cat's personality to the more difficult text, *Greedy Cat* (1983), as Mum teaches the cat an important lesson with a pot of pepper!

Supports Personal Writing

As children openly and thoughtfully discuss the decisions writers make in their stories, the lessons will influence their own writing as they try using the writers' techniques. After reading a trio of books by Richard Byrne, *This Book Just Ate My Dog* (2014), *We're in the Wrong Book!* (2015), and *This Book Is Out of Control* (2016), writers may want to write their own book with a disappearing character or ones that move from book to book within the book itself. Or, the organization and layout of *Some Writer! The Story of E.B. White* (2016) may inspire a writer to interview a family member, collect pictures and objects representing his or her life, and design a biography in the same style as Melissa Sweet.

Studying Craft During Guided Reading

The instructional context of guided reading offers rich opportunities for calling attention to the craft of writers and illustrators. During your introduction of a new book, invite children to share their initial responses to the style of the illustrator or the topic of the book. Point out unique features of the book that readers should be thinking about while they are reading. During Nikki Woodruff's introduction to *Trash or Treasure* (Clyne & Griffiths, 1999) [Level H], Trinity, one of the first graders in the group, looked closely at the pictures and noticed the dust Mom created while cleaning house to find things to donate to the school fair. Trinity spontaneously read the speech bubble showing the little girl, Jess, saying, "Achoo." This action led to more discussion of how the dust and Mom's cleaning efforts were important parts of the story's plot, and it helped prepare the young readers for the surprise ending as Jess bought all of Mom's donations the next day at the fair.

You can plan for such introductions by thinking about the craft of the writer and illustrator and deciding on a point or two that will facilitate children's understanding while they are reading. For example, when introducing *Dad Didn't Mind at All* (Naden, 1989) [Level F] to her first graders, Sue Brown discussed the author's use of the days of the week on most of the pages as a way to describe the family's week of vacation camping at the lake. The children also talked about the author's repeated use of the refrain, "Dad didn't mind at all," by linking it with the title. The special qualities of books representing a variety of levels are shown in the chart below as examples of ways to incorporate literary elements into book introductions and discussion at the end of the lesson.

Learning About Craft During Book Introductions

Title, Author, Level	Teacher's Questions or Prompts	Craft Lesson
The Little Red Hen, Cowley, Level B	"Look for changes in the pig, cat, and dog."	• Plot changes • Use of dialogue
My Bike, Martin, Level D	"Watch for words the author repeats to help us understand when the story takes place."	• Days of the week to indicate sequence and time
Sam's Mask, Cachemaille, Level E	"Look for how the author and photographer explain the steps Sam used to make his mask."	• Links between the text and illustrations • Plot sequence
Each Peach Pear Plum, Ahlberg and Ahlberg, Level G	"What storybook characters do you notice in the illustrations?"	• Intertextual links in both the illustrations and the text
The Enormous Watermelon, Parkes and Smith, Level H	"Notice the different sizes of pages. Why do you think the illustrator did that? Be ready to talk about the pictures after you read."	• Contribution of the format of the book to meaning
Do Like Kyla, Johnson, Level I	"Think about the repetition of the title throughout the story. What makes this a good title?"	• Repeated refrain linking the plot together
Frog and Toad Are Friends, Lobel, Level K	"There is a problem in each of the five chapters of this book. Read to learn more about the characters as each of the problems is solved."	• Plot development and resolution • Characterization
George Washington's Mother, Fritz, Level M	"George Washington and his mother are the two main characters in this story. Be thinking about how they are alike and different."	• Character development • Compare/contrast writing style

After the reading, you have another opportunity to talk with students about literary concepts. First, go back to what you discussed during the introduction to see if children have further insights into how the story developed, the contribution of the illustrations, or the particular quality readers were to look for during their reading. Then open invitations can encourage children to share their initial responses. In contrast to asking children if they liked the story or other questions that inspire brief yes/no responses, these invitations are broad.

You can extend open invitations with questions such as:

- What part did you like best? Why?
- What special part do you want to talk about now?
- What other books did you think of while reading?
- How does this story compare with other books by _____?

The intent behind such open invitations is to establish the expectation that children's thoughts and feelings about what they read are important and should be shared with the group. Often, young readers' insights into texts and illustrations represent fresh, new approaches that adults have never considered. Your role at that point is to encourage open response and follow the lead of the children—supporting, encouraging, and valuing each contribution. These conversations, however, are also rich opportunities for you to extend the literary awareness of young readers by "shooting literary arrows" (Peterson & Eeds, 1990) with a well-crafted question or comment directing readers to a particular quality of the writing or characteristic of the illustrations. See the chart below for examples at various text levels.

Learning About Craft After the Reading

Title, Author, Level	Teacher's Questions or Prompts	Craft Lesson
Splish Splash!, Cowley, Level B	"Let's talk about the sounds the words make when you say, 'Splish Splash!' What other words can describe what the children did with water in this story?"	• Onomatopoeia, words that sound like what they describe
It Looked Like Spilt Milk, Shaw, Level E	"What do you notice about the pictures in this book? What was special about the ending?"	• Use of collage • Surprise ending
The Lion and the Rabbit, Randell, Level F	"What did the lion learn from his experience?"	• Theme: appreciating what you have
Greedy Cat, Cowley, Level G	"Look back through the pictures and see if you can find messages created by the illustrator. How is this book like the other stories you have read about Greedy Cat?"	• Linking with styles found in other books by the same author or illustrator
Emma's Problem, Parker, Level H	"How do the author and illustrator tell readers about when the story takes place? Why can Emma touch the branch now, but she couldn't at the beginning of the story?"	• Subtle use of the seasons and inference that Emma grew taller over time
Amazing Grace, Hoffman, Level L	"What stories did you think about while you were reading? What did Grace learn about herself?"	• Intertextual connections • Theme of achieving success with self-confidence
Anansi and the Moss-Covered Rock, Kimmel, Level M	"How did you learn about what Anansi is like? How would you describe him? What do you learn through the pictures? How Anansi talks? How the other animals talk?"	• Character development through dialogue, illustration, and narration

Studying Craft During Interactive Read-Alouds

The chart below lists recent picture books that offer many opportunities to think about craft. This list was created to explore the unique characteristics of each book and identify the "literary arrows" teachers might use as they read each book aloud to their students. Those literary arrows, listed as questions, invite children to go back into the text and illustrations to develop new, deeper insights into the meaning of the story.

An added benefit of an Interactive Read-Aloud is the fact that the discussions are likely to link with similar talk during the other components of the language/literacy framework. For example, children who are already familiar with nursery rhymes, having fully explored Mother Goose collections such as *Here Comes Mother Goose* (1999) by Iona Opie, will be able to read nursery rhymes on chart paper during shared reading with greater ease. Discussions can focus on the interpretations of the nursery rhymes as reflected in the large, colorful illustrations by Rosemary Wells compared with illustrations students make of the rhymes for their poetry notebooks. Similarly, familiarity with folktales such as Janet Stevens' *The Three Billy Goats Gruff* (1987) or Paul Galdone's *The Three Little Pigs* (1970) will support children's readings of easier variations of such stories often found in publishers' collections of little books for guided reading and support students as they write folktale variations. Introducing literary aspects of writing or illustrating during an Interactive Read-Aloud can heighten the quality of the conversation during guided reading, support students as writers, and deepen readers' understanding of both the craft and the story itself.

Recent Books to Read Aloud and Discuss

Book	Teacher's Questions or Prompts	Teacher's Questions or Prompts
The Jelly Bean Tree by Toni Yuly	**THEME:** What can we learn from this story? **CHARACTERIZATION:** What do you know about Jelly Bean from this story?	**WRITING STYLE:** Why did the author write *long* three times while describing Jelly Bean's nap? **ILLUSTRATIONS:** How do the collage illustrations relate to the meaning of the story?
Playing from the Heart by Peter H. Reynolds	**PLOT:** How did the author use words and illustrations to show the passage of time? **MOOD:** How did the author use color to show the feelings of the little boy and his father?	**WRITING STYLE:** What are your favorite words and phrases from this book?
Wet by Carey Sookocheff	**PLOT:** How does the writer explore this single word, *wet*? **CHARACTERIZATION:** What have you learned about the boy from the story?	**ILLUSTRATIONS:** What did you notice about the author's use of blue in the illustrations? **FORMAT:** Why do you think the writer chose to have this book wide and thin?
Starry the Giraffe by Andy Bergmann	**PLOT:** How did the last four pages surprise you? **THEME:** What can we learn from the giraffe in this story?	**ILLUSTRATIONS:** What do you notice about the picture of the snake that ate two apples? **FORMAT:** Why did we have to turn the book on its side to see the picture of the giraffe getting the last apple?

Recent Books to Read Aloud and Discuss

Book	Teacher's Questions or Prompts	Teacher's Questions or Prompts
Long May She Wave: The True Story of Caroline Pickersgill and Her Star-Spangled Creation by Kristen Fulton; Illustrated by Holly Berry	**PLOT:** How did the author relate the making of the flag to the Revolutionary War? **MOOD:** How did the author use color and words like *Bang! Boom! Bam!* to show the British attack?	**WRITING STYLE:** What did you notice about the author's use of the song, "The Star-Spangled Banner?" **FORMAT:** How do the dust jacket and end papers contribute to the meaning of the story?
Be Quiet! by Ryan T. Higgins	**PLOT:** How do the antics of the friends move the plot along? **MOOD:** How did the author show the feelings of the main character?	**WRITING STYLE:** What literary words did you learn from this book? **ILLUSTRATIONS:** What is the role of speech bubbles in carrying the message? **FORMAT:** How do the dust jacket and end papers lead the reader into the story? How do the final end papers contribute to the story?
Nerdy Birdy Tweets by Aaron Reynolds; Illustrated by Matt Davies	**PLOT:** How do you learn about the problem in this story? How did the friendship change over time? **MOOD:** How do the illustrations show the increased frustration of the vulture?	**ILLUSTRATIONS:** How did the illustrator use color, pictures in boxes, and close-ups to show meaning? **THEME:** What is this story really about? What can we learn?
Someone Like Me by Patricia MacLachlan; Illustrated by Chris Sheban	**SETTING:** How do you know when the setting changes? **THEME:** What can we learn from this story? **CHARACTERIZATION:** What do you know about the little girl?	**ILLUSTRATIONS:** How can you describe the illustrations, and how do they add meaning to the story?
Cecil's Pride: The True Story of a Lion King by Craig Hatkoff, Juliana Hatkoff, and Isabella Hatkoff; Photographs by Brent Stapelkamp	**SETTING:** What did you learn about the setting from the text? Photographs? Sidebars? **MOOD:** How does the color and design of the paper behind the text add to the mood? **CHARACTERIZATION:** What did you learn about Cecil from the text and photos?	**ILLUSTRATIONS:** How do the full-page photographs and the smaller sidebars contribute to the story of Cecil? **FORMAT:** How do the size of the photos add to understanding Cecil's life and death?

Conclusion

Studying the writer's craft should be a daily, natural, enjoyable shared experience between readers. At times, children may take the lead based on their personal responses to a text or something special they have noticed in it; other times, you may purposefully shoot literary arrows to stretch the thinking of the group. I am not implying that you should think of literary elements such as mood, plot, and characterization as items to "cover" in the curriculum during certain grading periods or with certain texts. Rather, literary devices are tools to help readers more fully explore the meaning of texts by studying the unique characteristics of each author or illustrator. Consider this work as a way to foster both a love of books and an appreciation for the choices writers and illustrators make, while also having fun talking about books and their creation with your students.

Lucy Calkins once spoke about the child who read Jane Yolen's *Owl Moon* straight through and simply closed the book as if to say, "I'm done. What's next?" She argued passionately that children need the influence of talented writers such as Yolen and need to approach these writers' texts with the following question in mind: "What am I dying to talk about?" Reading is much more than getting through the book, closing it, and asking, "What's next?" You can make sure that a celebration of wonderful words, delicious sentences, and amazing art is what's next—and that children approach their reading knowing that this celebration is coming.

Suggestions for Professional Development

1. Meet with other teachers to read copies of your favorite guided reading books and discuss the literary arrows inspired by the text and illustrations.

2. Review the books in your book room to see if there are collections of leveled texts in need of a higher quality of writing. Discard books with limited interest for children or poorly written text and replace with paperback collections of quality children's literature.

3. Create a school-wide chart in your book room of quality books to read aloud that are particularly good examples of literary elements such as plot, theme, mood, characterization, setting, format, or point of view. Maintain a lending collection of those books in the book room for all of the teaching staff to use.

4. Invite your colleagues to join a book club that meets several times a month to talk about new books. Write a grant for funds to provide your group with new copies of children's literature for your enjoyment, professional growth, and classroom use. Look carefully at the writers' and illustrators' craft to think about how the book's characteristics will influence your teaching. Think together about how to share each book. Later, share your students' responses to the book with the group to continue the discussion about the unique characteristics of the book and ways those characteristics can support students as readers and writers.

5. Schedule two meetings a year to read and discuss the award-winning books selected by the International Reading Association's Children's Literature and Reading Special Interest Group (SIG) and the National Council of Teachers of English, respectively. Children's Literature and Reading SIG (http://clrsig.org/) lists Notable Books for a Global Society, announced each May, and the Children's Literature Assembly's Notable Books for the English Language Arts (http://www.childrensliteratureassembly.org/notables.html) are announced each November. Both lists contain excellent books for elementary grades.

CHAPTER 3

Comprehensive Literacy Framework: An Overview

Shelly Schaub

> "The three-block framework, consisting of language and word study, Reading Workshop, and Writing Workshop, is a conceptual tool for organizing instruction. The framework is flexible, allowing numerous variations in content, student groupings, daily timeframes, and the level of teacher-directed instruction."
>
> **—The Ohio State University Literacy Collaborative**

Foundations for a Comprehensive, Balanced, and Responsive Framework

As researchers deepen our understanding of how children learn, synthesize this information with historical research, and assimilate 21st century skills, teaching practices will continue to be refined and redefined. The framework within which teachers teach language, reading, writing, and word study must provide multi-text experiences that are carefully utilized to meet the needs of each student. In *Change Over Time in Children's Literacy Development* (2001), Marie Clay states, "Constructive children use the scaffolds which teachers provide to lift their progress. It is not the parent, or the teacher, or the politician, or the administrator, or the publisher who builds the neurological power pack: that can only be done by the child" (p. 2).

A well-designed literacy framework positions students as participants in active thinking, engaging conversations, and authentic reflections about texts that are purposefully chosen to meet the variety of needs and interests of students. The foundation of these experiences begins with high-quality children's literature and a systematic way to use the literature, which includes whole-group, small-group, and individual reading and writing contexts.

While classroom designs for comprehensive literacy instruction continue to evolve, the notion of "strategic" teaching within any kind of framework design is open to a wide variety of interpretations. School administrators may require *strategic* questioning, *strategic* planning, and *strategic* response as a means of facilitating deeper understanding of abstract concepts for the ultimate goal of increasing learning and performance on standardized tests. What does it mean to be strategic? How does a teacher provide strategic instruction that meets the needs of a spectrum of learners?

Teaching For Strategic Activity

Teaching for strategic activity evolves from the understanding that children have the potential to possess a strategy, or "in-the-head neural activity initiated by the learner, and hidden from the teacher's view" to aid in problem solving (Clay, 2001, p. 128). As young children encounter the problem-solving process while reading and writing, they develop knowledge of strategic activities for maintaining meaning and problem-solving unknown words as texts become increasingly more difficult. In an attempt to explain the failure of some children to learn to read or write, Clay (1991) investigated high progress readers to determine what helped proficient readers and writers continue to make gains as a result of their own efforts. This forward thrust in reading and writing achievement has long been explained by "…phonological skills and rapidly expanding vocabulary brought about by quantity of reading" (Clay, 1991). Clay poses the question, "What is the generating power controlled by the independent reader that gives him or her such easy access to quantities of reading, and what processes does that reader need to control to get a rapid expansion of vocabulary?" (1991, p. 4) Clay looked beyond controlling letter-sound relationships and learning more words (skills) to the processes that are managed by self-extending readers (strategic activity).

THE ZONE OF PROXIMAL DEVELOPMENT

In addition to understanding the processing involved in acquiring literacy, a teacher must possess a depth of knowledge about how children learn and ensure that the framework design implemented in the classroom is grounded in a strong learning theory. According to Vygotsky's Sociocultural Theory (1962), learning alongside others plays a major role in development, leading it forward as children receive instruction from more expert others in tasks within their Zone of Proximal Development (ZPD). As a child masters a particular concept, their ZPD is expanded. An observant teacher determines what the student knows and what they need to know next in order to keep the student on the cutting edge of their learning. Additionally, it is important for the teacher to provide scaffolding within each child's ZPD.

Wood, Bruner, and Ross (1976) propose that the more capable other provides scaffolding within the child's ZPD to enable the novice to perform at a higher level. Effective scaffolding encourages the production of strategic behaviors in readers and writers. Scaffolding does not change the task, but what the learner initially does is made easier. Gradually, the level of assistance decreases as the learner takes more responsibility for the performance of the task. For example, as a young

> An observant teacher determines what the student knows and what they need to know next in order to keep the student on the cutting edge of their learning.

child learns a nursery rhyme, the more capable other has all the responsibility of singing the song for the child. As the child hears the rhyme again and again, he begins to join in taking some of the singing responsibility. Eventually, the more capable other withdraws support, just as the scaffolding of a building is taken away as the walls are capable of standing alone. The next time the child sings the rhyme, the experienced singer helps him at points of confusion soon allowing the child to successfully sing alone.

The task of educating a classroom filled with various needs and fluctuating ZPDs can be challenging to the most experienced and well-intending teacher. Beyond developing a thorough knowledge base about how children learn the reading and writing process, it is essential that a teacher provide his or her students with a balanced, comprehensive, and responsive approach to teaching. This expectation leads to two very important questions: (1) What is a balanced, comprehensive and responsive teaching design? (2) What does it look like in the classroom?

To define balanced or comprehensive literacy, we must investigate various theorists in order to develop a definition that is compatible with the research about how children learn and work within the constraints of a classroom. Honig (1995) maintains that a balanced literacy program provides separate, explicit skill instruction and language-rich literature instruction. Instruction should be flexible to meet the needs of individual students. Tompkins (1997) describes literacy balance as integrating the language arts with a focus on children's literature. According to Tompkins, alphabetic knowledge and phonics skills are both a prerequisite and a consequence of learning to read. Therefore, instruction using a whole-part-whole model would be most beneficial. A high level of teacher scaffolding with individuals and small groups, as well as whole-group instruction, should be present in the well-balanced classroom.

Fountas and Pinnell (2017) provide this precise definition: "A comprehensive literacy design offers opportunities for language and literacy learning with an underlying coherent theory of the reading and writing process. Instructional routines are built on understandings about learning and how students develop as readers, writers, and language users" (p. 584). Additionally, Fountas and Pinnell (2017) discuss the importance of a literacy design that is responsive:

> Effective teaching is responsive to learners. It means that you are able to notice the strengths of individuals and notice their competencies. Instead of expecting them to be where you are, you have to bring the teaching to where they are… Responsive teachers have real conversations with students; they value their thinking and opinions; they encourage talk. Lessons are carefully planned and systematic; but there is always room for moment-to-moment adjustments given student response (p. 578).

Although there are several definitions for comprehensive, balanced, and responsive instruction, they all share these essential understandings: 1) children's literature is central to learning; 2) explicit and embedded phonics instruction is necessary; and 3) teacher support should be varied to meet the needs of all students. Understanding the theory behind learning ultimately leads to investigating what a comprehensive, balanced, and responsive design looks like in the classroom.

Putting Theory Into Practice

Just as a basketball coach strategically positions his or her team to execute a game-winning three-point shot, so must a teacher strategically position elements of a comprehensive, balanced, and responsive design into the classroom. To meet the individual needs of all students, a variety of instructional modes and levels of support is critical. In this chapter, I will outline three broad instructional contexts: whole group, small group, and independent learning. Within these contexts, I will briefly discuss elements of a literacy design including: Interactive Read-Aloud/literature discussions, Reading Workshop, Writing Workshop, shared reading, shared and interactive writing, and word study. Within each context, I will share photographs with a description of the environment, a brief discussion of the context, and a reference to another chapter in the book to learn more about that particular element of the framework. All of these elements incorporate authentic opportunities for reading and writing arranged on a continuum ranging from high to low teacher support with the ultimate goal of independent readers and writers.

Whole-Group Teaching

Interactive Read-Aloud and Literature Discussions

Reading aloud and discussing literature is the foundation of a comprehensive, balanced, and responsive classroom literacy design. Of the various types of reading, reading aloud provides the most teaching support. In most cases, the Interactive Read-Aloud is a whole-group experience that is designed to expose readers to quality children's books that are engaging, complex, and beautifully illustrated. Student engagement and learning during Interactive Read-Aloud is facilitated when the content of text is appropriate for the age and interests of the students and when discussion about the text happens before, during, and after the reading. Texts which are read aloud become mentor texts for reading, writing, and word exploration. A careful selection of literature ensures a variety of genres and reflects our diverse society. Texts should be rich in meaning and language, and class favorites should be read again and again (see Chapter 9) and used as a base for other literacy activities (Fountas & Pinnell, 1999).

PHOTO 3.1 Interactive Read-Aloud is a whole-group setting where the students are seated in a circle or a horseshoe to facilitate conversation among students about the text being read by the teacher.

> "Reading aloud to children is not a luxury, it is a necessity."
> — **Irene C. Fountas and Gay Su Pinnell**

The Commission of Reading stated, "The single most important activity for building knowledge required for eventual success in reading is reading aloud" (Anderson, 1988). Reading aloud is an advertisement of reading for pleasure (Trelease, 1989), stimulates student interest, and creates appreciation for quality literature. According to Trelease, "Early experiences with the richness and variety of reading materials seems to give children reason to read, teaching them not only how to read, but to want to read" (1989). As the teacher reads aloud, he or she demonstrates how to think and act as a reader, and provides insight into writing. When children hear written language read aloud, they can focus on meaning and ideas and enjoy the language (Fountas & Pinnell, 1996).

Allington and Johnston (2002) suggest that by the time a child reaches fourth grade, most of the basic skills for literacy have already been learned; however, the learning challenges continue. By the middle grades, the excitement students experienced in learning to read in the first grade has given way to boredom and frustration for some. This can lead to a negative impact on reading. Once the basic skills are taught, the only way to increase reading levels is by reading (Trelease, 1989). According to Lemme (1976), permanent reading habits develop between the ages of 10 and 12. Therefore, it is critical for educators to do everything possible to instill positive reading habits in students during this period. However, in many schools, once students reach the middle grades, little time is allocated for children to read and be read to. This is ironic because this is the time when children "learn to love reading" (Huck, 1987).

Do's and Do Not's of Reading-Aloud Design

Do's	Do Not's
• Begin reading to children as soon as possible.	• Don't read stories that you don't enjoy yourself. Your dislike will show in your reading.
• Continue reading through the grades.	• Don't continue reading a book once it is obvious that it was a poor choice.
• Read as often as you have time.	
• Remember that the art of listening is an acquired one.	
• Read above the listener's intellectual level occasionally, and challenge his mind. Listening comprehension outpaces reading comprehension!	• Don't feel you have to tie every book to classwork.
	• Don't overwhelm your listeners. Challenge them but always consider their emotional, intellectual, and social sophistication.
• Remember that even older students love a good picture book.	• Don't start reading if you aren't going to have enough time to do it justice.
• Allow time for discussion before, during, and after the reading.	• Don't confuse quantity with quality! Read favorite books again!
• Practice reading aloud. To do it well and with ease, you must practice.	
• Read slowly enough for listeners to build mental pictures of what he has just heard you read.	

The stories teachers read to children need to be chosen carefully. It is imperative to be thoroughly familiar with the books we have chosen before reading them to children. Teachers must know what book is to be read to children and why. In this way, the right books and materials can be selected to suit curricular needs as well as the needs to the students. Children need to hear a wide variety of language structures including formal, informal, and neutral registers in written language before they can be expected to expand their reading range.

Adapted from Trelease (1989)

Children need to hear a wide variety of registers in written language before they can be expected to expand their reading range. There are many benefits to balancing the read-aloud component with a variety of texts. These include:

1. Develops flexibility in children's reading

2. Supports critical thinking and problem-solving

3. Nurtures ease and facility in reading for information with an early exposure to expository text

4. Increases the use of expository text

5. Balances the types of communication used in reading

6. Develops the concept that all types of texts can be functional, enjoyable, and challenging

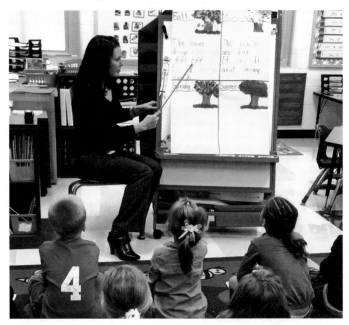

PHOTO 3.2 Shared reading is typically a whole-group setting where the students can clearly see the enlarged text being shared. The texts can be a wide variety of types including books with large print, digitally displayed texts, poems on charts, etc.

Discussion before, during, and after the read-aloud provides an opportunity to expand comprehension. Discussion is guided by the interests of the students and learning objectives of the teacher based on student need. Conversation occurs between the teacher and students and/or between students by turning and talking to one another in pairs or triads.

A large part of the educational research and practice over the last few decades confirms conclusively that the best way to raise a reader is to read to that child— in the home and in the classroom. This simple, uncomplicated exercise is not only the greatest intellectual and emotional gift that can be given to a child, it is the least expensive, most effective way to ensure the longevity of a culture and a love for reading.

> "Shared reading allows teachers to use engaging texts and authentic literacy experiences to help children develop strategies necessary for effective, independent reading."
>
> **—Kathryn Button and Margaret Johnson**

Shared reading allows the teacher to introduce, read, and study aspects of print through an enlarged text. Readers of all ages encounter a variety of complex texts that provide unique challenges. "When the teacher wants a group of children to share a story, she takes a text which is beyond the reading level of the group and, in the manner of the lap story, she introduces it in a way that the discussion calls up most of their prior knowledge that could be directed to the story" (Clay, 1991). Shared reading gives students opportunities to have exposure to print through big books, poetry, enlarged messages, and multiple copies of one text. In conjunction with strategic scaffolding on the part of the teacher, the stage is set to analyze text and prepare children for independent reading of more complex texts. And sharing a literate experience builds community and provides opportunities for everyone to feel successful and supported (see Chapter 11).

Shared and Interactive Writing

Shared writing, first developed by Moira McKenzie (1985), is an important part of a comprehensive, balanced, and responsive literacy design because the teacher models and demonstrates the process of putting children's ideas into written language (Fountas & Pinnell, 1996). This is the time where the teacher guides the children to compose a message and acts as their scribe. Emphasis is not only placed on composing a text but on constructing a text that the children can read later (McCarrier, Pinnell, & Fountas, 2000).

PHOTO 3.3 Shared writing is the context where the students and teacher negotiate the content of a message to be written by the teacher on a large chart for the class to see and reference at a later time. Shared writing may also be used in digital form where the teacher is typing the negotiated message and projecting it on to a screen.

Interactive writing grew from shared writing and is similar in many aspects. In both group-writing contexts, the text is planned collaboratively between the teacher and students and share the same general purposes—with the emphasis on composition. The defining aspect of interactive writing is the "sharing of the pen" at strategic points in the construction of the text. Based on the writing needs of the group, the teacher determines direct participation by the children. With each writing lesson, the teacher must direct the student's attention to the specific conventions of written language that need to be learned or reinforced (see Chapter 15).

"Shared writing is a collaborative process between teacher and children, and children, and children. Children begin to 'get in on' the craft of writing."

—Moira McKenzie

McCarrier, Pinnell, and Fountas (2000) describe the five functions teachers and students must consider when composing and constructing a text through interactive writing—see chapters 6–8 of *Interactive Writing: How Language and Literacy Come Together, K–2*:

1. PLANNING

Teacher and students work together to determine an authentic purpose, audience, genre, and type of communication they will write together.

2. DECIDING THE PRECISE TEXT

The teacher engages the children in conversation while they negotiate meaning, attend to specific or alternative words, think of different ways of putting words together, keep their audience in mind, and structure a text that coincides with the time and space available to them.

3. UNDERSTANDING HOW PRINT WORKS

The teacher and children work together to write the words, arrange words on the page, and use conventions such as space, punctuation, and capitalization to create a readable text.

4. SOLVING WORDS

Within the context of writing a continuous text, the teacher chooses specific and purposeful opportunities to draw attention to how words work.

5. CONNECTING READING AND WRITING

Interactive writing emphasizes frequent rereading while a text is being constructed as well as when the piece is complete. The completed text can be used as a reference throughout the school year.

PHOTO 3.4 Interactive writing is a similar context to shared writing with the distinct difference being that the students contribute to the printed message at times where the teacher determines there to be substantial learning for the students.

During shared and interactive writing, it is important to be clear about the aims and purposes of the writing with the children as this will impact the style and content. Typically, shared and interactive writing are a part of an ongoing study of content or children's literature. In both elements, the teacher and children work together to plan the text. However, the teacher assumes more than an equal role—she takes on a teaching role that enables children to develop and organize ideas. The emphasis is on the message or story they are creating. The children share ideas, and through the teacher's comments and questions, she sustains their interest and production of ideas. Through the collaborative nature of shared and interactive writing, students begin to construct their own understandings about written language, and use this knowledge on their journey to becoming independent writers.

"Helping children make an early, meaningful, and joyful entry into literacy is of paramount importance. And, in our journey towards this goal, one tool we find indispensable is interactive writing."

—Andrea McCarrier, Gay Su Pinnell, and Irene C. Fountas

Reading, Writing, and Word Study Workshops

Teaching within the workshop model builds upon teaching methods designed to meet the needs of all students in the classroom setting. These methods include three distinct parts:

Part 1: An explicit teaching focus (mini-lesson)

Part 2: An opportunity for application of the new learning by the students while the teacher engages with small groups and/or independent learners to provide differentiated support

Part 3: A group share of learning, which is typically a celebration of new learning from applying the mini-lesson. Figure 3.1 illustrates teaching methods within the reading, writing, and Word Study Workshop.

The Workshop Model

	Reading Workshop	Writing Workshop	Word Study Workshop
Part 1	Reading Mini-lesson (Whole Group)	Writing Mini-lesson (Whole Group)	Phonics/Spelling/ Word Study Lesson (Whole Group)
Part 2	**Student Role:** Application of lesson through: • Independent Literacy Work (K–1) • Independent Reading & Writing About Reading (2–8) **Teacher Role:** • Guided Reading • Reading Conferences	**Student Role:** Application of lesson through: • Independent Writing **Teacher Role:** • Guided Writing • Writing Conferences	**Student Role:** Application of lesson through: • Independent & differentiated word work **Teacher Role:** • Guided Word Study
Part 3	Group Share	Group Share	Group Share

FIGURE 3.1

Whole-Group Teaching Within the Workshop Model

MINI-LESSONS

Mini-lessons are based on student need, preplanned, short, and explicit instruction on any aspect of reading, writing, and word study. Typically written on chart paper for easy reference, children are expected to apply the lesson to their reading, writing, or word study application independently and immediately following the lesson (see Chapters 17 and 18).

> "Mini-lessons are short, concise, very purposeful lessons."
>
> **—Irene C. Fountas and Gay Su Pinnell**

Readers use evidence from
the text to support predictions.

I think..... because......

I think the bear is going
to eat the wolf because
the bear said DINNER.

PHOTO 3.5 Mini-lessons involve writing a brief learning objective on a chart paper, supported by an example that may come from a previously read piece of literature, student work, or other form of shared experience.

Small-Group Teaching Within the Workshop Model

GUIDED READING

During guided reading lessons, students do most of the reading work. The teacher may help the student recall and problem-solve but does not share in the actual reading of the story (Clay, 1991). Students are placed in a small group according to their reading development and are able to read about the same level of text. With individual copies of the text, each student is expected to read the entire text. The emphasis in guided reading is on reading increasingly challenging books over time. Students are regrouped according to their needs in a dynamic process involving ongoing observation and assessment (Fountas & Pinnell, 1996).

> "Guided reading is a context in which a teacher supports each reader's development on effective strategies for processing novel texts at increasingly challenging levels of difficulty."
>
> **—Irene C. Fountas and Gay Su Pinnell**

Since the purpose of guided reading is to enable children to use and develop strategies "on the run," there must be particular attention paid to selecting an appropriate text, effectively grouping students based on their instructional needs, and strategic teaching, prompting, and/or reinforcing before, during, and after the reading (see Chapters 13 and 14).

The framework of a guided reading lesson and a brief description of each element is outlined in the chart on the following page.

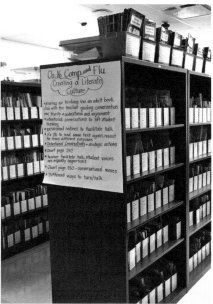

PHOTO 3.6 (left) A book room is a space, typically centrally located in a school, where leveled books to be used for guided reading are organized. The book room contains shelves with magazine files, or book boxes are used for easy access to borrowing leveled texts for guided reading groups.

PHOTO 3.7 (right) Often, the book boxes are clearly labeled with the level and titles of the texts. Well-stocked book rooms include a variety of genre and text types within each level. Approximately 50 titles per level will provide plenty of texts for teachers to borrow.

Framework of a Guided Reading Lesson

	Element of the Lesson	**Purpose of the Element**
Before the Reading	Select a text	• Ensure that the selection is in students' Zone of Proximal Development through sensitive and systematic assessments such as running records. • Provide variety in genres, text type, authors, illustrators, and publishers.
	Introduce the text	• Provide a sense of meaning in a brief discussion without giving away the entire story. • Draw attention to some unfamiliar concepts about print, structure of text, or specific words or punctuation. • Encourage students to read with a purpose in mind.
During the Reading	Students read the entire text at their own pace. Teacher listens in and teaches, prompts, and/or reinforces, as needed.	• Promote meaning-making and opportunities to encounter problem-solving through active reading of the entire text. • Create a collaborative, problem-solving relationship between teacher and student at point of difficulty through sensitive observations as children read.
After the Reading	Discuss the text	• Invite students to discuss the text to assess comprehension and encourage conversations with others to expand thinking.
	Teaching for Processing Strategies	• Revisit the text to teach or reinforce any aspect of reading related to use or neglect of strategic processing.
	Word Work	• Teach any aspect of word analysis that is needed based on your observations and appropriateness within the current text level.
	Extend the Meaning (optional)	• Use writing, drawing, or extended conversation to extend understanding of the text.

PHOTO 3.8 Guided reading is a small-group context where the students are seated at a kidney-shaped table. There is a space for the teacher to direct student attention to aspects of a text as a group or individually.

PHOTO 3.9 The guided reading area should be free of clutter and well organized with bins for books, folders for record keeping, and materials such as magnetic letters, wipe-off boards, markers, etc., ready to use, as needed.

> "Writer's Workshop enables children to learn and utilize the stages of the writing process with the support and guidance of a more capable other."
>
> **—Ralph Fletcher and JoAnn Portalupi**

GUIDED WRITING

During Writer's Workshop, the students have opportunities to work on individual writing pieces. Based on sensitive observation during individual writing conferences, the teacher may notice needs that are trending with small groups in the classroom. To be efficient with time and instruction, the teacher will bring this group together temporarily for instruction on a similar aspect of writing.

PHOTO 3.10 A guided writing group can meet at the guided reading table while the rest of the class is writing independently. It is important to have sharpened pencils, plenty of paper, and access to any support materials for writing. Students should bring their writing folder containing their current writing piece and any other helpful writing tools that have been introduced to the class.

> "Because most students in a given classroom vary in their word knowledge, instruction should accommodate different needs. Small-group instruction provides an alternative (to whole-group instruction), enabling students to explore the spelling features they are beginning to use but are using inconsistently—those within their zone of proximal development."
>
> **—Kathy Ganske**

WORD STUDY GROUPS

Through careful assessment and observation, a teacher may decide to bring a group of students together who are similar in their word study development that they can be taught together. By working with a small group, the teacher is working efficiently and is able to tailor instruction to the needs of the small group. Over time, teachers can expect these groups to change as learners encounter new challenges and take on new learning at individual rates (see Chapter 19).

PHOTO 3.11 A small group of students meets with the teacher for word study.

Individual Teaching Within the Workshop Model

INDEPENDENT READING, WRITING, AND WORD STUDY CONFERENCES

Within a well-designed literacy framework, teachers take frequent opportunities to circulate throughout the classroom to have individual interactions with students. Over time, individual conferences about reading, writing, and word study provide valuable information about student learning and next steps for teaching. Immediate feedback to the child from the teacher reflects personal interest in the child and stimulates a desire to respond to the teacher's expectations and teaching (see Chapters 17, 18, and 19).

"Conferences are conversations. Conferences, like many other conversations, have a point to them, have a predictable structure, pursue a line of thinking, have conversational roles, and show students we care about them."

—Carl Anderson

PHOTO 3.12

Independent Literacy: Grades K–1

Children have an opportunity to practice what they are learning during independent reading, writing, and word study. With strong routines and systems that encourage managed independent learning, children interact with one another and socially extend knowledge. Teachers may briefly check progress at learning centers between reading groups and discuss learning as well as self-management during a short sharing class meeting after independent learning time (see Chapters 6 and 7).

"Managed independent learning can be particularly effective in helping children develop the self-management skills that they will increasingly need as they go through school and life."

—Irene C. Fountas and Gay Su Pinnell

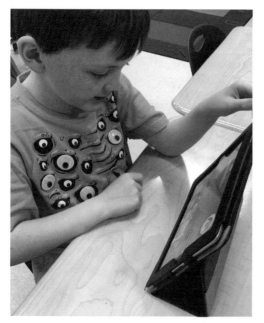

PHOTO 3.13 Young students explore a variety of literacy options, including independent learning on personal learning devices.

PHOTO 3.14 Students work together at literacy centers to promote 21st century problem-solving and speaking and listening while expanding their literacy knowledge.

PHOTO 3.15 Classroom libraries are organized to promote a wide range of student interests through children's literature, technology, and inquiry-based learning.

PHOTO 3.16 Students take ownership in organizing and labeling the classroom library to increase the accountability for using and caring for precious classroom materials.

Reading, Writing, and Word Study Group Share

Whole-group sharing may happen several times a day after students have worked independently or in small groups during the Reading, Writing, and Word Study Workshops. Group share is a short discussion, five minutes or less, highlighting aspects of learning that is connected to the mini-lesson for the day. Students are strategically selected so that the sharing of their learning can enhance the understandings of the whole group.

> "Self-management is even more critical for older students; and, like younger students, they need to be taught how to learn within a classroom community."
>
> —**Irene C. Fountas and Gay Su Pinnell**

PHOTO 3.17 Classroom libraries are spacious, clutter-free, and clearly labeled so students can make choices based on interest for their independent reading.

PHOTO 3.18 Small areas throughout the classroom encourage comfort and are inviting to students during independent reading time.

PHOTO 3.19 Group share occurs at the end of the Reading, Writing, and Word Study Workshop. Typically, the whole group returns to the meeting area to celebrate the independent work that was accomplished. Many times, the teacher strategically chooses a student to share work that is a good example of the learning objective from the mini-lesson.

"Sharing is an opportunity for students to come together as a community; students learn from their fellow classmates; teachers revisit the mini-lesson and highlight good decisions made by various students during the workshop."

—Patricia L. Scharer and Gay Su Pinnell

Independent Reading and Writing About Reading: Grades 2–6

Beginning in second grade, students spend a sustained amount of time reading self-selected books independently. Students and teachers work together to build reading stamina with the goal of achieving a substantial block of time of independent reading while the teacher is working with guided reading groups and conducting individual reading conferences. In addition to reading independently, students are writing about their reading and applying the mini-lessons to their independent work (see Chapters 7 and 8).

PHOTO 3.20 Students spend the majority of the Reading Workshop reading independently from a wide variety of books of choice.

Conclusion

Teaching children within a multi-textual, comprehensive literacy framework provides a vast array of learning opportunities. Students connect with one another through conversation about texts read to them, with them, and ones they read independently. They engage in authentic reading and writing that inspires inquiry through choice and variety. A range of text complexity within a multi-text literacy framework presents just the right amount of challenge and practice opportunities. The responsive teacher works to make connections across the elements of the framework in order to make new learning accessible for all learning styles.

Suggestions for Professional Development

With a group of colleagues,

1. Discuss your current practices about teaching literacy.
   - Which element(s) do you have in place?
   - Which element(s) of a comprehensive framework are new to you?

2. Choose one area of the framework to study together.
   - View the video example from the chapter at Scholastic.com/RLResources.
   - How will you apply what you see to your grade level?
   - What materials are required to teach this element?

3. Teach a lesson from your chosen area to study.
   - Video or audio record your lesson.
   - Reflect on the lesson:
     - How did the children respond?
     - What surprised you?
     - What will you try again?
     - What will you refine?
   - Share your learning with your colleagues.

CHAPTER 4

The Role of Emotion in Memory and Comprehension

Carol A. Lyons

> "All that quiet time reading stories chosen for me by an adult who loved me changed me forever— and granted me passion for stories and the ability to read fast and with feeling."
>
> **—Nancie Atwell**

The goal of all reading instruction is to develop children's capacity to read increasingly more complex texts with ease and understanding. We want them to take charge of their learning and to develop self-extending systems, or strategies, to improve and expand literate behaviors through successful reading. When that happens, we know that individuals have become self-regulated. They are experiencing success as readers and writers—success that has both cognitive and emotional significance.

Research on brain functioning shows that cognition and emotion are closely linked through experience. The meaning we take from all experiences has power, not only because we are taking on new information, but perhaps even more because of the emotional responses experiences trigger. The same is true for reading.

This chapter explores the role of emotions in an individual's ability to think and remember, as well as how emotions are critical in a student's ability to engage in self-regulating behaviors. I will make the case that the meaning children bring to and take from their experiences in learning to read, and their ability to search for and gain meaning while reading, are related to their ability to invest positive emotions while reading.

I focus on children who are struggling in reading and draw on my own experiences as a Reading Recovery teacher. Reading Recovery is a short-term (12–20 weeks, 30 minutes per day), one-on-one early intervention for the lowest achieving first-grade students. Unfortunately, when it comes to reading, many children have high levels of negative emotions. Skilled teaching, supportive relationships, and the experience of success can turn this situation around. These are lessons that can help all of us become better reading teachers.

A Russian psychologist, Lev Vygotsky, developed a theory of self-regulation (Vygotsky 1978). According to Vygotsky, self-regulation is encouraged by a specific type of interaction children have with a caregiver or teacher, one that actively engages the child as a collaborative partner in problem-solving activities just beyond the child's independent capacity. This zone represents what the child can nearly do. With adult support, the child can experience success with the task, creating positive emotions in the process.

Self-Regulation: Will and Skill

Self-regulation is defined as the child's capacity to plan, guide, and monitor his or her behavior from within and the flexibility to adjust according to changing circumstances (Diaz, Neal, & Amaya-Williams, 1990).

There are two properties associated with the term "capacity": will and skill. Will means choosing to act, a desire, controlling your own actions, or volunteering to participate. Will is associated with pleasure, energy, and enthusiasm, representing the affective side of human development. From a neurophysiological perspective, these properties reside in brain structures that are associated with emotional development.

Skill, on the other hand, represents expertise that comes from instruction, training, acquired ability, or proficiency. Skill is the development of knowledge, understanding, and judgment, and represents the cognitive side of human development. These properties reside in brain structures that are associated with cognitive development.

What does this have to do with reading comprehension? Just about everything. To expand their strategies, readers are required to solve problems. But the problems should not be so great (e.g., too many hard words) that they cannot attend to meaning. Ideally, every experience a child has in reading should be successful and full of meaning.

> Ideally, every experience a child has in reading should be successful and full of meaning.

The teacher's job is to figure out the child's plan for problem-solving because it drives what the child does at times of difficulty. A plan might refer to any kind of problem-solving. It is a repertoire of possible actions. Consider a simple example: When a child comes to a word he or she doesn't know, the plan is a series of actions to be tried. Included in the plan might be actions categorized as *plans to abandon efforts*, as well as actions categorized as *plans to attempt*.

Plans to abandon efforts indicate little will to attempt to solve a problem. They include:

- **Looking to you for help.** You certainly have experienced this behavior: The child's head swivels toward you in appeal.

- **Creating a diversion** by claiming a need to go to the bathroom, blowing his or her nose, or taking a break. One child we know claimed to be having a heart attack.

- **Looking into the air or at the ceiling.** One child said he was praying to Monica (a character on the TV show *Touched by an Angel*).

- **Crying.** We hope that this does not happen, but sometimes when children face difficulty, emotions can reach this level.

- **Quitting.** One child commented, "I can't think anymore; I'm too upset." Another said, "I am having a bad hair day."

Plans to attempt include:

- Examining the print and illustrations on a page
- Rereading
- Looking at the first letter
- Looking at the picture
- Looking at the end of the word
- Looking at the word parts or chunks of letters
- Trying a word that makes sense
- Thinking of a known word that looks like the word in the text

Any of these plans to attempt will be inefficient if it is the only weapon in the reader's arsenal. To read and comprehend texts, children must have a range of problem-solving strategies, not just for word-solving but for all reading strategies. The plan the child uses, revealed through his or her behaviors, will help you interpret his or her capacity (both will and skill). For example, the five plans to abandon efforts are not only ineffective but charged with emotion. They represent little will to try, perhaps because the child does not have the tools for success.

Helping children develop various ways to problem-solve will result in flexible, broad-based plans to resolve problems. You teach for strategies that develop the skill component of self-regulation but that also have implications for the will component. If a child shows you he is using only one plan (reread and look at the first letter), he is on shaky ground. That plan will not serve him well, especially when the texts are more challenging. That child will not succeed, and he will know it. And when the child encounters failure over and over again, the will to continue is jeopardized.

In his book *The Emotional Brain*, Joseph LeDoux (1996) suggests that continued emotional distress can create deficits in a child's intellectual abilities, crippling the capacity to learn. What does this mean for us as teachers? We must do powerful teaching of the skill component while at the same time attending to will. It is so important to look for and support the child's approximations or partially correct responses and then show how to complete the processing. In any new learning, all of us need encouragement to take risks and approximate. Without will, the child will not learn to read and write.

> When you teach children how to use multiple strategies for reading and writing text and see to it that they are successful in their attempts, they learn how to learn.

When you teach children how to use multiple strategies for reading and writing text and see to it that they are successful in their attempts, they learn how to learn. The *will* to learn is *charged*, something like charging your cell phone for longer, more effective use. Success builds emotional support, confidence, and the willingness to try—a *can-do* attitude. That attitude motivates children to continue to work with you, and in the process they become self-regulated as their circumstances change. How do you know if children are developing self-regulatory strategies? One way is to observe what they do at a time of difficulty. For each child, you may be thinking, What is the child's plan? Are there multiple plans? Do different plans guide and monitor behavior flexibility when circumstances change?

David: From Learning Disabled to Successful Reader

Let's look at an example drawn from one child I taught who was having severe difficulty in reading. David was classified as learning disabled (LD) in kindergarten and first grade by two separate teams of professionals. David had all the behaviors and supporting tests needed to be classified as LD. His brother and father had been classified and placed in learning disability classrooms in the primary grades, so it was assumed that his dyslexia ran in the family. When David experienced difficulty learning letters in preschool and did not make much improvement after five months in kindergarten, his well-intentioned parents wanted to get help immediately. In February of David's kindergarten year, he was classified as LD at Children's Hospital. Later, he was one of the first children tested by the school psychologist for a learning disability in the fall of first grade.

The results of David's tests by the school psychologist and doctors at Children's Hospital indicated that David was language delayed and LD with attention deficit hyperactivity disorder (ADHD). It was recommended that he attend speech and language classes three times a week and be placed on the waiting list for the primary learning disability room. While waiting for space in a primary special education classroom, David was placed in a regular education first-grade classroom. I began working with David because I had specifically asked to teach Reading Recovery students classified as LD.

David's scores on *An Observation Survey of Early Literacy Achievement, Third Edition* (Clay, 2013) revealed that he was the lowest-achieving student in the class. David could identify 37 of 52 letters by name; he could not identify F/f, G/g, Y/y, P/p, W/w, M/m, or U/u. He did not read 1 of 10 words on the Ohio Word Test, but he did look at the first letter to attempt several words; he read "two" for "the" and "there," "dad" for "did" and "down," and "you" for "yes." David knew 5 of 24 Concepts About Print, indicating an understanding of the front of the book and the bottom of a picture, the concept of one and two letters, and the meaning of a question mark and capital letter. Although David could not write one word, he did write the first letter of his first and last name, but he wrote the letter D backward. The dictation test revealed that when asked to write the sentence, "The bus is coming it will stop here to let me get on," David heard 4 of 37 phonemes. The text reading score placed David at Level A, indicating that he could point and read the words "No, no, no" when reading *Where's Spot?* (Hill, 1980).

David entered Reading Recovery on September 26 and exited the program February 28. He was in the program 21 weeks and had 99 sessions. His reading growth is shown in Figure 4.1.

David entered the Reading Recovery program reading text Level 1 and exited the program reading text Level 16, equivalent to the end of first-grade basal reading material. He could also write 66 words in 10 minutes and could hear and record 37 phonemes when asked to write, "The boy is riding his bike. He can go very fast on it." At the end of the year, David read at text Level 22 (with 94 percent accuracy), which is equivalent to third-grade basal reading material. David's total reading score on a standardized test placed him in the 99th percentile for first-grade students. David also exited the Reading Recovery program without three labels—LD, ADHD, and language delayed.

Weekly Record of Book Level

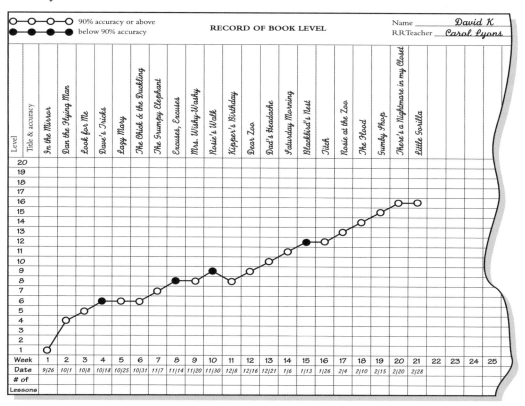

FIGURE 4.1

David's Classroom Teacher's Perspective

His classroom teacher commented that David was a completely different child at the end of the school year than he had been at the beginning. In October, she said that his attention span was about four minutes long. He showed little interest in any classroom activities. He appeared uninterested in the books she read to the class. When she read to the children, David had a difficult time sitting still, and he either stared into space or looked out the window. When she asked him how he enjoyed a story, he would say, "It was OK." But when asked what he thought was the best part of the story, he did not know. During the first month of school, David consistently drew pictures rather than attempt to write anything.

David's speech teacher had similar concerns regarding his attitude, behavior, and interactions with his friends or herself in speech class. She had a difficult time getting him to attend to any of the hands-on activities she organized. He volunteered little information about himself. He had a lisp and difficulty pronouncing some letters. For example, he would say "tick" for "sick," "tool" for "school," "pease" for "please," and "wif" for "with."

On the playground he seemed to have little difficulty talking to his friends, suggesting that his speech did not get in the way of communication. He seemed to have fun and to enjoy his many friends. How could this good social behavior manifest itself in instructional contexts?

David's Shifts in Behavior

After about four weeks in Reading Recovery tutoring, David's classroom and speech teachers noticed a major shift in his behavior. This once fidgety, overactive, disengaged child, who seemed reluctant to talk in class, was beginning to settle down and become more task-oriented and communicative with his teachers and classmates. He listened to the stories and willingly discussed why he liked or did not like them. He also wanted to share and write about personal experiences. He would tell a story about a picture the children were discussing in speech class and became involved in activities. His parents even noticed a positive change in his attitude about going to school, and that he seemed to pay more attention when he was read to before bed.

Factors Contributing to Change

What caused this sudden change of behavior? The classroom and speech teachers believed it was the individualized attention he received during the first four weeks of Reading Recovery that made such a dramatic difference and contributed to David's success in the classroom and in speech class. But I wanted to further analyze how individualized instruction helped to change David's attitude, motivation, and engagement.

> David and I were establishing a relationship that was having an impact on emotional learning.

Recently, I reanalyzed videotapes of David's Reading Recovery lessons with a new set of eyes. I was looking for evidence of David's emotional response to our interactions and sought to discover the impact that this response might have had on his thinking and subsequent behavior. As I analyzed the tapes, I noticed that more was going on than teaching for cognitive strategies. David and I were establishing a relationship that was having an impact on emotional learning. Below I share three insights that emerged from this analysis—insights that suggest ways that you can positively impact children's emotional and cognitive development.

1. SHOW THROUGH YOUR ACTIONS THAT YOU ARE GENUINELY INTERESTED IN WHAT CHILDREN THINK AND DO.

How do you do this? By engaging in genuine, relevant conversations focused on their interests. Have real conversations with the child. In this case, David and I talked as we walked to and from the lesson. We discussed what he was doing and/or interested in at home and in school. I got to know him as a person. If your own experience with such conversations is initially one-sided, keep trying—it will pay off in the long run.

A major breakthrough came for me when I asked David for advice about what to get my son for his birthday. He had several ideas, but the best gift he could think of was a puppy. The most important thing was that I wanted his opinion, and he knew it. He acted surprised that I had asked for advice. David offered many reasons why a puppy was the best present of all: puppies are alive and always happy. They do not grumble and are always willing to play. We kept this conversation going for weeks. He said, "I thought of the best reason why your son should get a dog. They don't crab at you or get mad when you make a mistake." That comment certainly revealed something about this child's own experiences.

These conversations were pivotal to David's change in attitude, his increased interest in reading, and his feelings about working with me. I valued his opinion and cared about him as a person, and he sensed it.

2. SELECT BOOKS AND GENERATE SENTENCES THAT REFLECT CHILDREN'S INTERESTS.

Carefully selecting texts that are *just right* for children (that is, are within the child's instructional level) helps to ensure success in processing them. You also should consider their interests and show that you really care about what they like. Using the children's own interests to guide your selection makes it much easier for them to read the text and comprehend it. David's interest in puppies was evident in his writing. For many weeks, he wrote about how to take care of a puppy—how often to feed it, how to train it, the kinds of things you can teach a puppy, where you can take it for a walk, and the games you can play with it. David was successful, and he knew it. Every little success motivated him to continue to engage in reading and writing. He had recaptured the will to continue learning.

3. PREVENT INAPPROPRIATE BEHAVIOR FROM OCCURRING.

Sometimes children must unlearn behaviors that are getting in the way. It is not always easy to help children unlearn inappropriate behaviors without causing emotional stress. You must know the child well and anticipate moves that signal the onset of an inappropriate behavior. The goal is to prevent a habituated pattern of behavior from occurring and engage the child in a new pattern of behavior to replace it.

For example, David routinely wrote the capital *D* in his name backward. I would watch him closely and as soon as I saw that he was going to start writing the *D* backward, I intervened by taking his arm and hand through the appropriate movements while verbally describing the movement. I prevented the inappropriate behavior from occurring until he could manage without guidance.

This support was matter-of-fact rather than critical or punitive and it was very important. Why? Because the more an inappropriate response is repeated (in David's case, making a backward *D*), the more the neural linkages in the brain are strengthened and the more difficult it becomes to unlearn what has been regularly done. David was a quick responder, labeled impulsive by the school psychologist and classroom teacher; that behavior needed to change. The backward *D* was only one example of many. If I did not catch him in time to stop his movement, he would become upset and frustrated, so frustrated that he would make holes in the paper with his pencil. This action caused a downward spiral; he became angry and mad at himself for not remembering. His emotions took over and he was unable to use what he knew. Instruction stopped. His anger was an emotional response to a mistake, but it was so strong that he had difficulty regrouping and attending to the rest of the lesson. Research reported by Greenspan (1997) shows that, for some children, getting off course causes a downward spiral which often is very hard to stop and reverse.

The bottom line is to recognize a student's feelings; talking is not sufficient for boosting problem-solving and getting the learner back on track. Saying, "You can do it" is not enough. The solution for a learning problem is not to attend to cognition alone but to address the inseparable fusion of emotions and cognition. Telling the child he is smart will not solve the problem; chances are, a child like David will not believe you anyway. David had to learn to act as a reader and writer, as one who had mastered part of the process. The changes in his actions also changed what he thought and how he felt.

Thinking About Cognition and Emotion

Neuroscientists now know that there are multiple memory systems in the brain, each devoted to different memory functions. The brain system that allowed David to make a capital letter *D* quickly and accurately is different from the one that allowed him to learn how to form the letter, and different still from the system that made him tense and anxious when he wrote the *D* backward. Though these are each forms of long-term memory (memory that can last for a lifetime), they are mediated by different neural networks.

Antonio Damasio (1994, 2013), a neurologist, has uncovered convincing evidence of neural networks in the brain. These networks support and provide the foundation for cognitive processing and are also associated with emotions. The connections between cognitive processing and emotions emerge from the unique experiences of individuals.

When there is an upset to one's routines, for example, such as getting lost while driving to a destination, the emotional responses—often unconscious, automatic, and involuntary—are activated in various parts of the brain. This activation is actually a full-body activation of the endocrine system, which includes the heart, blood pressure, and other regulations of the body that affect cognition and emotion. This evidence indicates that it is not simply the brain but the totality of the mind and body that makes up the unified whole of thinking.

Furthermore, because the emotional system can act independently of the neocortex (cognitive system), emotional reactions and emotional memories can be formed without conscious, cognitive participation at all. You remember most clearly those times when you were scared or when you experienced a psychological response. In the past, educators have thought about learning at the cognitive level. Now we need to broaden our understanding of learning and to remember that there is an inseparable relationship between emotion and cognition. In order to understand this relationship, we will look at the neural networks that integrate emotions and cognition.

Neurons

Recent pediatric research (Damasio, 1994; Greenspan, 1997; Carter, et al., 2014) has concluded that infants' and young children's learning involves emotional, social, and cognitive functions that are not *hierarchical*. They are not acquired in sequence, nor is one function more important than the others. Instead, emotional, social, and cognitive functions are *synergistic*; they are a combined and correlated force of united action. This synergy is the building block of all learning from birth and throughout life.

A mother cannot see what is going on inside a newborn's brain. She cannot observe the electrical activity as a neuron in the infant's retina makes a connection to a neuron in the visual cortex in his brain; but when this happens, her face becomes an enduring memory in the infant's mind that will last for a lifetime. She cannot observe the release of a chemical substance called a neurotransmitter as a neuron in the baby's ear, carrying the electrically encoded sound of "*Mom*," connects to a neuron in the auditory cortex of his brain. But when this happens, the sound of "*Mom*" creates a cluster of neuronal cells in the baby's brain that will respond to no other sound but his mother's voice for the rest of his life (Bagley, 1997).

The child's brain continues to form microscopic connections every day, connections that are responsible for feeling, learning, and remembering. The brain is hard wired from birth to direct everything it is supposed to do (e.g., walk, talk, think, reason, remember) without actually knowing how to do it. Neuroscientists are now realizing that experiences after birth, rather than something innate, determine the actual wiring of the human brain. This means that early childhood experiences exert a dramatic impact on a child's development, physically determining how the intricate neural circuits of the brain are wired. These early experiences influence the very structure and organization of the brain itself (Bagley, 1997; Carter, et al., 2014).

We know that in order for the necessary connections to be made—allowing a child to register his mother's face so that he can distinguish her from every other female he encounters, and to recognize the sound of her voice so that he can distinguish it from every other voice he hears—the child must be attending. The attentional system regulates all incoming sensory information. When a child is not attending, he will not learn. When tasks are too difficult, learners do not attend. We all experience positive and negative synergy while learning something new. We cannot prevent this from happening, because it occurs within our brains as neurons communicate with each other.

AN EXAMPLE OF LEARNING

A clear memory for me is the negative emotion connected to learning trigonometry in high school. My teacher would routinely ask every student to come to the blackboard to work out trigonometry problems, which she orally gave to the class. There were only 16 students in the class, so there was plenty of room for all of us to have a place at the board. We had to write out all of the steps in the process we used to solve the problem. I dreaded going to the board because I usually did not get the problem right. The teacher, Sister Agatha, would ask the class to look at my work and identify where I had made the mistake.

I always prayed that I would get the problem right, and that if I were wrong, she would not single out my work for everyone to examine. When she did, I was embarrassed because my errors seemed so obvious to my classmates. I was too emotionally involved to listen to the teacher while she explained the steps for getting the correct solution. I dreaded going to class for the first month. Finally, I asked my father for help.

Dad watched me working on several different types of equations, and then asked me to talk about what I was doing. He pointed out an error in my reasoning that was causing me to consistently make similar mistakes. My teacher had probably explained my pattern of errors the same way Dad explained it to me, but at the time I was so upset and embarrassed that I did not listen. My lack of attention made it hard for me to understand and remember what she was saying. Through my father's interest and help, a negative experience became positive, and I could continue to increase my understanding of trigonometry. Without his support I do not know what would have happened.

The negative experience that occurred during the first few weeks of class triggered a stress response as soon as the teacher said, "Let's all go to the board." As soon as she said those words, I felt myself flush, my stomach started to churn, my heart beat faster, and I started to sweat. In other words, physiological changes in my body took place. These physiological changes occurred because previous experiences going to the board to solve trigonometry problems had not been positive; stress interfered. I remember this high school experience vividly, which is not surprising because emotional memory takes precedence over every other type of memory. And emotional response interferes with thinking. The structure of the brain helps us understand how this works.

Structures of the Brain

The cortex is the outer layer of the brain. The inner layers of the cortex contain neural structures essential to learning and memory. Incoming information is processed through the reticular activating system (RAS), which is located at the top of the brain stem. (See Figure 4.2.) The RAS sends messages coming from the five senses to the thalamus, which sorts the information and sends it to three organs or lobes of the brain: the temporal lobe, which processes auditory information; the occipital lobe, which processes visual information; and the parietal lobe, which processes sensing and motor information. The information is processed in the manner described below.

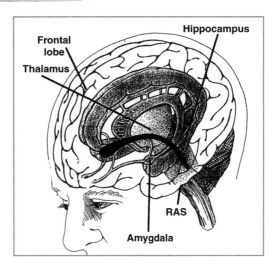

FIGURE 4.2

Short-Term Memory

Incoming information first goes to *short-term memory*. Short-term memory lasts only for 15 to 30 seconds. Some researchers say that you have limited space for short-term memory; the older you are, the more space you have for short-term memory. You can generally hold up to seven items in short-term memory before those items go to *working memory*.

Working Memory

Working memory is located in the prefrontal cortex. It can be used for hours, and it gives you the ability to form more lasting, *long-term memories*. We have all used our working memory to cram for a test. We study really hard the night before, and this information is stored in working memory long enough to take the test, but forgotten after we take the test. In fact, we would have a difficult time recalling the information the following week.

If information is not meaningful or allowed to form patterns in the brain, it will be lost. Short-term memory and working memory represent only temporary storage.

Long-Term Memory

After moving through working memory, information is sent to the frontal lobes, where it is decided whether it will be stored in long-term memory. Information sent to long-term memory is sorted and sent to two different structures critical to learning and memory: the hippocampus and the amygdala. These structures are found deep inside the medial part of the temporal lobe. The amygdala lies adjacent to and underneath the hippocampus.

THE HIPPOCAMPUS

The hippocampus catalogs, files, and stores factual information and communicates this information back to the surrounding regions of the brain. To maintain the stored information for a few years, the components of this system must also store the memory trace, which is maintained by interactions between the temporal lobe system and the frontal lobes. Gradually, over years, the hippocampus relinquishes its control over the memory and the memory appears to remain as long as it is a memory, which may be for a lifetime.

This model of memory has helped physicians and neuroscientists better understand what occurs in a mind afflicted with Alzheimer's disease. The disease begins its attack on the brain in the temporal lobe, particularly in the hippocampus, thus explaining why forgetfulness is the first warning sign. But the disease eventually creeps into the cortex, suggesting why, as the disease progresses, all aspects of memory (old and new) are compromised. Understanding how Alzheimer's disease affects the mind and brain in tandem is helping researchers figure out approaches to prevent, arrest, or reverse the disease.

THE AMYGDALA

The amygdala catalogues, files, and stores emotional information and determines if it is emotionally important for long-term storage. Each route that leads to the amygdala—sensory thalamus, sensory cortex, and hippocampus—delivers unique information to the organ. According to LeDoux (1996, 2015), the amygdala is a critical site of learning because of its central location between input and output stations.

Emotional responses begin in the amygdala before we completely recognize what it is we are reacting to or what we are feeling. Because the neural emotional system can act independently of the cortex (frontal lobes), some emotional reactions and emotional memories can be formed without any conscious, cognitive participation at all. What this means is that an emotional response can precede a cognitive perception and response. The amygdala's response to a situation can drastically affect how well it is remembered.

Thus, incoming information is coded two ways: emotionally and cognitively (Greenspan, 1997). It is coded in two different regions of the brain, each specifically designed and responsible for learning and memory. The hippocampus files, catalogues, and stores *factual* information; the amygdala files, catalogues, and stores *emotional* information. The hippocampus is responsible for planning, problem-solving, and reasoning related to factual information; the amygdala is responsible for telling us how we feel about that information, which is then stored in our emotional memory. Emotional and cognitive memories are stored and retrieved in parallel, and their activities are joined seamlessly in our conscience experience (LeDoux, 1996).

Learning—Emotional and Cognitive

LeDoux (1996) and Jensen (2009) suggest that neural pathways are set so that a learning situation may evoke either an emotional response that may be helpful, or a rapid, negative emotional response that can impair learning, memory, and thinking even before engaging cognition.

Understanding how the hippocampus and amygdala function in learning and memory may provide an explanation for what happened in my high school trigonometry class. I could not think because I was worried that I would get the problem wrong again and Sister Agatha would ask the rest of the class to examine my work. I could not hide the steps I took to resolve the problems because they were written on the board for everyone to see. As soon as Sister Agatha said, "Everyone to the board," I panicked. Her words were sent immediately to the amygdala (seat of the emotional brain), bypassing the thalamus, which would have sent it to the frontal lobes to examine the situation. When this occurred, neurotransmitters (chemical signals) were released and my body started to prepare for flight. My heart raced faster to get my blood flowing quickly. This stress response was triggered by a few words from the teacher, words that I associated with embarrassment and failure. The stress response can save your life or it can cause you great embarrassment, which it did in my case.

> Remember that the emotional memory takes precedence over cognitive memory. The brain always gives priority to emotions.

Likewise, David's emotional reaction to instruction in reading and writing, with which he was seldom successful, may have had a physiological root. *Remember that the emotional memory takes precedence over cognitive memory. The brain always gives priority to emotions.*

The Nature of Long-Term Memory

Long-term memory consists of information stored for an indefinite period of time. Five different but interrelated facets of long-term memory are critical to learning and comprehension. Procedural, automatic, episodic, semantic, and emotional memory are all used to access and store information.

PROCEDURAL MEMORY

Procedural memory is located in the cerebellum. It includes sequences that are consistently repeated until they become automatic routines. That means you can execute these sequences without thinking about what you are doing. Consider such automatic behaviors as riding a bike, driving a car, or running your finger along a line of print. Procedural memory allows you do two things at once; for example, driving a car and listening to a book on tape. It allows you to divide your attention. When reading, you simultaneously recognize visual symbols and imagine what characters in a novel look like and feel.

AUTOMATIC MEMORY

Automatic memory resides in the cerebellum. Certain stimuli evoke a conditioned-response memory automatically. After you hear the first few words of a song from years past, you might remember all the words of that song. Other things you have stored in automatic memory include letter names, letter sounds, multiplication tables, high-frequency words, and so on.

EPISODIC MEMORY

Episodic memory is located in the hippocampus. Episodic memory may be triggered by your automatic memory. For example, you sing a song from your youth and just a few words from the song trigger a memory of the circumstances in which you heard the words for the first time. You remember where you were and who you were with when you first heard it. The words of *Camelot* may trigger a memory of President Kennedy; then you may remember where you were when you heard that he had been assassinated. Some children will remember when a teacher showed irritation or anger when they could not remember how to make a letter or the letter sound after it had been taught to the class. Your responses to children's inability to recall information may impact their memory more than you will ever know.

SEMANTIC MEMORY

Semantic memory, located in the hippocampus, holds information learned in words. Most of our educational experiences involve semantic memory. When we receive new information, it may be connected to previously learned information and sent to working memory. Working memory will continue to sift and sort the old and new information. Through prior knowledge and interest, the new information will be added to the old information to form more long-term memories. This process can be called *synthesis*. Synthesis will be repeated several times before long-term memories are formed. Semantic memory is stimulated by associations, comparisons, and similarities; building semantic memory is the heart of the comprehension processes.

EMOTIONAL MEMORY

Emotional memory exerts a powerful influence on thought processes. Emotional memory registers and retains positive and negative responses, and brings up these responses if circumstances are repeated (as the trigonometry experiences were). If the child repeatedly reads or senses disapproval in the teacher's response to an error, he will be reluctant to put himself in that circumstance again. He won't take the risk; he may think, "I can't learn how to read." The will to learn is gone. Embarrassment and fear of making a mistake may prevent the child from trying again. All of us remember our mistakes. You can give an hour-long talk that was perfect for 59 minutes, but the one minute you forgot what to say and fumbled the words may never be forgotten. For some individuals, that one minute of fumbling prevents them from ever speaking in front of a group again.

> If the child repeatedly reads or senses disapproval in the teacher's response to an error, he will be reluctant to put himself in that circumstance again.

Emotions affect short-term, working, and long-term memory. Negative emotions can impair the activity of the prefrontal cortex, the area involved in working memory. This interference offers a reason why, when we are emotionally upset, we cannot think straight. It also explains why continued emotional upset can cripple the capacity to learn. Positive emotions, on the other hand, can facilitate working memory that is critical to long-term memory and thus basic to comprehending strategies. All of this means that children's capacity to think and problem-solve is heavily dependent on positive affective experiences.

Social Forces Are Critical to Learning and Memory

Experience is a major factor in the development of an infant's ability to reason and make sense of what she hears and sees in the environment. Social interaction, through language, is the means through which this cognitive ability is developed. Language researchers, such as Bruner (1983) and Lindfors (1999), have shown that a toddler's vocabulary is strongly correlated to how much the parent talks to the child. Furthermore, only a *live* voice, not the electronically produced voices of television, increases a child's vocabulary and language structure because language must be used in relation to an ongoing event. Otherwise, the sounds are just noise.

Language is embedded in an emotional context that seems to stimulate neural circuitry more powerfully than information alone. The child will more readily learn the concept of the word "more" if it refers to the happy prospect of more milk, or the concept of "later" if it is attached to a frustrating wait for a trip to the playground. Or she may understand the word "again" when it is associated with the happy experience of rolling the ball to Mom again. Happy and sad emotions contribute to vocabulary development and memory. If abstract words such as "more," "later," and "again" were presented outside of a meaningful context, in isolation from things the baby cares about and wants to know about or do, they would not be remembered. In this way feelings, concepts, and language begin to be linked to form memories, even as early as seven months (Gopnik, Meltzoff, & Kuhl, 1999; Gopnik, 2016).

The infant cannot tell you about what she has learned because she does not have control of the necessary language to do so. But she has a memory of what she has learned, and so she can show you that she knows. Especially when they are hungry, children know what they want to eat and what they do not want to eat. Parents read the intonation of the child's voice and interpret the child's wishes. I remember giving our son a pickle, and he hated the taste of it. From that day on, whenever I put the pickle jar on the table he became upset.

We continue to form memories in a similar way throughout life. Adults form memories much more readily if the new information is accompanied by emotional content. Most adults can easily recall happy occurrences, such as their wedding day or the birth of a child, and tragedies, such as the death of a parent or child, or the day the space shuttle carrying Christa McAuliffe exploded.

> If David had not successfully learned how to read, he would probably have been labeled LD and ADHD for the remainder of his school years.

If my father had not stepped in to help me with trigonometry, I probably would have dropped the class. Who knows how that negative experience would have changed my educational life? If David had not successfully learned how to read, he would probably have been labeled LD and ADHD for the remainder of his school years. This designation may have had an impact on his progress throughout his schooling, even throughout his life. Instead, David had a good academic record in school and is a college graduate.

Conclusion

The brain strengthens frequently used neuronal connections by pruning connections that are not used. Experience determines which connections will be strengthened and which will be pruned. Connections that are activated most frequently are preserved and stored in long-term memory. Emotion, the brain's primary architect, facilitates this process. Learning depends on memory, and the most powerful learning takes place if multiple memory areas (procedural, automatic, emotional, semantic, and episodic) are involved.

The brain at a young age is flexible, like plastic. The plasticity of the brain enables students such as David, who once had difficulty learning, to reorganize the brain's activity. In his case, he became a good reader and writer. The downside of the brain's great flexibility Is that it is acutely vulnerable to stress and trauma. Experience may alter the behavior of an adult, which was apparent in my experience in trigonometry class, but it literally provides the organizational framework for the brain of the child—the brain's organization reflects its experience. If a child experiences fear and stress, then the neurochemical responses to these emotions become powerful architects of how that child's brain is organized. If a child has experiences that are emotionally overwhelming, and has them again and again, the structure of his brain is changed (Greenspan, 1997).

We cannot prevent or stop the synergy among the emotional, cognitive, and social forces that influence children during learning. What we say and do, and how we say and do it, makes a difference. It is therefore important that we remember to:

- Show through your actions that you are genuinely interested in children, in what they think and what they do.

- Select books and generate sentences that reflect children's interests.

- Prevent inappropriate behavior from occurring.

Suggestions for Professional Development

1. Have fun probing your own memories and emotions. With a group of friends, think of at least one of the following:

   - A song that immediately comes to mind when you think about high school or college.

   - An object that you treasure even though it has little monetary value.

   - A time you love to remember because you were so happy.

2. Share your memories and the emotions connected with them. Now think of something that you found very hard to learn, e.g., skiing, public speaking, playing the piano, or calculus. Share the emotions connected with your struggle.

   - Did emotions ever get in the way?

   - Did you abandon the effort or keep struggling until you learned?

   - How did you deal with your feelings? What helped you?

3. Now think about one or two struggling students in your class. Plan to observe these students carefully over several days to determine when emotions are working *for* them in terms of learning and how their emotions might be working *against* them.

4. If possible, have a colleague observe you as you work with these students (e.g., in guided reading). You want students to work so that they will learn, but not to *struggle* so much that they experience negative emotions. Becoming sensitive to negative emotions will help you sense when to give a little extra help or more demonstration and explanation.

CHAPTER 5

Fostering Literate Identities

Wendy Sheets

"During a time when I felt like an outsider, the characters I met in books I read affirmed my existence."

—**Marcelle M. Haddix**

Think about yourself for a moment. What are your identities? I identify in several ways: as a mom, a teacher, a literacy trainer, a grandma, a literacy coach, a Sunday School teacher, a writer, a researcher, a presenter, a learner, a doctoral student, a daughter, a singer, a swimmer, a traveler, a friend. Notice that all of those identities are social constructions that shift (or are solidified) within my social interactions with others. Our identities are always in flux as our narratives shift, and they depend upon what stories we choose to tell about ourselves and to whom (Moje & Luke, 2009).

What about your students? What are their strengths? What are their interests or hobbies? Their ways of interacting? Their favorite movies, video games, or toys? In what traditions, routines, and rituals do they engage with their families? What languages do they speak? It is important for us to not only know who our students are, but to make space for their identities that are typically revealed outside of the classroom. When we value students' cultural and home-based resources, we may promote those resources as tools for literacy learning. Students are then better able to identify with reading and writing practices, which fosters their identities as learners (Dyson, 2003).

PHOTO 5.1 Choice is one aspect of a reader's identity.

When I consider students as learners, I consistently hold onto the goal of helping them develop positive literate identities. Isn't that what we all desire for our students? We want children to engage as readers and writers with a sense of agency that propels them in meaning-making, knowing they have power as thinkers.

Literate beings

The Stories We Tell About Ourselves

The stories our students tell about themselves as "literate beings" (Rogers & Elias, 2012, p. 260) are shaped, in part, by their literacy experiences and active participation in our classrooms. While many constructs, such as habits, values, beliefs, cultural practices, traditions, language, gender, race, class, experiences, and others' perceptions make up and impact one's identity, I believe classroom discourse also plays a large part in that growth. Vygotsky (1978) argued that children "grow into the intellectual environment around them" (p. 88). As teachers, we have the opportunity to facilitate positive constructivist classrooms where meaningful interactions make way for students' voices to play a valuable role in agentive spaces like the two girls in Photo 5.2. As we engage in meaningful interactions, constructing conversation through listening and speaking, we co-create understanding with one another. When we consider ways students develop identities as literate beings, it is often impacted by what is communicated, or the discourse, within the classroom.

PHOTO 5.2 Dialogic interactions between learners have the potential to position self and others in multiple ways.

Widening the Classroom Walls

For instance, Sue, a fifth-grade teacher I know, provides opportunities and space for her students to engage in literacy in many ways, including bringing items from home at times. When that happens, she allows them to share with the class in meaningful ways. For example, one student had purchased several graphic novels with a gift certificate she had received to a bookstore. She brought them in to read during independent reading, and soon was discussing and sharing the books with other students and teachers as well. Another student brought in arrowheads and stone tools found on his grandfather's farm. Though there wasn't a scheduled "show and tell" time, Sue understood the importance of those opportunities for her students to be represented as knowers whose voices mattered. When students are encouraged to talk, and to draw upon their own "home-based genres of argument and explication," they practice and hone their discursive tools (Michaels, O'Connor, & Resnick, 2008, p. 286). After all, according to Brian Street, "literacy is a social practice" (Coronel-Molina, 2003, p. 77).

discursive tools

It is not enough to view literacy as a set of skills or something that is bounded by school-based acts of reading and writing. What ways do you value what your students bring to the classroom in order to build bridges between spaces? Think about ways your students engage in acts of literacy outside of your classroom walls. How do they use new media or other non-academic social practices? According to Vygotsky (1986), ignoring important social and cultural resources that children bring to their schooling experience places them at risk for academic failure. When students are able to flexibly transfer or generalize learning from one space to another in meaningful ways, their

PHOTO 5.3 Learners mediate their identities as readers and writers when they share their work (and what matters to them) with one another.

identities expand as learners. Let's find ways to expand those valuable aspects of their identities, focusing on what already exists to build on those assets.

What Stories Are Told by the Teacher?

I recently visited two different classrooms in the same district. Like many teachers, Elaine (whose name has been changed for this chapter) was working hard to maintain classroom management. Desks were in rows and students were monitored in their ability to sit down and stay quiet. Admittedly frustrated, she shared that students hadn't learned as much as she had hoped at that point in the school year. As I observed, I noticed Elaine was often the sole speaker, hence the authority, in the classroom. Although students cooperatively raised their hands to answer her questions, Elaine was looking for specific, *right* answers, and students didn't have opportunities to elaborate on their thinking. Once she found a student who was able to provide the answer for which she was looking, she confirmed: "Right! That's what the character wanted in the story." I watched as students, who had previously had enough agency (Johnston, 2012) to share their thinking, now stopped offering their ideas. In this way, the teacher missed an opportunity to allow for the construction of meaning through social interactions. Instead, her questions and her thinking were privileged above everyone else's, and there wasn't room for collaboration. During guided reading, I observed Elaine taking the lead to share her thinking about the topic. Below, I share the conversation that took place during the introduction of a text about difficult times.

Teacher:	What do you think it would be like to live in a time when people didn't have enough money to buy clothes and food and even a place to live?
Student 1:	We do have that time now. It's called homeless people. No offense. But when I grow up…
Teacher:	You are right.
Student 2:	Before my grandma died, we saw a homeless person…
Teacher:	This book we're going to read, just everybody was in that situation. It was called the Great Depression, and the title is called…
Student 1:	(flipping through the book, seeing Henry Ford) And they made a car?
Student 2:	Looks like they built it out of scraps.
Teacher:	This was the time period. It was in the 1920s. Look on pages 2 and 3. You'll see some pictures. That's what the environment looked like at that time, but there was a big boom, and people were spending a lot of money.
Student 1:	The big bang?
Teacher:	No. They were spending more money than they had, and that's what caused the Great Depression. Look on page 11. Another thing that was happening was called the dust bowl.
Student 2:	It looks like a sand thing.
Teacher:	Yeah, around the 1930s the Midwest looked like a big dust bowl cuz there was a drought.
Student 1:	Looks like a tornado.
Teacher:	All sand.
Student 1:	Is a sandstorm enough to blow down a whole building?
Teacher:	Could cover up a building, and at that time, the president was Franklin Delano Roosevelt and he came up with a plan, an idea of how things could be better, called the New Deal, on page 13. I want you to notice how the author uses lots and lots of details to help us understand all these multiple things in this text, all about the great depression, but numerous things are happening.
Student 1:	How can they spend more money than they earn?
Teacher:	Go ahead and start reading.

Elaine begins the introduction with a genuine question that appears to elicit student interest, background knowledge, and/or connections. When students respond, however, Elaine doesn't pursue their thinking to help them better understand the text. Throughout the interactions, we see readers attempting to construct meaning by sharing their thinking and wonderings. However, it doesn't fit in with the teacher's agenda, and she misses opportunities to support students in making meaning. Inadvertently, Elaine is encouraging students to engage in what some researchers call "procedural display," where students simply go through the motions of what is expected of them in order to participate in school tasks rather than authentic learning.

In another classroom where desks were arranged in groups, I found Lenore (whose name has been changed) calling her students to engage in an Interactive Read-Aloud like the teacher and students in Photo 5.4. In their small classroom, they had found a way to utilize the constructive, powerful context of sitting in a circle to engage with one another. Students quickly move their chairs into a large oval through the center of the classroom. Learners and their teacher are all positioned in the same way; everyone can see one another. All voices matter.

PHOTO 5.4 When students contribute to the meaning-making during the practice of Interactive Read-Aloud, they show agency as literate beings as they construct meaning through language. The responses offered by others also impact literate identities in various ways.

Lenore introduces Chris Van Allsburg's (1986) *The Stranger* and begins reading. After the first four pages, a student interrupts. See below for an excerpt of the interactions:

Student 1:	I think I get it.
Teacher:	What do you get?
Student 1:	I think she feels the draft cuz he's blowing.
Teacher:	Hmmm. Look at his eyes, too. (Teacher reads another page.)
Teacher:	(with a puzzled look) Stop and build a conversation about what you're thinking.

Students turn and build conversation in pairs, and then they are called back together to share.

Student 2:	I think the rabbits looked back cuz this man lives out in the woods far away from people and he knows about animals, so they looked back cuz they thought he'd follow them.
Teacher:	I never thought of that, but maybe he has a connection with the animals because they thought he was a hermit?
Student 2:	The rabbits wanted him to come back to the woods cuz they might be used to him.
Teacher:	What do the rest of you think? Agree? Disagree?
Students:	I agree.

Teacher reads.

Student 3:	(interrupts) I told you. Ohhhh!
Teacher:	What made you say, "Oh," Devon?
Student 3:	Cuz he's probably used to working out in the wild…
Teacher:	Hmmm.
Teacher:	(reads more pages, then stops) What are you thinking? Turn and talk to each other.

Students turn and build conversation in pairs, and then they are called back together to share.

Student 4:	He's probably gonna change it with his memory.
Teacher:	Why do you say that?
Student 4:	Cuz he couldn't remember his memory, but he's probably getting his memory back.
Student 5:	I think he controls the seasons…the fall…
Teacher:	Interesting.
Student 6:	I think since it's all happy and cheerful at their farm, everywhere else is changing cuz they're probably used to waiting, probably just letting the seasons pass by this farm, since it's so happy and cheerful.

Teacher:	How can that happen?
Student 6:	I don't know…
Teacher:	So, based on what you know as a reader, do you think it's a fantasy book? (students raise hands and agree before some discussion about the genre)

following students' line of thinking

prompting students to tell more

Share the authority in constructing meaning

Teacher continues reading.

During this segment of the Interactive Read-Aloud, we see Lenore following students' line of thinking, even prompting them to tell more. In doing so, students are represented as knowers, sharing the authority of contributors to the construction of meaning within the classroom discourse. Lenore sends the message to students that their thinking is important, which encourages them to take risks to contribute to the conversation, lifting the thinking of everyone in the class like the teacher and students in Photo 5.5. Lenore is genuinely interested in understanding her students' thinking; not only that, she pushes to expand the context so that multiple perspectives may be shared. In this classroom, students are less hesitant to take risks because they share the authority in constructing meaning.

The instructional decisions that teachers make are based on what they believe about readers' identities and also contribute to the personal identities possessed by students (Anyon, 1981; Sarris, 1993; Johnston, Woodside-Day, & Jiron, 2001). It is evident

PHOTO 5.5 When a teacher listens, she conveys that she believes they have something of importance to say.

that Lenore believes her students have something valuable to contribute to the conversation, and because of that, she is intentional in opening the door for their thinking to be shared. At times, students have difficulty articulating their thinking clearly, and Lenore invites them to tell more, while everyone listens intently. The conversation is not simply teacher to student, but students build on each other's ideas, allowing for some problem-solving and more abstract thinking to be shared. When teachers follow the give and take of conversation as meaning is constructed, they become better informed about their students' understanding. "Seeing more deeply, realizing the importance of others' words (and names), utilizing speech and action, and collaborating for transformation are fundamental principles by which to deeply and deliberately listen to and with others" (Kinloch & San Pedro, 2014, p. 7). These classroom interactions make learning much more meaningful, but also afford opportunities to the teacher to mediate learning as a more knowledgeable other.

PHOTO 5.6 Students learn to truly listen to one another, honoring each other's thinking.

Elaine's current understandings about her students and her role as a teacher drive the instructional decisions she makes. While both groups are similar in demographics, it appears that Elaine's students are not given the same opportunities to build understanding as the students in Photo 5.6. They are positioned in ways that shut down explorations, conversation, and inquiry. Elaine's discourse style and expectations make her the only expert in the classroom, which may disempower students, hiding their literacies (Delpit, 1988; Dyson, 2008). Through ongoing coaching, however, Elaine's beliefs related to students as contributors to meaning-making have the potential to shift, thus impacting students in positive ways.

The Power of Teachers

According to McCarthey and Moje (2002), power has a role in how identities are enacted and how students are positioned. Because power always exists in relationships, teachers can use that power "to enhance learning and help children to extend their existing ways of being, or…to demonstrate to children our perceptions of the limits of their capabilities" (Dyson, 2003, p. 74). Every interaction we have with a student sends a message of one type or another about who we say they are. We must be cognizant of our language with and about students, along with the decisions we make that affect them. Something as simple as interrupting a student who is speaking, or taking out the red pen to mark up a child's piece of writing, or telling a reader unknown words before he has had an opportunity to problem-solve, may undermine students' literate identities.

Think about the messages inherent in identifying children by reading levels. I don't know about you, but I never walk into the bookstore looking for Level Z texts! As a reader, I'm not limited by a label that is confined by a level. Not only that, I sometimes choose to enjoy easy books that are far below my instructional level. At other times, I seek information from a text that may be challenging for me. Perhaps it relates to a favorite topic or content area, and as a reader, I access pieces of information for specific purposes. While levels are valuable for teachers in making assessment and instructional decisions for guided reading purposes, our students need to view themselves as readers, not as levels. "It is detrimental to a student's self-esteem and to their love of reading when they are encouraged to measure their own progress by 'moving up levels'" (Fountas & Pinnell, blog post, 9/29/16). The signals we send to readers about levels are counter-intuitive to the behaviors that are important for growing as readers. For more information, see: http://blog.fountasandpinnell.com/post/a-level-is-a-teacher-s-tool-not-a-child-s-label.

PHOTO 5.7 When the classroom becomes a community of learners who understand the value of their work, learners may go about their work alongside one another. Interactions become purposeful as they reflect together, lifting the thinking of others in the group.

What Stories Are Told by the Classroom?

· traffic pattern
· safe access to materials
· spaces within the classroom

Everything that is communicated within the classroom also creates realities related to literate identities. What messages are conveyed through the classroom discourse? As teachers, we are so thoughtful about the way we organize our classrooms. We consider the way we arrange desks or tables to provide for cooperative learning experiences. We consider traffic patterns to allow for easy, safe access to materials and spaces within the classroom. We create whole-group, small-group, and individual spaces in order to meet the needs of our students in various learning contexts. We plan our schedules to include opportunities for teaching and learning across contexts. All of those decisions carry a message about who we believe our learners are and what their capabilities are as well. If, for instance, we arrange desks in rows, might we convey a belief that students are not to be trusted to interact with one another in productive ways? Or that we do not want them interacting? Think about the resources we make available to our students. If I don't have a well-stocked, organized classroom library, what message does that convey? That reading isn't highly valued in this room? If tools for Writing Workshop aren't provided (various forms of paper, pencils, crayons, etc.), might that send the message that publishing writing pieces is not a serious expectation? Or if students have only a short time to write independently, is it really important? If we come together for an Interactive Read-Aloud or a mini-lesson and my

PHOTO 5.8 When we come together for an Interactive Read-Aloud or mini-lesson, we want learners to be positioned in a way that allows for the construction of meaning. Within a circle, everyone may see and hear one another, and the playing field is level. We don't want anyone marginalized socially or physically.

students are all seated in a clump on the floor facing me, am I conveying that I am most important and my thinking holds the most weight? Or that our interactions should be limited to teacher to student? Consider how the teacher and students sitting in Photo 5.8 helps them to value each other's thinking.

The texts I choose to share, along with the discussion for which I prompt, carries meaning as to what is important as well. The interactions around and interpretation of literature are social acts (Lewis, 2006) as we construct knowledge together. The text itself, along with the views shared in the classroom are part of the discourse that shapes individual and group identities. If students are interested in pursuing a difficult topic during a discussion around text, for instance, I allow for a constructive context that becomes the canvas upon which their voices may paint.

Conclusion

Peter Johnston (2004) says that our language is our most powerful tool. Every gesture I make, along with what I say, is affected by my feelings and attitudes. Therefore, my emotions convey information about how I see particular students or all children in general, how I view various subjects (whether it's math or guided reading or poetry or immigration), and what I find valuable or otherwise. The tone of voice I use carries meaning. Even a pause or a sigh might indicate the way I view a student or his thinking. When our speech or emotions position students in negative or positive ways, we should expect them to begin to take on those narratives—of themselves and of each other. I once noticed a sign hanging in a classroom that stated, "In this classroom, we speak English." What message, I wondered, did that send to our English language learners? If I privilege one thing—a language, a gender, a particular socio-economic status, a sport, a viewpoint—I create a false dichotomy that positions other things as less valuable. While I'm not suggesting we stop showing enthusiasm for our own passions, I hope to raise an awareness of the power we have as teachers.

We are responsible for the classroom discourse in our spaces. The literate identities that our students take on affect their progress over time. If we open the space to constructive conversation with and between our learners, and our messages convey a genuine interest in our students and their lives, along with our belief in their

PHOTO 5.9 When students recognize who they are and who they want to become as readers and writers, their work becomes more purposeful and efficacious.

competence as learners, they will begin to view themselves and each other as knowers and contributors to the meaning-making in the classroom. With respect for one another's thinking, the boundaries of their own thinking will be broadened.

Within this context, students connect with one another and with the content with purpose, perseverance, empathy, kindness, and responsibility. Aristotle once said, "Educating the mind without educating the heart is no education at all." When the discourse within our classrooms opens the doors to rich opportunities for communication and growth, our students are more likely to develop positive literate identities. Because dialogue is central to meaning-making (Bakhtin, 1935/1981), conversation and social interactions are a necessary part of learning. As significant members of a classroom community, students view their work as readers and writers and thinkers and speakers as purposeful, not confined by the institution of school. They become problem-solvers who pursue learning with passion, inquiry, agency, and flexibility.

> When the discourse within our classrooms opens the doors to rich opportunities for communication and growth, our students are more likely to develop positive literate identities.

PHOTO 5.10 When classroom walls are filled with tools for authentic reading and writing behaviors, along with showcasing the work of our readers and writers, we position that work as being highly important.

PHOTO 5.11 Readers and writers should have many opportunities to share their thinking and their work. It is our desire that they find their work meaningful, so we must privilege the sharing of it.

And they learn to enact their literacies in ways that are carried beyond the borders of the classroom and into all aspects of their lives. Isn't that what we all want for our learners?

Suggestions for Professional Development

1. Host a professional book study to read and discuss one of Peter Johnston's books: *Choice Words* (2004) or *Opening Minds* (2012).

2. Lead teachers in generating a list that describes their own identities. Encourage them to consider multiple aspects of identity. Then have them think about ways those aspects of their identities contribute to who they are as learners, and how they use those assets within various experiences.

3. Reflect after reading this chapter and work with a colleague to implement ways to support positive literacy identities in your classrooms.

PHOTO 5.12 There is such power in teachers coming alongside one another to reflect upon instructional decisions.

4. After surveying students to learn more about their interests outside of school, have teachers come together to make decisions about how to build on student assets.

5. Consider a few students from your classes who are progressing slowly or are disengaged within the classroom. Come together to closely discuss the students as a staff, generating understandings about the children (their interests, family life, cultural aspects, ways of interacting with others, etc.). Take an inquiry approach to generating possibilities for engaging children in more holistic ways, to tap into their strengths and interests, and to build upon their identities.

6. Have teachers videotape a segment of teaching and learning within their classrooms. They may individually or within pairs view the video in order to analyze their language and the ways students are positioned by the teacher, by other students, or by the classroom itself, along with ways students position themselves. Being analytical during this noticing and reflecting should result in more intentional language in order to provide greater opportunities for constructivism and agency in the classroom.

SECTION TWO:
ORGANIZING FOR LEARNING

Professional videos and downloadables are available at Scholastic.com/RLResources

CHAPTER 6

Managed Independent Learning: What Makes It Work?

Justina M. Henry, Barbara Joan Wiley, and Shelly Schaub

"Children grow into independence as they develop as literate learners."

—**Peter H. Johnston**

It's early September, and the topic of conversation in the teachers' lounge in an elementary school in central Ohio is Managed Independent Learning. Typically framed as a one-and-a-half to two-hour literacy block, Managed Independent Learning supports kindergarten and first-grade students working independently in centers while their teacher instructs small groups of children in literacy.

At first, the teachers' conversation focuses on why they want to try Managed Independent Learning. A first-grade teacher states, "By working with small groups of students with similar abilities, I can provide books with just the right amount of challenge to help them learn." He adds, "And what the rest of the children are doing during those 20 minutes is important. They need to be working independently, reinforcing learning about reading and writing, and fully engaged in the task at hand. Kindergarten and first-grade students need to be able to move around and engage with peers while productively learning at a variety of centers." The teachers sitting around the table nod their heads in agreement.

One summarizes the issue, "Because students typically spend an hour or more of the literacy block working independently in centers, and only 20 minutes or so with their teachers in a guided reading lesson, their independent time needs to be as valuable and productive as their time with the teacher. That way they'll make steady progress."

Another teacher offers a challenge. "I've noticed that Managed Independent Learning is highly successful in some classrooms; but in others, teachers struggle with activities that are at best unproductive and at worst chaotic." Again, teachers nod in agreement. The conversation shifts to questions: How can I teach the children to work independently at centers? How can I be sure that the students are reinforcing learning when they're in centers and not just "doing" activities? How can I get students to care about their learning and work hard when they are at centers?

Leslie, a teacher who successfully implemented Managed Independent Learning during the last school year, joins the conversation. "It works for me and my students." The conversation breaks up and Leslie invites the teachers to stop by her room so that she can share with them what she's learned about Managed Independent Learning.

This chapter is a description of what the teachers learned when they visited Leslie's classroom as she explained and demonstrated how to initiate Managed Independent Learning.

What Makes Managed Independent Learning Work?

Leslie is a reflective teacher who problem-solved issues related to independent learning on a daily basis. She wanted to know how to teach the routines effectively so that her students with varying abilities in reading could work alone without her assistance. Once they were independent workers, she wanted to be certain that their learning was productive as they worked independently. So, she asked herself a series of questions.

Leslie's Issues and Questions		
Issue:	**Definition:**	**Questions:**
Routines	A series of activities performed according to standard procedures.	How can I teach the students to work independently during reading time?
Just Right Content	Work that offers just the right amount of challenge—not too easy and not too hard.	How can I make the independent work activities more powerful?
Self-Regulating Behavior	The child's ability to organize and monitor his or her own behavior.	How can I teach the students to manage their own learning?

How Can I Teach the Students to Work Independently During Reading Time?

Although Leslie's goal was to eventually release control of centers to her students in the first few weeks of school, independent work time in her classroom was highly structured and carefully monitored. Centers were introduced gradually, one or two a day. It was only after her students could care for supplies, successfully complete tasks, and maintain a comfortable noise level that she would introduce a new one. In addition, she provided activities that were ongoing so that she didn't need to teach too many new routines each day. Leslie paid particular attention to her explanations and expectations for work in the centers. She wanted her language to be explicit and to provide helpful feedback.

Use Explicit Language

At the beginning of each day, during whole-group meeting time, Leslie explicitly taught the children what they were to do in centers. During the first month of the school year, Leslie was faithful to the adage, "Less is best." She began by using a simple workboard that was easy for the children to follow; quality was valued over quantity. Some centers had an assigned task, and Leslie held the children accountable for a product. Each center also had several

workboard

PHOTO 6.1 An early workboard

activities from which the children could choose after they had finished the assigned task. They stayed in the center until they were told that it was time to move on. Each child was assigned a partner with whom to work (see Photo 6.1).

After the children had spent about 20 minutes in centers, Leslie asked her students to clean up and come to a community meeting. The purpose of this group time was to share learning experiences and address issues that may have occurred at the centers. For example, in September, during the group discussion, Leslie taught her students to value the routines of putting their names and the date on their papers. She encouraged them to use good handwriting so that she could read what she wrote. At this time she also shared that she appreciated their working well together and keeping busy. Leslie knew that her students were eager to please and that they would do what was expected of them if they

- knew what the teacher wanted,
- knew why the teacher wanted it, and
- were treated respectfully.

Leslie's language was always explicit and respectful when she offered rationales and feedback. She knew this kind of language enabled her students to follow and internalize routines. Below is an example of explicit language that focused on routines that took place early in the year during a community meeting after reading period.

Leslie:	Everybody was working very nicely with their partners. I cannot say enough about how well you worked together. That's how you learn. People were following the directions on the cards. I saw Jacob going to the card at the Reading Center. He found the card, read it, and did his job there. One of the things I want to talk about again is this: When you are done with your job at the center, turn in your paper and do something else productive at that center. I was talking to Cody about that. Cody, can you tell everyone some of the things they can do at the Word Study Center when they are finished there?
Cody:	Link letters, magnetic letters, pictures.

Leslie:	Good. You can see what Cody did. (Holds up Cody's paper from the Word Study Center.) He remembered to put his name and the date on his work so I can see it. You can see how nicely he worked. And again, his handwriting is really nice. I am able to read it. I can tell that he said the words slowly and put down the sounds that he heard, and most of his words are spelled right. What productive work! Really nice job. Who would like to share something that they did today? Hannah?
Hannah:	I wrote a letter.
Leslie:	Hannah was at the Writing Center, and the job was to write a letter to a friend. Hannah wants to share her letter. If you notice Hannah's work, she has her name and a date on it. Very nice handwriting. You can tell she took pride in her work. Now she is going to read us her letter.

Give Feedback

After participating in this community meeting, the children moved on to the second center of the day. As the students worked, Leslie walked around the room and monitored what was happening. She recognized what her students were doing right. One day, early in the year, Leslie told the children, "Wow, what organized students you are! You got right to work on your job. When you were done, you found something else to do at the center. Really nice." Leslie would also offer reminders and suggestions as needed. Her goal was to eventually work herself out of the job of closely monitoring her students.

Increase the Complexity

Over time, Leslie knew that the workboard gradually needed to become more complex. To help with the transition, many of the Literacy Centers became ongoing activities rather than short-term ones that would last only a day or two. The children went to these centers every day and knew exactly what to do, making time-consuming, daily explanations unnecessary. This also freed Leslie from having to create new centers each week. For example, when working in the Browsing Box Center, the children read four books from the box, alone or with a partner. At the Writing Center, they wrote letters, poems, notes, or journal entries.

PHOTO 6.2 A more complex workboard

The children quickly internalized the expectations for these ongoing centers. They learned the meaning of the center icons: what to do, what was expected, and what the rules were. For every student, the last icon each day was independent reading. So, when Leslie glanced around the room and noticed that the majority of the students were reading at their desks, she stopped what she was doing and called an end to center.

Leslie felt that the effort she made organizing and managing centers early in the year, and making the process easy for herself and her students, was time well spent. As the children learned to monitor their own behavior and learning, Leslie began to assess their individual abilities. By the third week of school, she had completed and analyzed their baseline assessments, and she began conducting guided reading lessons. This was her payoff.

When her students knew what to do, she was free to teach them what they needed to learn next in small reading groups.

How Can I Make the Independent Work Activities More Powerful?

Once Leslie's students understood the routines for independent time, it was time to up the ante. Leslie began to focus a greater portion of her attention on challenging each child appropriately every day in every work area.

Create Just-Right Challenges

Early on, at the beginning of the year, Leslie had asked herself, "What can these children do alone?" She observed each child closely, every day, and analyzed the information she was collecting to assess what each student could do independently. Then she used her district's goals to determine what her students needed to learn next; for example, one curriculum goal was that her students write a poem. So, early in the year, she asked herself, "What is an initial step that these children can take right now that will eventually lead them to this goal?" She decided to have the children memorize a different poem each week for a month, hoping that they would learn more about poetic devices such as rhyme, meter, images, and sound. This knowledge would take them one step closer to actually authoring a poem themselves.

Leslie kept striving for just the right amount of challenge. She knew that if the work was too easy, the children would spin their wheels. If it was too difficult, it would be a waste of their time and they would stop trying. Her driving maxim was, "Give them challenges they can successfully meet, because that's when the lightbulb of learning goes on." Leslie realized that independent work time is quite different from the centers that her students were used to in kindergarten. Kindergarten children move from center to center, exploring magnetic letters in the ABC Center and looking at their favorite books in the Library Center. In first grade, there is more sustained reading and writing time. For example, during work time, first grader Connor would be investigating the rain forest by reading books and writing interesting facts on index cards. He later categorized these cards and used them to prepare a project that summarized his learning, which he shared with the class.

Offer Authentic Problem-Solving Activities Using Rich Literature

Next, Leslie began working to make sure that the learning that was taking place in centers and other independent work was knowledge that could be transferred from one context to another. She did not want her students merely to memorize items of knowledge. Instead, she wanted them to engage with a wide range of rich literature and become strategic problem-solvers through reading, writing, speaking, and listening. By engaging in meaning-making, problem-solving behaviors, her students would develop self-extending systems to help them to get better at something the more they practiced it. For example, when the class was studying about states in the Research Center, Kevin brought from home a huge book filled with information. While reading the book, he gleaned many interesting facts. He noticed that multiple states had the same state bird. He wanted to categorize the states by their state birds and create a bar graph to display his knowledge. He also wanted to learn the year that every state joined the Union and put them in chronological order. He was not just learning isolated facts; he was using the problem-solving strategies of focused attention, logical thinking, and deliberate memory to synthesize something new.

Leslie considered the kinds of activities she would avoid using at centers, such as contrived activities, which rely on "texts" that do not represent rich literature.

> By engaging in meaning-making, problem-solving behaviors, her students would develop self-extending systems to help them to get better at something the more they practiced it.

Examples of Contrived Activities

- Worksheets
- Dated, poorly written photocopies
- Busy work designed to keep students occupied and quiet

Provide Open Activities Using Choice and Inquiry

Leslie also began to provide more and more opportunities for the children to have a choice in what they read, wrote, and studied. She felt that the eagerness that resulted from having choices would support learning at a higher level. One center that she wanted to implement was a "Challenge Me Center." Here children were asked to investigate something that they really cared about, such as a favorite animal or flags of different countries. Their work could go on for several days or several weeks, depending upon the students' goals and their plans for sharing their learning with the rest of the class. First, students selected their personal challenge and wrote a few sentences about what they would learn and why they wanted to take on this challenge. When their challenge was completed, the students shared their project with the rest of the class, which usually inspired even more students to take on challenges. Aubrey, for example, became deeply engaged in learning how to count and spell in Spanish and in so doing was learning about a different culture. Offering students choices empowered them to learn.

Leslie realized there were times when she would need to limit choices at some of her centers in order to maintain order. For example, Leslie would assign one story to listen and respond to at the Listening Center. Likewise, she would assign programs that would most benefit learning at the Computer Center or assign words for a particular word sort for individual students. Even in this type of closed center, one with limited choice, Leslie tried to include opportunities for open response. Leslie avoided designing center activities that forced students into a right or wrong answer. If there were activities that had a correct answer, Leslie ensured that the students had the opportunity to check their own work and learn from any mismatches.

After Leslie realized that her students were working smoothly and learning, because the work was on their level, she saw a need to refine their attitudes about how to work more diligently in centers.

How Can I Teach the Students to Manage Their Own Learning?

In order for her students' independent learning to accelerate, Leslie felt that they needed to understand more fully their roles as students. She accomplished this by valuing independent learning, using process words, and teaching students about expectations.

Value Independent Learning

This teaching shift—from routine procedures to work habits—was particularly evident in the many interactions Leslie had with her students that focused on the value of learning. The value of learning, and thus self-regulatory behavior, became Leslie's focus in her interactions with her students because she knew these interactions supported independent learning. These conversations often took place during the community meeting at the end of Managed Independent Learning. Leslie typically prefaced each exchange with a child using the question, "What did you learn today?" Essentially, this discussion highlighted what the children were learning, how they were learning, and why they were learning. Leslie felt that when children fine-tune their work habits, they learn more and they learn faster. For example, a community meeting at the end of workboard time included interactions that focused on self-regulatory behavior by defining the role of a student.

Leslie:	I am going to start out by asking what you learned today, Hannah.
Hannah:	I found a Golden Retriever that was named a different name.
Leslie:	What state were you researching?
Hannah:	Maryland.
Leslie:	Right, this book says that Maryland's state dog is the Chesapeake Bay Retriever. Some retriever dogs are similar but have different names, just like the rocks we are looking at in the Science Center. One is sandstone, and the other is limestone. Now, let's look at what Hannah does because I always like how Hannah takes her time when she works. She concentrates and finishes whatever she does,

Leslie: *continued*	and always, always tries her best without being told. Did you find a book over there that was useful to you to find this information? Was it the green one? (Hannah nods.) So she found that the green dictionary that I showed you this morning was very useful in finding information she needed. (Hannah shows and reads her research booklet.)
Leslie:	I like how well you worked on it. You are such a hard worker. Who else learned something today? Brett.
Brett:	I learned at the Research Center that North Carolina is not just smooth; it is also bumpy.
Leslie:	Yes, Brett, let's share your book. I think you are another good example of someone who always focuses on his work and reads very carefully to see what he is supposed to write.

Teach Using Process Words

Many of Leslie's conversations were also peppered with process words that support self-regulatory behavior, like "concentrate" and "try." Using these words encouraged her students to learn the strategies of focused attention and self-regulation. By talking about the meaning of such words as "focus," "self-control," and "concentrate," Leslie was demonstrating the type of language her students needed to develop self-regulatory behaviors. Leslie knew that her students could more readily take on the behaviors when they had a term for them (Bodrova & Leong, 1995).

Review Teach Expectations

Leslie reviewed expectations, helped the children evaluate their own behavior, and asked them to share what they had accomplished at every community meeting after workboard. Leslie knew that her students had self-regulatory behaviors when they did what was expected of them without being told or monitored. Negative class management was not an issue because she had taught her students (1) what she wanted; (2) why she wanted it; and (3) how to use respectful language. Discipline in her room was neither a power struggle nor a free-for-all.

Once Leslie's students knew what was expected of them (what to do), this internalization freed them, and their teacher, to concentrate on content (what to learn) and behavior (how to learn). Together they had problem-solved what makes Managed Independent Learning work.

Conclusion

Leslie is a reflective teacher. She began the year by asking herself, "What do I think students can do independently?" Once she answered this question, she moved on to ask, "How can I up the ante so they can learn new things?" When she was certain the children were working with just the right amount of challenge, she began to ask herself, "How can I support them in taking on the role of a serious student who is a self-regulated and self-motivated learner?"

The answers to these questions guided Leslie to start the year by teaching her students the routines of centers. As the children internalized the procedures for independent work time, her focus shifted to providing her students with successful challenges. Next, she helped her students value their learning and take on the role of a serious student. Her shift was from other-managed to self-managed behaviors.

Leslie's thinking does not stop here. The process is both an ongoing and a recursive one. Her observations of the students in her room will continue to drive her practice from day to day, month to month, and year to year. She does this because she knows that effective teacher decision-making is directly related to what the students know and what they need to know next. By checking on her students' learning, Leslie was also checking on her teaching.

Each time Leslie addressed a problem and solved a problem with her students, she led them one step closer to her goal of making Managed Independent Learning work in her classroom. She saw value in her students becoming independent learners who get better at what they do every time they do it because they know how to learn.

The teachers Leslie invites to her classroom to learn about how she successfully implements Managed Independent Learning soon come to realize that even as many of their questions are answered about how to implement Managed Independent Learning, more emerge regarding how to teach successfully.

They agree with Leslie that a teacher's job is to continually ask the important questions: What do these children know? What do they need to know? And how can I teach them what they need to know next? They believe that this is important because it's how teachers check on their teaching through their students' learning.

Suggestions for Professional Development

1. Think of a new center or activity that you want your students to be able to do independently while you work with a small group in guided reading. (Alternatively, think of a center that is not working well in your classroom and start over to make it more effective.) Select an activity that will be productive in terms of reading or writing—one that all students can do simultaneously the first few times they work on it.

    - Ask a colleague to observe your classroom (or join you at lunch or after school) to look at the physical arrangements and materials in the center.

    - Together, analyze in detail exactly what the children will have to do to use the center effectively. Walk or talk through the sequence of expected actions while your colleague takes notes.

    - Plan the introduction of the center or activity. Questions and procedures that will help include:

- What materials will students need? Organize the materials in the place where students are expected to complete the activity or in an accessible place if all students are working at their desks or tables. Eliminate clutter by making sure that all materials are separated into containers. Label the containers and the place on the shelf where they are supposed to go.
- What is the sequence of actions the students will be expected to undertake from beginning to end? Plan how you will demonstrate the actions.
- Is the activity simple enough that the students in your class can easily learn it? If not, simplify the sequence of actions.
- How long will it take for students to learn the routines? If necessary, plan how you will establish the routine over several days.
- How can students be involved in their own learning? Plan to have students self-evaluate their performance of the activity each day. Also, ask them to talk about what they have learned. This follow-up discussion is important in helping students become self-managed and take ownership for their learning.

- Implement your plan over a period of two weeks. Gradually withdraw your supervision and support as students become more independent, but keep a watchful eye. Reteach routines as needed.
- Meet with your colleagues to share what you learned from the experience. Remember, as students learn more of these routines, they *learn how to learn* them, and it will take less time to teach them. Every new activity, though, will require some teaching.

2. Analyze your center activities using the matrix below. Assign each center to one of the four quadrants.

Center Activity Matrix	**Open Activity** Opportunity for choice and inquiry; variety of responses possible	**Closed Activity** Little or no opportunity for choice; correct or incorrect responses possible
Authentic Activity Real or genuine reading, writing, listening, speaking, and learning opportunity; wide range of continuous texts; problem-solving opportunities	#1	#2
Contrived Activity An unnatural or false appearance or quality; texts are not representative of rich literature	#3	#4

- How many of your activities are Open & Authentic (Quadrant #1)?
- How many of your activities are Closed & Authentic (Quadrant #2)?
- How many of your activities are Contrived (Quadrants #3 & #4)?
  - Discuss with colleagues to generate ideas to adjust contrived activities so the learning for students is more authentic.
  - Work to eliminate contrived activities from your student learning centers.

CHAPTER 7

Second-Grade Transitions in Independent Literacy

Shelly Schaub and Denise Rowe

*"*Like a child's first words and first steps, learning to read and write should be an exciting, fulfilling, and rewarding experience.*"*

—Lesley Mandel Morrow and Diane H. Tracy

This chapter is based on a wide range of second-grade experiences we have had as we have studied the transition from first grade to third grade. Our expectations for students in second grade have changed recently as we have learned how to support students' development of stamina for reading and writing continuous texts. These abilities enable students to have deeper experiences with a wide variety of texts and supports their development as writers as well.

Thoughts from Shelly

I have been an educator for over two decades. During that time, I have spent most of my career teaching first grade and kindergarten. After extensive training in Literacy Collaborative at The Ohio State University, I began to work in many second-grade classrooms. What I learned from working with a multitude of second-grade teachers is that second graders are unique. All children and grade levels have individual qualities, of course. However, the most intriguing question in second grade seems to be in the area of independent literacy. Independent literacy is that time of the day when the teacher is working with small groups of students at the guided reading table and the rest of the class is working independently. Should second-grade classroom routines for independent literacy involve a variety of centers like in the primary grades or should second-grade students be working toward longer stretches of independent reading and writing about reading like in the intermediate grades? My experiences in a variety of school settings as a professional developer and literacy coach have shaped my understandings related to this issue.

Recently, I began teaching and coaching in a building which housed second through fifth grade. Kindergarten and first grade were in a different building on campus. I worked in 16 second-grade classrooms with 16 incredible second-grade teachers and learned more than I ever thought possible! In addition, I began learning more about teaching within a Reader's Workshop from the school's Intermediate (Grades 3–5) literacy coach. During professional development sessions where second- through fifth-grade teachers worked together, we began to wonder how student achievement would be impacted if we began transitioning to more sustained reading and writing about reading during independent literacy in second grade. The second-grade teachers and I began to work together to improve the reading stamina and quality of writing about reading. After implementing this model in second grade for four years, teachers reported a high degree of satisfaction with how their students were responding, and student achievement in reading and writing as measured by third-grade achievement tests soared!

I began to wonder if this sort of success was specific to the district in which I taught or if another district with different demographics, teachers, and students would find similar results. I began working with Denise Rowe, District Literacy Collaborative Trainer (an expert in the field of literacy), who agreed to implement this kind of Independent Literacy transition in second grade classrooms in her district. The impact on student achievement and positive literacy experiences was astonishing and very similar to the increases noted in the school in which I taught.

Throughout this process Denise and I learned valuable lessons that are transferable to other second-grade classrooms:

1. Second graders are capable of sustaining their reading for longer and longer stretches of time if the expectation is clear and connected to real learning.

2. Second graders are able to write about their own reading if they are given clear guidance about what to write about related to their thinking while reading.

3. Second graders enjoy choosing texts to read based on their interests, because this is often the first full year where they have reading abilities allowing for a wider variety of choice if a variety of texts are provided.

4. Second graders begin to develop a level of literary maturity which allows them to transfer understandings from a mentor text to an independent text with clear expectations and instruction.

5. Second graders are becoming more capable writers and are able to write constructively about their thinking related to a text they are reading independently when strong routines and expectations are established and maintained.

Throughout this chapter, Denise and I will share our journey transitioning second graders to a Reader's Workshop model. We will explore the role Interactive Read-Aloud plays to help students write about their reading as a whole group and how that thinking transitions to independent reading and writing about reading.

Interactive Read-Aloud and the Second-Grade Transition

One of the most powerful learning experiences for me was when Mrs. Kirven, a second-grade teacher, asked me to join her as her class studied biographies because she wanted to understand more about how to use children's literature to increase student ability to think about and write about their reading.

Biography Study

Our learning goals for the study included but were not limited to:

- Notice and remember the important events in chronological sequence.
- Learn (synthesize) new concepts and ideas from listening to nonfiction texts.
- Use background knowledge of history to understand simple biography.
- Relate important information and concepts in one text, and connect to information and concepts in other texts.
- Infer the importance of a subject's accomplishments.
- Understand that a biography is the story of a person's life written by someone else.
- Understand that biographies are often set in the past.
- Draw and write to relate important information/ideas within a text or to other texts.
- Use some academic language to talk about genres.
- Use some academic language to talk about literary features.

Mrs. Kirven is a lover of children's literature and came to the planning session with a wide variety of biographies to be used as mentor texts. We decided to share the books with the students and begin talking about the features of biography. We also wanted to investigate which of the texts the students really enjoyed because this would become the mentor text for our writing about reading. It didn't take long for the students (and teachers) to fall in love with *Henry's Freedom Box: A True Story from the Underground Railroad* by Ellen Levine and Kadir Nelson. This biography about a slave's life and escape to freedom provided the backdrop for authentic exploration of the student learning goals. Student inquiry and defined learning expectations led to rich discussion and a depth of writing about reading through interactive writing (see Chapter 15 for more information about interactive writing). After reading *Henry's Freedom Box* multiple times, the teacher and the students together

- decided that this story needed to be shared with other second-grade classrooms.
- chose the main events in the story that would accurately illustrate Henry's life (biography).
- analyzed Henry's character throughout these events and identified how he changed with each event.
- retold each event in their own words through conversation and negotiation of how to best communicate the information.
- wrote the retelling on chart paper for the whole class to see.

When Henry was a little boy he was a slave. He felt sad because he was a slave and he didn't even know his birthday!

When Henry got a little older his master called him into his bedroom. At first Henry thought he was going to be free so he was excited! Then Henry was disappointed because he found out that he was getting sold to the master's son.

Henry was very sad because he had to say goodbye to his mother. He watched a bird fly and it made him think about being free!

PHOTO 7.1 The illustration captures three of the nine episodes that the students chose as important events in Henry 'Box' Brown's biography. The students, guided by the teacher, composed and constructed the text using a variety of vocabulary to describe how Henry changed throughout his life. The illustrations were inspired by those in the text and were collaboratively constructed by ripping colored paper and placing them strategically to form each image.

- wrote the retelling in their own personal notebook while it was being written on the large chart.
- worked in small groups to illustrate the events that were written.

While the students were studying biographies using Henry 'Box' Brown as their mentor text, they were reading biographies of their choice during independent literacy. Mrs. Kirven provided a range of texts at a range of levels for the students to explore while she worked with guided reading groups. Mrs. Kirven used a modified workboard (see Photo 7.2) to help the students move through their independent literacy tasks. As the school year progressed, the Independent Reading and Writing About Reading icons were the only ones used because the students built enough stamina to read and write for the entire independent literacy block, which is approximately one hour in length.

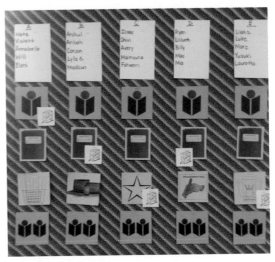

PHOTO 7.2 Modified workboard supporting independent literacy time

Each heterogeneous group begins the independent literacy time reading for a sustained amount of time from their personal texts (purple icon). Next, they write in their Reader's Notebook about their reading and, often, in response to the mini-lesson for the day (green icon). Then the students move to a variety of different centers, including poetry box, computer, choice, handwriting, or Writing Center (blue icons). Finally, students end the independent literacy time sharing a book or their Reader's Notebook entry with a partner (orange icon). At this point, the teacher is completing the last guided reading group, and the class meets in the common meeting space for sharing time.

PHOTO 7.3 (top) Students take their independent reading material and find a quiet spot in the classroom to read.

PHOTO 7.4 (left) Logan is enjoying the time to reflect upon the lesson and write about his thinking in his Reader's Notebook.

The students were not restricted in their choice of books based on reading level or ability. They were free to choose any biography they found interesting to browse. The expectation was that all children began independent literacy reading independently. Their books included biographies, other choice texts, and some books from their guided reading lessons.

After reading for an established amount of time (which got longer as the school year progressed), all students responded to their reading in their Reader's Notebook. Mrs. Kirven used the learning goals as a focus for the students to write about. For example, after choosing the important events of Henry 'Box' Brown's life, the students were to find the important events in the life of the person they were studying independently.

The role of Interactive Read-Aloud is critical to provide strong examples of how readers read, think, and respond. This guided process allows children to practice different ways of analyzing a variety of texts with teacher and peers and opens a world of possibility for responding and connecting to texts. The release of responsibility for the students to practice a particular learning objective on their own text of choice allows students to apply new learning independently.

Transitioning to a Reader's Workshop Model

Denise Rowe, coauthor and District Literacy Collaborative Trainer, established a strong Reader's Workshop with second graders in her classroom. The example below is a description of one day in Denise's workshop.

Mini-lesson

By connecting her mini-lesson to a previously enjoyed Interactive Read-Aloud, Denise is able to give a strong example of her learning objective.

Independent Reading and Writing About Reading

While Denise meets with guided reading groups, students read and write about their reading with a focus on responding to the mini-lesson.

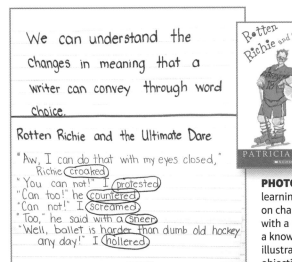

PHOTO 7.5 Denise's learning goal is written on chart paper along with a portion of a known text that illustrates the lesson objective.

Sharing

After spending time reading and writing about their reading, students gather in the common meeting space to share how they connected the mini-lesson to their own independent text. Some students are asked to share by the teacher, while others may get to share with a partner or small group.

PHOTO 7.6 (top) Leila is thinking about the book she read and is writing about it. She is using a reference guide provided by Mrs. Rowe to support her writing.

PHOTO 7.7 (left) Denise revisits the mini-lesson by choosing a student to share the work that he completed during independent literacy.

Writing About Reading and the Second-Grade Transition

According to Fountas and Pinnell (2017), "students' written responses to what they have read provide evidence of their thinking. When we examine writing in response to reading, we can make hypotheses about how well readers have understood the text. Through writing, readers can express and expand their thinking and improve their ability to reflect on a text" (p. 74). In second grade, students should have the opportunity to write about common read-aloud experiences in whole-group contexts using shared and/or interactive writing as well as write independently about their own reading in a Reader's Notebook. As the year progresses, the whole-group experiences become less frequent and the independent experiences become a part of the daily literacy routine.

In the example about *Henry's Freedom Box*, the students were writing independently in response to the mini-lesson provided by the teacher. Often this response is written in the Reader's Notebook and is shared with the class or with a peer during the sharing time to conclude the Reader's Workshop.

Another kind of written response is a dialogue letter that is written between a student and the teacher about a text that the student is reading independently. See Photos 7.8 to 7.10.

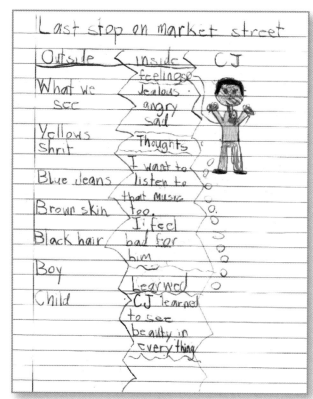

PHOTO 7.8 After a mini-lesson about describing character traits, this student chose a character in her independent reading book and analyzed the character traits using a T-chart.

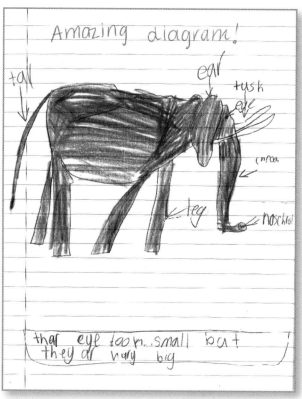

PHOTO 7.9 After a mini-lesson about understanding the use of diagrams and labels in nonfiction texts, this student created a diagram of an animal that she was reading about in her independent text.

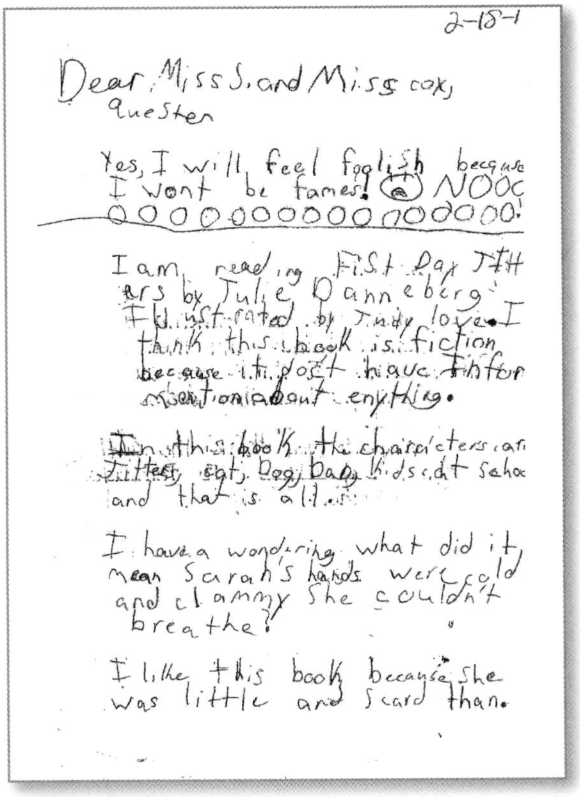

2-18-1

Dear Miss J. and Miss Cox,
Quester

Yes, I will feel foolish because I wont be famers! NOOO
OOOOOOOOOOOO NOOOOO!

I am reading FiSt Day JHH ers by Julie Danneberg Fllustrated by Judy love. I think this book is fiction because it doesn't have Tnfor msation about anything.

In this book the characters are Jitters, sgt, Deg Dady kids at saho and that is all.

I have a wondering what did it mean Sarah's hands were cold and clammy She couldn't breathe?

I like this book because she was little and scard than.

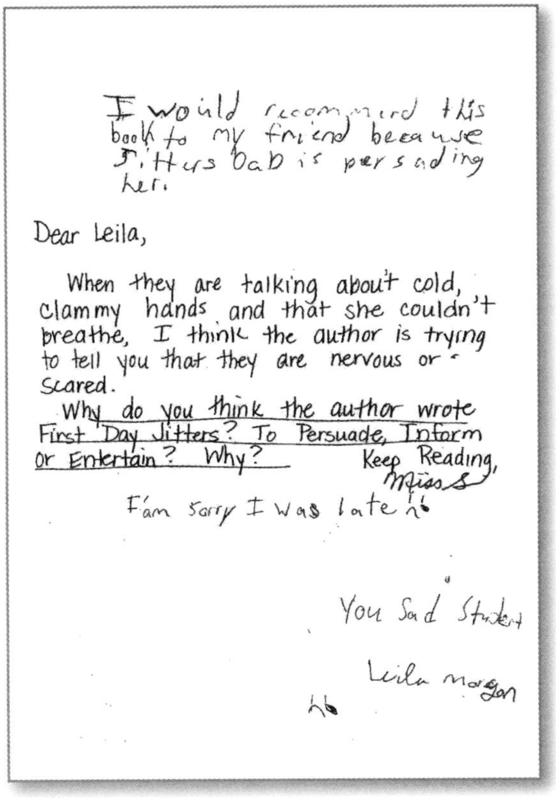

I would recommend this book to my friend because Jitters Oab is persading her.

Dear Leila,

When they are talking about cold, clammy hands and that she couldn't breathe, I think the author is trying to tell you that they are nervous or scared. Why do you think the author wrote First Day Jitters? To Persuade, Inform or Entertain? Why?   Keep Reading,
                                                    Miss J
     I'am sorry I was late.

          You Sad Student

          Leila morgan

PHOTO 7.10 This dialogue letter represents a conversation between teacher and student. The student shows evidence of thinking about the text in a variety of ways. With her teacher as her audience, she is free to express wonderings and insights with authenticity and expectation that the teacher will respond.

                                          Date

Dear _____,

   Answer any questions that _____ asked you in your last letter.

   I am reading <u>Title of book</u> by Authors Name. This book is fiction/non-fiction.

   In this book (tell us what is happening, who the characters are, and what you are learning about).

   I like/do not like this book because (give at least 1 reason why you do or do not like the book).

   I wonder (share at least 1 wondering that you are thinking).

   I would/would not recommend this book to my friend…

                         Your Student,
                         Your Name

FIGURE 7.1 This is an example of a skeleton of a dialogue letter used to support the students in Mrs. Rowe's classroom. As the students progressed, this example would become more complex.

Teachers can provide scaffolds to help students write dialogue letters as shown below. Start with short expectations for writing letters, and as the students begin to show mastery, you can increase expectations for their responses.

Dialogue Letters

The title is…	I was wondering…	I really liked…
The author is…	It made me excited when…	I didn't like…
The genre is…	It made me upset when…	My favorite part was…because…
The setting is…	It bothered me when…	My least favorite part was…because…
The characters are…	I was surprised when…	I thought the beginning was…because…
In the beginning…	The character changed…	I thought the ending was…because…
In the middle…	The character I am most like is… because…	I would (not) recommend this book because…
In the end…	The story reminded me of…	I know this because the author…
		I feel this way because the author…
		The author wrote this to (inform, entertain, persuade). I know this because…

FIGURE 7.2 Stems like the ones in the chart help the students in writing about their reading.

Conclusion

Our experiences with teachers and students continue to refine our thinking and our work. This chapter reflects a set of experiences that have positively impacted the lives of many students and have redefined how second graders are perceived in many ways. All classrooms are as unique as the students inside. It is important for teachers to consider how to best transition students towards longer periods of sustained reading and writing about reading. Many teachers have been surprised at how well their students have risen to the increased expectation of the Reader's Workshop. Setting a strong set of routines and remaining consistent with expectations that are high yet realistic is critical.

Suggestions for Professional Development

1. Gather a group of second-grade teachers. Consider the following questions:
   - How many minutes do your students read independently each day?
     - What is the value of sustained reading?
     - What are the obstacles or challenges?
   - Do your students read from independently chosen texts each day?
     - If yes, discuss why and how it works in your classroom.
     - If no, discuss why.
   - What kinds of writing about reading do your students experience?
     - How often do they write about their reading?
     - How do you provide feedback on their thinking?
   - What kinds of activities are your students doing while you work with small groups?
     - Which parts of your current practice is meeting the needs of your students?
     - Which parts of your current practice could transition into a Reader's Workshop model to better meet the needs of your students?

2. Based on your discussion, review the ideas in this chapter and consider ways you can begin to increase stamina in reading and writing about reading in your classroom. Transitions may occur at different paces and in different ways for teachers. Some options might include:
   - Create a timeline for transitioning that would work for you.
   - Choose one aspect that you feel comfortable trying and implement slowly.
     - Dedicate time to student reading and increase that time little by little.
     - Build opportunities for student choice into independent reading.
     - Implement Reading Mini-lessons and Sharing.
     - Implement Responding to Mini-lessons.
     - Try writing Dialogue Letters with a few students about their reading.
   - Visit the classroom of an intermediate level (third grade would be best since it is closest to your grade level) colleague who teaches in a Reader's Workshop.
     - Which aspects seem appropriate for second graders?
     - What would the teacher recommend for getting started based on his/her experiences?

CHAPTER 8

Creating Independent Readers, Grades 2–6

Sherry Kinzel and Wendy Sheets

*"*Readers' minds are living other lives, learning to pose the questions that are worth asking, and filling up with the knowledge of the world.*"*

—Nancie Atwell

As learners move into intermediate grades, there are greater opportunities for them to take on additional independence as readers and writers. The Reading Workshop is structured such that learning is scaffolded in a variety of ways, while students are afforded time and space to practice what they are learning within a supportive, literate community. There are multiple links shared across the literacy block with many opportunities for reading, writing, thinking, listening, and talking about books.

Reading Workshop is a highly productive, structured time within a classroom. Typically a 60-minute period, the workshop often begins with a book talk or two. Book talks are like commercials for books, so sell the books you know your students may not ordinarily choose for themselves, along with books you know your readers will love!

Reading Mini-lessons

Reading mini-lessons are a crucial daily practice within the Reading Workshop. Brief but powerful, you may want to provide mini-lessons on any explicit principle related to reading behaviors and the reading process. Mini-lesson statements are explicit, and are often stated in a way that tells what readers do, and how or why they do it. For example, a mini-lesson statement focusing on noticing character traits may look like this: *Readers consider the traits of characters by noticing what the characters say and do, along with what others say about them.* Then, examples are shared using mentor texts (books that have been previously shared within Interactive Read-Aloud) in order to provide clear demonstrations. Readers are expected to take on the reading behavior, trying it out with their own independent reading texts. Because the task is related to an authentic reading behavior—rather than an isolated assignment—readers simply apply the thinking to their reading.

READER'S NOTEBOOK

Readers should be prepared to share their learning after independent reading time. You may ask readers to jot down their thinking on a sticky note or a "thinkmark," or they may record their thinking in a Reader's Notebook. Doing so holds students accountable, provides valuable feedback to you, and helps readers prepare for sharing time. We highly recommend using a Reader's Notebook to capture the thinking readers do while reading and reflecting on texts. Whether a teacher uses published notebooks or creates her own from blank composition books, spiral notebooks, or binders, these notebooks are excellent tools for noting progress over time for individual readers and a wonderful space for readers to record their thinking about their reading. The notebook provides a space for readers to keep an ongoing reading list, to respond to mini-lessons, and to write about their reading through a variety of written responses. Often, readers will produce a weekly letter or other form of response (graphic organizer, summary, etc.) to share their thinking about their reading. When writing about what they read, readers comprehend at a deeper level. Teachers then reply to weekly responses, generating a written reader-to-reader conversation that continues to lift students' thinking.

SUSTAINED INDEPENDENT READING

During independent reading time, readers are typically reading self-selected texts that are just right for them. Intermediate readers should be able to build momentum in order to sustain their reading for longer periods of time, building up to about 45 minutes within an hour-long Reading Workshop. Because of this, readers are no longer engaging within centers, but are either reading or writing about their reading. They should have time to read independently and try out the learning from the mini-lesson, and could also be working on a reading response or engage within a guided reading group or book club on a given day. During independent reading, you confer with readers, work with guided reading groups, or meet with book clubs.

DAILY SHARE

The workshop concludes with a daily share time. Bringing readers back together to reflect upon their learning is a powerful way to extend the literate community, monitor student understanding to inform instructional decisions, and hold students accountable for their learning. Though brief (usually 5 minutes), it is such an important time to come together and bring closure to the Reading Workshop.

Many teachers often wonder, "How do I establish this goal of independence in my readers?" The following is a collection of 30 mini-lessons to help create an atmosphere of independence. It includes specific language to communicate what is expected of readers, examples of using mentor texts, and behaviors to notice when students are sharing their learning. The order of the mini-lessons mirrors Fountas & Pinnell's "Getting a Readers' Workshop Started in Thirty Days" (2017). While the sequence is useful, you may want to adjust it based on the needs of your readers. You may also need to repeat a mini-lesson or revise it a bit in order to build independence and understanding within your classroom.

Starting a Reading Workshop: The First 30 Days

After establishing a Reading Workshop during the first month or so of school, reading mini-lessons continue on a daily basis and are guided by the needs of learners, along with expectations for standards for particular grade levels. Fountas and Pinnell's *Literacy Continuum: A Tool for Assessment, Planning, and Teaching* is an excellent resource for determining behaviors and understandings to notice, teach, and support within reading mini-lessons across the school year.

DAY 1: Our Classroom Library Organization	
Goal	Introduce the organization of the classroom library. Help students learn how to select and return books. Explain voice levels.
Mini-lesson Statement/ Sample Anchor Chart	Readers use the classroom library in certain ways to make independent reading time enjoyable. • Select books you find interesting. • Return books to the correct place. • Read silently. • Reading is thinking!
Language to Support Goal	This year you will have many opportunities to choose books from our classroom library! What do you notice so far about the way the books have been organized? (Follow students' lead to discuss their noticings about ways books are categorized— by author, genre, topic, series, award winners, or other categories you've established (not levels). Show students how to take books out and return them facing the correct direction.) You'll notice that all of the books have been carefully placed in bins, and we'll talk more about their labels tomorrow. For today, you will get to browse the classroom library and choose one (or two) books that you find interesting. Be sure to note which bin you take books from so that you may return them to the right bins. That way, we may all be able to find and use them easily. Once you've chosen your books, please find your seat and get started with your reading. We'll all read silently so we may do our best work, because reading is thinking! Please don't talk with others, because I want you and your peers to be able to do your best thinking while reading. When we come back together, we'll share the books we've enjoyed.
Share Reiterate the goals of the mini-lesson. Debrief the effectiveness of students taking on independent reading behaviors.	Students share the books they have chosen (title, author, and something about the book). Behaviors and understandings you might notice and note: • Students' interests • Students' individual processes in choosing books • Students' awareness of genre, authors, and previously read books

DAY 2: How to Choose a Book You'll Love

Goal	Help students understand how to choose books.
Mini-lesson Statement/ Sample Anchor Chart	Readers thoughtfully choose books in a variety of ways. • Topics that are interesting • My favorite genre • My favorite author • Books in a series • A friend's recommendation • Award-winning books • Saw the movie about the book • Researching a topic
Language to Support Goal	Let's think about and list all of the different ways readers choose books. Think about yourself first. What do you think about when you choose a book? (Generate ideas together and write student responses on chart. The above is an example of possibilities that could be generated.) So, today you'll have another opportunity to choose books from our classroom library. When you choose a book for independent reading today, I'd like you to think about the ways you made your choice. You may think about one of the things we listed here, or you may choose a book for another reason. When we come back together to share, I'd like you to be ready to discuss the way YOU chose your book(s). Remember, reading is thinking, so read silently to give everyone an opportunity to enjoy reading and think deeply.
Share Reiterate the goals of the mini-lesson. Debrief the effectiveness of students taking on independent reading behaviors.	Students share the books they have chosen (title) and tell the way(s) they chose their book. (Honor new ideas by adding them to the chart.) Behaviors and understandings you might notice and note: • Students' individual processes in choosing books • Students' awareness of the classroom library and its organization (genre, author, series, topics, etc.) • Students' awareness of aspects of texts (as noted on chart example above) • Students' ability to clarify misconceptions

DAY 3: Finding Your Just-Right Book

Goal	Show students how to make good book choices.
Mini-lesson Statement/ Sample Anchor Chart	Readers choose just-right books to make independent reading productive and enjoyable. • Select books you find interesting • Return books to the correct place • Read silently
Language to Support Goal	Today we are going to think about some ways we can be sure we're choosing books that are just right for us as readers. Some books may be easy or challenging for different readers. For instance, a challenging book may be one that you're just not ready for YET. And that's okay. Let's start by thinking about what makes a book easy. Sometimes we enjoy reading easy books. They might be familiar to us and don't require a lot of effort. How can you tell when a book is easy? (Elicit responses from students and record on chart. See possibilities listed in the example above.) Now let's talk about challenging books. There may be times we choose challenging books to look for specific information or because we're curious. We may enjoy the illustrations or perhaps someone has told us about the book. Even though you may decide to dip into a challenging book to read a portion or find some facts, we want to choose books more often that are just right for us so we may grow as readers. How can you tell a book is challenging? (Generate and list ideas.) How can you tell when a book feels just right for you as a reader? (Generate and list ideas.) It's really important that you choose books that are just right for you as a reader so that independent reading time will be productive and enjoyable. When you're reading your books today, I want you to be aware of whether the book is easy, just right, or challenging for you, and be ready to share that when we come back together. You've been reading silently and doing your best thinking, and we want to continue so our independent reading time is most successful. Let's be sure to continue to read quietly and thoughtfully today.
Share Reiterate the goals of the mini-lesson. Debrief the effectiveness of students taking on independent reading behaviors.	Students share the books they have chosen (title) and explain why the book was easy, just right, or challenging. Honor new ideas by adding them to the chart. Behaviors and understandings you might notice and note: • Evidence of students choosing just-right books • Students articulating why a book was easy, just right, or challenging • Students' ability to clarify misconceptions

DAY 4: Reading Is Thinking

Goal	Ask readers to think about their reading.
Mini-lesson Statement/ Sample Anchor Chart	Reading is thinking! Readers should always be aware of what they are thinking while they are reading and how they feel about it. • The character or event reminds me of a personal connection. • The author's style reminds me of another book I read. • I notice something the author or illustrator did that I liked/didn't like. • I notice how my own thinking is changing.
Language to Support Goal	Remember when we read *Saturdays and Teacakes* by Lester Laminack during our Interactive Read-Aloud yesterday? We were doing lots of great thinking and sharing our thoughts as we discussed that book. As a reader, I was thinking about the boy and his mammaw making tea cakes together, and it reminded me of the times when my grandmother and I baked cookies together. I understand how he must have felt. That connection helped me to think more deeply about the boy's relationship with his mammaw, since my own relationship with my grandmother made me feel special. Can you see how I am aware of my thinking and can talk about it? That's one way I might think about my reading. As a reader, you might be thinking about what you know about the topic, or thinking about how this is like another book that you've read. You could be wondering about the characters or the author, or you could be making a prediction about what might happen next. What are some other ways you might be thinking while you're reading? As you're enjoying books during independent reading today, I'd like you to jot down two of your thoughts on sticky notes. So, in two places jot down some of your thinking and stick those notes right into your book. When we come back together to share, I'd like you to talk about those with a partner. We can add some of those ways of thinking to our chart during our Share time.
Share Reiterate the goals of the mini-lesson. Debrief the effectiveness of readers taking on independent reading behaviors.	Readers share their thinking listed on their sticky notes. (Honor new ideas by adding them to the chart.) Behaviors and understandings you might notice and note: • Students articulating their thinking about their text • Students thinking literally, inferentially, and/or analytically about text • Students looking at and listening to one another

DAY 5: Building Conversations

Goal	Help readers talk with others about their thinking.
Mini-lesson Statement/ Sample Anchor Chart	Readers build conversations with other readers so they can deepen their understanding of texts. Language to Build Conversation • I agree because… • I wonder… • Tell me more about… • Do you mean…? • I can add to that… • I disagree because… • What else were you thinking?
Language to Support Goal	Some of the ways we grow as readers are by talking and listening to other readers. Imagine that you have three blocks and all of your friends have three blocks. What would you be able to build with your three blocks? (Discuss.) What if you put all of your blocks together? (Discuss. Blocks could be used to demonstrate this powerful object lesson.) Yes, you're right! You would be able to build many different things— bigger and better things—if you all put your blocks together rather than you using just your three blocks. Conversations are like that. We build our own thinking when we listen to the thinking of others and share our thinking. Often we get thinking that is bigger and better than we had with just our thinking alone. When we really listen to each other and talk about our ideas together, we construct meaning in powerful ways. Everyone's thinking is valuable. We are helping each other as a community of readers when we share our thoughts, feelings, and understandings with others. So, here are a few language starters that can help us get a conversation started or keep it going so that a lot of great thinking is shared. (Share chart listed in example above.) Enjoy your reading during independent reading today and know that when we come together as a class for our Share, you will be building conversations with other readers. Be prepared to share your thinking,
Share Reiterate the goals of the mini-lesson. Debrief the effectiveness of readers taking on independent reading behaviors.	Readers have a conversation about what they have read and practice using language starters from the chart as needed. Class debriefs their engagement in conversation and the effect it had on their thinking as readers. (Honor new ideas by adding them to the chart.) Behaviors and understandings you might notice and note: • Students articulating their thinking about their text • Students thinking literally, inferentially, and/or analytically about text • Students looking at and listening to one another as they build conversation • Students using the language starters that were listed on the chart as needed

DAY 6: It's Okay to Abandon a Book That's Not Working For You

Goal	Help readers understand that they can abandon a book if they have a reason.
Mini-lesson Statement/ Sample Anchor Chart	Readers sometimes abandon a book after giving it a good try. • Not interesting at all • Too challenging • Too scary • Not what I thought it was going to be • Way too emotional • Personally offensive • No new information
Language to Support Goal	Sometimes when we choose a book and have given it a good chance, we find that it just isn't what we had expected. If we aren't enjoying a text, it could be that it isn't interesting to us, or that it's challenging right now. Perhaps it is confusing or scary, or maybe we really want to read another book right now. Can you think of any other reasons you might abandon, or give up on, a book? (Elicit responses and add to chart.) It's important that we give books a chance before making a decision to abandon them. And we don't want to abandon too many books. If that happens, we may need to make better choices. But there are times when readers choose to abandon books. If you have a book that you're thinking about abandoning, it's important to think about your reason. Is it too hard right now, for instance? Ask yourself if you've given it a good chance, because sometimes books get better once we get into them. During independent reading today, you'll have time to continue reading and thinking about your book. When we come back together for our Share time today, we'll talk about decisions we've made to abandon a book—either today or on another day. Go enjoy your reading!
Share Reiterate the goals of the mini-lesson. Debrief the effectiveness of readers taking on independent reading behaviors.	During Share, discuss occasions when readers have chosen to abandon books and the reasons for the choice. Add new thinking to the chart. Behaviors and understandings you might notice and note: • Students articulating their thinking about abandoning books • Students' rationale for abandoning books • Students giving books a good try before abandoning • Students looking at and listening to one another as they build conversation

DAY 7: Fiction and Nonfiction: What's the Difference?	
Goal	Show readers that they can choose books from a variety of fiction and nonfiction genres.
Mini-lesson Statement/ Sample Anchor Chart	Readers recognize the differences between fiction and nonfiction texts to help them think about them. Fiction Story that is not true; sometimes sounds like it could have happened Nonfiction True story or information that is accurate
Language to Support Goal	You've been choosing books from our classroom library, and we will continue to make choices throughout the year. Some of the books are fiction— meaning they are not true stories, although they sometimes sound realistic; some of them are nonfiction—true stories with accurate information. Let's take a look at the Books We've Shared chart showing all the books we've experienced together during Interactive Read-Aloud. (Discuss some of the titles and determine together whether they are fiction or nonfiction.) During independent reading today, I'd like for you to notice whether the book you're reading is fiction—a story that is not true, or nonfiction—a true story. Be ready to discuss your thinking about the kind of book it is and how you know when we come back together for our Share.
Share Reiterate the goals of the mini-lesson. Debrief the effectiveness of students taking on independent reading behaviors.	Readers share their thinking about whether their texts are fiction or nonfiction and how they know. Behaviors and understandings you might notice and note: • Students thinking critically about whether texts are fiction or nonfiction • Students articulating clear rationales for their thinking • Opportunities to clarify understanding

DAY 8: Getting to Know the Genres of Fiction

Goal	Help readers understand that there are different genres of fiction books.
Mini-lesson Statement/ Sample Anchor Chart	Readers recognize that there are many different types of fiction by noticing the characteristics of text. Realistic Fiction Stories with characters experiencing typical modern-day problems Historical Fiction Stories that show how people lived in the past and focus on problems and issues of a particular historic time period Traditional literature (fables, fairy tales, legends, myths, etc.) Stories passed down in written or oral form throughout history; similar story may appear in many cultures (e.g., Cinderella) Modern Fantasy (Animal Fantasy, Science Fiction) Imaginative stories that might include settings in another world, talking animals, magic, etc.
Language to Support Goal	Yesterday, we talked about the differences between fiction and nonfiction texts. Today, I'd like us to think more about all of the different types of fiction texts we might be reading or that we may read this year. When we talk about the specific type of text we're reading, we are referring to its genre. (Discuss each fiction text shared during Interactive Read-Aloud and listed on the Books We've Shared chart to determine what genre it is. Label each one with the genre codes: RF for Realistic Fiction; HF for Historical Fiction; F for Fantasy; TL for Traditional Literature.) Example: "For example, *Fly Away Home* by Eve Bunting is a fictional text. It's not a true story, although it could have happened, and could be happening today, so it is considered realistic fiction. I'll write RF next to the title so we can remember that. Another example is *Henry's Freedom Box* by Ellen Levine. It takes place during the days of slavery and is based on the true story about a real man who was a slave named Henry. The character and some of the events of the past are real, but some of the events came from the author's imagination. It seems real and took place in the past or in history, and so it is considered historical fiction. I'll write HF here. Books that are fictional and tell about supernatural events are called science fiction. Those would be shown with SF. Another example is *Pete and Pickles* by Berkeley Breathed. It is an example of a fiction book that includes unrealistic elements, such as talking animals. Its genre is fantasy. We can write an F to show fantasy. *continued on next page*

DAY 8: Getting to Know the Genres of Fiction *continued*	
Language to Support Goal *continued*	Remember when we read *Rumpelstiltskin* by Paul O. Zelinsky? That is a book that was passed down orally throughout history. It comes from the Traditional Literature genre, which includes traditional stories like folktales, fairy tales, myths and legends. Both fairy tales and folktales are traditional tales, but fairy tales have magic in them. Folktales are old stories that people tell, and sometimes they have a lesson in them. I'll mark this with "TL" for traditional literature. (Continue to share a variety of genres during Interactive Read-Aloud, noting the genre codes during brief discussions following each Interactive Read-Aloud.) As you read today, think about the genre of your book before you begin reading. Know that you may change your mind as you get into the book based on the characteristics of the text. Be ready to share what type of fiction book you are reading and to explain why you think it is that genre.
Share Reiterate the goals of the mini-lesson. Debrief the effectiveness of students taking on independent reading behaviors.	Readers share the books they are reading and tell what fictional genre they believe they are, along with reasons why they believe that. Know that some texts may be categorized within more than one genre. Being able to support one's decision with a strong rationale is most important. Behaviors and understandings you might notice and note: • Students articulating their thinking about fictional genres • Students' rationale for choosing genre labels • Misunderstandings related to genre • Opportunities to build genre understandings • Students looking at and listening to one another as they build conversation

DAY 9: Getting to Know the Genres of Nonfiction

Goal	Help readers understand that there are different genres of nonfiction books.
Mini-lesson Statement/ Sample Anchor Chart	Readers recognize there are many different types of nonfiction texts by noticing their characteristics. Biography The story of a person's life written by someone else Autobiography A person writes the story of his/her life Memoir The story of a significant experience or event in someone's life, usually autobiographical Narrative Nonfiction Text that uses a narrative (story) structure to provide info Expository Text Logically organized text that gives info about a topic Procedural Text "How-to" texts that give directions; they may teach or describe a process Persuasive Text A text that tries to convince the reader to do something or agree with an opinion.
Language to Support Goal	Yesterday, we talked about the different types, or genres, of fiction texts. Today, let's talk about the different types, or genres, of nonfiction texts. Remember, nonfiction texts are true and contain accurate information. Let's start by thinking about the nonfiction texts we've read during Interactive Read-Aloud. For example, think about *Saturdays and Teacakes*. Mr. Laminack tells us about his life when he was a young boy, not his whole life. In that text, he tells us about his memories of spending time every Saturday baking teacakes with his grandmother and how it made him think and feel and the power of his memories. Saturdays and Teacakes is an example of the memoir genre. Now think about *Wilma Unlimited: How Wilma Rudolph Became the World's Fastest Woman*. It's a text about the life of Wilma starting when she was a baby and following Wilma through her adult life. Wilma isn't telling this story. Mrs. Krull is sharing facts about Wilma's life and what we can learn from her struggles and triumphs. This text is an example of the biography genre. Many biographies are told in a chronological order and are examples of narrative nonfiction. *continued on next page*

DAY 9: Getting to Know the Genres of Nonfiction *continued*

Language to Support Goal *continued*	*A Drop of Water* by Walter Wick is another genre known as informational text. Remember how we learned lots of facts about the qualities of water and what it can do? Informational texts usually focus on one topic and share a lot of facts in order to learn something new or explore ideas. Nonfiction books may be organized to share information in categories. These books have an expository structure.
	Now, let's think about the nonfiction books you've read so far. Do you know what type of nonfiction they are? If so, what makes you think that they are that specific genre?
	(Discuss and add examples of titles of nonfiction genres to the chart.)
	Today, as you're reading, think about the genre of your text and be prepared to share your thinking about the genre during our Share.
Share Reiterate the goals of the mini-lesson. Debrief the effectiveness of readers taking on independent reading behaviors.	Readers share the books they are reading and tell what nonfiction genre they believe they are, along with reasons why they believe that. Know that some texts may be categorized within more than one genre. Being able to support one's decision with a strong rationale is most important. Behaviors and understandings you might notice and note: • Students articulate accurately a nonfiction genre • Students make an attempt to articulate the characteristics of the genre they have read or are currently reading • Students contribute to the conversation

DAY 10: Getting to Know Your Reader's Notebook

Goal	Introduce the Reader's Notebook to the students.
Mini-lesson Statement/ Chart	Readers prepare to write responses to their reading in their Reader's Notebooks as they record their thinking.
Language to Support Goal	**PART ONE:** We've been doing some great thinking and talking about the books we've been reading. Today we're going to learn to share some of our thinking in writing, and it will be a reader-to-reader written conversation. (Display a Reader's Notebook.) The Reader's Notebook is a very special tool we will be using this year to help us think deeply as readers. Let's turn to the section titled Writing About Reading. Here, you're going to be sharing your thinking about books you read by writing your thoughts in letters to me, and I will be writing back to you as well! Let's set the notebooks aside for a bit while I share an example of a reading response letter that I wrote. Your letters will be similar, except you'll tell about a book you've read. (Share example of a teacher-written letter based on a recent Interactive Read-Aloud text. See example at Scholastic.com/RLResources.) What do you notice about how this was written (letter format/structure: date, greeting, body, closing, signature; title of text is underlined; author's name included; paragraphs)? Where do you see evidence of my thinking shared in the letter? (Lead a discussion about the ways thinking is shared. Note examples of connections made, predictions, inferences, synthesis, analyzing, and critiquing.) **PART TWO:** (This is an additional scaffold that is recommended for students who have not consistently engaged in the practice of reader response entries and may require an additional day.) Now that we've thought about the example of the letter I wrote, let's work together to construct a written conversation about the book we shared this morning during Interactive Read-Aloud. (Engage in an interactive writing of a reading response letter with students contributing to the construction of meaning. Support the understanding of a letter format, including the date, greeting, body, closing, and signature. Support students in writing a brief summary that includes the title and author. Focus on the decisions involved in communicating thinking about the text in meaningful ways.) *continued on next page*

continued on next page

DAY 10: Getting to Know Your Reader's Notebook *continued*

Language to Support Goal *continued*	**PART TWO:** Today, I'm going to provide sticky notes again, and they'll be available from now on during independent reading. As you read, there may be some places where you're aware of your thinking, and it might be something you would want to include in a reading response letter. Go ahead and jot down your thinking on a few sticky notes when that happens so that when you begin writing your letter, you'll already have some ideas generated. However, don't let the sticky notes be a distraction. If you find yourself using more than two or three, you're probably interrupting the flow of your reading too much. When we come to Share today, you'll have an opportunity to build conversation about your thinking.
Share Reiterate the goals of the mini-lesson. Debrief the effectiveness of readers taking on independent reading behaviors.	Readers share their thinking about their texts, drawing upon the notes they've jotted down. They should keep their notes to support letter-writing tomorrow. Behaviors and understandings you might notice and note: • Students articulating their thinking about texts, particularly evidence of strategic behaviors (thinking beyond and about the text) • Students having jotted down thinking on sticky notes in order to share their thinking • Opportunities to support students in noticing ways they may use their sticky notes to support their letter writing tomorrow

DAY 11: Learning About Reader Response Letters

Goal	Ask readers to write a letter to you in their Readers' Notebooks. (Refer to your model letter and the one constructed interactively with the class.)
Mini-lesson Statement/ Sample Anchor Chart	Readers write response letters in their Reader's Notebooks each week to share their deep thinking. Ideas For Deep Thinking • Share thoughts/opinions about characters or plot or topic • Share connections you have • Share something the writer did well or something you didn't like about the text • Share questions or things you are wondering about. (You can find an example of such a response letter at Scholastic.com/ RLResources.)

DAY 11: Learning About Reader Response Letters *continued*

Language to Support Goal	(Pass out Reader's Notebooks.)
	Today, we're going to start writing those reader response letters for which we've been preparing. Let's talk about some of the things we need to remember to write thoughtful response letters. (Elicit student responses to generate a chart, listing ideas for thoughtful responses.)
	As you write your own letters today, you'll want to keep these things in mind. Also, there's a wonderful list of suggestions in your Reader's Notebook if you aren't sure about what kind of thinking you might share. Let's look at that together (see or create a list of suggestions for thinking inferentially and analytically about one's reading).
	Today, you will all be writing your first reader response letter to me in your Reader's Notebook as we start our written conversations about books we're reading! You'll write your best thinking in the form of a personal letter addressed to me. If you're in the middle of a book right now, go ahead and share your thoughts about the book up to that point. Start your letter on the first clean page in your Reader's Notebook section marked "Writing About Reading."
	When we come back together for our group Share, you'll get to read your letter to a partner and also listen to your partner's letter. You'll be able to talk about the places where you both notice evidence of deep thinking. Make sure you manage your time during Reading Workshop today so that you have enough time to complete your letter. I can't wait to read them all at home tonight and write back to each of you!
Share Reiterate the goals of the mini-lesson. Debrief the effectiveness of readers taking on independent reading behaviors.	Readers share their letters with a partner or in a triad. Readers provide feedback to each other about the kind of thinking shared. Be sure to collect Reader's Notebooks in order to read letters and respond to students tonight.
	Please note: This is the only time you will need to take home all Reader's Notebooks on the same day. Know that with your support, the quality of responses will improve over time. Your response should not only model correct letter form, but thoughtful communication about texts. Rather than taking an evaluative stance, a reader-to-reader conversation will be most productive in building strategic thinking.
	Behaviors and understandings you might notice and note: • Students use a letter format • Students include the title and author • Students briefly summarize their reading • Students share their authentic, strategic thinking about the text (literal, inferential, and/or analytical comprehension) • Students offer constructive feedback to others

DAY 12: Exploring Deep Thinking in Your Reader's Notebook

Goal	Invite students to talk about their letters and your response.
Mini-lesson Statement/ Sample Anchor Chart	Readers build their understandings by communicating with other readers using a Reader's Notebook.
	Use an example of a student's letter from your class that illustrates deep thinking about a text and the teacher's response, which includes the teacher prompting for more thinking in a reader-to-reader conversational way. Share an enlarged example so the class can have a shared experience, which will facilitate more productive conversation. You can find some examples of student letters at Scholastic.com/RLResources.
Language to Support Goal	In just a moment, I'm going to return your Reader's Notebooks that you turned in to me yesterday. We want to notice how this type of communication helps us to think more deeply about the texts we are reading.
	First, let's think together with an example. Carolyn gave me permission to share her letter with you. Let's read her thinking and build some conversation around how she is thinking about her book. Next, let's read my response to Carolyn's thinking. What do you notice about my thinking?
	(Additional prompts: Does it sound like I'm interested in her thinking? Does it sound like I'm giving her a quiz about her reading? Are there places in my response where I prompt her to do/share more thinking?)
	Now I'll pass out your Reader's Notebooks. I want you to read your letter first. Then read my response to you. Ask yourself these questions: What do I notice about the teacher's response to my thinking? Is she asking me to share more of my thinking? If so, underline or put a star beside my words that are asking you to share more thinking so you remember to share it when you write your next letter.
	Today, before you start reading independently, I want you to take a few moments to respond to my letter to you. Then you can continue reading and preparing for your next letter in your Reader's Notebook.
Share Reiterate the goals of the mini-lesson. Debrief the effectiveness of readers taking on independent reading behaviors.	Readers share with a partner/triad the letter that the teacher wrote to them AND their response for more thinking. Each reader provides input as to whether the students' responses met the teacher's request. Behaviors and understandings you might notice and note: • Students are able to identify requests for more thinking/information about their own reading • Students respond appropriately to requests for more evidence of thinking

DAY 13: Keeping Track of Our Reading

Goal	Teach students to keep a record of their reading in a Reader's Notebook.
Mini-lesson Statement/ Sample Anchor Chart	Readers can make a list of the books they've read to keep track of the quality and quantity of their reading.
Language to Support Goal	Today, in our Reader's Notebooks we are going to start keeping track of all the books we read independently this year. Readers become stronger readers by reading a lot of books and by also reading a variety of books. Think about your diet. You don't eat the same thing for every meal every day. We know that we need to eat a variety of foods to stay healthy. Reading a variety of books is sort of like that. We get to experience many different genres, authors, and topics. We'll always have our favorites, but reading a variety of books over the year will make us stronger readers. Turn to the section of your Reader's Notebook that says "Books I've Read." In this section, you are going to write the title and author of each book you start reading in independent reading. Take care to write the title and the name of the author correctly and neatly because we will be talking about the books you are reading independently when you and I confer about your reading. You may also want to recommend a book to another reader. Writing the title and author's name correctly is also a way of honoring the work he or she has done. When you finish reading a book, write the date that you finished your book in this column and take a moment to think about whether the book was Easy, Just right, or Challenging. Use codes listed in your Reader's Notebook to show what you thought about the book. E = Easy, JR = Just right, C = Challenging You can also use the code "A" if you chose to abandon the book. So, today before you start reading, go ahead and write the title and author of the book you are currently reading in your Reader's Notebook. Enjoy your reading! (Note: Readers may choose to add the titles and authors of books they have finished since they began Reading Workshop with you this year.)
Share Reiterate the goals of the mini-lesson. Debrief the effectiveness of readers taking on independent reading behaviors.	Readers share their first entries in their Reader's Notebook with a partner or in a triad. Behaviors and understandings you might notice and note: • Students record information in the section "Books I've Read" • Students honor the work of the writer by spelling the title and author's name correctly • Students make a connection between the chart previously created about choosing just-right books and the codes (E, JR, C) they will use in their Reader's Notebooks upon completion of reading a book or abandoning it (A)

DAY 14: Guidelines for Our Reading Workshop

Goal	Teach students the guidelines for continuing within a Reading Workshop. (Note: This may be a mini-lesson that is taught sooner within the sequence of the first 30 days.)
Mini-lesson Statement/ Sample Anchor Chart	Readers follow specific guidelines during independent reading so that ALL readers can do their best thinking. Our Guidelines for Reading Workshop <ul><li>You must always be reading or writing your thoughts about your reading.</li><li>You need to work silently so that you and your classmates can do your best thinking.</li><li>Select books that you think you will enjoy and abandon books that aren't working for you after you've given them a good chance.</li><li>Use a soft voice when conferring with the teacher.</li><li>List the book info (title, author) when you begin, and record the date when you finish. Use the codes E, JR, C, and A to describe your reaction to the book.</li><li>Always do your best work.</li></ul>
Language to Support Goal	Readers, today we are going to discuss some guidelines for Reading Workshop. These guidelines will help us make sure that we use our time wisely and that everybody has an opportunity to do their best thinking as readers. Let's look at the guidelines one at a time and build some conversation about how each one will be helpful to us and to others. (Discuss guidelines.) Are there any other really important guidelines that you think we should add to make Reading Workshop more productive? (Allow for additional guidelines if needed, but this should not be an exhaustive list. Keep it simple and easy to follow.) Okay, these are our guidelines to help us make Reading Workshop productive and enjoyable for everyone, so make sure you are following them during our independent reading. When we come together for our Share, we'll talk about how well we followed our guidelines.
Share Reiterate the goals of the mini-lesson. Debrief the effectiveness of readers taking on independent reading behaviors.	Readers discuss how effectively they believe the class was able to follow the guidelines of Reading Workshop and problem-solve any issues that prevented the group or individuals from maintaining the guidelines. Behaviors and understandings you might notice and note:<ul><li>Students worked quietly and independently</li><li>Students were engaged in reading texts or writing about their reading</li><li>Students returned or selected text from the class library efficiently</li><li>Students did not distract their fellow classmates</li><li>Students did not require the teacher's support to follow the guidelines and engage in independent reading</li></ul>

DAY 15: Writing About Our Reading

Goal	Teach students to write one thoughtful letter (or other form of writing) a week on the assigned day: Monday, Tuesday, Wednesday, or Thursday.
Mini-lesson Statement/ Sample Anchor Chart	Readers write about their reading to share their thinking about a text with other readers.
Language to Support Goal	Readers, we know that our job during independent reading is to read texts and write about what we are reading. I would like you to share what you are thinking about your reading with me once a week in writing. Remember when we worked on writing a letter? What did we say we should include in order to share our best thinking? (Refer to charts with examples of letters if necessary. Display examples of letters and a list of what to include in letters.) Notice our chart called "Reader's Responses are due on…" This will be a reminder that you are expected to share your best thinking about the text(s) you are reading on the day of the week listed on this chart. If you are absent on the day that your response is due or we don't have school on the day it is due, you may turn it in a day early or the day after it is due. (Display "Reader's Responses are due on…" chart.)
Share Reiterate the goals of the mini-lesson. Debrief the effectiveness of readers taking on independent reading behaviors.	Readers share their thinking and/or writing about their reading with the whole group or a triad. Constructive feedback can be offered by classmates or the teacher. Behaviors and understandings you might notice and note: • Students include a variety of thinking (literal, inferential, analytical) in their responses • Students understand that a thoughtful response to their independent reading is required on a specific day of the week for the entire school year • Students understand that their responses are "reader-to-reader" responses, not a "quiz-like" response to prove that they read at a literal level or as a retelling of the text

DAY 16: Proofreading Our Letters

Goal	Teach students to proofread their letters before turning them in to the teacher.
Mini-lesson Statement/ Sample Anchor Chart	Readers proofread their writing to make sure their message is clear and easy to read. (Use an example letter that a student has written or generate a letter of your own to model proofreading.) Proofreading Checklist • Do all my sentences make sense? • Do all of my sentences begin with a capital letter? • Do all of the sentences end with the punctuation that helps me express my thoughts? • Are there words I need to check for correct spelling? • Do I have the correct format for my writing (e.g., letter, T-chart, etc.)? • Is my writing neat and easy to read?
Language to Support Goal	Readers, when we share our thinking in writing, we want to make sure it is clear and easy to read for other readers. What are some things that might make it difficult to read someone else's thinking? (Allow students to generate ideas.) Many of the things you mentioned could be fixed if we proofread our work. You may have used proofreading marks like the ones on our chart (display chart) when you were editing your writing or someone else's in Writing Workshop. These marks remind us to check our spelling of words, add or delete punctuation, capitalize words, or add missing words to help it make sense. Proofreading our written work helps us make sure nothing is getting in the way of us communicating our message/thinking clearly to others. Let's make a checklist of things we need to do when we are proofreading. (Allow students to generate a clear, concise list of things they should look for when they are proofreading. Display chart for reference and/or include a page-size chart for their Reader's Notebooks.)
Share Reiterate the goals of the mini-lesson. Debrief the effectiveness of readers taking on independent reading behaviors.	Readers share changes they made to make their message clear and easy to read. It could sound like, "First, I wrote it like this…but then I changed it to…." Behaviors and understandings you might notice and note: • Students are following letter format • Students include title, author, and summary • Students share thinking that shows evidence of thinking strategically (Thinking Within, Beyond, and About the Text) • Students use conventions of writing appropriately in order to convey meaning accurately • Students write legibly

DAY 17: Reading Responses: Sharing Our Deep Thinking

Goal	Help students understand that there are a variety of topics they can write about in letters.
Mini-lesson Statement/ Sample Anchor Chart	Readers write about a variety of topics or ideas when they share their thinking about a text so that other readers understand their deep thinking. • What are the characters like (their personality, motivations)? • How is your thinking changing about characters or events? • What predictions can you make about the text? • What personal connections can you make to the text? • What do you think about how the author wrote the text (language, organization, character development, etc.)? • Why do you like it or not like it? • Who do you think would really enjoy this text? Why?
Language to Support Goal	Readers, let's think about what makes our writing about our reading interesting to someone else. Sometimes we write a retelling of what we've read. A retelling would include who the characters are and what they did throughout the story. But we want to write about much more than that when we write weekly about our independent reading books. We want to include our own thinking about events and characters in a story like making predictions or connections, noticing what the author did to create the story, and noticing how our own thinking is changing as we read a text. If we are reading an informational text, we want to share what we've learned and how our new understandings impact our lives or thinking. If we are reading a persuasive text, we want to share what we are thinking about the author's stance and what techniques he or she used to persuade. Could you see yourself using those same techniques in your own writing? I am going to challenge all of you to think "deeply" about what you are reading. Not only will it make your writing about your reading interesting to read, but you will also be reading to find meaning and purpose for your own life. Reading is enjoyable when we find meaning and purpose in our texts. Readers, you have probably noticed when we share our thinking during our Interactive Read-Alouds that we share many different kinds of thinking. For example, when we read *Saturdays and Teacakes* by Lester Laminack, we talked about how a detailed description of the setting and language that the characters used made the story very authentic, and how Mr. Laminack helped us understand the relationship that he had with his Mammaw by the dialogue and the events that he chose to share. *continued on next page*

DAY 17: Reading Responses: Sharing Our Deep Thinking *continued*

Language to Support Goal *continued*	We were noticing the author's craft—what the writer did intentionally or purposefully. We also talked about the connections we made to our own lives while thinking about this memoir. Some of us shared how this book made us think about the relationships we value in our lives. Let's make a list of possible topics and ideas we could include when thinking and writing about a text. (Generate a list with the class. Note: Some pre-published Reader's Notebooks include a list of possible writing topics and ideas.) Readers, today let's try using our list to help us share our deep thinking about our reading.
Share Reiterate the goals of the mini-lesson. Debrief the effectiveness of readers taking on independent reading behaviors.	Readers share examples of "deep" thinking in whole group or triads. Behaviors and understandings you might notice and note: • Students make connections (text to self, text to text, text to world) • Students write a summary • Students make inferences about characters, plot, etc. • Students make predictions • Students show evidence of synthesizing a text (awareness that their thinking is changing) • Students analyze by noting and describing elements of the author's craft • Students critique by giving opinions and making evaluative statements

DAY 18: Collecting, Organizing, and Sharing Your Thinking

Goal	Teach students how to collect and organize their thinking in order to prepare for writing in the Reader's Notebook.
Mini-lesson Statement/ Sample Anchor Chart	Readers make quick notes about their thinking to help them prepare for writing about their reading. (Make a chart of sticky notes that includes ideas from a text recently read during an Interactive Read-Aloud.)
Language to Support Goal	Readers, today we are going to practice using sticky notes as a tool for helping us collect and possibly organize our thoughts about our reading. Readers have lots and lots of thoughts while they read because "reading is thinking." When we write about our reading, we want to be able to share the important ideas and understandings we are having, as well as how our thinking is changing as we read and what we are noticing about the way the writer chose to create her text. You can write some of these ideas/thoughts on sticky notes. You may choose to pause a few times during your reading and write your thinking on a sticky note. You can also give yourself a few minutes before the end of Reading Workshop to write your thinking down. Sometimes you might use both options. Only write a phrase or a few sentences on each sticky note—just enough to help you recall your thinking when you are ready to actually write your weekly response to your independent reading. Let's look at a few examples from a text that we shared during Interactive Read-Aloud…. So, today you will need to record your thoughts about your reading on two or three sticky notes. When we come together for our Share time, be ready to share what you wrote on your sticky notes and why you chose those particular thoughts.
Share Reiterate the goals of the mini-lesson. Debrief the effectiveness of readers taking on independent reading behaviors.	Readers share two or three sticky notes in triads. The teacher may ask a few students to share with the whole group. Behaviors and understandings you might notice and note: • Students limit use of sticky notes to two or three so that they do not break up the natural momentum of their reading • Students record their own thinking and do not copy info from the text indiscriminately • Students can articulate a clear purpose for why they chose to record specific thoughts/ideas; they should avoid "collecting random thoughts" that will not lead to deeper comprehension

DAY 19: Keeping Track of Your Reading Interests

Goal	Teach students to create a list of their reading interests.
Mini-lesson Statement/ Sample Anchor Chart	Readers keep a list of books, authors, and genres that they would like to read in order to plan ahead for their reading or choose a new book quickly. (Display books that the teacher would like to read but hasn't yet.)
Language to Support Goal	Have you ever heard someone talk about a book and then said, "Wow! That sounds really good! I want to read that book too," but you're already reading a book and you know that you won't be finished anytime soon? When that happens, you can create a list of books you would like read in the future. In fact, most readers have a list. Here are a few of the books that I would really love to read. It would be frustrating for me to start a new book when I'm already reading a book, so I put the books I want to read on my list. I write down the title and author's name so that when I'm ready, I remember those books to read. You have a section in your Reader's Notebook that you can use to create your very own Books I Want to Read List. Listen carefully when I share a Book Talk or a classmate shares a book recommendation. Then decide if you want to add that title to your list. You can add the title of a book and author's name at any time throughout the year. From time to time when I confer with you, we'll take a look at your Books I Want to Read List together. If you already know of a book you want to add to your list, go ahead and add it today. Enjoy your reading today.
Share Reiterate the goals of the mini-lesson. Debrief the effectiveness of readers taking on independent reading behaviors.	Readers share any titles they have added to their lists. Behaviors and understandings you might notice and note: • Students are recording the title and author's name accurately • Students know where to find the Books I Want to Read List located in their Reader's Notebooks

DAY 20: Recommending Books to Others

Goal	Teach students how to make book recommendations for others.
Mini-lesson Statement/ Sample Anchor Chart	Readers often recommend books to other readers to share enjoyable stories, exciting topics, or writers they appreciate. (Share an example of a written book recommendation for a previously read Interactive Read-Aloud. You can find some examples of student-written book recommendations at Scholastic.com/RLResources.)
Language to Support Goal	Readers, have you ever read a book and thought, "I bet my friend would love this book, too?" Have you ever had someone recommend a text to you? I think making book recommendations is something that readers do naturally. I know that when I have a good experience with a book, I want to share that with other people. Sometimes I want to tell everybody I know about a special book, and sometimes I just tell one specific person about a book that I think might be especially meaningful to her. Today, we are going to learn how to make book recommendations. Here's an example of my recommendation for *Flying Solo* by Ralph Fletcher. We've already read this text during Interactive Read-Aloud, so you will already be familiar with the story. Read the recommendation to yourself. Then let's talk about what you are noticing and how this type of writing, a book recommendation, is different from other types of writing about your reading. (Discuss what students are noticing and generate a chart of possibilities for creating a strong book recommendation.) Using some of the ideas from our chart and your own ideas, I would like for each of us to write a book recommendation. It can be the book you are currently reading or one of your favorites from the past. Today your audience for your writing will be our class, so keep them in mind while you are making your recommendation. Think about what information you can share that will make them want to read the book you are recommending. When our recommendations are complete, we will write them on index cards and put them in a place where they will be available to anyone who is looking for a great book. We will have a chance to write book recommendations several times over the course of our year together.
Share Reiterate the goals of the mini-lesson. Debrief the effectiveness of readers taking on independent reading behaviors.	Readers share their written recommendations with a triad. Then the teacher asks for two or three volunteers to share recommendations with the class. Behaviors and understandings you might notice and note: • Students write one or two paragraphs • Students use the Book Recommendation chart for support • Students share their thoughts in an attention-getting or persuasive way

▶ **You can find guidelines for Days 21 through 30 at Scholastic.com/RLResources.**

Conclusion

At times, it can be challenging to develop independence within intermediate-age children. However, with thoughtful planning of classroom routines and time to teach, prompt, and reinforce the behaviors that lead to self-motivation and self-reliance, you can gradually release students to act and think as independent readers. It is our hope that you create a collaborative learning environment in which students view themselves as readers with the motivation to find a message for their lives in everything they read. It is our dream that your students become lifelong readers who positively impact our world because you chose to support them in their growth as independent readers.

Suggestions for Professional Development

1. Working with a partner, teachers can assess their classroom libraries. Note the quality and quantity of the books currently available to readers. While assessing classroom libraries, you might consider the following:

   - Organization and space for library
   - Categories, such as genre, authors, topics, award winners, series, etc. (not by level)
   - Percentage of fiction and nonfiction
   - Number of texts at each genre
   - Range of reading levels within each genre

   Discuss what you are noticing about your libraries in terms of strengths and needs. Make a list of the types of texts needed for future purchases.

2. Working together, teachers will collect and share mentor texts (usually texts that were previously read during Interactive Read-Aloud). Thinking about the needs of their own readers, they can plan future mini-lessons using the mentor texts. Give each teacher an opportunity to share how she used the mentor text within the mini-lesson.

3. Working together, teachers can develop mini-lessons to support readers beyond the first 30 days of mini-lessons to create independence. Considering the needs of your class, write mini-lesson statements that use the same structure as the mini-lessons presented in this chapter. First, address the *audience* as Readers. Next, tell *what* the readers do (the behavior you want them to practice). Then explain *how* or *why* readers do it. For example: *Readers infer what a character is like by noticing what he does, what he says, and what other characters say or think about him.* Then choose mentor texts to demonstrate the mini-lesson, pulling out pieces of text to share with readers.

SECTION THREE:
READING

Professional videos and downloadables are available at Scholastic.com/RLResources

CHAPTER 9

Interactive Read-Aloud: The Bedrock of the Literacy Block

Lisa Pinkerton

> **"When all the members of the classroom share deep and intimate knowledge of a small collection of books, a new level of communication about reading and writing becomes possible."**
>
> **—Lester Laminack**

If we compare the literacy block to a solar system, then Interactive Read-Aloud (IRA) is the sun around which all the other heavenly literacy bodies orbit. IRA is a critical component of any instructional system for literacy; it informs and supports every other part of the literacy framework. In fact, Fountas and Pinnell (2006) maintain that the practice "is not a luxury but a necessity," and they view IRA as "an essential foundation of a good language and literacy program" (p. 215). Whole-group IRA experiences build students' ability to think and talk critically about texts during guided reading and independent reading. IRA experiences may also generate ideas for composing messages during community writing or Writing Workshop and provide rich resources for writing about reading. In every grade level I have taught, from preschool to upper elementary school, Interactive Read-Aloud has been a vital part of my students' daily literacy experiences. Even my college students take great delight when I read aloud to them. Students of any age can benefit from this highly engaging literacy practice.

Defining Interactive Read-Aloud

During a *traditional* read-aloud (Trelease, 2013), the text is read orally by the teacher, perhaps with some teaching commentary, but students are not deliberately called upon to think and talk about the text. In contrast, during an Interactive Read-Aloud, the teacher and students take an active stance, engaging in conversation together. The intent of this reading content is to "spark discussion around the reading

(Fountas & Pinnell, 2017d, p. 38). According to DeFord (2002), during an Interactive Read-Aloud, "there should be intentional, ongoing invitation to students to actively respond and interact *within* the oral reading of a story" (p. 133, italics in original). Students are invited, in a planned and purposeful way, to build conversation and share their thinking about a text read aloud by the teacher. Thus, a traditional read-aloud, while an important part of any literacy program, is different from an Interactive Read-Aloud.

Interactive Read-Aloud is grounded in Marie Clay's (2001) Literacy Processing Theory. According to Fountas and Pinnell (2006): "A literacy processing system is an integrated set of strategic actions by which readers extract and construct meaning from written language" (p. 13). Within the systems of strategic actions, readers think strategically within, beyond, and about texts. During an IRA, the teacher reads the text aloud to students, managing the thinking within the text (literal understanding), which frees the students to think beyond (inferential thinking) and about (analytical thinking) the text, promoting deep literacy processing and meaning-making. When students are "[f]reed from the challenge of processing print, they can concentrate on the language and meaning" (Fountas & Pinnell, 2006, p. 217).

PHOTO 9.1 Denise Rowe, the Literacy Collaborative District Trainer for Newark City Schools, reads *Horrible Bear*, by Ame Dyckman, to a group of students.

The Context of Interactive Read-Aloud

Interactive Read-Aloud takes place during the context of whole-group teaching. The teacher holds one individual copy of a carefully selected text, most often a picture book, and students sit close to the teacher, listening to the story while viewing the illustrations. Texts may cover a variety of genres, formats, authors, illustrators, topics, themes, and the craft of writing and illustrating. Of all the reading contexts available during the literacy block, IRA offers the highest level of instructional support. The reading level of the book is typically above the instructional reading level of the majority of the students in the class, and the texts are often more complex than those students could read independently. Interactive Read-Aloud:

> …levels the playing field, ensuring that readers in the classroom experience rich, interesting texts that are age and grade appropriate, *regardless* of their independent or instructional reading level. *All* students can think and talk about the text even if they can't read it for themselves (Fountas & Pinnell, 2006, p. 216, emphasis added).

Thus, IRA is a highly democratic literacy endeavor, one that makes space for all learners, irrespective of their reading ability (Dewey, 1916/2009).

Setting

Many teachers designate a community meeting space designed so that students may gather together in order to both see and hear the book as it is read aloud. A comfortable rug can set this space apart from the rest of the classroom. Students need to sit close enough that they

can turn and talk to one another in pairs or triads. We highly recommend that children sit in a circle. A circle is conducive to supporting authentic and natural conversation, as students can see the face of whomever is speaking. In a small classroom with older students, two circles can be formed, with the inner circle of students sitting on the floor and the outer circle sitting in chairs. The teacher will need a bit of space around her so that students immediately next to her can see the illustrations. Above all, it is critical that the setting foster the development of a strong and supportive literacy community.

PHOTO 9.2 Turn and Talk during Interactive Read-Aloud

Structure

An Interactive Read-Aloud typically lasts 15–20 minutes. Fountas and Pinnell (2017) divide the structure of an Interactive Read-Aloud into three main sections: *before* (text selection and preparation); *during* (reading aloud, embedded teaching, and text talk); and *after* (discussion and self-evaluation, record of reading, and an optional written or artistic response).

BEFORE READING

Selection

- Select a text based on students' literacy needs and your learning goals.
- Choose a text you enjoy and one that you anticipate your students will also enjoy.
- See "Text Selection" guidelines later in this chapter for more specific recommendations.

Preparation

- Read the text, responding first as an authentic reader.
- Analyze the text for the unique thinking possibilities it offers readers.
- Plan 2–3 intentional stopping places to engage students in thinking and discussion.

Rudine Sims Bishop, Professor Emerita of Education at The Ohio State University, created a powerful metaphor that helps guide how teachers might think about the selection and preparation of texts for Interactive Read-Alouds. Bishop (1994) maintains: "…children need literature that serves as a window onto lives and experiences different from their own and literature that serves as a mirror reflecting themselves and their cultural values, attitudes and behaviors" (p. xiv). All students need a balance of both kinds of books, seeing themselves and others in the literature they read. Children from marginalized cultural groups often have very few mirror books available to them, an experience that can send them a damaging message of devaluation by society (Bishop, 1990a). Conversely, when children from dominant cultural groups have an excess of mirror books, they see mostly reflections of themselves in the books they read, an experience that may allow them to grow up "with an exaggerated view of their importance and value in the world—a dangerous ethnocentrism" (Bishop, 1990b, p. x). Teachers have a responsibility to ensure that all students have access to both window and mirror books in their classroom reading experiences, including those encountered during Interactive Read-Alouds. IRA has the power and potential to give students books that both validate their own lived experiences and expose them to experiences outside their own. I share Bishop's (2012) belief that "children have a right to books that reflect their own images and books that open less familiar worlds to them" (p. 9).

> IRA has the power and potential to give students books that both validate their own lived experiences and expose them to experiences outside their own.

DURING READING

Opening

- Briefly introduce the book in order to build students' interest.
- Activate students' prior knowledge when appropriate.
- For a list of "Opening Moves," see Fountas and Pinnell (2006), p. 226.

Reading Aloud

- Read the text aloud in a genuine, engaged, and expressive manner.
- Focus on bringing the story to life, making eye contact and using gestures.
- Use voice tools to direct students' attention (pitch, tone, volume, stress, and pace).

Embedded Teaching

- Stop at several places in the text to ask genuine questions and build conversation.
- Focus students' strategic activity on thinking beyond and about the text.
- Be prepared to respond to what students wonder about and notice in the text.

Text Talk

- Facilitate student talk around key thematic ideas in the text.
- When appropriate, ask students to turn and talk about the text.
- Foster strategic activity by asking students to explain their thinking.

Vygotsky's theory of teaching and learning "suggests that learning occurs most powerfully in situations that are highly social, and in which children are engaged with one another and the teacher in meaningful activities where there is a great deal of talk" (Sipe, 2008, p. 39). The Interactive Read-Aloud setting provides valuable opportunities to expand meaning-making through text-based talk (Fountas & Pinnell, 2017). IRA helps to promote a shared language for talking about texts as well as responding to the thinking of others.

PHOTO 9.3 Listening to the teacher read during the Interactive Read-Aloud

According to Sipe: "Literary understanding is a social construction, with children bringing their own unique perspectives, thus extending and refining one another's thought" (p. 236). During IRA, students learn how to talk about books with fellow readers. This shared talk about texts supports students in learning how to build upon and appreciate the thinking of their peers (Fountas & Pinnell, 2017). Thus, the literacy community supports each individual in creating a deeper understanding of the text than they could create on their own.

As the more knowledgeable other, the teacher can facilitate the talk of her students through the use of teaching, prompting, and reinforcing language. IRA develops the capacity to use academic language with which to talk about texts (Fountas & Pinnell, 2017). The teacher puts such language into the linguistic reservoir, allowing students to hear and then appropriate such language for their own text talk. Whole-group IRA experiences build students' ability to talk critically about texts during small group and individual reading contexts. In fact, Sipe (2008) reports that "educational researchers and practitioners generally agree that reading stories to children and talking with them about stories is a very important factor in ensuring their development as independent readers and writers" (p. 5).

Talk acts as a window through which students reveal their meaning-making process (Sipe, 2008). Talk during an Interactive Read-Aloud provides the teacher with valuable insight into how students are taking on strategic thinking about texts. Essentially, talk acts as formative data—which informs instructional decisions. For thinking *beyond* texts, talk can demonstrate evidence of students' ability to predict, make connections, infer, and synthesize. For thinking *about* texts, talk can provide evidence of students' ability to analyze and critique texts as art objects. Likewise, a lack of quality text talk can signal to the teacher that students need more teaching, prompting, and reinforcing as they learn how to think and talk strategically about texts.

AFTER READING

Discussion

- Provide opportunities to expand thinking around meaningful conversational threads.
- Invite students to make connections within and across the text and other texts.

Self-Evaluation

- Ask students to evaluate their thinking and learning during the IRA.
- Ask students to evaluate their individual contributions to the conversation.

Record of Reading

- Record the title of the book on the classroom record of reading experiences.
- This record becomes a resource of mentor texts for reading and writing mini-lessons.

Written or Artistic Response (Optional)

- Students may write about their reading experience.
- Students may respond artistically to their reading experience.

Louise M. Rosenblatt's Transactional Theory of the Literary Work can help inform the overall Interactive Read-Aloud experience. Rosenblatt (1995) defines a reading experience as a particular event involving a particular reader and a particular text at a particular moment in time under particular circumstances. Rosenblatt (1978/1994) conceives of reading as a creative transaction, the "coming-together of a human being…and a text" (p. 143). During a reading transaction, "an interdependent relationship in time" is built between a reader and a text (Rosenblatt, 1998, p. 888). Essentially, a reader and a text come together to produce a reading experience. In Interactive Read-Aloud, it is a teacher, a *group* of readers, and a text that create the transactional reading experience:

> The fire of literacy is created by the emotional sparks between a child,
> a book, and the person reading. It isn't achieved by the book alone, nor by
> the child alone, nor by the adult who's reading aloud—it's the relationship
> winding between all three, bringing them together in easy harmony.
> (Fox, 2001, p. 10)

The aim of Interactive Read-Aloud is to engage readers in the creation of a shared transactional reading experience, one that builds relationships between students, books, and teachers.

Planning for an IRA Lesson

Text Selection

It is important to know your students and their unique identities in your reading community. This knowledge will help guide the selection of texts that will most interest and engage your students. First and foremost, choose a text that you love. Your passion for the book will be contagious, creating shared book joy in the literacy community. There are so many rich texts to choose from that teachers should never have to read a book to their students that they themselves do not enjoy. Additionally, choose a text that you anticipate your students will also take delight in. Select a range of both fiction and informational texts. Within fiction, strive for a balance of realistic, historical, and speculative fiction. Look for award-winning picture books featuring lyrical language and outstanding art. Texts featuring high-quality writing and illustrations will offer students opportunities for deep thinking and rich discussion, as well as nurture an appreciation for picture books as aesthetic art objects. You may also wish to choose texts that connect to your grade level's curriculum or standards. Reading books by writers or artists that your students have previously enjoyed can lead to an author/illustrator study. Texts that have the potential to expand students' knowledge of the world are especially worthwhile. See the appendix for an extensive list of high-quality picture books for Interactive Read-Alouds.

Lesson Planning

The preparation for an Interactive Read-Aloud is purposeful; the teacher does not simply pluck a book off the shelf and begin to read. Rather, the IRA is an intentionally planned literacy lesson, one that is carefully designed to meet the particular needs of a particular group of learners. Kiefer's (1982) groundbreaking research into children's responses to picture book illustrations found that the teacher's role is crucial in supporting children in their process of understanding the meaning of picture books. Teacher knowledge about literature helps to promote student talk that is substantive (Sipe, 2008).

STEP ONE

The first step in planning an effective IRA is to choose a book that you personally love. For example, one of my favorite picture books to read aloud to students of all ages is Ame Dyckman's *Tea Party Rules* (2013), illustrated by K. G. Campbell. At first glance, the book is light and humorous, but a careful reading reveals powerful themes and messages. Campbell's sepia marker and colored-pencil illustrations bring the entertaining characters to life. According to the book jacket:

> When Cub follows his nose through the woods, he discovers a backyard
> tea party…with cookies! He is just about to dig in when the hostess of the
> tea party shows up. And she has several strong opinions on how
> Tea Party *must* be played. Cub tries to follow her rules … but just how
> much can one bear take, even for cookies?

A high-quality story offers a multitude of opportunities to engage students in thinking inferentially and analytically. *Tea Party Rules* invites students to think strategically by predicting, making connections, inferring, synthesizing, analyzing, and critiquing.

STEP TWO

The second step is to experience the book as an authentic reader. The teacher is the book's first reader. Strive to be aware of your own strategic activity as you read the book. Ask yourself: What impacted me? Where was I most drawn into the story? Where were my emotions engaged? What did I notice and wonder about? Answering such questions will help uncover key thematic ideas in the text.

For example, the first time I read *Tea Party Rules*, I was surprised at the little girl's response after closely examining Cub, who has taken the place of her stuffed teddy bear at the tea party table. Instead of yelling "A bear!" or "You're not my teddy bear!" and running for safety, the girl calmly states: "You're grubby." I realized that throughout the book, the girl's responses to the real bear are not what the reader expects, subverting the reader's predictions and inviting deep thinking and discussion around whether or not the girl knows the bear cub is real.

STEP THREE

The third step is to think analytically and critically about the text and the unique possibilities it offers for meaning-making. Consider what the story is *really* about: What are the big ideas? What unique possibilities does this text hold for strategic thinking? What truths does the story tell about what it means to be human? The answers to these questions will help guide you to places in the text that will provide opportunities for your students to think strategically about key thematic ideas.

For example, in *Tea Party Rules*, Cub puts up with a great deal, from being given a bath to being dressed in doll clothes, in order to get what he wants—cookies! The girl ignores a great deal, most notably that she is interacting with a real bear, in order to get what she wants, which is someone who will follow her tea party rules. Dyckman helps readers consider big ideas and questions such as: What do we put up with, even ignore, to get what we want? One of my favorite memories of sharing this book as an Interactive Read-Aloud took place in a sixth-grade classroom. After one student pointed out all the visual differences between the real and stuffed bears, I asked: "Do you think that the girl knows the bear is real?" Another student responded: "Of course she knows he's real. She is carrying him up the stairs to her house. He is breathing! His heart is beating! He has real fur!" When I followed up with the question: "Then why is she pretending that he is her stuffed bear?" The student stated, in a slight tone of disgust at my obtuseness: "Cuz she wants what she wants." This sixth-grade student was able to think critically and strategically about a deeper meaning in the story, uncovering a truth about what it means to be human. She taught me that any book containing powerful messages for readers to discover through shared talk will make a powerful IRA for any grade level, even if the content seems more suited to younger children.

STEP FOUR

Choose several places (usually 2–3) in the book to invite conversation and discussion. You may consult the IRA "Selecting Goals" section of *The Literacy Continuum* (Fountas & Pinnell, 2017) to confirm your planned points of inquiry, and refer to *The Prompting Guide* (Fountas & Pinnell, 2012) as a resource for language with which to write your questions and/or thinking prompts. Four general questions that scaffold strategic activity are: "What are you thinking?" "What are you noticing?" "What are you wondering?" and "What are you feeling?"

Natural stopping points in *Tea Party Rules* occur whenever the girl's reactions to the real bear cub are not what the reader anticipates. For example, when the girl tells Cub that the last tea party rule is to eat daintily, Cub can't believe it. The text states: "This was too much for a bear. So Cub helped himself." The illustration shows the bear grabbing the cookies and stuffing them into his mouth while the girl reacts in astonishment. I stop and ask: "What do you think the girl will say when she sees that the bear is eating the cookies?" Invariably the students predict that the girl will finally yell something about the bear being real because he is moving right in front of her. I keep reading and we discover that instead, the girl shouts: "YOU'RE NOT FOLLOWING THE RULES!" which always leads to a rich discussion about why the students think she says what she does.

STEP FIVE

Plan how you will invite students into the book. Think about how you will engage their attention and prepare them for active listening and response. Possibilities include drawing students' attention to the author and/or illustrator, the genre or format, a specific theme or topic, or a connection to a previously shared text. The primary goal is to activate students' interest in listening to the book. When I introduce *Tea Party Rules*, I like to let my students know that Ame Dyckman is one of my favorite authors. I share that she writes light-hearted

hearted books full of humor and big ideas. In fact, I love launching an author study with this book. My students adore *Wolfie the Bunny* (Dyckman, 2015), *Horrible Bear!* (Dyckman, 2016), and *Read the Book, Lemmings!* (Dyckman, 2017) all illustrated by Zachariah OHora, as well as Dyckman's (2017) newest book: *You DON'T Want a Unicorn!*, illustrated by Liz Climo.

Planning Caveat

Careful planning is key to ensuring a successful Interactive Read-Aloud lesson. However, it is also important to be prepared to deviate from the plan based on students' responses. While teachers do plan several stopping points for the IRA, they should remain tentative and open, ready to respond to what the children wonder about and notice in the text. Such "teachable moments" are "stimulated" by the comments and questions generated by students in response to the reading experience (Sipe, 2008, p. 214). These moments cannot be specifically planned for because they are natural responses during the actual read-aloud experience. However, if the teacher reads the book carefully first, thinking about her own reactions to the story and the possibilities it holds for meaning-making, she is "more likely to see the potential in the children's comments" because of her own personal reading experience of the book (Sipe, p. 214).

The Benefits of the Interactive Read-Aloud

IRA *engages* students in:	• shared book experiences • strategic thinking about texts • rich and meaningful conversation about books	IRA develops students' "ability to think, talk and write about texts that fully engage their interest…" **(Fountas & Pinnell, 2017d, p. 11).**
IRA *expands* students':	• knowledge of literature • complex language structures • vocabulary and conceptual knowledge	"Recognize the importance of reading aloud to children. Let children hear text structures that expose them to language beyond their control. Reading aloud to children of any age will sketch for them a landscape of features into which their own language usage may expand" **(Clay, 2004, p. 10).**
IRA *exposes* students to:	• models of fluent, phrased reading • the aesthetic craft of picture books • mentor texts from a range of authors/illustrators in a variety of genres and formats	"Reading aloud supports learning in every other area. It is a way of nourishing the intellect of your students, expanding background, vocabulary, and language, developing an appreciation for inquiry, and creating a literary community in your classroom" **(Fountas & Pinnell, 2006, p. 215).**
IRA *promotes*:	• the joy of reading • the expansion of world views • the development of a reading community	Literature invites children "to insert the texts they hear and read into the texts of their own lives, and to broaden their view of what is possible" **(Sipe, 2000, p. 88).**

Benefits of Interactive Read-Aloud

There are a multitude of benefits to a daily practice that promotes the oral language and literacy of students (Fountas & Pinnell, 2006). A single high-power Interactive Read-Aloud can address a multitude of higher literacy standards. For example, whenever I read *Tea Party Rules* to a group of students, regardless of the grade level, we invariably cover 20–25 bullets under "thinking *beyond* the text" and "thinking *about* the text" in the "Selecting Goals" section of the IRA Continnum (Fountas & Pinnell, 2017).

Additionally, when readers personally experience literature, they "develop the imaginative capacity to put themselves in the place of others—a capacity essential in a democracy, where we need to rise above narrow self-interest and envision the broader human consequences of political decisions" (Rosenblatt in Karolides, 1999, p. 169). Sipe (1999) explains this phenomenon: As students move through experiences with literary texts, they forge links between the literature they experience and their own lives. These personal links "have the potential to be both informative and transformative for their developing sense of themselves as individuals and members of society" (p. 127). Walking in the shoes of characters with experiences unlike their own can help to expand students' understandings of what it means to be human, building empathy for others. Thus, IRA is a highly political endeavor, one with the potential to transform the ways in which students view themselves and their world (Sipe, 2008).

Cautions

First, students do not need a lengthy introduction to the book. The purpose of the opening is to prepare students to actively engage in, and respond to, the reading experience. It is not always necessary to build students' background knowledge. A high-quality book will fill in the gaps in student knowledge. My favorite way to introduce a book is as follows: "I'm so excited to share this new book I found with you! I loved reading it, and I hope you will too!"

Second, it can be tempting to stop and define every vocabulary word new to students. While one of the benefits of Interactive Read-Aloud is that it builds students' vocabulary, it is not a vocabulary lesson. Spending too much time defining words detracts from the flow of the IRA. If there is a word that you feel students must understand in order to comprehend the story, stop for just a moment to briefly define the word, and then continue reading. IRA is not the context to call on random students to define words; this practice wastes valuable discussion time. Rereading of favorite texts, however, will naturally build students' exposure to, and understanding of, new vocabulary.

Third, it is paramount that the students do most of the talking during the read-aloud, rather than the teacher. The teacher's role is to facilitate and support the thinking and conversation of students. While the teacher can model her own thinking aloud, it is critical that the majority of the conversation comes from the students. When necessary, teachers can use prompting and reinforcing language to scaffold the thinking and text talk of their students.

Finally, only two to three stopping points are recommended so that the Interactive Read-Aloud does not lose momentum. Stopping to discuss every possible point will interrupt the flow of the story, causing students to lose interest and engagement in the reading experience. A book that offers a variety of valuable stopping points can be reread during a subsequent IRA lesson.

Conclusion

Mem Fox (2013), a fierce advocate for reading aloud to children, reflects on the memories her students shared with her regarding their read-aloud experiences in her college courses:

> I'm pleased they remember because underneath all that joy they also heard wonderful words and ways to use them; stunning sentences and ways to construct them; memorable stories and how to shape them; linguistic problems and how best to solve them. They also heard bold beginnings and deeply satisfying endings. And in amongst it all, from the stories they listened to, they learnt life's lessons and how to be good and caring citizens (p. 8).

My students, from kindergartners to college undergraduates, have felt that same read-aloud joy. Interactive Read-Aloud brings the magic of stories alive in vibrant classroom communities. The benefits from this highly supportive classroom practice, one that takes just 15–20 minutes a day, are exponential. I invite you to make Interactive Read-Aloud the center of your own literacy block, around which all the other literacy practices may orbit.

Suggestions for Professional Development

1. Setting for Interactive Read-Aloud
   - Assess your community meeting space. Is there room for the students to sit in a circle? (If not, work with a colleague to arrange the IRA space so that students can see one another while building collaborative conversation.)
2. Materials for Interactive Read-Aloud
   - Visit your school's library or the children's section of your local library.
   - Explore picture books by the authors and illustrators in the Interactive Read-Aloud book list in the appendix.
   - Begin creating a list of your own favorite picture books to read aloud to students.
3. Team IRA Planning/Teaching/Reflecting for Interactive Read-Aloud
   - Meet together as a team of teachers, either at grade level or across grade levels.
   - Choose a picture book for an Interactive Read-Aloud and plan the lesson together.
   - Take turns observing one another conducting the Interactive Read-Aloud.
   - Meet together after everyone has taught to reflect on the IRA experiences.
     - How did each teacher facilitate text talk?
     - How did the classes respond differently to the book?
     - How did the groups of students take on strategic thinking?

CHAPTER 10

Teaching for Phrasing and Fluency: Connections to Comprehension

Andrea McCarrier

"Prosodic reading is fluency's link to comprehension.**"**

—Timothy V. Rasinski

When good readers process print aloud, the way it sounds provides a window into how those readers are constructing meaning. They pause to set off parenthetical expressions, use falling tones at periods, let their voices rise for questions, and get slightly louder for emphasis at exclamation points. They set off dialogue and make it sound like talking. They divide language into phrases and adjust both the speed and level of sound that indicate their interpretation of the author's intended meaning. Good readers also process text with momentum—at a rate that allows listeners to make sense of the language. Good readers are not simply fast; phrasing, pauses, and inflection also figure strongly into the quality of their reading.

When individuals read silently, we assume that they are also processing the text fluently and, at some level, getting a sense of phrase units even though they may not be consciously aware of the process. They are accessing the meaning of the text, or comprehending. As Fountas and Pinnell (2017) stated, "…comprehending is an active, meaning-making process, not simply an isolated outcome or product after reading" (p. 469). There is a deep relationship between what the reader does to comprehend and what the reader does to sustain fluency and phrasing. As a teacher, I find that it is important to notice and encourage fluency and phrasing as a way of supporting children as they make sense of reading, even when they are just beginning.

Factors That Contribute to Fluent Reading

As an adult, I am a fluent reader, but at times I can become disfluent. Consider these two sets of directions:

1. Directions for making oatmeal cookies.

2. Directions for changing oil in your car.

Which set of directions would be easier for you to read with fluency and understanding? Reading a recipe is much easier for me because I know the format and vocabulary. Usually there is a list of ingredients followed by a set of step-by-step directions for combining ingredients. I can process the directions quickly because my years of experience in reading recipes helps me know what to expect when I read this sort of text. Also, I am familiar with the terms used in cooking. I do not need to ask someone what to do when the recipe reads, "Sift the dry ingredients."

On the other hand, following the directions for changing oil in my car is much harder for me. I lack the prior knowledge about changing oil that would help me anticipate what should come next. I falter over unfamiliar vocabulary. My reading slows down because I have difficulty making sense of the directions. Comprehension eludes me! To read the directions with greater understanding I need an orientation to the material—an overview of what happens in an oil change, for example, or a brief explanation of some unfamiliar terms.

Good readers are both accurate and fluent. When good readers make errors in reading, they typically distinguish between the errors that change the meaning of a passage and those that do not. They monitor their reading for meaning-changing errors and self-correct them, while ignoring the unimportant errors. Highly fluent readers seem to be able to extract the author's message from the text through effective problem-solving of errors that can cause breakdowns in meaning for less fluent readers (Clay, 2016). This assumes that there is a match between the text being read and the reader's instructional level. If the book is too hard, the reader will have to spend so much time in problem solving at the word level that it will be difficult to fully comprehend the text.

> Highly fluent readers seem to be able to extract the author's message from the text through effective problem-solving of errors that can cause breakdowns in meaning for less fluent readers (Clay, 2016).

Knowing the content of a text and how it is organized allows us to predict what we will be reading. A text that does not match our expectations prompts problem-solving behaviors such as rereading a phrase, a line, or even an entire paragraph. As proficient readers, we are constantly monitoring whether we understand what we are reading and whether we need to search for more information. We fix errors and clear up confusion using all sources of information available to us. Background knowledge and awareness of text structure help us gather this information more quickly and precisely. Many other factors influence fluency and comprehension as shown below.

Factors Related to Sustaining Fluency and Phrasing

- Recognizing and solving words in a quick, automatic way.

- Recognizing phrase units.

- Being aware of and using punctuation.

- Activating and using background knowledge.

- Understanding and using the organizational structure of the text.
- Using meaning and language structure to monitor reading (making sure reading makes sense and sounds right).
- Predicting at the word, phrase, and text level.

Knowledge of the topic, text structure, language structures, and vocabulary all aid the reader in constructing meaning. These kinds of knowledge also aid the reader in predicting and confirming his or her reading more quickly, because he or she can use everything he or she knows about the topic to read in an efficient and flexible way.

Teaching for Phrasing and Fluency in Reading Across Instructional Contexts

If we value phrased, fluent reading, then we need to teach for it. Children will not automatically develop a sense of phrasing and fluency. You can teach for phrasing and fluency across every context in the comprehensive literacy framework.

Teaching for Phrasing and Fluency Across Contexts

Instructional Context	Teaching to Support Phrasing & Fluency
Interactive Read-Aloud	• Demonstrate phrased, fluent reading. • Talk with students about how meaning influenced the reading.
Shared Reading	• Demonstrate phrased, fluent reading. • Students read together using phrasing and fluency. • Discuss how to interpret texts to influence phrasing and fluency.
Guided Reading	• Demonstrate phrased, fluent reading during the introduction, if needed. • Select a text that supports phrased, fluent reading. • Teach for fluency individually or to the group.
Independent Reading	• Provide a rich collection of quality books for students to select to read independently. • Encourage buddy reading to practice fluency.

The four instructional contexts listed above offer varying degrees of teacher support to help students build a reading process and become fluent readers.

Interactive Read-Aloud

Reading aloud provides the highest degree of support because you model what good readers do when they read. Good readers also read for a purpose—to enjoy a story or gather information. When you read aloud to children, you demonstrate that reading is a meaning-making process that is facilitated when the reading makes the author's message clear. Most often, you will read to the entire class as a way to build a community of readers who share common knowledge about particular stories and topics. Because your students will ask for favorite stories over and over, they will quickly join in on repeated phrases such as, "I'll huff, and I'll puff, and I'll blow your house down." Here, the children are participating in reading from their memory of the text and respond with fluency and expression based on how you have read the story. Reading aloud reveals your interpretation of the text based on your phrasing, intonation, and fluency.

Through Interactive Read-Alouds, you teach students that reading is a message-getting process (Clay, 1991). Simultaneously, you foster the conditions for meaning-making through your phrased, fluent, and expressive reading. You model the kind of reading behaviors you want students to exhibit when they are reading their own books by demonstrating that reading is meaningful. Because of how you use your voice, the narrative sounds like storytelling, and the dialogue sounds like talk.

Some books are better than others for demonstrating phrased, fluent reading. Books that contain dialogue offer excellent opportunities for expressive reading. For example, think of how you would use your voice to portray the characters in *Little Red Riding Hood* (Hyman, 1983), showing the innocence of Little Red Riding Hood, the sneakiness of the wolf, and the frailty of the aged and sickly grandmother.

The following example is from a second-grade classroom with many English language learners. Sharon, the teacher, prefaced the reading of the book she selected, *The Korean Cinderella* by Shirley Climo (1993), with an explicit demonstration of how to construct meaning about the story from illustrations and prior knowledge. The class had previously read several versions of *Cinderella*.

Sharon:	This is *The Korean Cinderella* by Shirley Climo. (She opens the book to show both the front and back covers as a double-page spread.) As I look at the illustrations, they remind me of Korea. The colors are very rich and deep, and I love that. (She closes the book to show just the front cover.) If you look at the character on the front, she looks like she is dressed for… something special.
Jorge:	A wedding.
Sharon:	A wedding. It could be.
Tana:	A princess.
Sharon:	A princess? Yes, that's possible.
Sujata:	Is Korea in China? (Many of the children in the class are from Southeast Asia.)

Sharon:	No. It is in Asia. Let's look at a globe. China is in Asia, also. They are both in that part of the world—on the continent of Asia.
Sujata:	Oh!
Sharon:	(She points to the fan on the cover.) She's using something to hide a part of her face. We'll find out what's going on.
Jorge:	She's ugly.
Sharon:	You think she looks ugly and that's why she's hiding her face? Hmmm. Is Cinderella usually ugly?
Sujata:	No!
Jorge:	Yes!
Sharon:	Well, maybe at the beginning. She's not really ugly, but she's not dressed well.
Elizabeth:	She's shy.
Sharon:	She's shy?
Sujata:	She's dirty. But why is she dirty?
Elizabeth:	Because she has to clean the house so much.
Sharon:	Yeah!
Chamrong:	She doesn't take a bath.
Sharon:	Could it be she doesn't have much of a chance to take a bath?
Chamrong:	(His voice sounds as if he is reconsidering his comment about baths.) Yeah.
Sharon:	(She points to the flower in the illustration.) Notice this flower. This is sort of a little clue here.
Bunthean:	Lotus blossom.
Sharon:	It is a blossom. Not a lotus blossom. What kind of blossom do you think it is?
Sujata:	Pear blossom.
Sharon:	Pear blossom. You're right. (Sharon turns to the endpapers.) Even the endpapers are a deep, rich color. Look at this symbol. It's the same one that is on the fan. Another student told me that people have this symbol hanging in their cars. Have any of you seen that?
Children:	Yes!

Sharon:	Do any of you have something like that?
Children:	No.
Sharon:	There's that symbol again. See it on the fan? (She indicates the illustration on the page opposite the title page. She turns to the first page of the story.) Look at the illustrations now. Look at how important the illustration must be because the writing is only in this little white box. Almost the entire page is taken up with illustrations, so the illustrations must be very important. (She points to animals.) And you see animals. So animals must play a very important role in this story. This story begins, "Long ago, in Korea." So this story begins: "Long ago" instead of "Once upon a time." *(Sharon begins to read again.)*
	"Long ago in Korea when magical creatures were as common as cabbages, there lived an old gentleman and his wife."

As Sharon continued to read the story, she drew the children's attention to key parts of the illustrations to help them understand how pictures can be used to predict or anticipate what will happen next. She also helped students follow the story through the way she read dialogue. Children could tell by her voice whether the frail father, the matchmaker, or the mean stepmother was speaking. Sharon clearly modeled how her understanding of the story influenced how she was reading about each character.

Shared Reading

Shared reading is an instructional context that also offers a high degree of support to students because you and the students share the task. An essential feature of shared reading is an enlarged text. The text can be

- a big book, which is an enlarged version of a text.
- a piece of interactive or shared writing with large, legible print.
- a teacher-made chart.
- a text from the Internet projected on a whiteboard.
- a poem projected on a screen by a document camera.
- a text used for a dramatic reading.

Shared reading is different from an Interactive Read-Aloud in that students are attending to the enlarged print and reading along with the teacher (see Chapter 11). Shared reading lessons may begin with reading the text to the students so they are familiar with the content. Older students preparing for a dramatic reading may be able to join in right away. The initial focus is on meaning and enjoyment. After students have heard and talked about the text, revisit it to develop specific skills or strategies. For example, students may talk about how to read a poem to reflect their interpretation of its meaning. Should this part be loud or soft, read quickly or very slowly to build suspense? These activities directly link fluency to meaning.

Shared reading provides an excellent opportunity for modeling phrased, fluent reading. When young children start to read, they must learn to think about language in a different way. Now they must learn that the flow of speech is actually made up of separate units, called words. Think about the phrase "peanut butter and jelly." When we talk, we say it as if it were one word: *peanutbutterandjelly*. In order to learn how to read, the young child must learn how to map speech onto print. Clay (1991) writes:

> Young children are trying to discover how the flow of speech can be cut into word segments. It is false to assume that the child knows that his oral sentences are composed of word units. He has to discover what the word units of his speech are. He learns to break his speech into words separated by pauses and tries to match units of speech to patterns in print. (p. 162)

PHONOLOGICAL AWARENESS AND WORD AWARENESS

Our task as teachers is to help the young child develop phonological awareness and break up the flow of speech into word units. One way is to teach the child word-by-word matching; that is, to point to each word as they read it. The coordination among eye, hand, and voice helps the emergent reader break the stream of language into individual words. Young children often confuse multiple-syllable words as being more than one word. So, we teach children how to break up the oral language *peanutbutterandjelly* into the individual words "peanut butter and jelly" by demonstrating word-by-word matching and encouraging them to do it themselves.

When word-by-word matching is well under control, however, we want the eyes to take over the process. We want readers to begin to combine words into meaningful phrases as their eyes move quickly across them. This is the time to move away from external mediators such as the finger or a pointer, which ultimately can interfere with fluency.

TRACKING PRINT

During shared reading lessons, you can help students make the transition away from using an external mediator to track print. Instead of crisply pointing to each word, sweep the pointing stick across the page. The sweeping motion guides the readers' eyes to move more quickly. Another way to encourage your children to use their eyes to track across a line of print is to point only to the beginning of each line. When the children finish reading a line of text, move the pointing stick to the beginning of the next line to support their return sweep and to maintain momentum and unison in their reading. Teaching children to put words together into meaningful phrases is key to developing their ability to read fluently with comprehension. We want to teach them to recreate the stream of language with phrasing consistent with the meaning of the text. Phrases within the sentence are often separated by the briefest of pauses. Sentences are indicated through slightly longer pauses and changes in pitch.

PHOTO 10.1

One teacher wrote the text on sentence strips and then cut the strips apart into phrase units, placing them in a pocket chart. Notice in Photo 10.1 how she left space between the phrase units in order to emphasize that each group of words must be read together. The teacher and the class revisited this poem several times, so that the children would get a feel for reading in phrases. The poem was left in the pocket chart so that they could practice phrased reading during buddy reading or independent reading. You could also write out a text and have the students decide the best places to cut the text into phrase units. The texts you select for this purpose should be easy for all children in the group to read so that they can process the text quickly, with a minimum of problem-solving, so that their full attention is on phrasing.

EXPRESSIVE READING

You can also use shared reading lessons to teach students to be expressive readers. Again, it is important to choose a text that is easy for students to read. Stories with dialogue work especially well in teaching expressive reading. For example, *The Little Red Hen* (Galdone, 1973) is a familiar story for many children. When children read the dialogue they can be taught to change the pitch and inflection in their voices in order to make the personalities of characters come alive. Part of what we are teaching children is that we read dialogue differently from narrative. There are many texts suitable for older students to prepare a choral reading of the text by working in small groups to interpret the text to guide their performance.

In the following example, the teacher chose to teach for expressive reading by using a refrain from one of the class's favorite read-aloud books, *Kate and the Beanstalk* by Mary Pope Osborne (2000). Like other Jack tales, the giant repeats a refrain throughout the book. The author has varied the giant's traditional refrain. Her giant roars:

> *Fe, Fi, Fo, Fum'in,*
>
> *I smell the blood of an Englishwoman.*
>
> *Be she alive or be she dead,*
>
> *I'll grind her bones to make my bread.*

One of the twists in Osborne's variant of the Jack and the Beanstalk tale is that the giant's wife, the giantess, has a refrain of her own. When Kate first comes knocking at the castle door, the giantess opens the door, grabs Kate, and chants:

> *Help me!*
>
> *I need a servant!*
>
> *The last one stole*
>
> *our hen*
>
> *and ran away!*

The next time Kate knocks, the giantess repeats the refrain except for the phrase "our hen." The giantess does not know that Kate, who is in a new disguise, is the thief, so she hires Kate to replace the servant who stole the bag of coins. The giantess laments her dilemma by repeating the refrain, replacing "our hen" with "our money bag" in the text.

The teacher wrote both refrains on enlarged charts. In order to follow the story line, she wrote "our money bag" and "our hen" on separate sentence strips so that it would be easy to match the story line with the correct text. Before she read the story, the children and teacher talked about how the giant and giantess felt. The giantess was desperate. The giant was hungry and looking for something good to eat. Then the children practiced how each character might have sounded.

The first time the children read the parts of the giant and the giantess during the Interactive Read-Aloud, they all read both parts. Later, the teacher divided them into two groups. One group read the part of the giantess, and the other group read the part of the giant. The refrains provided a powerful opportunity for teaching for phrasing, fluency, and expression.

USING PUNCTUATION

Writers use punctuation to indicate meaningful breaks in the text. For example, writers use quotation marks to indicate that someone is talking. They use commas to indicate that the reader should pause briefly, and periods to indicate the end of sentences. When children ignore punctuation, meaning-making is often distorted and disrupted.

Dialogue can be just as powerful for teaching children to attend to punctuation as it is for teaching expressive reading. Poetry is another excellent choice for teaching children the importance of punctuation.

Shared Reading With Informational Texts

When students become more skilled in using organizational tools, such as tables of contents, they can spend more time attending to information rather than searching for information. Knowing how to use organizational tools aids comprehension.

USING BIG BOOKS

Many commercially produced science and social studies curricula include big books for teaching key concepts. These big books are excellent tools for teaching how to read expository texts. Often these books have a table of contents, an index, section headings, and captions or sidebars. The primary purpose for big books is to teach content included in the course of study—but they are also excellent materials for teaching children how readers use text features to aid in comprehending the text. For example, the table of contents not only helps the reader locate information, but it also gives the reader an idea of what the author thinks are the important concepts in this topic.

If you do not have enlarged texts for teaching children how a table of contents works, you can use a document camera to project the table of contents from standard-sized trade books. For example, the study of the life cycle is part of the course of study in many primary grades. In the following lesson, the teacher enlarged the table of contents from the book *The Life and Times of the Honeybee* (Micucci, 1995).

The children and their teacher looked through the titles listed in the table of contents. The group decided that the section with the title "From Egg to Bee" was probably about the life cycle of the honeybee. When they turned to page eight, they found just what they were looking for. Throughout the year, the teacher took every opportunity to demonstrate that readers can use the table of contents to find out how the book is organized and what topics the author included or chose not to include.

> Shared reading is a powerful instructional context for teaching children how to become more skillful readers across a range of genres.

Shared reading is a powerful instructional context for teaching children how to become more skillful readers across a range of genres. Teachers provide important models for how reading sounds so students read fluently on their own.

Guided Reading

Guided reading differs from the first two contexts in three ways:

1. Unlike Interactive Read-Aloud and shared reading, students are grouped according to their instructional needs. Most teachers will have four or five groups of four to six students each.

2. Teachers select books for each group that match their instructional level and needs.

3. Teachers support students by orienting them to the book, but each student reads the text independently. Teachers listen to individuals read, closely observe how they are processing the text, take notes, and provide teaching points when needed.

During guided reading, you support each student's ability to comprehend the text and to read with phrasing and fluency in two ways—book selection and book orientation.

SELECT THE TEXT

First, carefully select a text that matches the student's instructional level. If a book is too difficult, both fluency and comprehension will be affected. Next, plan an introduction that provides enough background information to support meaning. You may also need to demonstrate how the book is structured or point out any unusual language usage or vocabulary. The orientation should support students' reading yet leave enough reading work to help each learner become a better reader on the next book.

For example, consider the book *Mr. Putter and Tabby Pour the Tea* by Cynthia Rylant (1994) [Level J]. Most children can read this book at the end of first grade or the beginning of second grade. The story is divided into three sections. The title of the first section is "Mr. Putter." In this section we find out that Mr. Putter is lonely and decides to find a cat to keep him company. The second section is called "Tabby." This section explains how Mr. Putter selected Tabby—a cat just like himself. The last section, "Mr. Putter and Tabby," describes the relationship between Mr. Putter and Tabby and why it is so satisfying for both of them.

DURING READING

Before I introduced this story to a group of children I worked with, I asked if they had read other Mr. Putter books because that knowledge would shape my introduction. I wanted them to understand the relationship between this story and other stories they may have read. In this case, the children had read several other Mr. Putter stories. Before reading the book, I asked them to talk about what they already knew about the relationship between Mr. Putter and Tabby. I told them that this is the story about how the friendship between Mr. Putter and Tabby began.

Level J books tend to be longer stories, containing episodes that relate to one another in some way. Tools such as a table of contents or chapter headings help readers get a sense of the organization and structure of the text. In the case of *Mr. Putter and Tabby Pour the Tea*, I knew that reading the section headings would help the children understand what each section was about and support both fluency and comprehension. To highlight the book's organization, I placed each of the three headings on a piece of chart paper to provide an overall picture of the book, and I drew their attention to the way the story was divided and helped them to form expectations.

Then I talked about the first section, "Mr. Putter." I encouraged them to think about why Mr. Putter might feel lonely so they could understand and empathize with his problem. Then I asked them to consider the next section heading, "Tabby," and predict what might happen in this section. Could a cat be the solution to Mr. Putter's problem of being lonely?

I knew that the children would be able to solve most of the words in the story, but that the meaning of "company," as applied to a cat, might be challenging. Most eight-year-olds would think of Tabby as a pet. They might not equate pets with companions or company, so this literary language might be unfamiliar. I also thought that most of the group would not be familiar with the concept of clipping roses, so I talked about gardens and what gardeners do, using the language of the text. This background knowledge and their familiarity with language would help the children maintain a stream of meaning as they read these stories.

Notice how the text layout supports phrased reading in the following text:

> *All day long as Mr. Putter*
>
> *clipped his roses*
>
> *and fed his tulips*
>
> *and watered his trees,*
>
> *Mr. Putter wished for*
>
> *some company.*

AFTER READING

After the children had read and enjoyed the story, I wrote the above text on chart paper and taught for phrasing. I pointed out that the single sentence extended over several lines of text. We read the sentence together and talked about its meaning. Then we practiced reading it in phrased units until our reading sounded phrased and expressive. I asked the children to read several pages of the story aloud during their independent reading and to monitor themselves for phrased reading. You could also use a document camera to project the text so everyone can easily see it.

The teaching point at the end of the lesson is also an opportunity to teach fluency depending on the needs of the group.

Independent Reading

Independent Reading provides students with opportunities to practice reading. You may not be there to support each student as they read, but you have provided support in terms of making appropriate books available and guiding their selection of texts. Texts used during independent reading vary from texts young students have read in shared reading lessons or written during interactive writing lessons to books that older students have read in their guided reading lessons or selected based on the recommendation of another student. Because students are choosing books that are easy for them to read, independent reading provides time for them to practice phrased, fluent reading. Children need opportunities to practice fluent reading every day. They can read books from your classroom library, or reread interactive writing or poetry that is displayed on charts in the classroom. They can also read with a reading buddy or listen to recordings of stories, especially those that lend themselves to expressive reading.

Conclusion

Research indicates that there is a relationship between fluent reading and comprehension. Reading fluently, with phrasing, reflects recognition of the writer's intended meaning in combination with the reader's interpretation of the text. Fluent, phrased reading also reflects the joy of reading for meaning. As teachers, we can support fluency, phrasing, and comprehending through careful selection of texts and through teaching for these components across the language and literacy framework.

Suggestions for Professional Development

1. Meet with grade-level colleagues to discuss fluency and phrasing in reading. Have each participant prepare for the meeting by bringing a recording that illustrates one minute of fluent, phrased oral reading from a student in her or his class. Be sure that the student was reading without pointing and has full control of word-by-word matching. Also, be sure that the recording was made on the second reading of the book, after the student had read it once either orally or silently. Bring the written text so that listeners can follow along and notice punctuation.

   • How do the readers sound?

   • What evidence is there that they are noticing phrase units?

   Discuss teaching ideas from this chapter and select a goal to try one or more ideas to strengthen your teaching of phasing and fluency.

2. Identify two or three students in your class who have difficulty demonstrating fluent, phrased reading and record two minutes of them reading. Work intensively with these students for a two-week period. Do not increase the level of difficulty of the text, but try different ways to support phrased, fluent reading. Record two minutes of reading again to share with colleagues and discuss what you have learned.

CHAPTER 11

Shared Reading: Essential for All Grades

Patricia L. Scharer

> "Shared reading provides an excellent support for students as they interact with, interpret, and analyze increasingly challenging texts through close reading."
>
> —**Adria Klein**

Don Holdaway (1979) has been called the "father" of shared reading. Based on his observations of young readers, Holdaway noticed the early literacy behaviors children appeared to learn while "lap reading" with a parent or caregiver, much like the child in Photo 11.1. These experiences with books begin quite early as adults read board books to infants and toddlers; some requesting favorites over and over. I once gave a copy of *Goodnight Moon* (Brown, 2002) in French (*Bonsoir Lune*) to a colleague as a baby gift since both she and her husband were fluent in French and planned to speak French at home. She later reported to me that her 11-month-old son would not go to sleep without repeated readings of this favorite book. For some children, these daily experiences with books enable them to become fluent readers before entering school. For others, the enjoyment of having a story read to them, sometimes over and over, instilled a love of books, an appreciation for reading, and excitement to become a reader. Initially, shared reading was typically found in primary classrooms. More recently, however, shared reading has become an important link to guided reading and to close reading in the upper grades as well.

PHOTO 11.1 Mother reading to her preschool daughter

What Does Shared Reading Look Like?

An enlarged text in print or projected digitally—with students seated so they can all see the text—is the essential beginning of shared reading. The text may be a commercially made big book or chart poem, a student-teacher collaboration created in the classroom through interactive or shared writing, or a poem written on chart paper by the teacher.

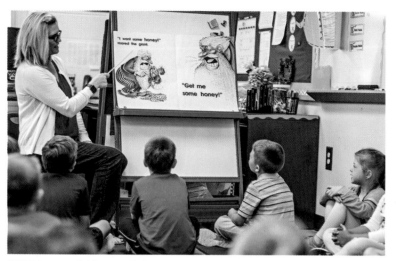

PHOTO 11.2 Children read about the giant with enthusiasm.

The teacher and students read the text together while the teacher points to the print. The teacher uses a thin pointer to help students notice the beginning of each word during the reading. Later, the teacher may only point to the beginning of each line when students can track the print independently. Shared reading is a time to enjoy stories and poems together and learn not only about text features but also learn how to interpret the text in ways that change how it is read. For example, in Photo 11.2, the class has talked about how to read the giant's words. What do we know about the giant that will help us know how to read it? He is large, angry, and very hungry! So, that's how the words must be read. These early interpretations of text set the stage for deeper understandings in more difficult texts.

Organizing for Shared Reading

It's essential for the setting to be organized so that each student can easily see the print. In Photo 11.2, the teacher uses an easel to hold the book and students are seated on the carpet. You can also use a document camera to project the print onto a screen or whiteboard. Just be sure that the text can be seen easily by the child seated farthest away. I once watched a lesson where the teacher wondered why the students weren't chiming in during the reading. She hadn't realized that the glare from the window on the shiny surface had made the text very difficult to read. So, be sure to consider the students' perspectives when arranging a space for shared reading.

Pointer

Resist the temptation to buy a fancy pointer with a butterfly or flower at the end of it that covers up the print and doesn't clearly point to individual words or letters. The only pointer needed for shared reading is a thin, inexpensive dowel rod, which can be purchased at any hardware store. You may want to have several different lengths—a longer one for texts projected on the screen or whiteboard and a shorter one for big books and poems. The teacher in Photo 11.3 has her pointer all ready for the shared reading lesson.

PHOTO 11.3 Getting ready for a shared reading lesson

Materials for Shared Reading

There are other materials needed for shared reading beyond the text and a pointer. Some teachers keep a small box on the shelf under their easel to store sticky notes, highlighter tape, and Wicky Stix. The sticky notes can cover all or part of a word to teach children how to read an unfamiliar word. For example, a teacher could cover up *potatoes* in Photo 11.4, a story about a boy trying to lose a tooth, and have the class think about what the word might be. The picture could be of some help, but showing the first letter in the word would narrow it down to words starting with the letter *p* like *potato* or *pudding*. Finally, totally removing the sticky note could reveal the word so students can take a close look to confirm if the word was *pudding* or *potato*. This teaches students to think flexibly when figuring out new words by using the picture or meaning of the story, looking at initial letters, and then using the entire word to confirm if they are right. Students can use highlighter tape to identify rhyming words in a poem or circle all the words that start or end the same using the Wicky Stix, thin flexible sticks that attach temporarily to paper. These materials help teachers to focus attention on a particular section of print and help students learn to problem-solve words independently.

I ate some bread.
My tooth did not come out.

I ate some potatoes.
It did not come out.

PHOTO 11.4 From *My Loose Tooth*

It is also important to have a small whiteboard, Magna Doodle, or chart paper available for a few minutes of word work during a lesson. If your easel is large enough and there is room above the big book, keep whiteboard markers handy in case you need to write a word the class knows, like *and*, to help them read *band*. Having materials close by ensures that valuable instructional time is not lost tracking down your Magna Doodle.

Shared Reading Lesson

A shared reading lesson features seven essential components. Working together, the teacher and students:

1. Reread familiar texts.

2. Are introduced to a new text.

3. Read the new text together.

4. Discuss the meaning and illustrations of the text.

5. Focus on one teaching point.

6. Notice features of the new text.

7. Reread the new text.

A shared reading lesson begins as the class selects several familiar texts to reread and enjoy. You may want to select a particular text but the students can choose, too. This is a time to enjoy favorite books, songs, poems, and charts. Next, the teacher introduces a new text to read. For example, in a kindergarten class where the students are ready to learn about reading more than one line of text, the teacher may select a big book like *Wishy-Washy Sleep* (Cowley, 2012). If students are already familiar with other books about Mrs. Wishy-Washy, they will certainly notice the main characters on the cover—Mrs. Wishy-Washy, the cow, the pig, and the duck—and talk about what they know about each. Then, the teacher may read the book for students, inviting them to join in the repetitive refrain "I am asleep" that each animal says until, of course, Mrs. Wishy-Washy says, "Food! Food!" By the end of the book, the children will beg to read it again, this time joining their voices with their teacher on each page. The class will want to talk about the story, perhaps wondering why the animals wouldn't respond to Mrs. Wishy-Washy at first or noticing how the illustrations show how the animals are feeling.

PHOTO 11.5 Cover of *Wishy-Washy Sleep* by Joy Cowley

PHOTOS 11.6 First pages of *Wishy-Washy Sleep*

Mrs. Wishy-Washy called, "Bath! Bath!"

"I am asleep," said the cow.

PHOTO 11.7 Rereading a big book during independent literacy time

PHOTO 11.8 Shared reading of a BIG KEEP BOOK with a small group

The teacher may want to direct students' attention to some particular features of the text such as the two lines of teaching requiring return sweep to read, or the exclamation point. Then students can share what they notice about each two-page spread. Brian may find *Bath* which starts like his name; others may find *said* on several pages. The lesson ends by reading the book one more time, ensuring that students will be able to read it independently the next day like the children in Photo 11.7.

It's important to remember that shared reading can also take place in a small-group context. In Photo 11.8, the teacher is using a large version of a KEEP BOOK to teach return sweep to a small group of students. When the students are successful at reading the large version together, they will each receive a small copy of the same book to read independently and put in their personal browsing box before taking it home to keep.

Benefits of Shared Reading

During shared reading, students:

- experience fluent reading success.
- read texts beyond their independent levels.
- learn about early literacy behaviors, how words work, word solving, genre features, and writer's and illustrator's craft.
- experience the joy of reading.
- build community.

Shared reading is a rich learning context for all ages. It's a time when every student can experience success while joining their voices with the teacher's. The text is of greater difficulty than the class can read independently but, over time, they are able to successfully process the text. The voices of classmates support children who are not quite ready to read the text with the teacher's support and the repeated reading of the text. For young children, this is a time to experience texts much like Holdaway's lap reading (1979). But shared reading is not only for the young. Older students can join their voices to read selected pages of chapter books, nonfiction, or poems to learn about inference, genre characteristics, interpreting the

City Dog, Country Frog

SPRING
- waiting for a friend
- dog/frog meet at the rock
- dog/frog played

SUMMER
- dog teaches frog how to play
- dog/frog were best friends

FALL
- Frog/dog memories (thinking)
- tired (Frog)

WINTER
- dog is alone on the rock
- dog is sad

PHOTO 11.9 Kristy Staten's kindergartners' summary of *City Dog, Country Frog*

text, or the writer's craft. Shared reading should be a joyful time to read, interpret, and discuss interesting texts. Every text read by the class builds a community of readers who share a knowledge of children's literature.

For example, Kristy Staten's kindergartners loved listening to *City Dog, Country Frog* by Mo Willems (2010) during Interactive Read-Aloud lessons and created a chart summarizing the book during shared writing. However, the class did not like how the book ended so they decided to write their own book about the dog and his new friend, the chipmunk. Over several weeks, the class wrote the book during interactive writing and illustrated it. Both the chart and the book became favorite texts for shared and independent reading. Kristy commented that the class probably would have been happy to continue reading and writing about the book for several more weeks but she finally decided to move on to other topics! This authentic reading and writing experience truly built a literate community within Kristy's classroom and shared reading was at the core of it.

PHOTOS 11.10 Pages from a big book written by Kristy Staten's kindergarten class

Selecting Books for Shared Reading

The criteria for selecting big books is similar to choosing quality children's literature. A strong story line and interesting illustrations will ensure both the attention and delight of the readers. In some cases, big books with rhyme, rhythm, and repetition support early readers who will revisit the books again and again. Of course, the books must have print large enough for students in the back to easily read.

Not all big books are suitable for shared reading. Since big books tend to be expensive, be cautious about your purchases. Many books are printed in an enlarged size but the print is still too small for students to read from the back of the group. The value of these books may be that the illustrations would be easier for students to see while the teacher is reading but the texts should not be used for shared reading. Big books also differ relative to the potential for teaching. For example, the single line of text and two-word sentences on each page of *Butterfly* (Moeller, 2013) are excellent choices for early readers working on locating the print, one-to-one word matching, and using the picture to figure out an unknown word.

PHOTO 11.11 Pages from *Butterfly*

Readers ready to learn about return sweep, how to move from the end of a line to the beginning of the next, will enjoy and learn from *Wishy-Washy Ice Cream* (Cowley, 2012).

Other books may support expressive, fluent reading such as a big book about the wolf who says, "Little pig, little pig, let me come in." Enlarged versions of plays also make great texts for shared reading as students work together to interpret how a character would say a certain line. These sessions could lead to performances for other classrooms.

More and more nonfiction big books are becoming available with different purposes—both for content and to illustrate the unique characteristics of that genre. Photo

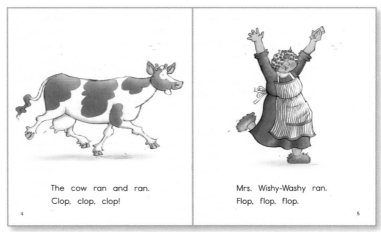

PHOTO 11.12 Pages from *Wishy-Washy Ice Cream*

11.13, for example, is a page from *Animals Everywhere* (Bennett-Armistead, 2015) with several features commonly found in nonfiction texts—labels and bolded vocabulary in addition to narrative text. For teaching science concepts, the teacher may slow down the reading of this

PHOTO 11.13
(left) Page from *Animals Everywhere* with narrative text, labels, and bolded vocabulary

PHOTO 11.14
(right) Diagram from *Growing Things*

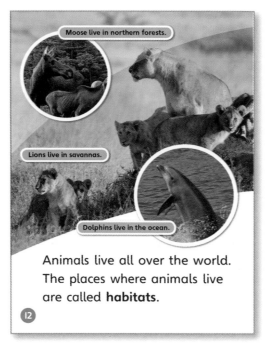

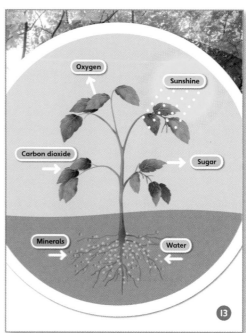

text to also thoroughly discuss the photographs and how the labels and bolded words help with understanding concepts.

Photo 11.14 illustrates another type of text and picture commonly found in nonfiction—a diagram. This big book, *Growing Things* (2015), also by Susan Bennett-Armistead, can be used to introduce students to the concept of a diagram so they can discuss not only the content, but also why it's important to study such illustrations. Both big books have other features such as a table of contents and a glossary, which are important concepts to teach as well.

Organizing Big Books

Given the different purposes for enlarged texts, it's important to organize them in efficient ways. Some schools keep big books in their book room alphabetically or in a single wooden box. I suggest a different system. Try putting all the early concept books in one area and the more difficult books with texts that can be seen by the whole class in another area. Depending on the number of books, you may decide to separate each of these types into further categories. The books that are large versions of children's literature should be stored close to the interactive reading collection. Also, sort out the nonfiction big books and organize them according to content and your curriculum. This method will ensure that teachers can find the "just right" big book when they need it!

Other Texts for Shared Reading

Big books aren't the only texts used for shared reading. Photo 11.15 illustrates how one teacher used sentence strips to write nursery rhymes. When the students were familiar with the rhyme, the teacher mixed up the sentence strips and the students worked together to put the rhyme back together (like Humpty Dumpty!) using a pocket chart.

Class big books like Kristy Staten's class made are excellent texts for shared reading. Similarly, other products of both interactive writing and shared writing can be used during shared reading lessons. Charts of favorite songs are also excellent texts for shared reading. By using a document camera, you can project pages of individual books for everyone to see. Be careful with your selection as some cameras project a fuzzy image that will not enable students to read along. The document camera can also be used for shared readings of texts from the Internet, historical documents, speeches, and news stories.

PHOTO 11.15 Nursery rhyme on sentence strips

Shared Reading of Poetry

In K–6 classrooms, poetry comes alive as teachers enlarge and share using a document camera or on chart paper or sentence strips. Teachers might first introduce poetry by reading aloud from a collection, such as the classic, award-winning *A Jar of Tiny Stars: Poems by NCTE Award-Winning Poets* (Cullinan, 1996), which features children's favorite poems from ten winners of the National Council of Teachers of English Award for Poetry for Children. During multiple expressive readings by the teacher, children can enjoy the "heavy" words used by Barbara Juster Esbensen in her poem about the elephant or Valerie Worth's description of a lawnmower, "Spitting out a thick/Green spray."

Such poems provide exciting opportunities to talk about word choices within a concise text by discussing how the poet selected just the right word to express a meaning larger than the poem itself. Word selection also can be discussed relative to the mood created by the poem leading to reading the poem with expression based on the interpretation. The light, rhythmic calypso beat of *No Hickory, No Dickory, No Dock: Caribbean Nursery Rhymes* (1995) by John Agard and Grace Nichols may be contrasted with the slow, deliberate pace of some of the animal poems by Esbensen in *Words with Wrinkled Knees* (1986). Readers of Esbensen's poems about the elephant or the dinosaur will need to take a plodding, weighty tone quite different from the Caribbean rhythms.

As children experience multiple readings of their favorite poems, you can write their favorites on chart paper and read the poems together. Seeing their favorites in print ensures successful readings and a new opportunity to study the writer's craft. As they see the poems,

readers may want to talk about what they notice about the patterns, rhythms, rhymes, word choices, or format.

Some poetry collections offer themes for readers to explore. These books are particularly valuable as a starting point to discuss how writers convey meaning using different formats and word choices within the same topic. Spirals in nature is the topic of the single poem found in Joyce Sidman's *Swirl by Swirl* (2011) and the shape of poems is the focus in *Wet Cement: A Mix of Concrete Poems* (Raczka, 2016). Sibling rivalry is explored in *No Boys Allowed: Poems About Brothers and Sisters* (2006), a compilation by Jon Micklos, Jr. From the simple, partially repetitive format of Mary Ann Hoberman's "Half-Whole-Step" to the dialogue and drama of "Who Ate the Last Five Cookies?" by David L. Harrison, these poems provide readers with the opportunity to study the craft of many authors, each writing a poem or so about the same topic.

Connection Between Shared Reading and Guided Reading

Shared reading is a powerful instructional context for setting students up for success in guided reading. The lesson parallels the organization of a guided reading lesson through the selection of a "just right" text, introduction by the teacher, reading of the text, discussion, and word study. Becoming familiar with this routine will facilitate guided reading lessons. Shared reading is an opportunity for children to see and read literary language, which

> Shared reading is a powerful instructional context for setting students up for success in guided reading.

they will see in guided reading such as "once upon a time." The reading your students experience through shared reading models the kind of fluent reading expected during guided reading, softly read by the younger students but gradually becoming a silent, inner voice more rapidly for more expert readers. Shared reading is a chance to teach specific ways to approach unknown words, which will transfer to both guided and independent reading such as searching for context clues or analyzing word parts. For very young readers, shared reading may be when the child learns the difference between pictures and words, where to start reading, and how do one-to-one matching with words so they are ready for guided reading texts. For older students, shared reading is a time to explore more sophisticated aspects of text such as idioms, conversational text, foreshadowing, and character development.

Shared Reading and Close Reading

Waters (2014) writes that "…shared reading emphasizes accurate and fluent oral reading through repeated readings, while close reading focuses on deep comprehension of main ideas and central themes by returning to the text" (p. 9). But shared reading has an important contribution to close reading. Fisher & Frey (2008) recommend interactive shared reading, which "allows the teachers to instruct through modeling by demonstrating how a skill or strategy is applied to reading. After modeling, the teacher asks questions to foster discussion and provides prompts to scaffold students' understanding as they read text that is initially new to them" (p. 37). When a teacher selects a piece of text for shared reading, the rereading and discussion deepen comprehension. Waters (2014) concluded that "a shared reading approach not only enabled special needs students, English language learners, and other struggling readers to increase fluency and accuracy in oral reading, but also empowered them to deepen their comprehension and their understanding of the implicit message within the narrative through reading excerpts closely" (p. 20).

Conclusion

Shared reading is an important and powerful learning context for all grades. It is a rich opportunity to teach not only reading and writing but also to teach other content as well. Most classrooms today have access to both enlarged texts and the technology to project and enlarge texts. The key is to select texts carefully with your students in mind and enjoy every minute of the time you spend reading together!

Suggestions for Professional Development

1. Gather the big books teachers have in their rooms or in the school book room and critically evaluate the set. Discard old, torn books and then sort the books according to the best way the book can be used. Is this a book to teach early reading behaviors? Fluency? Performance reading? Poetry? Nonfiction? Decide on a way to organize and share your books across classrooms.

2. Examine the poetry books in your school library and pull out those that would be good to project using a document camera. Consider marking them a unique way so they are easy to find when you need a "just right" book. Then, try out several poems with your class and share what students discussed and learned from this experience.

3. Read this chapter and discuss with your grade-level team. Think about goals you might set to increase the use of shared reading in your classroom. Talk about your goals, how this chapter might support your goals, and how you can support each other as you try out new ideas.

CHAPTER 12

Using Data to Make Instructional Decisions for Readers

Sherry Kinzel

> "Effective literacy instruction is based on knowing what children need and understanding literacy development so that teachers can offer expert teaching."
>
> —**Richard L. Allington**

What is the purpose of assessing students? This critical question is one that we too rarely discuss. While I believe that most educators would agree that assessment should drive classroom instruction, we seem to get caught up in the practice of assessing students as a means to an end or something that we are required to do for accountability. When this attitude toward assessing prevails, assessments are rarely used to inform future instructional decisions for students. They may be summative assessments, which have their own value. However, summative assessments rarely help a teacher predict where she needs to go next with her students. No one wants to believe that the time and effort spent assessing students results in simply recording the results on a form that is then filed away. The purpose of assessing has to be greater than just collecting data.

I believe that any one specific assessment should be viewed as one specific piece of the puzzle for understanding what a reader is capable of doing at that point in time. And there are many pieces to a puzzle. It is the teacher's role to fit the pieces together to create a whole picture of a reader's ability to process a text effectively, and it is the *responsive* teacher who then makes instructional decisions based on what she has learned about her readers. How do we embrace our essential role as instructional decision-maker?

Embracing My Role as Instructional Decision-Maker

One way to do that is to consider how we view the act of assessing. Assessing readers and writers should be viewed as an investigation or exploration. It is an opportunity to learn, confirm, and/or adjust your understandings about what a reader can do, can almost do, or is not able to do yet. The teacher is positioned as learner to find out as much as possible about each student if he views assessment as a form of inquiry.

Ask yourself the following questions to place yourself in a learner stance when analyzing student responses on assessments:

1. *What does this assessment tell me about this child as a **reader**?*

2. *What information/data or previous understanding about the reader does this assessment confirm?*

3. *What did I learn about this reader that I did not know before?*

4. *Are there recognizable patterns across this collection of individual or class data?*

Imagine that you are sitting down to have a parent-teacher conference. Instead of just showing the parents the child's scores on a variety of assessments, you begin the meeting with this statement: *Thank you so much for taking this time to talk with me about Evan's literacy development. This is what I know about Evan as a reader*…. How would you finish that statement? What would you want his parents to know about him as a reader?

Looking at assessments through the lens of what that one piece of the puzzle conveys about this child as a reader has the potential for helping us identify what a reader is doing successfully, what a reader can almost do (possibly within his zone of proximal development), and what a reader cannot yet do. Recognizing when reading behaviors fall into one of these three categories can help us determine whether the reader needs additional instructional support. Using this lens for analyzing assessments can become a responsive approach for teachers to inform their instruction. To further develop this approach, you might consider using a form like this one.

After using this lens over time, teachers tend to develop a habit of mind for viewing assessments this way.

Documenting a Student's Reading Behaviors

Reading Behaviors the Reader Uses Successfully	Reading Behaviors the Reader Can "Almost Do" or Can Use With Support	Reading Behaviors the Reader Shows No Evidence of Using

Working in the Zone

Lev Vygotsky introduced the concept of the zone of proximal development (1978), where a learner can almost act successfully on his own. The student may show evidence of being able to partially use certain behaviors. However, the student needs the support of a "more expert other," someone with a little more knowledge or experience, such as a teacher, to take on the behavior independently. In other words, teachers are working on a student's edge of learning when they are working in a child's zone of proximal development. Working with readers at their edge of learning creates the greatest potential for growth.

When you are using formal published assessments or teacher-created assessments, it is important that you look past a score or a level to consider each of the four questions previously mentioned. If not, you could run the risk of using that score or level to simply label that reader. For example, it is not unusual to hear teachers refer to readers as being "on grade level" or "a Level S reader." However, neither of those labels tells me what the reader can do or helps me to determine my next instructional moves. Oftentimes, informal assessments can be done by teachers quickly and require little preparation. Best of all, informal assessments can be linked to the work that students are already doing, and there is no need for a teacher to locate an additional passage from a random text. For example, a teacher might listen in to a child while he reads an authentic piece of text, such as the book he is reading independently during Reading Workshop. Informal assessments, such as running records or reading records, can provide great insight into what a reader is doing when he is processing text. The following is an example of how I use informal assessments to inform my instruction.

While conferring one-on-one with Evan, I took an informal running record while he read aloud a text he had chosen from the class library. I simply asked him to read while I took a few notes about the things he does while he's reading. The first running record you will see is my original record of his reading. It was done "informally" on a blank sheet of paper. The check marks indicate that Evan read the word correctly. If he did not read the word correctly, I recorded what he said or did using a coding system (Clay, 2013). The second running record is the same as the first one. I modified it so that you could see the actual text that Evan was working to read.

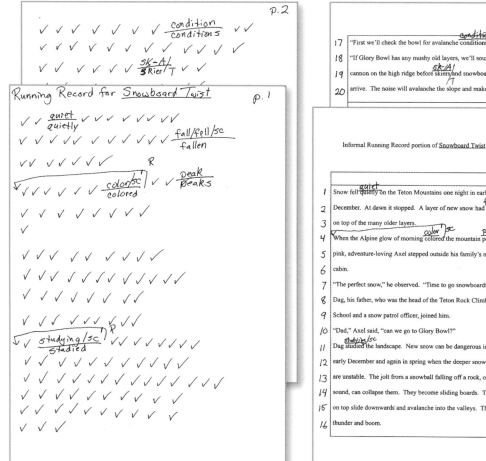

FIGURE 12.1 Original reading record

FIGURE 12.2 Modified reading record with text

Full-sized versions of these examples and forms are available at Scholastic.com/RLResources.

Analyzing the Reading Record

Using this reading record, I asked myself three questions:

- What does this assessment tell me about this child as a reader?
- What information/data or previous understanding about the reader does this assessment confirm?
- What did I learn about this reader that I did not know before?

Let's investigate each one in turn.

What does this assessment tell me about this child as a reader?

When I considered my notes, I noticed a pattern emerge. Evan made errors, like *quiet* for *quietly*, *fall* for *fallen*, *color* for *colored*, *peak* for *peaks*, *studying* for *studied*, and *condition* for *conditions*. He replaced words in the text with other words that were visually similar. (I recorded the letter *V* in my notes when I inferred that he was using a visual cueing system to make an error or make a self-correction.) It appeared that he doesn't attend to the endings of words. Errors like *peak* for *peaks* may seem inconsequential in that it may not affect comprehension yet. However, it happened frequently enough in his reading that I knew that not attending to endings in the future could drastically affect comprehension. I also noticed that Evan was able to self-correct errors, like *color* for *colored* and *studying* for *studied*, after he reread the portion of the sentence that came prior to the error. (See lines 4 and 11 of the running record with the text included.) I assumed that he was thinking that something didn't sound right, as though that is not how we would say that using our English language structure. I recorded this information on my Reading Behaviors form in Figure 12.3.

Reading Behaviors the Reader Uses Successfully	Reading Behaviors the Reader Can "Almost Do" or Can Use with Support	Reading Behaviors the Reader Shows No Evidence for Using
- uses visual info to attempt words i.e. *quiet* *quietly* - able to read in 3 to 5 word phrases when prompted	- use visual and structural info to self-correct - knowing when to adjust rate for a natural pace - attend to punctuation - notices some craft of writer	- characteristics of science fiction - understanding of realistic fiction - noticing text to text connections

FIGURE 12.3 Reading Behaviors form (available at Scholastic.com/RLResources)

What information/data or previous understanding about the reader does this assessment confirm?

As I listened to Evan reading, I also made notes on the right side of the original running record to indicate what I noticed about his fluency. In the beginning, his rate was too fast, like he was running a race. This caused him to ignore punctuation and not read in natural phrases. Readers often do this when they think they are being timed. Unfortunately, some equate good reading with fast reading. The unnatural rate and lack of attendance to punctuation that Evan demonstrated concerned me because in his previous reading I did not hear those behaviors. After the first page, I prompted him to read naturally, like he was talking. My notes indicate that he was able to adjust his reading rate to a more natural pace. He also began attending to punctuation by pausing appropriately and reading in natural phrases. These behaviors were also noted on my Reading Behaviors form for Evan. I was able to confirm that he is capable of fluent reading. However, I noted that he seems to need support in this area also. I was curious if he would be able to adjust his rate in order to read in natural phrases and attend to punctuation *without* being prompted to do so. I want him to be able to demonstrate those behaviors independently as a reader.

What did I learn about this reader that I did not know before?

Next, I asked Evan to read the rest of the story on his own and write me a letter about the story when he finished. Evan was accustomed to writing letters about his independent reading each week. He knew our class followed a format of including the title, author/illustrator, a summary of the book or portion of a longer text, and the reader's own thinking about the text. Below is Evan's response.

By reading Evan's letter, I was able to confirm some reading behaviors that he uses and identify areas where he needs support. Evan was able to provide a clear, concise summary. He was also able to notice part of the writer's craft of "teaching you something" about avalanches even though he believes this piece is fiction. He even uses information and words from the text with his own words to explain his thinking ("a snowball" or "a loud sound" can create an avalanche; "deep layers of snow" slide down the mountains). He does have some confusion about the science fiction genre. He even sounds a bit tentative in choosing that genre when he says it's "maybe science fiction." I can infer that he is making a connection with the occurrence of an avalanche happening in nature, or being weather-related, to the studying of such events in science class. He will need to explore multiple science fiction texts to begin to understand the true characteristics of science fiction. I think he shows some evidence of analyzing the author's craft again when he makes the following statement: "I think Mrs. George ended the book with a happy ending…." He realizes this a choice that the author purposefully made, and he infers why she may have made that choice by adding "she doesn't want people to be afraid of going snowboarding or playing in the snow." Knowing that Evan has read another book by George called *Firestorm*, I was quite surprised that he didn't make connections between the two texts. Both books have a great deal in common, like being adventure stories with potential danger, as well as the character of Axel. They are both written with a similar structure and style. This makes me wonder if he did not notice those similarities or is not used to making text-to-text connections.

September 10

Dear Mrs. Kinzel,

I just finished reading *Snowboard Twist* by Jean Craighead George. It's a picture book illustrated by Wendell Minor.

It's a story about a boy named Axel who wants to go snowboarding with his dad, a friend, and his dog. There's an avalanche but thanks to Grits the dog everybody is safe.

One thing I thought was cool about this story was it told how an avalanche happens. Kind of like it's teaching you something. Did you know that a snowball or a loud sound can make deep layers of snow slide down the mountains? It can smash trees and bury you in snow.

I think this book is maybe science fiction cause it talks about avalanches. At first I was kind of worried something bad was going to happen to someone because it was talking about testing for avalanches. But nobody got hurt. I think Mrs. George ended the book with a happy ending cause she doesn't want people to be afraid of going snowboarding or playing in the snow.

Your friend,
Evan

FIGURE 12.4 Evan's letter

Using Assessment to Plan Instruction

I have been able to get to know Evan much better as a reader through this careful observation of his reading behaviors. Based on what I know about him, I can support him in different teaching contexts including whole-group mini-lessons, small-group reading instruction, and one-on-one reading conferences.

One-on-One Reading Conference

In my next reading conference with Evan, I plan to listen to him read whatever he is currently reading independently. I will be looking and listening to see if he is attending to the endings of words. If the pattern continues, I will have him pause so that I can prompt him to "look all the way through the word," and explain that endings can change the meanings of words so we have to read the word as it is in the text. An *-ed* ending in a word like *thanked* can tell us that something has already happened in a story. An *-s* ending in a word like *boys* can tell us that more than one boy is involved in something in the story. I want him to use the visual information in the text. I also want him to ask himself, *"Does that make sense and sound right?"* to help him self-correct when he ignores the endings. I will listen for his fluency. I don't want him to go back to the habit of reading too fast and

PHOTO 12.1 Powerful reading conferences are based on careful assessments.

ignoring punctuation. If that behavior reoccurs, I will ask him to adjust his rate so that it sounds more like talking. I would explain that reading in phrases will help him remember more of what he has spent time reading. If he does read fluently, I will take a moment to specifically reinforce that behavior with the previous statement about phrasing.

Guided Reading

Evan meets regularly with a small guided reading group of readers with similar characteristics. One of those characteristics is developing their fluency by pausing appropriately with punctuation and reading in longer phrases. To support Evan and the rest of the group, I have decided to intentionally choose a couple of texts with dialogue that will encourage them to read it the way it would sound if they were talking. I plan to use texts with dialogue for two to four guided reading lessons. Then I will transition into texts without dialogue, possibly expository text, to see if they can maintain reading in phrases without the support of dialogue. All the while, I will teach or prompt them to notice the phrases and say the words together like phrases as they are constructing meaning.

Looking at Patterns Across Class Data

There are times when you are observing readers in one-on-one conferences or small groups and you begin to notice similar needs among many of your readers. Whole-group contexts like mini-lessons and Interactive Read-Alouds are powerful ways to help meet those needs. For example, Evan was one of many students who was confused about various types of fiction. Therefore, I chose to use a genre study approach to help readers understand that there are different types of fiction. Over the course of the year, we took time to explore realistic fiction, historical fiction, and science fiction. We began each study by reading several examples of that type of fiction during Interactive Read-Aloud. Readers shared what they thought might be a characteristic of the genre, and the class eventually crafted its own definition to explain how that type of fiction was unique. Each genre study culminated in each student, including Evan, writing his own example of that genre.

Conclusion

Each day with your students is an opportunity to learn more about them as readers and writers. Consider what you are currently using or could be using in your classroom to answer the question: *What am I learning about this child as a reader?* Trust yourself to make good observations of what readers are doing successfully and can almost do with your support. Record all that you are learning about individuals and look for patterns across your data and then teach responsively. You are the instructional decision-maker. And those decisions powerfully affect student learning.

Suggestions for Professional Development

1. Have a group of teachers bring an example of each of the following for one student: authentic student work, anecdotal records, formal assessment, and informal assessment. Ask them to share what each of the four items taught them about this reader.

2. Examine one particular assessment prior to administering it. Make a list of all the reading behaviors the assessment requires a reader to use in order to be successful. Reflect upon what can be learned or not learned by using this assessment.

3. Share across grade levels the assessments that are used to assess various types of comprehension (e.g., literal, inferential, analytical).

— Individually assess students (informal, formal assessments)

CHAPTER 13

Building Strategic Activity Through Guided Reading

Nikki Woodruff

"Guided reading is a small-group instructional context in which a teacher supports each reader's development of systems of strategic actions for processing new texts at increasingly challenging levels of difficulty."

—**Irene C. Fountas and Gay Su Pinnell**

Excitement is in the room as the elementary classroom is filled with literacy buzz. Some students are talking with other students about their independent books; some are deep in a discussion about a word study principle; still others are using their Reading Notebooks to respond to their thinking about a text read aloud by the teacher. In the corner of the room there is also excitement building around a kidney-shaped table. It is there that the teacher sits in the middle of the group and is introducing a high-interest book to the students. With one glance you can see the joy on their faces as well as the excitement in their voices as they build conversation surrounding what they might know about this text prior to reading. Guided reading happens at this table. Irene Fountas and Gay Su Pinnell state that "guided reading offers a context within which students engage with a variety of texts and are taught how to build an effective and efficient reading processing system" (2017, p. 4). In this form of small-group instruction, children are flexibly grouped together based on their reading abilities. It is a time when the children read a continuous text supported by the teacher through a book introduction, prompting for problem-solving, and explicit teaching.

PHOTO 13.1 Introducing a guided reading text

Marie Clay defines reading as "a message-getting, problem-solving activity which increases in power and flexibility the more it is practiced" (Clay, 1991, p. 6). Because of the complexity of reading, we need to approach teaching children how to read with a focus on making meaning of the text. It is not about teaching individual words; rather, it is teaching the child to know how to approach novel texts with the overall goal of making meaning. This chapter will discuss the essential components of guided reading, the responsibilities of both teacher and student, and how to teach for strategic actions before, during, and after the reading of a new book.

Essential Components of Guided Reading: An Overview

Before getting started with guided reading, teachers need to assess students and place them in homogeneous groups. Assess for reading-level accuracy, fluency, and comprehension. With the analyzed assessment as a guide, group your children who are similar in their development. Ideally, the group should have three to five students to allow for flexibility across groups. If the need arises, you may have six students in a group temporarily while making grouping decisions. After grouping the children, work on a schedule to see three or four guided reading groups per day. It is also important to flexibly group the students to allow movement between groups based on the progress of each student.

Before the guided reading group begins, carefully and thoughtfully select a text that will be appropriate for the readers based on their strengths and needs. Then, write a book introduction tailored to fit the experiences, interests, and needs of each group. The introduction needs to include discussion surrounding the meaning of the text and introduce the structure of the text including sentence structure and text characteristics. In addition, the book introduction needs to guide the reader into thinking about the information in the book including new vocabulary and searching for new and partially familiar words or high-frequency words that will help the reading processing.

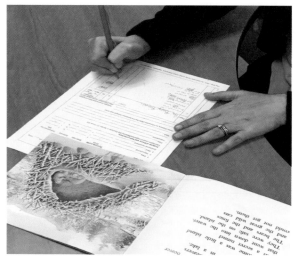

PHOTO 13.2 A teacher analyzes a running record to prepare for the next guided reading lesson.

Familiar Read and Running Record

The 15- to 20-minute guided reading group begins with the children reading a familiar book at the table. This time for familiar reading activates the children's brains and provides the teacher an opportunity to take a running record on one child's reading. (See Clay, 2016, for information about how to take running records.) A running record enables the teacher to analyze the reading for evidence that the reader is thinking about the meaning, structure, and visual information in the text. After the running record, the teacher selects one or two teaching points to support the student's processing strategies.

New Book Introduction

The next step is to introduce a new book at the children's instructional level. First, give an overview of the meaning of the text and introduce some structural components of the book. The focus on structure is teaching children how books work. For example, there may be a part of the book where the words are in italics or the language is unique to the text. Take some time to teach this during the introduction. Finally, spend some time on the visual information in the text locating known words or having the children find new words based on the initial sounds.

Comprehension Conversation

After the introduction, the children read the entire text independently. This is done with each child reading at his or her pace. This is not the time to have the readers each read a section of the text, like round robin reading. Round robin reading does not support reading for meaning, fluency, or active engagement. While the students are reading independently, observe, teach, prompt, and reinforce based on the behaviors that the children exhibit on the text being read. Provide some explicit and individualized instruction during the reading of the text as needed. After all of the children have read the text, have a comprehension conversation designed to engage children in the meaning of the text. Then, provide an explicit teaching point or demonstration based on the behaviors observed during the reading of the text (see Photo 13.3).

PHOTO 13.3 The teacher listens to one child read the new text to teach, prompt, and reinforce effective reading behaviors.

Word Work and Writing About Reading

At the end of the lesson, guide the students through a one- to three-minute demonstration of a word work principle based on the visual processing needs of the students in the group. One optional component of the guided reading lesson is having children writing about their reading of the new book in a Reader's Notebook.

    The structure of the guided reading lesson does not change over time; however, it is important to plan in advance for the lesson based on student need. The planning includes analyzing data to learn students' strengths and needs, choosing a book that will be at their instructional level (not too difficult, not too easy), and planning a book introduction based on the strengths and needs of the reader. This book introduction needs to be concise while providing the support for the readers to successfully read the text for meaning.

Guided Reading Lesson Components

Familiar Read and Assessment (Running Record)

New Book Introduction and Reading of New Book

Comprehension Conversation and Teaching Point

Word Work

Writing About Reading (optional)

Assessments to Guide Instruction

Small-group guided reading instruction is a time for explicit teaching based on the needs of the children in the group. The information from your initial assessments will guide decisions about how to group your children based on their instructional reading level. In addition, valuable information is gained on how students process text as you listen to them read. The teacher gathers information including accuracy, word solving, monitoring, fluency, and meaning-making. All of this information is used to group students into homogeneous groups for guided reading instruction and plan future lessons.

After guided reading begins in your classroom, it is important to take daily running records on one child in each group while reading the book you introduced the day before. If you take one running record per group per day, you should have a running record on most of the children each week. These running records provide valuable information about the reading strengths and needs of your students. They serve several purposes:

- The running record provides evidence of a child's processing of a familiar text.

- It gives another opportunity for the teacher to gather more information on meaning-making through a comprehension conversation after the reading of the text.

- After the reading and conversation, the teacher has an explicit teaching point based on the reading of the text.

- The information gathered in this running record (as well as the information during the guided reading group) provides information to help plan the next guided reading lesson.

- These running records also serve as evidence of successful processing and serve as documentation to help the teacher make flexible grouping decisions (when to move students up and down a level based on the data).

Teacher decision-making during guided reading needs to be tentative, flexible, and based on the careful observation of children. It is important for teachers to consider all parts of the framework when planning for guided reading, which might include anecdotal records from shared and performance reading, interactive read-aloud, and independent reading. These data will enable decisions about flexible groupings. For example, in my classroom, I initially assessed a reader at Level J. This child quickly demonstrated, however, through running record analysis, guided reading discussion, and also classroom observations, that the Level J books were too easy. So, I moved this student up to a Level K and was tentative about that decision as well. I wasn't sure if Level K or Level L would be right. Immediately after moving the child, I could confirm his ability to read at Level K through informal observation, running records, oral reading, and conversation.

Periodic and daily assessments help teachers understand the ways each student is processing text. Running records are particularly effective at identifying how students are processing within the text by recording self-monitoring, self-corrections, searching behaviors, word-solving abilities, and fluency. The discussions during guided reading will provide insights into how the child is constructing meaning of the text. Then, based on these observations, teachers can plan effective lessons to support students in learning more sophisticated systems of strategic actions while reading increasingly more difficult texts from a range of genres.

What Is Strategic Activity?

In the 1970s, Clay published *Reading: The Patterning of Complex Behavior,* in which she suggested that learning to read was not a simple matter of attaching letters to sounds to words. Rather, learning to read was a complex act requiring the use of multiple sources of information, such as knowledge of letters and sounds, structure of the language, and the emerging meaning of the text. From close observation of young children's reading behavior, Clay theorized that reading involves using meaning and language, searching for information, self-correcting when error is detected, and forming an internal set of "rules" that help to fuel further learning. She didn't use the words *strategies* or *strategic actions*, but was clearly describing the complex operations that are going on in the young reader's head.

Clay pursued this theoretical perspective in a later publication, *Becoming Literate: The Construction of Inner Control* (1991), and argued for a model of reading different from models that focus on teaching the sounds of letters or individual words. Rather, although understanding letters, sounds, and how they work are important, "what the child acquired was not merely a set of information but a network of strategies for operating on or with text. It assumes that in order to read with understanding, we call up and use a repertoire of strategies acting upon stores of knowledge to extract messages from print" (pp. 325–6).

Ten years later, in *Change Over Time in Children's Literacy Development* (Clay, 2001), she described young proficient readers as building "systems" within which they work with different types of information simultaneously. As students read, they make decisions based on coordinating information from print, from language, and from the meaning they construct using not only the text but their own prior knowledge. As they do so, they actually learn more. She states:

> Several kinds of perceptual/cognitive systems are critical for extending literacy processing power, and that they enable us to learn to read by reading, and to learn to write by writing (p. 91).

More recently, Fountas and Pinnell (2006, 2017a, 2017b) have detailed "strategic actions" in 12 major categories "because teachers need words to talk with each other about what they think is going on in the brain" (2017b, p. 362). They caution, however, that we cannot directly observe these "in-the-head" actions but can assume them when we see evidence in the way readers behave, what they say, and what they write. Fountas and Pinnell have detailed such evidence in their *Literacy Continuum* (2017a), which helps teachers support students' development and expansion of three categories of strategic actions: (1) *thinking within the text;* (2) *thinking beyond the text;* and (3) *thinking about the text.*

- **Thinking within the text.** What are the processing behaviors I observe as the student reads? Is there evidence that he is searching for information, self-monitoring, and using a range of strategies to solve words? Does he read fluently and can he remember what he read that is important?

- **Thinking beyond the text.** Is there evidence that the reader is applying prior knowledge and both social and emotional intelligence to help him understand the reading? Does he voice predictions? When he talks about his reading, is there evidence that he is making inferences and gaining new knowledge?

- **Thinking about the text.** What does the reader notice about the text? In talk or writing, does he notice how it is organized or how the writer uses language? Does he apply understanding of genres and forms? Does he recognize and use structures such as compare and contrast.? Does he engage in critical thinking?

To these three categories, I would add a fourth—**Experiencing the book.** What feelings emerge while reading the text? What does the reader say, do, or express to indicate that the text has created an emotional response? Is there increased motivation to find out how the book ends? Does the reader feel the emotions of the characters? Is the reader caught up in the plot?

Planning to Support Teaching for Strategic Actions in Guided Reading

Reading is a complex process; it is much more complex than identifying individual words. Teachers need to consider this when choosing a book and planning a new book introduction. Introducing an instructional level text to students requires intentional and thoughtful planning, taking the following into consideration:

- Strengths and needs of the students in the group

- Text selection including the 10 text characteristics: genres/forms, text structure, content, themes and ideas, language and literary features, sentence complexity, vocabulary, words, illustrations, book and print features (Fountas & Pinnell, 2017c)

- Meaning of the text: theme, characters, problem, solution, illustrations

- Structure of the text: how books work, including language patterns, character names, book structures, and language structures that may be new to the children

- Visual information in the text: locating new and/or complex words in text

After choosing a new book that will provide the appropriate amount of challenge for readers, thoughtfully write a book introduction. First, write down how you will briefly introduce the meaning of the story and invite conversation among the children. The book introduction should be a natural conversation with all children actively engaged in meaning-making. Next, consider what parts of the book structure will need to be introduced. Does the book have repetitive language? Are there text patterns children need to learn? Consider where the words are on the page: bold text, text on both sides of the page, etc. Teaching about a book's structure helps students know how books work. Also, consider visual information. Are there high-frequency words that aren't quite secure that you want to draw attention to? Is there a word that would be unfamiliar to these children that they would have to locate and think about the meaning? Write down how you will introduce the book, thinking about meaning, structure, and visual information. List page numbers where you will want to stop. It is not necessary or appropriate to have the children look at every single page of the book. If the text is at their instructional level, there isn't a need to give away the ending. In an instructional level text, the child should have many periods of accurate and fluent reading as well as opportunities to problem-solve unfamiliar words.

Teaching for Strategic Actions Before, During, and After the Reading of a New Book

Let's take a look at the teacher and student responsibilities before, during, and after the reading of a new book in guided reading to dig deeper into the teaching of the new book. Then, we are going to explore a transcript of a guided reading group that I taught to analyze the new book through the lens of teaching for strategic actions.

Before the Reading

Teacher Responsibilities	Student Responsibilities
Before	**Before**
• Introduces the new book, paying close attention the meaning, structure, and visual information in the story. • Begins a conversation thinking within, beyond, and about the text so children are engaged in the text through the introduction.	• Listens actively to the introduction. • Brings background to the story and starts to make connections prior to the reading. • Gathers meaning from the text. • Engages in thoughtful conversations with peers and teacher about the new book.

PHOTO 13.5 The teacher leads a discussion about *The Lion and the Mouse* (Level G) prior to the children reading this new book in guided reading.

Teaching for Strategic Actions

We are going to use parts of a transcript of a guided reading group that I taught in a first-grade class to investigate how to teach for strategic actions before, during, and after the reading of a new book. The new book was titled *The Lion and the Mouse* (Level G) and is based on the traditional tale of the lion catching the mouse, but letting her go despite his desire to eat her. The mouse ends up helping in the end when the lion gets caught in a trap and the little mouse is the only animal in the forest that can help.

Conversation During the Book Introduction

Teacher	Student	Instructional Goal
Your new book is called *The Lion and the Mouse*. This story is about a big lion who never thought the little mouse could help him out. Tell me about a time when you were too little to help or when someone thought you were too little to help.		Providing a summary of the text and drawing readers into the theme by making connections.
	One time when I was little I was too little to help my mom clean the kitchen.	
	One time I couldn't help my sister wash the dishes.	
	One time I was too little to help my mom. I was too little too.	

When planning for a book introduction, I want to engage my readers in a discussion of the meaning of the story. One of the themes in *The Lion and the Mouse* is "being too little to help." During the opening of this book introduction, I engaged the children in a discussion of the theme. I summarized the story and then guided the conversation along through a discussion of the theme. The children could relate to this theme, which helped build background knowledge.

Conversation Supporting Meaning

Teacher	Student	Instructional Goal
In this story, the mouse is not too little to help this big lion. Turn to the beginning of this book, *The Lion and the Mouse*. Look at page 2. What do you think is happening?		Making meaning through inferring and synthesizing new learning in anticipation of reading the text.
	The lion is really sleepy.	
	I think the mouse is trying to talk to him.	
What makes you think that?		Using the pictures to infer and draw meaning.
	Because he is on his nose and the mouse's mouth is open.	
Yes, the little mouse ran over his nose and woke him up.		
	Oh, that's not good (*said with concern on her face*).	Making predictions about what is to follow. Expressing feelings about the predictions made using summary from the teacher and also picture evidence.

After a brief introduction, the readers open the text and start to gather meaning from my prompting. We can see from this exchange that my questions are open-ended and focused on beyond-the-text thinking such as inferring, synthesizing, and predicting. The readers are making their own meaning from the teacher's guiding questions and the pictures.

Teaching the Structure of the Text

Teacher	Student	Instructional Goal
Let's turn the page and see.		
	Oh… I was right. The lion is going to eat the mouse.	
	"Yes, he said" (*reading from the book*), "I am going to eat you."	Synthesizing and inferring from evidence in the text, in pictures, and the written text.
Look at how the author used those words on that page (bold and larger font).		Drawing attention to the writer's craft to make meaning.
	Yes, because the lion is really mad.	
He is really mad. Do you think the lion is going to let that mouse go?		Making a prediction.
	No, because he is angry.	
	And hungry.	

As we dig deeper into the introduction of the text, I drew the readers' attention to the text structure. In the reading they will encounter the bold words, and I wanted them to notice the words to support their comprehension. I prompted them to think about the meaning of the story and analyze the author's craft. While they are reading, it is important for them to think about why the author used bold words when the lion was speaking. I followed up with a question asking them to predict based on what they know now.

Teaching to Solve New Words

Teacher	Student	Instructional Goal
If you were going to write the word *please*, what two letters would it start with?		Teaching reciprocity of reading and writing through solving words.
	Students: *PL.*	
Yes, it starts like the word *play* that you know. Find *please*.	Students find the word *please*.	Using initial sound-letter relationships to predict and locate words in text.
That word is *please*. This is going to help you in your reading.		
Turn to page 6. On page 6, the lion kind of sings a song. Do you see all of these words that are slanted? *(Teacher points to the italicized words.)* They are called *italics*. He says: You're too little to help me. You're too little to eat. Go away, you silly mouse, but beware next time we meet.		Using academic language to talk about the print features in the book. Modeling fluent reading.

In this part of the introduction, I first supported the readers in solving new words. I was purposeful in this interaction. I did not want to just tell them the word and show them the word. Instead, I modeled the thinking that I expected them to do when they come to a word that might be difficult. I want them to use analogy to solve words; therefore, I linked the new word to a word that they knew how to read and write. I modeled this to support independence in word solving. Finally, I knew the italicized text would also be new for these readers, so I drew attention to the words and read the passage aloud. My goal was for this exchange to serve as a model for fluent reading as well as supporting them in their comprehension of the text.

Creating Meaning Through Discussion

Teacher	Student	Instructional Goal
	Look! He's going to eat him!! (*the reader said with a surprise in her voice and facial expressions*)	Feelings of surprise while drawing meaning from the pictures in the text.
	That looks like a trap (*looking closely at the picture*).	
Look what Eric noticed. It looks like it could be a trap.		Synthesizing information to make predictions.
	Look at the food in the picture.	
	And the food…that is what lions like.	Making inferences based on the picture clues and background knowledge.

When we look at this excerpt from the book introduction, it is clear that I am leading the discussion with input from the children. My invitation into the book serves a very important purpose. We are introducing the book together while gathering meaning through the pictures and the visual information on the page as pointed out by the teacher. For example, the children naturally inferred and predicted based on the pictures. I also took the time to intentionally point out the bold, enlarged font and italics so they could analyze why the author might have written those words in that way. In addition, I planned a specific place in the text to encourage word-solving behaviors. One of the needs of this group is that they just stop when they come to an unknown word. I asked them to locate the word *please* after relating it to their writing as well as a known word (the word *play*). We can also see in this part of the introduction I am embedding the teaching of the meaning, structure, and visual information in the story introduction.

Teaching Vocabulary and Setting a Purpose for Reading

Teacher	Student	Instructional Goal
Turn to page 20.		
	The mouse is there. He is hunting and he can help the lion.	
	You know how mice chew through the wall.	Making connections based on understanding of the text and background knowledge.
	They can chew everything.	
	So he can help him.	
So that little mouse is helping him. In this story is the word *gnaw*. It means just what you said, "chew through."		Introducing new vocabulary.
	It means he is going to take little bites of the trap.	
Yes, he is going to take little bites so the lion can be rescued out of there.		
(Writes the word gnawed *on the whiteboard.)* The word *gnawed* starts with the letter *g*. The *g* is silent. It means "to chew a little."		Modeling the writing of new vocabulary to support the readers in solving unknown words.
	I think that the mouse should be biting the top of the trap so he can get right out.	
We are going to see what happens in this story and how this little mouse helps the lion. Read to see how this little mouse helps this big lion.		Gives purpose for the reading of the text linking it back to the theme from the first part of the book introduction.
As you read, you need to be thinking about the story as you come to a word you don't know. Take a look at the first letter or letters and go back and reread to think about the story.		Teaching the children to use their strength in visual information as well as the meaning of the story to problem-solve at difficulty.

During the end of the book introduction, I am teaching a new vocabulary word, *gnawed*, as we build common understandings through the pictures and discussions. In addition, I chose to write the word on the board to emphasize the different orthography, or the way the word looks. This grand demonstration will serve as a reminder when the readers get to that page in the text. I end this introduction giving them purpose for reading, saying, "We are going to see what happens in this story and how this little mouse helps the lion. Read to see how this little mouse helps this big lion." This gives them something to read for and also will help guide the comprehension conversation at the end of the reading. In addition, I leave them with some explicit teaching based on their needs. I know that these readers notice when they don't know a word; however, they need to reread to gather meaning to make a meaningful prediction based on the visual information presented. I told them what I expect them to do when they come to an unknown word. "As you read you need to be thinking about the story as you come to a word you don't know. Take a look at the first letter or letters and go back and reread to think about the story...."

During the Reading

Teacher Responsibilities	Student Responsibilities
During	**During**
• Listens to the children read the text.	• Reads the text while problem-solving and actively constructing meaning.
• Teaches for, prompts for, and reinforces effective processing of text.	• Emergent and beginning readers will read softly (Levels A–H). Readers of Levels I through Z will read the texts silently.
• Stops periodically to support meaning-making and check for understanding.	
• Supports the reader thinking within the text through teaching points related to problem-solving while reading the text.	
• Takes notes on readers' behavior to use when planning a teaching point and the next new book.	

Prior to the selection of this text, I had analyzed students' anecdotal and reading records on this group. I noticed that the children were not going back and rereading for meaning to assist in their word-solving. They would stop at the error and either wait for an explanation from the teacher or to make an attempt at word-solving letter by letter. The students were noticing before the error, which was a strength; however, they didn't know what to do other than a letter-by-letter sound analysis. This was not efficient processing. My goal for this lesson was for the students to take a quick look at the visual information and then go back and reread to think about the story. We reread to gather meaning. These children needed to understand that. As we explore this transcript, it further illustrates my efforts for these students to think about the meaning of the story.

Looking at the following conversation, we can see how I was immediately responsive to the needs of this child through my concise teaching and prompting. We can also see that the prompting language I used was the same as during the book introduction.

Text reads: *Lion was angry. "I'm going to eat you up," he roared.* Picture depicts the lion with an angry face grabbing the tail of the mouse.	
Reader:	Stops at the word *angry*.
Teacher:	Prompts for meaning, saying: *Think about the story, look at the first two letters and go back and reread.*
Reader:	Successfully reads the text after rereading to gather meaning and thinking about visual information.

Text reads: *Little mouse began to gnaw.*	
Reader:	Reads: Little mouse b- be be.
Teacher:	Listens in to see if there are shifts in problem-solving behavior. Then says: *You looked at the first part, now go back and reread.*
Reader:	Successfully reads: Little mouse began to gnaw.

In both of these instances, the readers were prompted to reread to gather meaning and were successful. This is further evidence that my prompts were responsive and just what the readers needed. One of the reasons I knew that this was a challenge for them is because I was diligent in my record keeping—taking observational notes, analyzing running records, and observing carefully while students read familiar and new books. My book introduction was intentionally planned to heavily support the meaning-making in this story. These two examples demonstrate responsive teaching based on the known needs of the readers both in the preparation of the book introduction as well as during the reading.

If we take a look at another teacher-reader exchange, we can see a different decision I made.

Text reads: *Little Mouse began to gnaw. She gnawed and gnawed and gnawed.*	
Reader:	Stopped at the word *gnaw*.
Teacher:	Says: *The g is silent in this word. That word is* gnaw. (Teacher runs finger under the word *gnaw* and says it slowly.)
Teacher:	*What is the mouse doing in this picture?*
Reader:	*Biting.*
Teacher:	*Right, we talked about how the author chose to use the word* gnawed, *meaning little bites from the mouse.* Teacher reads: *Little Mouse began to gnaw. She gnawed and gnawed and gnawed,* demonstrating fluent reading behavior.
Teacher:	*Now, you go back and reread that.*
Reader:	Reads accurately, but with finger and word by word.

Teacher:	*Go back and read like you are talking.*
Reader:	Reads the rest of the text without pointing and fluently.

If we deconstruct this exchange, we see that I made a different decision than when the reader stopped at difficulty. I made the decision to tell the student that the word *gnaw* had a silent *g*, teaching this reader that the English language has silent letters and then telling the word *gnaw*, an unfamiliar word. I followed up with a discussion of the meaning since this was new vocabulary for this reader. When the reader stopped at this unknown word (similar to the above scenarios), I did not prompt the reader to reread and try again because this word had a silent letter and was new vocabulary so more support was needed.

We can see from these excerpts that my instruction was mainly focused on within-the-text behaviors. The rationale for this is because the readers needed the most support on this text thinking within the text. The readers noticed when they came to a word they didn't know, but then did not know what to do next that would help them in their problem-solving. My focus was to teach the readers that when they encountered a difficulty, they needed to take a look at the visual information (to word-solve), but to immediately reread to gather meaning. The data I had collected before this guided reading group indicated that these readers had strong knowledge of visual information, but they were not using meaning with the visual information to predict the word. I wanted them to learn to cross-check the visual information with the meaning of the story (Clay, 2016).

After the Reading

Teacher Responsibilities	Student Responsibilities
After	**After**
• Engages the readers in an intentional conversation about the text, focusing the teaching on the three ways of thinking: within, beyond, and about the text.	• Uses evidence from the text; the readers engage in a comprehension conversation with the teacher and others in the group.
• Delivers a teaching point designed to increase processing strategies based on the needs of the readers in the group.	• Listens actively to the teaching point.
• Demonstrates explicit word work based on the processing development of the readers in the group.	• Engages in word work.
• Supports readers in writing about reading experiences (optional).	• Writes about reading (optional).

After the reading of the text, I engaged the children in a natural conversation through summarizing and synthesizing the text. I ended the book introduction with these words: *We are going to see what happens in this story and how this little mouse helps the lion. Read to see how this little mouse helps this big lion.*

Thinking about the theme of the text, I opened the conversation after the reading this way:

Teacher:	Before we started reading we talked about how the little mouse was so little the lion never thought the little mouse could help. What happened?
Reader 1:	The mouse wasn't too little. I can go back into my book and show you. (Reader turns back to the page where the mouse is gnawing the net). The mouse is nibbling the net.
Reader 2:	The mouse gnawed that net so the lion could get out.
Reader 1:	Yes, here (points to the picture), so the lion could get out.
Reader 3:	And on this page (turns to the page where the lion gets released), the lion got out.
Reader 2:	Yes, in the end the lion was so happy to be out.
Teacher:	What was the lesson that was learned from this story?
Reader 1:	That the mouse can help you.
Reader 4:	Tiny people can help you, just like us. We can help.

Throughout the reading of the text, I noticed that this particular part of the text (with the mouse gnawing the net) piqued the interest of the readers. There were a couple of sidebar conversations during the reading by several readers. I chose to take the readers back to that part of the story for this reason. Embedded in that conversation were opportunities to teach readers how to respond to text through going back into the text to search for evidence in the text and pictures. In addition, I linked the introduction to the discussion by talking about the theme of the text.

Following the comprehension conversation, I moved into my teaching point, which was very purposeful. Prior to this lesson, I had evidence that the readers struggled with what to do at difficulty. The foci of many of my prompts during the reading of the text were on monitoring and correcting. Because of this, I made the decision to call their attention to a place in the text and recreate the teaching point that I made with a student in the group. The strength of the readers in this group was that they could look at visual information in an effective way. It just wasn't enough information to solve the words. They were not using meaning to make a meaningful prediction based on the visual information.

The teaching sounded like this:

Reader 1:	I have a question. (Turned to page with text: *Little Mouse began to gnaw.*) I got stuck on these two words (*began* and *gnaw*).
Teaching Point	Sally did some really good reading work. She worked so hard here. (Opened text to page of difficulty where text reads *Little Mouse began to gnaw.* During the reading the child was stuck on *began*.) She said, "Little Mouse /b/." Then I said, "Look at the first part." I covered the *-gan* so just the *be* was showing. What does the first part say?

Readers:	Be (several responded).
Teacher:	Then I told her to go back and reread to think about the story. She said, "Little mouse be-gan to gnaw." It just came out of her mouth because she was thinking about the way that word looked and she was thinking about the story. When you get stuck, you have to go back and reread to think about the story.

I used very concise, specific language with the readers as I wanted to teach them how to reread to gather meaning after looking at the visual information. They needed to learn how to monitor and correct as well as how to search for and use more than one source of information when they are reading.

Conclusion

Guided reading is a powerful teaching context for readers to come together to read a book with the support of the teacher. It requires the teacher to be a keen observer of readers to be responsive to the needs of the readers in the group. This includes the analysis of the observation through running records, choosing of a new book that is appropriate based on the needs of the group, planning of a new book introduction providing the right amount of support, prompting and reinforcing during the reading of the new book, leading the comprehension conversation, and teaching after the reading of the new book. Guided reading is a powerful context to teach students systems of strategic actions and to increase their reading abilities while reading interesting texts.

Suggestions for Professional Development

1. Work as a grade-level team to analyze a classroom set of data. Once you have analyzed all of the assessments, work together to put them in initial reading groups based on the developmental needs of your classroom.

2. Analyze the running records of one guided reading group in your classroom. Write down the strengths and needs of the readers in your group. Use this information to choose a new book based on where the teaching needs to go in guided reading. Plan a new book introduction that will support the strengths and needs of the group.

3. Record a book introduction on video. Analyze the book introduction and think about how you supported the readers in thinking about meaning-making and processing strategies. Use the guided reading section of *The Fountas and Pinnell Literacy Continuum* (2017) to guide your thinking and discussion.

CHAPTER 14

Scaffolding the First Reading of Books for Young Readers

Mary D. Fried

"The goal of teaching is to assist the child to construct effective networks in his brain for linking up all the strategic activity that will be needed to work on texts, not merely to accumulate items of knowledge."

—**Birdie Raban**

As we consider introducing a new book or story to children, most of us draw on a wealth of experience—we have introduced hundreds, even thousands, of books to students. In this chapter, I invite you to examine some important understandings that underlie the practice of introducing stories to young readers. A book introduction can be a powerful tool that scaffolds their first reading of a new and more challenging text. The support in an introduction takes many forms and can focus on just about any aspect of reading, but the ultimate goal is to help students expand their comprehending strategies. I begin by discussing the traditional method of introducing texts and then focus on some new and different concepts to consider when introducing new books to young readers in guided reading.

Building on Our Past Experience as Teachers

The practice of introducing a text should not be daunting, because it is not entirely new. Like me, you may have used a basal reading system. If so, you probably are able to call up the prior knowledge embedded in your repertoire of teaching practices. These practiced responses have served us well over the years. The traditional framework for introducing a story using a basal reading system approach would usually begin with building interest for reading the story. For example:

Traditional Framework for Introducing Storybooks
- Select next story in basal.
- Engage students' interest.
- Introduce new concepts.
- Look at the pictures.
- Predict what might happen.
- Establish a purpose for reading.

Teacher:	We are going to read a funny story called *The Smoke Detector*.

Linking the concepts of the story to the students' own background of experience is the next step. Some of the children might be asked to share their own experiences that relate to the story:

Teacher:	Do you know what a smoke detector is?
Student 1:	We have one in our house, and you have to push this little red button to see if it is working, and it goes BEEP real loud.
Student 2:	Yeah, our smoke alarm went off one time when Daddy was cooking bacon. Oooo, it was loud.
Teacher:	So everyone knows what a smoke detector is?

If any of the concepts in the story are unfamiliar to the children, you would take time to introduce and explain the concept:

Teacher:	Do you know what a smoke detector is?
Students:	(No response)
Teacher:	Well, a smoke detector is a small plastic box in the ceiling or on the wall that is like the fire alarm you hear at school when we have a fire drill. It makes a loud noise when it detects smoke, so it warns everyone to get out of the house because there might be a fire.

The next component of the traditional introduction might be to look at some of the pictures and predict what is going to happen in the story. Often, only the picture on the cover or those on the first few pages will be used. Many times you might not refer to any other pictures and would end the discussion of the major concept of the story with a question or a statement to establish the purpose for reading the story:

Teacher:	Read this story, *The Smoke Detector*, to find out what happens when Rayshawn and Grandpa hear the smoke detector go off.

This traditional book introduction will vary slightly based on your teaching style and your students, but the basic components will remain fairly consistent.

Scaffolding: A Concept for Thinking About Book Introductions

Consider what Marie Clay (1991) says about introducing new books to young readers in guided reading:

> As the child approaches a new text he is entitled to an introduction so that when he reads, the gist of the whole or partly revealed story can provide some guide for a fluent reading (p. 335).

The word *entitled* should be stressed because it is critical for young, beginning readers to have a great deal of support as they begin the complex journey of becoming literate. The established, basal format is a good background for beginning, but we want to move away from the traditional introduction in some important ways. The kind of support I will describe can be thought of as "building a scaffold" for a successful first reading of a new book.

What Is a Scaffold?

What is the origin of the concept of *scaffolding*? The dictionary defines *scaffold* as a temporary platform for supporting workers. The key word in that definition is *support*. The word *temporary* should also be noted, as it implies that the need for support will change over time. As students learn more and more about how to read, they need less support for reading at an easy or instructional level or for a familiar kind of text. The term *scaffolding* used in an educational sense was introduced in an article written by Wood, Bruner, and Ross (1976). They described scaffolding as "a process that enables a…novice to solve a problem, carry out a task, or achieve a goal which would be beyond his unassisted efforts" (p. 90).

The scaffold you build makes it possible for the student to carry out the task of reading the new book independently or with very little assistance from the teacher. The scaffold makes it possible for them to read the hard or challenging book. The scaffold is considered selective assistance, a concept explored by Tharp and Gallimore (1988):

> Scaffolding, however, does not involve simplifying the task; it holds the task difficulty constant, while simplifying the child's role by means of graduated assistance from the adult/expert (p. 33).

If the appropriate level of difficulty is considered when selecting a book for emergent, early, or transitional readers, then your job is not to simplify the book or rewrite the story. Your job is to focus the children's attention on critical aspects of reading the story by highlighting what they need to take into account and learn about before they begin to read. Building a scaffold for the successful reading of a new book is a critical skill for teachers of beginning readers. As Wood (1988) states: "Built well, such scaffolds help children learn how to achieve heights that they cannot scale alone" (p. 80).

Characteristics of Readers Along a Continuum of Development

As a foundation for building the scaffold to prepare children effectively for a new story, understanding the terms "emergent," "early," and "transitional" readers will be helpful. Fountas and Pinnell (2017) provide detailed discussions and charts to clarify characteristics of readers and their behaviors along a broad continuum of development. I will highlight key concepts to differentiate these three achievement levels of beginning readers.

Characteristics of Emergent Readers

"Emergent readers" refers to children who are just acquiring very early concepts of literacy. An emergent reader may be a child who only looks at the pictures and is not yet aware that we read the print. It is wonderful when young children at home (or in preschool or beginning kindergarten) pick up a book and pretend to read by saying a story as they look at the pictures. In order to become readers, eventually these children will need to learn to attend to the details of print and understand how print operates. Emergent readers may know some words (for example, their names in all capital letters, *mom*, *dad*, or a sibling's name) as well as some letters, but they do not yet understand how the letters go together to make words, and that we are reading those words when we read books.

As teachers, it is our job to build a foundation by selecting appropriate books for emergent readers to read during guided reading. Select from books that have the following characteristics:

- Familiar concepts.
- A small amount of easy-to-see print.
- Appropriate font and spacing between the words.
- Print that is clearly separated from the pictures.
- Pictures that clearly illustrate the text message.

The page layout from *Zoo Animals* (Fried, 1999) [Level A] illustrates the simplicity of books that are appropriate for use with emergent readers (see Photo 14.1).

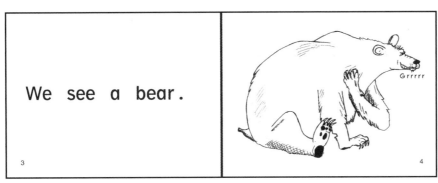

PHOTO 14.1 Page layout from *Zoo Animals*

BUILDING A SCAFFOLD FOR EMERGENT READERS

As in the traditional approach to introducing new books, it is important to tap into the children's background experiences that relate to the story. In the case of *Zoo Animals*, the teacher builds a scaffold for her students before they begin to read the story:

Teacher:	Have you ever gone to a zoo? Talk to a partner, someone sitting close to you, about going to the zoo.
Students:	(Students turn and talk to each other about any zoo experiences they might have had, or anything about a zoo or zoo animals. The conversation buzzes.)

As the teacher listens in, she can determine the extent of the children's zoo experiences while the children talk to each other instead of responding to the teacher's questions. Some students may be asked to share what their friend said, or they might share an idea of their own. This brief activity is different from the traditional approach in which the teacher poses the discussion questions, then calls on individual children to respond by taking turns. When building a scaffold for reading the story, all children have the opportunity to talk and share experiences. Using oral language to relate personal experiences to new learning is a basis for comprehension.

The introduction continues:

Teacher:	Here is the title of our story (pointing to each word to help focus the children's attention): Zoo Animals.
William:	That is the word *Zoo*!
Markesia:	*Z Z Z*!
Teacher:	That's right. That is the word *Zoo*, and there's the *Z*.

This primitive print connection is reinforced and praised by the teacher. With the background experiences related to the story and some of the words used to focus on the print, she will now tell the children what the story is about. She shows the cover of the book (see Photo 14.2).

The teacher provides the main idea of the story and is careful to use some of the language structures of the book. Next, she and her students do a thorough review of the book as she highlights some of the important sources of information the children should use as they read the book independently:

PHOTO 14.2 Cover of *Zoo Animals*

Teacher:	This story tells us about the different animals we see at the zoo. Look at the pictures on the front cover. Think about what zoo animals might be in our story.
William:	I like the monkeys. They are funny hanging around.
Teacher:	(She turns to the book's first page.) Oh, look, we see a tiger. Say that word *tiger*. See him in the picture. The tiger goes: Roar-r-r-r! Let's all roar like a tiger. Softly. Roar-r-r-r.
Students:	Roar-r-r-r (all join in roaring).
Teacher:	Now let's all say: We see a tiger.
Students:	We see a tiger.
Teacher:	These are the words that say (she points and reads), "We see a tiger." (She focuses the children on the print.) Here is the word *We*. See the big *W*. It's like in William's name. Everyone say "we" as I point to it. And here is the word *tiger*. See the *t* for *tiger*. Watch while I point and read the words: "We see a tiger." (The teacher provides a clear demonstration of pointing with her index finger under the words.) Turn the page. Now we see…what?
Students:	A bear…a bear!
Shawn:	He's scratching himself. He's got fleas.
Teacher:	Yes, we see a bear. And Shawn says he has fleas. What do you think?
Tina:	No, he's just itching, I think. Like I itch and I don't have fleas.
Shawn:	He's got an itchy flea.
Teacher:	Now what do we see?
Students:	Monkeys!
Teacher:	Yes, monkeys. We see monkeys. Let's think about the word *monkeys*. Say "monkeys" slowly.
Students:	M o n k e y s.
Teacher:	*Monkeys* starts like somebody's name. *Monkeys* starts like *Mark* and *Markesia*.

Markesia:	M M M!
Teacher:	That's right, *monkey* and *Mark* and *Markesia* all start with *M*. Let's look on this page (page 5) and find the word *monkeys* that starts with *m*. (See Photo 14.3.)
	(Some children now confuse uppercase *W* with *M*, and some go easily to the lowercase *m* for *monkeys*. To sort out the confusion and reinforce the *m* for *monkey*, the teacher points and says…)

PHOTO 14.3 Page layout from *Zoo Animals*

Teacher:	Everyone point to the word *monkeys*. See the *m*. Yes. We see monkeys… (She turns the page) …*everywhere*! Do you see monkeys everywhere? I'll pass the books around and you look at the last picture to see how many monkeys we can see. Count how many monkeys you see.
Students:	(The students begin to count and squeal out how many monkeys they see.)
Teacher:	Okay. Lots of monkeys *everywhere*. This is the word *everywhere*. Everyone point to that word. *Everywhere*! This story was not about the bear and his itching. This was about what zoo animals we see. And what animals did we see everywhere?
Students:	Monkeys! Monkeys everywhere.

In this introduction to *Zoo Animals*, the teacher wove pictures, words, letters, sounds of letters, book language structures, and the excitement and fun of the story into a scaffold for the children's first reading. She provided clear demonstrations; tried to sort out confusion; introduced important concepts of how our printed language operates at the letter, sound, word, and sentence levels; and encouraged the joy of literacy as the children prepared to read the book. As this example shows, the teacher's introduction varied greatly from the traditional new book introduction.

BUILDING A SCAFFOLD OF INFORMATION

The introduction was also more in-depth than and different from a "picture walk," which has had a surge of use in recent years. We do not use the term "picture walk" because it is somewhat misleading both for teachers and children. Yes, the pictures are discussed, but also the language structure of the book is shared and some of the words and letters are highlighted. Any part of the book's format may be clarified as the children and the teacher look through the book together for the first time.

Building a scaffold of information to use while reading the book is certainly more than a labeling of the pictures. Clay (1998) reminds us that "…although the interaction flows like a conversation and leaves room for the child's input to inform the teacher, it [the introduction] also includes deliberate teaching moves" (p. 175). In the example described above, both the conversational flow and the deliberate teaching moves are apparent. These types of demonstrations are critical when providing an introduction to children who are just beginning to learn how to use the print to read the message of the book.

> Clay (1998) reminds us that "…although the interaction flows like a conversation and leaves room for the child's input to inform the teacher, it [the introduction] also includes deliberate teaching moves" (p. 175).

For text introductions in the first guided reading lessons for emergent readers, many teachers like to hold the book so that all the children focus on the right page, word, or picture as the teacher points things out. As children learn the routines of guided reading, they also learn how to hold and use books independently during the introduction.

In summary, pictures are only a part of the focus and interaction when building a scaffold for a successful, independent reading of a story during guided reading. Instead of using only the pictures to predict what might happen in the story, the teacher can skillfully help emergent readers (who may still be sorting out that it is the print we read, not the pictures) focus on a variety of information sources: their background knowledge, oral language structures, the print itself, and the pictures. This distinguishes building a scaffold for reading a story from the traditional introduction, and includes more than the term "picture walk" implies.

As you might imagine, when the group of emergent readers are turned loose to read *Zoo Animals* on their own, the teacher will continue to provide supportive instruction, help, and individual guidance. Without a supportive scaffold for the first reading, the children may be at a loss and would perhaps continue to make up a story or invent text to go with the comical pictures. The supportive scaffold helped them begin to use the print as they enjoy reading a wonderful little story.

SUMMARY OF KEY CONCEPTS IN BUILDING A SCAFFOLD FOR EMERGENT READERS

In introducing texts to emergent readers, be aware of general characteristics of learners at this level. Consider the particular behaviors and strengths of the children you teach, as well as the characteristics of the text you are introducing. Some key concepts in building a scaffold for emergent readers are:

- Introduce the concept of the story to support comprehension.
- Encourage the children to talk to each other about the topic/concept.
- Share some of the comments/personal information.

- State the main idea of the story. Tell what the story is about.
- Discuss the story using the pictures, the language structures, the words, and the meaning of the story.
- Engage the children in looking at important aspects of the print (letters, words, punctuation, where to start, which way to go, etc.).
- Clarify any confusion.
- Provide clear demonstrations.

Characteristics of Early Readers

What are the characteristics of early readers? What are their strengths? What distinguishes them from emergent readers (see also Fountas & Pinnell, 2017)? Early readers have gained basic understandings of how print operates in the English language; that is, where to start, which way to move across a line of print, return sweep, and the basic concepts of letters and words. They use pictures as a source of meaning and have become adept at surveying the pictures before they read a book or page. Pictures are not the only information they use, however. At difficulty, early readers may quickly check the picture, but usually rely less on illustrations than emergent readers do. Early readers use more information from the print.

Most early readers have control of several high-frequency words and read familiar stories with phrasing and fluency. They often use the visual information of the print—what the letters and words look like—in combination with meaning and syntactic information to notice when they have made an error. They tend to work to integrate sources of information (meaning, language, and visual information from print), making them match in order to read accurately. Often, early readers can self-correct the errors they notice; self-correction is more frequent and more independent than for emergent readers.

The wolf blew down the house of straw.

6

The wolf blew down the house of sticks.

7

PHOTO 14.4 Page layout from *The Three Little Pigs*

BUILDING A SCAFFOLD FOR EARLY READERS

Early readers have more experience in reading printed language and bring a wider range of problem-solving strategies to processing texts, but they are still learning how to read and need the support of a well-built scaffold. Vary the amount and type of support you provide based on the familiarity of the story concepts and/or the difficulty of the level of the text. An easy version of *The Three Little Pigs* (Francis, 1995) [Level E],

for example, might need only a brief overview and a focus on one or two particular words before the children begin to read:

Teacher:	At our read-aloud time, you have listened to me read three different versions of *The Three Little Pigs*. Now you get to read a different version of the same story. Talk to your neighbor about what you remember about the three pigs stories.
Students:	(Students are quickly engaged in animated conversations of their favorite parts of the three pigs and big bad wolf stories.)
Teacher:	Wow! You know a lot about the three pigs. Look through the pictures in this book and think about the story. You can talk with a friend quietly as you look at the pictures. Let's look at page 6. What is the wolf doing?
Ronnie:	He huffed and puffed and huffed and puffed and blowed the house way up in the sky.
Terry:	He made a tornado!
Teacher:	In our story it says, "The wolf blew down the house of straw." Can you find the word that says *blew*?
Students:	(Some point to the word *blew* while others are pointing to the word *down*.)
Teacher:	(She writes the word *blew* on a whiteboard and talks a bit about the letter *b*.) This is the word *blew*. See the *b*. This is different from how you write the color *blue*. (She writes the word *blue* under the word *blew*.) They both have a *b* first, but this one is the one in our story. The wolf blew down the house of straw.

Good, everyone found the word *blew*. Turn to page 1. This story starts just like our first story of the three pigs: "Once upon a time." Everyone point and read that part with me: Once upon a time.

(The teacher needs to help two of the students match up the tricky book language with their pointing. Others use this opportunity to begin reading.) |

Because the children all had extensive prior knowledge about this familiar tale, the introduction focused on drawing their attention to the visual information along with the language structures on just two pages. The teacher provided a visual model of the irregular word *blew* and helped the children sort out what might have been confusing about the homophone *blue/blew*.

It is important to provide a concrete example when helping children to focus on the analysis of the print. In this example, the focus was on the positive similarities, for example, both words have a *b* as the first letter. (You should avoid having children compare very similar and easily confused first letters such as the *b* and *d* of *blew* and *down*.) Writing on the whiteboard provides a concrete example on which to focus the students' attention. Talking about the complexities of our language without a clear model (writing down text or pointing to print in the text) has the potential of creating confusion for children who are still at the early level of using the details of print as they read.

A book at the same level of difficulty but with unfamiliar concepts, *Growing a Pumpkin* (McCarrier, 1995) [Level E], might require a more thorough introduction before reading. Here, the introduction should help students to explore and develop the unfamiliar concepts of the life cycle of a pumpkin plant:

Teacher:	Our new book is called *Growing a Pumpkin*. If you were going to grow a pumpkin, what would you do first?
Students:	(*Several students shout out*) Buy a pumpkin!
Teacher:	Look at the cover of the book. In this story the little girl and her grandma want to grow a pumpkin. Why do they have shovels?
Students:	(Most students do not respond. The teacher hears one student ask, "What's a shovel?")

Based on the students' responses, the teacher quickly shifted her book introduction to a more detailed survey of the pictures and a discussion of the concepts around the life cycle of a pumpkin plant from the seeds, to the need for water, to the growth of little plants, and the blossoming of the flowers before the pumpkin makes its first, tiny appearance on the vine. Interwoven with this discussion of growing a pumpkin plant was a focus on some key words and how they look in the text, including *seeds*, *dirt*, and *poured water*.

Early readers are actively engaged in learning how to read and how to make sense of the abstract symbols of our printed language, as well as learning more about the many concepts in the day-to-day world of living and learning. Compared to emergent readers, they do not need as much protection from concepts that are a little more distant from their direct experience, but you should still provide as much of a scaffold as needed for successful reading and comprehension.

It is common for young children not to have a great deal of background to bring to their reading. Teachers have long been aware that informational books are usually more difficult for children to read than story narratives. When a lack of experience or knowledge base is noted, strengthen the support you give in your introduction so that students are actively engaged and learning at complex levels as they prepare to read the book. Another way to think about providing a scaffold is to weigh the concept level of a new book and

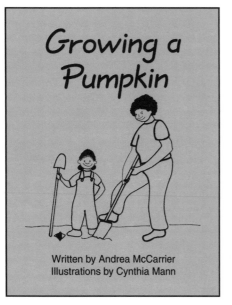

PHOTO 14.5 Cover of *Growing a Pumpkin*

estimate how to increase the support and teaching in the event the children do not have enough understanding of their own to plunge in and start reading independently. As Clay (1998) reminds us, "Book introductions enlarge the range of what children can do with whole stories at a first reading" (p. 175).

SUMMARY OF KEY CONCEPTS IN BUILDING A SCAFFOLD FOR EARLY READERS

As with emergent readers, preparing and providing an introduction for early readers is a complex process, one that requires you to consider the readers' strengths and needs as well as the features of the text. Some key concepts in building a scaffold for early readers are as follows:

- Weigh up the concept load when selecting a book.
- Prepare contingency plans to strengthen the introduction if prior knowledge needs to be supported before reading.
- Encourage the children to talk to each other about the topic/content.
- Allow children to share knowledge or engage in building knowledge if concepts are unfamiliar to all or some of them.
- Take an active role in building concepts; if they are unfamiliar, use more pictures and explanations as needed.
- Engage the children in looking at important aspects of the print (letters, endings, word parts, specialized vocabulary).
- Clarify confusions and build concepts.
- Provide concrete examples (written examples in the text or out of the text).

Characteristics of Transitional Readers

Transitional readers have made a definite shift to relying more on print as a major source of information while reading. The transition here is from the kinds of overt and sometimes sequential ways children attend to pictures and print to a smoothly operating process in which the reader uses multiple sources of information simultaneously to problem-solve and make meaning while reading continuous text. Emergent and early readers are learning to integrate the various sources of information available to them; their behaviors are overt and we can almost see them checking their information. For transitional readers, the process of reading is more automatic. They now control all of the basic concepts of print and are flexible enough in their knowledge to adjust to more unusual formats and layouts of the text.

Transitional readers have built up a large core of sight words that are frequently used in our language. This achievement means that they are required to give less attention to word solving. Rapid recognition of most words in a text helps them read in a fluent, phrased manner and to bring more expression to their oral reading. Transitional readers can search for and use multiple sources of information in an integrated way as they read, and can solve words "on the run," with greater efficiency and independence. Because they are reading longer, more complex texts that contain more multisyllabic words, irregular words, and descriptive adjectives and adverbs, transitional readers still need supportive teaching so that they can expand their word-solving strategies.

Providing a strong scaffold in the new book introduction is still an important aspect of guided reading instruction for transitional readers. You can help them bring the whole process together; the scaffold is temporary but important. As always when providing a scaffold, you are giving students the support that they need to move to the next level in their developing abilities. These transitional readers are moving toward silent reading. Soon, their reading processes will have become *learning systems* that enable them to expand their skills continually as they read a wider variety of increasingly more difficult texts. As this occurs, they will become what Clay calls *self-extending* readers (Clay, 2001).

Sometime toward the end of second grade or the middle of third grade, we can expect students to become self-extending readers. Of course, because we are always dealing with individual children, we understand the wide range of differences and time requirements that exist among them as they become self-extending readers. Some children learn rapidly and develop early, sprouting with seemingly little cultivation from the teacher. Others need a longer time and more instruction before bearing fruit.

BUILDING A SCAFFOLD FOR TRANSITIONAL READERS

A book introduction for a guided reading group of transitional readers would be similar to the components and the weighing-up of concepts discussed above for early readers. Take into account the concept level and demands of the text in relation to the experiences and learning of your students. The most important shift in planning the introduction of a new

---

Examples of Texts at Three Different Levels

EMERGENT: # We see a cat.

EARLY: ## We could not find the cat. It ran under the steps.

TRANSITIONAL: In the afternoon Mugs sits on the windowsill and watches the brightly colored birds flying in and out of the bird feeder. He twitches his tail.

FIGURE 14.1

---

book is for you to be aware of the increasing demands and complexity of the text. When there is a definite shift in the complexity of the language structures, your scaffold should be prepared to support this heavier load. Figure 14.1 provides examples of typical texts at the three different levels.

The differences between these three texts are obvious. The text for transitional readers makes more demands on readers. By analyzing it, you can determine the areas needing support or consideration for support. The following are questions you may raise about the text example:

- Are my students familiar with the concepts of *windowsill* and *bird feeder*?
- Should I call attention to the phrase "brightly colored birds" and/or "twitches his tail"?

It is impossible to predict whether the concepts of *windowsill* and *bird feeder* will be problematic for any one group of transitional readers. But, in general, modifying phrases that precede the noun can be a tricky business. Also, a word such as *twitches* might benefit from a closer examination of the two parts, even if the phrase is introduced as an unusual language structure.

Below are excerpts from a new book introduction for transitional readers:

Teacher:	In this story Mugs does whatever he wants to do. He always goes around twitching his tail. What does that mean?
Students:	He moves his tail back and forth.
Teacher:	Look on page 4. Can you find the word *twitching* or *twitches*?
Students:	(Students locate *twitches* in print and verify the ending.)
Teacher:	Yes, sometimes we add -*s* to the end of words and sometimes we need -*es*. Ronnie, at the end of reading group today could you please add that word to our chart of words we are collecting in the -*es* category? Thank you. Now, look at this picture of Mugs.
Sam:	He's looking at the birds. He's going to eat one of them.
Teacher:	Yes, he is looking at the birds, but in this story the author uses these words to describe the birds: *brightly colored birds*. I'll write the word *bright* on the chart paper. Who could come up to add something to the end to make it say *brightly*?
Zetta:	(Zetta adds -*le* to the end of *bright*.)
Teacher:	Okay. It sounds like it might be -*le*, but it's -*ly*. Can you fix that, Zetta? Good. We are going to be looking for more words that have -*ly* on the end of them. I think we can start another chart of all the -*ly* words we find. That should help us in our spelling also. Let's find and read that part on page 4 about the birds. Now look through the book before you start to read to help you think about the story and what old Mugs does all day long. Remember to read silently to yourself. I'll be around to listen to you read part of the story.

The teacher did the problem-solving and planning to prepare an introduction to *Mugs* (Pinnell, 1996) [Level H] for her transitional-level guided reading group. She helped them to advance their analysis of the increasingly complex visual information they would need in order to read this book successfully, and also to expand their strategies for word analysis in general so that they can apply them to other texts.

Her concern was not to have children learn the particular words *twitches* or *brightly* in order to read this text accurately, although she certainly values accurate (although not perfect) reading. The teacher supported children's learning of how these words and similar words work across many different and increasingly more difficult texts. Her work on word analysis will strengthen skills and understandings as students write independently and use word-solving strategies in spelling.

Introducing New Stories: A Decision-Making Process

Building a scaffold of support for reading a new story is a decision-making process based on careful observation of the children and an analysis of the text. As a teacher, you are the decision-maker who determines how strong the scaffold needs to be for any unique group of children. Planning a new book introduction becomes a challenge to customize the support you give your students based on their needs instead of a routine delivered the same way, time after time, for every group. Clay (1998) describes a book introduction as "a process of drawing the children into the activity before passing control to the children and pushing them gently towards problem-solving the whole first reading of the story for themselves" (p. 172). In guided reading, there is the expectation that teaching and prompting for strategies is provided during the first reading of the book. However, it is

---

Building a Scaffold for Successful Reading of a New Book: Planning Introductions in Guided Reading

- Select books based on children's knowledge of literacy concepts.
- Tell what the story is about.
- Connect to students' background experiences by inviting them to talk to each other (engagement and conversations).
- Review the book, highlighting multiple sources of information in the text (meaning/structure/visual information).
- Focus attention on some aspects of the print, using what children already know to connect to new learning.
- Gradually increase the difficulty of the text.
- Build a temporary scaffold, but remain flexible to increase the strength of the support when appropriate.

the intent of the book introduction to prepare each child in the group to read and problem-solve difficulties during the first reading as independently as possible, with only a limited amount of help. For emergent and early readers, comprehension is supported by the introduction of the story. Only after children have learned basic reading skills are they asked to read and comprehend stories more independently. When concepts are unfamiliar, however, you must provide additional support. You can download a Planning Guide for Scaffolding Book Introductions at Scholastic.com/RLResources.

Conclusion

Becoming an expert at introducing stories to children in guided reading is a learning process that takes time. It may be helpful to record your book introductions over several days or weeks. Then you can analyze them on your own or work with a colleague to evaluate your effectiveness, asking whether you provided the appropriate level and kind of support for children to process the text successfully. Remember that processing a text successfully does not mean reading every word accurately. We want children to notice most of their errors (monitor), initiate problem-solving, and use multiple sources of information to self-correct on the run without losing their focus on the meaning of the text. This Planning Guide for Scaffolding Book Introductions was designed to help you plan your book introductions for emergent, early, and transitional readers.

FIGURE 14.2 You can find this Planning Guide for Scaffolding Book Introductions at Scholastic.com/RLResources.

Planning Guide for Scaffolding Book Introductions

DATE _____ TEACHER _____ GRADE _____

READING ACHIEVEMENT LEVEL: ☐ EMERGENT   ☐ EARLY   ☐ TRANSITIONAL

BOOK/STORY TITLE _____

Key concepts to consider when planning book instructions for beginning readers:

MEANING
☐ Tell what the story is about / provide the main idea
☐ Draw upon students' experiences and knowledge by engaging them in discussions with each other / share some of their ideas
☐ Help students understand unfamiliar concepts
☐ Discuss pictures to build a framework of meaning and to spark interest and involvement in the story (more pictures for emergent / less for transitional)

STRUCTURE
☐ Introduce and let the students practice language patterns / character names / unfamiliar book language

VISUAL
☐ Point out any unusual aspects of text layout / unfamiliar punctuation marks
☐ Draw attention to some new and/or important words in the story
☐ Provide concrete examples to demonstrate how visual information is analyzed (letter, letter cluster, endings, syllables, irregular spelling patterns)

NOTES

Suggestions for Professional Development

1. Working in cross-grade-level groups, plan an introduction for at least two texts per grade level. Assume that you are working with a group of children who can read the text with 90 to 95% accuracy. For each text, you can consult the teacher at the appropriate level and use a group of children from that classroom as the focus for planning. Think about

   - the supports that are in the text.
   - the particular demands of this text.
   - concepts, language structures, or tricky words that you might bring to students' attention during the introduction.
   - what you might want to leave for them to figure out for themselves.

2. Bring the whole group together to discuss the following:

   - What is the role of the introduction in helping students read more challenging texts?
   - How does the introduction change as the texts become more challenging over time?

3. Leave the meeting with the goal of reflecting on your text introductions over the next two weeks.

4. Record several introductions for texts at different levels and reflect on how you created a scaffold for students.

5. Share your reflections and a recording or two with a partner to talk about the quality and effectiveness of your introductions.

SECTION FOUR:
WRITING

 Professional videos and downloadables are available at Scholastic.com/RLResources

CHAPTER 15

Interactive Writing: The Cornerstone for Writers

Jenny McFerin and Nikki Woodruff

> **"Writing can contribute to the building of almost every kind of inner control of literacy learning that is needed by the successful reader."**
>
> **—Marie Clay**

Children light up with excitement when they have a shared experience through an Interactive Read-Aloud. They gather together with the teacher at the easel excited to discuss the book that was shared. This is a natural time to use this excitement to write. In this kindergarten classroom, children listened to *Bunny Cakes* (1997) by Rosemary Wells several times during their Interactive Read-Aloud time. In *Bunny Cakes*, the reader follows Max and his bossy older sister, Ruby, in their quest to make their grandmother a birthday cake. Max and Ruby have very different ideas about what the cake should look like. This involves multiple trips to the grocery store and disasters along the way. In the end, a surprised grandma receives very different cakes, including Ruby's angel raspberry-fluff cake and Max's cake with Red-Hot Marshmallow Squirters, and can't decide which to enjoy first.

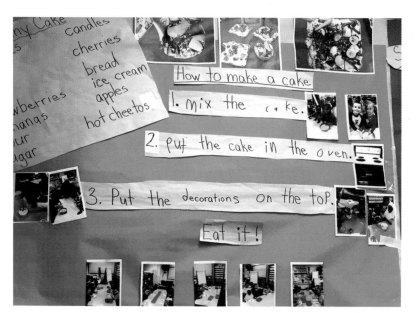

PHOTO 15.1 Interactive writing of *Bunny Cakes*

After reading *Bunny Cakes*, this kindergarten class decided they were going to make their own bunny cake, but needed to write down the recipe in case their friends wanted to make bunny cakes, too. First, they listed the ingredients that they were going to use (complete with hot Cheetos). After making the cakes in a shared cooking experience the children used their pictures to help write the directions for the bunny cake (see Photo 15.1).

This is an example of how the teacher used the Interactive Read-Aloud to have a shared experience and write about it. The children owned the entire process. They had a purpose for writing out the ingredients and the recipe because they were going to share this with their friends in the school building. And they learned all about the writing process while negotiating the text to select just the right words, and sharing the pen with the teacher while writing the message.

What Is Interactive Writing?

"Interactive writing is a dynamic, collaborative literacy event in which children actively compose together, considering appropriate words, phrases, organization of the text and layout" (McCarrier, Pinnell & Fountas, 2000, p. xv).

Interactive writing is an instructional time when the teacher and children share a pen while working together to compose and construct a text based on a common experience. Interactive writing provides support for negotiating the text as well as learning about letters and words and how they work during the text construction. The focus of this part of the literacy framework is explicit teaching, prompting and reinforcing the complex writing process based on the needs of the students. Interactive writing provides a scaffold of support for our writers in kindergarten through second grade.

Initiating Writing in Your Classroom

In the above example of the interactive writing in response to *Bunny Cakes*, the stage is set for a dynamic interactive writing lesson. The children are gathered on the carpet at the base of the easel; they are focused on composing their message together to write on the chart paper.

The interactive writing lesson takes 10–15 minutes of instructional time and a few materials. Choose black markers and white or light paper. This contrast encourages the writers and readers to look closely at print. A variety of color makes rereading a distraction. When selecting paper, consider landscape without lines for emergent writers. Emergent writers are learning letter formation so the lines on the paper are a distraction. The landscape paper gives early writers more room on the page to construct a sentence.

Having the appropriate materials organized and ready will allow you to focus on the needs of your students instead of the supplies needed during the lesson. This teaching context is fast-paced, and your attention needs to be focused on supporting the writers.

Materials for Interactive Writing

- Easel
- Chart paper, sentence strips (placed at eye level)
- Word wall
- Alphabet chart, consonant cluster chart
- Name chart
- Chart markers (black)
- Double-sided tape
- Dry-erase markers
- Whiteboards (magnetic are best)
- Magnetic letters
- Pointer
- Student data

PROFESSIONAL TEXTS:

Interactive Writing (McCarrier, Pinnell & Fountas, 2000)

The Continuum of Literacy Learning (Fountas & Pinnell, 2010)

FIGURE 15.1

Why Is Interactive Writing Important?

Interactive writing makes the writing process come alive for writers. As teachers, we need to provide a space each day to show writers how writing works. Through interactive writing, we demonstrate, guide, and invite students to give writing a try supported by our teaching and the collaborative efforts of their fellow writers. This authentic experience accomplishes multiple goals as it builds writers and expands comprehension while embedding phonics and word study.

Interactive Writing Fosters Independence in Writers

In Chapter 10 of *By Different Paths to Common Outcomes*, Marie Clay (1998) helps us understand the writing process in three steps: from ideas to spoken structures to written messages. First, writers form an idea in their head. Next, the idea is expanded upon when the writer talks about the idea and decides exactly what will be written. Finally, the writer is ready to record the message. Sometimes, the writer will go from the written message back to ideas or from ideas right to the written message (see Figure 15.2). This understanding helps teachers see how teaching interactive writing supports the writing process.

When teaching the writing process through interactive writing, it is important to think about the eight elements of interactive writing (McCarrier, Pinnell & Fountas, 2000, p. 73):

- Provide a base of active learning experiences
- Talk to establish purpose
- Compose the text
- Construct the text
- Reread, revise, and proofread the text
- Revisit the text to support word solving
- Summarize the learning
- Extend the learning

Each of these elements offers support for the writer in experiencing the writing process (see Figure 15.3).

Let's take a closer look at each element. Understanding how the elements work together will help teachers support writers in the writing process. In addition, teachers are able to scaffold support for writers based on their needs. The end result is purposeful lessons with high engagement during the interactive writing session.

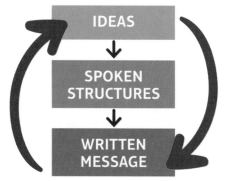

THE WRITING PROCESS

FIGURE 15.2 Adapted from *By Different Paths to Common Outcomes* by Marie Clay

A **base of learning experiences** is a common experience from which to share. This can be an inquiry study, series of Interactive Read-Alouds, or class experience. This should be an experience that the class is excited about and wants to share with others. Examples of this might include writing about reading, and taking field trips, such as observing animals or tracking plants' growth.

Next, the teacher and children **talk to establish purpose** of the writing so the children take ownership of the learning. As a community of writers, the audience, genre, and form of writing are clearly established. Who will read this writing? Will we write a story…a letter…a list… a book of facts?

After that, the writers need to decide on the message. It is time to **compose the text**. This is a time for the children, with the support of the teacher, to work together to negotiate the text. According to McCarrier, Fountas, and Pinnell (2000), "The composing process involves intentional teaching. In the planning process, you are deliberately trying to elicit a particular kind of writing, and you have in mind some of the characteristics of text that you want the children to learn. What they actually compose is the product of negotiation" (p. 85).

The Writing Process	Elements of Interactive Writing
Ideas	• Provide a Base of Learning Experiences • Reread, Revise, and Proofread the Text
Spoken Structures	• Talk to Establish Purpose • Compose the Text • Reread, Revise, and Proofread the Text
Written Message	• Construct the Text • Reread, Revise, and Proofread the Text • Revisit the Text to Support Word Solving • Summarize the Learning and Extend the Learning

FIGURE 15.3

There is much to consider here for the community of writers. What are the needs of our children? How do we want to relay our message? How should the text look on the page? What is the best way to say our message? What words will be best used in this message? The teacher intentionally piques the interest of the children through this common experience in deciding what to write about. After this decision is agreed upon, the teacher and children spend time negotiating the message—discussing the best way to convey meaning to their audience. For example, one child may begin with his or her thinking, and another child then works to expand the thought. Consider this dialogue from the kindergarten class planning the writing of *Bunny Cakes*:

Student 1:	We should say, *Step 3: Decorate the cake.*
Student 2:	How about we say, *Step 3: Put on the decorations?*
Student 1:	Yes, or maybe, *Put the decorations on the top.*
Teacher:	When I hear that last sentence it makes it clear where to put the decorations on the cake. Writers communicate clearly to their audience. We are going to write: *Put the decorations on the top.*

Once the message has been chosen, the group can **construct the text**. Construction involves the explicit teaching of letters, words, and how print works depending on the needs of the class. This part of the lesson is the most challenging; the teacher has to meet the word-solving needs of her writers while maintaining the engagement of the rest of the class. During this part of the lesson, the teacher is making rapid, careful decisions about what letters, letter clusters, and words she will write and what letters, letter clusters, and words the children will write. When the teacher knows her students well, watching text construction is like watching a maestro conduct a symphony.

Let's consider the chart of data in Figure 15.4 about the kindergarteners involved in the construction of this sentence from the bunny cake recipe in Photo 15.1: *Put the cake in the oven*. We can see that the teacher has collected data through her careful observations

Student Word-Solving Needs

Abby	AJ	Connor	Lauren	Lincoln
• Spacing • Initial consonants • High-frequency words: *the*	• Initial consonants • High-frequency words: *the, see, a, in* • Letter formation: starting from the top	• Initial blends and digraphs • Short vowels	• Letter formation • Spacing • Saying words slowly • Initial consonants	• Initial sounds • Saying words slowly • Spacing

FIGURE 15.4 Student data

of these children's writing. She used these data to make decisions about when to share the pen during the construction of the text. Since she did not know what the sentence would be before the lesson, she had to know what her children needed to solve words. Having this information allows the teacher to be flexible during the construction of the text and make decisions to meet the needs of the learners. The teacher was very purposeful in making her decisions about who is going to contribute. For example, we can see from Figure 15.5 that the teacher asked Abby to say and write the initial sound in the word *Put* because she is working on hearing and recording beginning sounds. Later, she asked AJ to write the word *in*. Likewise, AJ wrote *in* quickly. Connor would not have been a good choice for either of these words because he does not need work on initial sounds or the word *in*. The teacher's decisions in this example supported the needs of students' word solving.

As the text is constructed, the writers **reread, revise, and proofread the text**. Each time a new word or phrase is added, the writers reread the text. Sometimes the writers will decide to revise or edit text. Interactive writing can be revisited at a later time and reread for revising and editing purposes.

After the text construction of the bunny cakes recipe, the teacher reread the text with the class, explicitly pointing to each word as they read together. This emphasizes and models one-to-one correspondence on the reading of a text, which further supports the writer's use of spacing. In addition, time can be spent revising and proofreading the text after the construction to model this process.

Analysis of Teaching Decisions During Interactive Writing

Text	Teacher Support
Put	Abby wrote *P* after saying the word slowly. Connor contributed the short vowel *u*.
the	Written by the teacher, this word is known by most of the class. While the teacher is writing the word *the* on the chart paper, the children are saying the word slowly and writing it on their arms for practice writing high-frequency words quickly.
cake	Lauren used her hand to make a space after *the*. Lauren said *cake* slowly and wrote *c*.
in	Written by AJ. The teacher supported his learning of the high-frequency word *in* through demonstration on the Magna Doodle and having him practice several times before he wrote the word *in* on the chart paper.
the	Written by the teacher, this word is known by most of the class.
oven	The class clapped *oven*. The teacher wrote the *o*. Lincoln said *oven* slowly and heard *v* and *n*. Lincoln wrote *v*. The teacher wrote *e*. Lincoln wrote *n*. The teacher added the punctuation after Lincoln reminded her that this was the end of the sentence and they needed a period.

FIGURE 15.5 Teaching decisions

After the lesson, it is always good practice to **summarize the learning**. What were one or two takeaways from the lesson that you want your writers to continue to do in their writing? What was modeled and explicitly taught that they can take on in their independent writing? It could be thinking about the audience, using space between words, saying words slowly and writing down what is heard, or using an element of writer's craft that we noticed in a mentor text. The best way to summarize the learning is to think about what happened during the writing lesson that was important and worth reinforcing. In the bunny cakes example, the teacher summarized the learning by asking the children to locate known words in text (which she determined because recognizing high-frequency words was a goal for her kindergartners).

Sometimes the interactive writing enables you to **extend the learning**. Let's imagine that your students lost the class lunch basket, for example, and they decided to write a letter to the school describing the basket and asking if anyone had seen it; you might extend letter writing and invite your students to write their own personal letters. Or you might invite students to write their own "how-to" books during independent literacy centers.

Interactive Writing Extends Literature Experiences

Teachers can collect evidence of a reader's comprehension through conversation about a text, or we can ask a reader to draw or write about what was read. Interactive writing offers a high level of support that helps students learn how to put their thinking about what was read into written messages. Writing about reading can take many forms. Writing about reading can be done independently or in a whole-class setting like interactive writing. When readers write about their thinking before, during, and after their reading, we can understand what they are thinking and learn how to support them. Readers are able to show their understandings in different ways. Multiple expressions allow them to deepen their understandings (Fountas & Pinnell, 2017).

One kindergarten teacher and literacy coach, Angie Chandler, used an author study to teach her students multiple genres of writing. In late winter/early spring, Angie and her students began studying the author Mo Willems. They read many of his books, such as *Knuffle Bunny: A Cautionary Tale* (2004), the Elephant and Piggie books, *The Naked Mole Rat Gets Dressed* (2009), *Leonardo, the Terrible Monster* (2005), and *Don't Let the Pigeon Drive the Bus* (2003). Then, through the context of interactive writing, Angie was able to support her readers' thinking within, beyond, and about the text (Fountas & Pinnell, 2017). *Thinking Within the Text* is helping the reader to express the literal meaning of the story, like summarizing.

Thinking Beyond the Text is supporting the reader while making predictions, inferencing, and synthesizing. *Thinking About the Text* is making the reader aware of the writer's craft and analyzing the features like language, characterization, and structure (Fountas & Pinnell, 2017).

Examples of Writing About Reading Through Interactive Writing

- Drawing/Sketching
- Graphic Organizer
- Summary
- Prediction
- Letters
- Compare/Contrast

In Photo 15.2, Angie and her class wrote a persuasive letter to the school, hoping to encourage other students to check out the Mo Willems books from the library. Part of the letter is pictured here. Angie was teaching her students to express their understanding about these books and Mo Willems through a letter. By analyzing characters, writing opinions, and naming characteristics of the author, Angie is helping her readers show in writing how much they know.

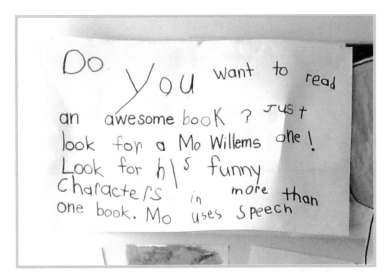

PHOTO 15.2 Mo Willems's persuasive letter

PHOTO 15.3 Piggie's speech bubble

PHOTO 15.4 Gerald's speech bubble

In the speech bubbles in Photos 15.3 and 15.4, the students share who Gerald and Piggie are. McCarrier, Fountas, and Pinnell state, "Interactive writing is a way to make visible to children the inner workings of texts and to raise their awareness of the relationships between genre and text structure" (p. 84). Through this interactive writing, children learned about the relationship between the speech bubbles that Mo Willems used in all of his Elephant and Piggie books and how that text structure was important in this narrative genre.

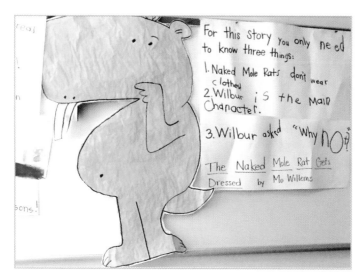

PHOTO 15.5 Naked Mole Rat's summary

PHOTO 15.6 Opinion of *City Dog, Country Frog*

In Photo 15.5, the children explain what has happened in the story and identify Wilbur as the main character. They were learning about characters and the big ideas in a story. For this writing, they used a list to create their summary. Finally, Photo 15.6 shows an example of the students' opinion about the book. For this interactive writing session, Angie and her students told why they enjoyed the book *City Dog, Country Frog* (Willems, 2010). The children made their own illustrations in the Art Center.

While all of the examples from this kindergarten class provided opportunities for students to extend their experience with literature, their comprehension was expanded through writing about reading. Figure 15.6 provides an analysis of the writing from this author study. We considered thinking within, beyond, or about the text as well as the form of writing. Over the course of the study, the children were exposed to multiple forms of writing and a variety of ways of thinking.

Analysis of Mo Willems Interactive Writing		
Way of Thinking	**Example**	**Form**
Thinking Within the Text	• Hello, I am Piggie. My best friend is Gerald. • My name is Gerald. My BFF is Piggie.	Speech Bubbles
	• List from Naked Mole Rat	List
Thinking Beyond the Text	• Do you want to read an awesome book? • Look for his funny characters in more than one book.	Letter to School
Thinking About the Text	• For this story, you only need to know three things:	List
	• This is a great book because it goes by the seasons.	Narrative

FIGURE 15.6

Constructing the Text in Interactive Writing: Supporting Phonics and Word Study Instruction

In their book *Interactive Writing* (2000), McCarrier, Fountas, and Pinnell describe the interactive writing process as a context in which the students "can explore written language for themselves" (p. 119). During the construction of the text, the children are learning about how letters and words work through demonstrations and prompting by the teacher. The goal is for children to learn about high-frequency words, phonemic awareness through hearing and recording sounds in words, and the orthographic principles of spelling through this dynamic writing experience.

High-Frequency Words

Interactive writing provides a natural context during the literacy block for children to learn high-frequency words. Children need to learn to write frequently occurring words quickly in order to retain the meaning of the sentence they are trying to construct. During interactive writing the teacher guides the children to learn high-frequency words in the sentence. After deciding which words the teacher is going to take to fluency, he or she can provide opportunities for children to learn the words in a variety of ways:

PHOTO 15.7 Teacher models high-frequency words

- Teacher models the writing of the high-frequency word on the whiteboard, Magna Doodle, or in magnetic letters for the group to see (see Photo 15.7).

- Students practice writing the word on individual whiteboards or on the carpet (see Photo 15.8).

- Teacher puts the word on the word wall so the children can access this word during independent writing time.

- The teacher may then also put these words in the Word Study Center to provide more opportunities for learning these words.

PHOTO 15.8 Student practices words on whiteboard

The purpose of learning high-frequency words is not only for children to learn the words, but also for the children to "develop a way of learning the features of words, noticing them in different contexts and using that knowledge as part of a writing or reading process." (McCarrier, Fountas & Pinnell, p. 114). In addition, these experiences help children learn ways to solve new words. High-frequency words need to be taught daily through many contexts:

interactive writing, word study lessons, guided reading, etc. Interactive writing provides a strong context for this powerful learning during the writing process.

Hearing and Recording Sounds in Words

Some words during the construction of the text in interactive writing are supported through hearing and recording sounds in words. Children first need to be taught how to say words slowly so they can hear these sounds. We encourage children to say words slowly as opposed to isolating sounds like /b/ /a/ /t/. This procedure helps the children to hear the sounds naturally and avoids over-articulation, which may result in creating extra sounds. Students must articulate these words out loud so that they not only hear the word and sounds, but also feel the way their mouth moves during this slow articulation. After saying the word slowly, children need to listen for sounds to identify letters associated with those sounds. This provides the students opportunities to think about the sounds they hear. This is also a time for the teacher to help support these writers in thinking about how these sounds connect to other words that are familiar. Many charts around the room can help with this process:

PHOTO 15.9 Name chart

- The **name chart** can be a good place to link words they know with unknown words. Children can hear the *K* in *Katelyn* and think about how that sounds the same as in the word *kite*. (See Photo 15.9).

- The **word wall** teaches high-frequency words as well as provides a resource for children to use in the room for correct spelling. (See Photo 15.10).

- **Alphabet charts** and **blends and digraph charts** are used by the teacher to link sounds and letters and provide opportunities for analogy work. For example, the word *sleeps* starts just like the word *slide* on our blend chart.

- **Labels** around the room are also used as a resource for correct spelling.

- **Other interactive writing pieces** displayed in the room provide opportunities for children to learn about high-frequency words and analogy.

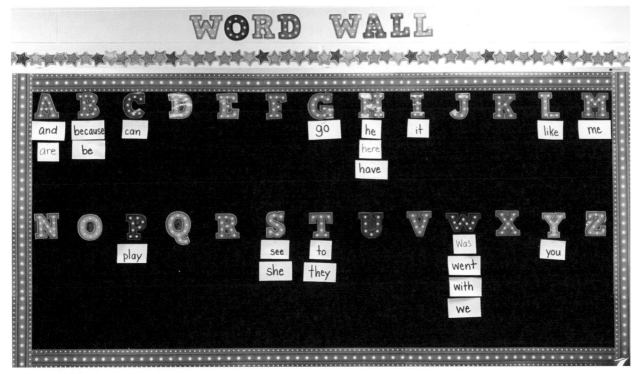

PHOTO 15.10 Word wall of high-frequency words

The emergent or early writer may not hear all the sounds in the proper sequence. For example, if the child was writing the word *kite*, the ending consonant may be the only connection the children can make. The teacher would then write the first part, and the children contribute what they hear at the end. As they proceed in their development this task becomes more complex, and we can expect the sounds and letters in sequence using both consonants and vowels to hear and record sounds.

Learning Features of Words

Children need to learn how words look and how to look at words. This includes thinking about distinguishing features of letters. For example, children need to learn how the letter *n* and letter *h* differ. Writers also need to examine the orthographic features of words and the conventional spelling of words. The focus of instruction here is how words look and can expand the learning through demonstrations saying words slowly, using Elkonin boxes and analogy (Clay, 2016).

Let's examine this teacher-student exchange where the teacher guided the students through a word-solving conversation.

Prior to the word solving, the teacher draws six boxes (one for each letter) on the whiteboard above the interactive writing (see Figure 15.6). Elkonin boxes help children to identify how many letters are in the word as well as think about how these words look. The children who help in the construction of this word are carefully selected based on needs. First, the teacher encourages the children to say the word slowly and think about

FIGURE 15.6 Example of Elkonin boxes

the sounds they hear. Then the class works from left to right through the word. The teacher calls a carefully chosen student to the board to help with the demonstration of each letter or several letters. The teacher knows that the student she called to the easel is working on the class blend/digraph chart to help with the initial blends (like the *sl* in *sleeps*). The teacher then goes on to demonstrate the analogy of *sleeps* and *slide* (on the blend/digraph chart). In addition, the teacher uses analogy to help with the long *e* pattern represented by *ee* like in the known words *see* and *tree*.

Teacher:	Say the word *sleeps* slowly.
Student:	Sleeps.
Teacher:	What two letters do you hear at the beginning of *sleeps*?
Student:	*sl.*
Teacher:	Yes, *sleeps* starts just like *slide* (points to the blend/digraph chart in the classroom). Write the *sl* that you hear up here (points to the Elkonin boxes).
Student:	(Says *sleeps* slowly and writes *sl.*) I also hear an *s* at the end of the word.
Teacher:	Yes, the *s* goes here (points to the last box).
Teacher:	Say *sleeps* slowly again. Sometimes when we add an *s* to a word it makes it hard to hear the last consonant. So we need to say the word without the *s* at the end. Say *sleep*.
Students:	*P.* I hear a *p*.
Teacher:	The *p* goes here, right before the *s*. Now, we have two more letters. Say that word slowly again. (Teacher slides finger under the word while the children say it slowly.)
Student:	I hear an *e*.
Teacher:	(Draws attention to the fact that they hear one sound, but there are two letters.)
Student:	Maybe an *ee*?
Teacher:	It is an *ee* just like the word on our word wall *see*.
Student:	And yes, just like the word *tree* that we wrote.

In this example, we can see how the teacher focused on saying words slowly, thinking about the sound sequence, and using analogy to solve the word *sleeps*. Elkonin boxes are used to provide a scaffold of support for these children who are beginning to think about the orthography of words.

Conclusion

We believe that interactive writing is the space that provides young writers opportunity to take risks with the support of the teacher. According to McCarrier, Fountas, and Pinnell (2000), "Interactive writing helps children on the way to reading and accelerates their learning in writing" (p. 234). Being a part of a community of writers is essential for young writers. Interactive writing provides this context.

Suggestions for Professional Development

1. Select a collection of writing samples from your class that includes two to three high-progress, two to three middle-progress, and two to three low-progress students. Analyze the writing, thinking about the students' strengths in writer's craft and conventions. What are your students' needs? Make goals for your interactive writing instruction based on your analysis.

2. Work with a group of colleagues to establish different opportunities for interactive writing extensions based on Interactive Read-Aloud texts. What texts are good for character analysis, summary, alternative endings, or innovation on a known text?

3. Videotape an interactive writing lesson. Watch with your colleagues and reflect upon the teaching of the writing process through composing, negotiating, and constructing the message while simultaneously guiding phonics and word study. How did the teacher support the writers in the writing process? How did the teacher scaffold learning? How did the teacher decide when to teach, prompt, and reinforce?

CHAPTER 16

Powerful Tools for Teachers of Writing

Sherry Kinzel

> **"Teach the writer, not the writing."**
>
> **—Lucy M. Calkins**

The Power of the Pen

Do you remember pouring your second-grade heart and soul into your two-page novel about your shiny red bicycle that you got for Christmas only to have the teacher return your work of art (your highest literary achievement to date) and find it covered with more red markings than your entire bike? You probably sat there staring at the paper with a steadily sinking feeling until you became aware that others might notice the red ink from across the room. Then you buried your paper, bloody from battle, under the stack of worksheets on your desk until you could give it a proper burial at home . . . in your trash can. You wouldn't dream of placing it on the refrigerator for all to see what a horrible writer you are.

The power of the marking pen is that it can inspire or demolish the human spirit. As teachers, we need to wield it with caution and care. Children of all ages consider their writing an extension of themselves, as do most published writers. As teachers of writing, we ask students to share their personal thoughts, feelings, memories, goals, desires, fantasies, fears, and accomplishments in their writing. We ask children to put themselves into their writing, so we must take care not to appear as though we are passing judgment on them or their lives when we assess their writing. There are many ways to honor the writer's work while providing instruction and assessment that will ultimately benefit the writer. In this chapter, I share the rationale for assessing writing— why do we do it? I also share practices and tools for effective assessment used by teachers in various grade levels.

Why Do We Assess Writing?

Every time you review, evaluate, and make notes about a student's writing, you are engaging in a form of assessment. In this chapter, I address several forms and purposes for the assessing of writing. Teachers need to consider their purpose for assessing prior to assessing a student's work. Oftentimes, teachers use assessments as a means to an end—they have taught a concept or strategy so now they will check on students' abilities to use the concept or strategy.

In general, the purpose of assessing is threefold: (1) to provide information about the students' abilities; (2) to use as accountability; (3) to drive future instruction. Assessing written works is no different. However, if we examine our purpose(s) for assessing, we may find ways to ensure that our purpose is not only accomplished more thoroughly but also has a greater impact on the writing lives of our students. For example, information about the abilities of a writer should be shared explicitly with the writer, not just collected. You may notice that I have used the verb form—*assessing*—more than I have used the noun form—*assessment*. We need to think of assessing as an active, ongoing process, not an end product. Assessing can also take many forms. Assessing in a variety of forms can ensure that the teacher creates a broader picture of what elements of craft the writer knows how to use effectively and that the writer can clearly articulate their message or purpose for writing.

Seeking Information

According to Richard Stiggins (1996), high-quality assessment starts with a vision of success. All writing teachers want their students to be successful writers. To ensure students' success, teachers need to have an understanding of where their writers are on the writing journey. Time and conversation allow us to get to know our students as writers and to see students' strengths and challenges for ourselves.

Time and conversation also help us develop mentoring relationships with our writers that, in turn, allow us to establish with them a collaborative vision that inspires progress.

Assessment must be an integral part of instruction. In fact, you can accomplish both assessment and teaching by observing and recording student behaviors during Writing Workshop. While the class is working independently on their writing pieces, teachers like the teacher in Photo 16.1 have one-on-one conversations with young writers. Individual conferring is a powerful component of Writing Workshop. In this one-to-one conversation, the teacher

PHOTO 16.1 Assessing during a writing conference

begins to develop the stance that "writing assessment is a habit of mind" (Anderson, 2005, p. 2). Before each conference, prepare by asking yourself, "What do I know about this child as a writer?" During the conference and immediately following it, record the responses to these questions: What did I observe about this writer that confirms what I already knew? What did I learn? What is my learner's next goal? How can I support him in reaching his goal? The goals you and your student set will create a path of progress.

Collecting Information

Teachers can collect assessment data in a variety of ways. Many teachers use individual conferences to record observations about a student's writing. While the student is sharing the writing, you have the opportunity not only to make quick notes about the written products, but also to record evidence of the student's self-awareness. These notes begin to build a picture of the developing writer.

I have found it helpful to use a master form in a way that makes it easy to monitor progress, plan future instruction, and share data with parents. You can house these materials in a binder with separate sections for each student or place them in hanging files. Tailor the master form to your own needs and purposes. The examples that follow are forms that classroom teachers have used successfully. You may want to use these examples as you develop your own form, realizing that sometimes it is very helpful for teachers across a grade level or several grades to use the same form. Above all, a recording form should be quick and easy to use. Also, you do not want the form to "take over" your conference time, during which the highest priority is your conversation with the student. The form should support the conferring process as well as allow quick notes that will help you use time effectively.

The recording form shown in Figure 16.1 provides space for brief comments about observations, as well as a section that allows you to keep track of which days and the number of days you have met with specific children. This information is helpful because it is easy to overlook an individual writer during a busy school week. The form also has space at the bottom in which to record the needs of writers in general terms—for example, notes on priorities for instruction based on patterns that are appearing in this writer's work that

Conference Record Form

Name	M	T	W	TH	F	Comments
Lori	X					Writing Memorie; iniates revision strategies
Mark	X					Info. Text; needs help organizing research
Randy	X					Looking for new topic; needs to try other genres
Kim		X				Personal narrative; help w/organizing para.
Tricia		X				Pamphlet; needs to consider audience
Andy		X				Looking for new topic; using writer's notebook
Marie				X		Publishing fantasy; punctuation for dialogue

Minilessons:
- Think about audience when you organize your writing.
- Organization of different genre.
- Writers need to think like readers.

FIGURE 16.1 Conference Record Form (see Scholastic.com/RLResources for the full-sized forms)

could be addressed with the whole class during mini-lessons. Using a form such as this one can help you notice when several students have the same needs. These observations can be invaluable in informing your instructional decisions as you plan mini-lessons with the entire class, guiding writing with small groups, and conferences with individuals.

The recording form shown in Figure 16.2 was created by a group of primary teachers to collect specific information about their young writers. They began with their own understanding of the process of learning to write. To create the document, they made a list of recognizable early writing characteristics that, based on research, they believed would lead to successful writing. They used the form to help them find evidence of progress over time. While conferring with a child, the teacher would indicate the level of competence by recording a minus (–) to show "no evidence," a plus (+) to "some evidence," and a plus enclosed in a circle to show "competence." Competence in an area indicates that the writer demonstrates control of this area and is able to perform it with ease. You can easily create a similar form using a list of standards as a start. Be sure to get as specific as you need to be and tailor it to meet the needs of your students and school.

Using an open-ended form such as the one in Figure 16.3 allows you to make notes capturing evidence in an ongoing narrative, yet the form also provides enough structure to enable you to make later interpretations. The left column allows you to record what you think is significant about the piece (e.g., the title, genre, purpose, audience, areas of strength and/or concern). In the right column

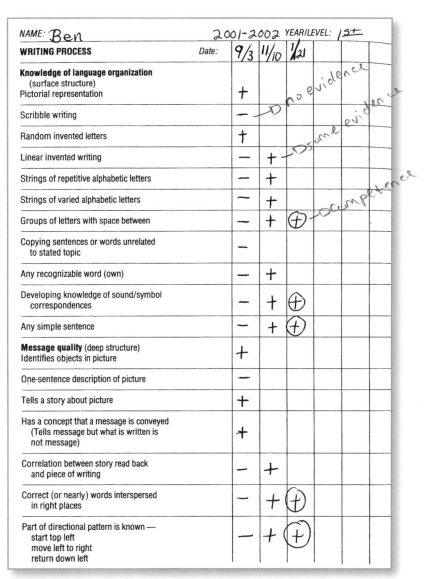

FIGURE 16.2 Recording form created by teachers (available at Scholastic.com/RLResources)

FIGURE 16.3 Blank recording form (available at Scholastic.com/RLResources)

Rubric Traits	
Ideas and Content	• Clear, well-focused message • Important details relevant to the topic • Interesting and easy to understand
Organization	• Beginning (lead) that hooks the reader and is easy to follow • Best way chosen to organize the message • Ideas link to main message • Strong conclusion
Voice	• Enthusiastic about topic • Sounds like writer talking • Holds the reader's attention
Sentence Fluency	• Easy to read • Sentences begin in different ways • Some long and some short sentences • Sounds smooth when read aloud (seems to flow)
Word Choice	• Some strong verbs or colorful phrases • Most precise words chosen • Uses unique words • Avoids repeating common words too many times
Conventions	• Spaces between words and sentences • Title written correctly • Correct punctuation • Correct capitalization • Proper spelling • Proper grammar • Paragraphs indented

FIGURE 16.4 Writing traits chart

you can record the teaching point that is needed to support the writer with this piece or a future goal. Also, rubrics can be used as tools to support the assessment of specific qualities or traits of writing. Once you learn to use them, rubrics represent a quick way to collect information about your writers since the criteria for a rubric are set. More and more states/districts are requiring the analysis of student achievement in writing using rubrics designed to measure competencies relative to various traits such as ideas and content, organization, voice, word choice, sentence structure, and conventions. The development of these traits supports your writers in many ways, as shown in Figure 16.4.

Such assessment may become the driving force behind the curriculum, so rubrics can be very influential. Teachers tend (or are required by administrators) to align writing instruction with these traits because many assessments are analyzing students' progress in these same or similar traits and teachers want their students to be successful on standardized writing tests. In some school districts, committees are asked to survey the standards in the areas of written communication and then create a standard-based tool for teachers to use during writing conferences. Evidence of progress toward meeting competency of a standard can be noted with a point value, a date, or a simple check mark. Figure 16.3 provides an example of using a standard to create an assessment tool.

Ruth Culham encourages the use of rubrics with students and has developed several rubrics that are teacher-friendly and easily understood when used with students. You may find her book *6+1 Traits of Writing: The Complete Guide for the Primary Grades* (2005) to be a supportive resource. It includes many examples of student writing to help you recognize the traits of effective writing. As with all forms of assessment, their strength lies in their ability to inform your instruction. The advantages and cautions about using rubrics are listed in Figure 16.5.

The writing process is complex and multifaceted, so our assessments must reflect this understanding. You want to create a clear, well-supported view of students' writing potential and progress, and using more than one form or tool to collect information on students as writers can help.

Getting Started

If you are new to systematic writing assessment and have not used tools such as those described previously, you may be a bit uncertain about what you should record. Trust your instincts; they are usually right. When a child shares his work, the most pressing issues will pop right out at you. Make a note of them, but do not dwell on them. Assess the work to determine the learner's needs, but also look for evidence of what the writer can manage on her own and the degree to which she does it successfully. You will find that evidence of the learner's strengths is highly valuable and gives you a conservative view of what the developing writer controls. Also, it is important to help writers use what they know to expand their learning.

Whichever tools you choose to use to collect information, make sure you remember that your goal is to "capture what students do well so they can do it again, and what they're not doing so well so you can help them do better next time" (Culham, p. 39). Communicating these ideas clearly to writers has a much greater impact than any number or score. The ongoing process of conferring is a routine that develops a sense of accountability in young writers.

Ways Rubrics Are Helpful	Cautions About Using Rubrics
<ul><li>Provide a way of collecting information or evidence of your students' learning</li><li>Quick and simple to use</li><li>Help build an ongoing picture of who your students are as writers</li><li>Cause you to continually reflect on your teaching</li></ul>	<ul><li>Using them to grade (evaluate) but not using them to inform teaching</li><li>Using rubrics that do not have language that is accessible for students</li><li>Using rubrics that do not help students understand the expectations for performance</li></ul>

what is it mean?

FIGURE 16.5 Advantages and cautions about rubrics

Building Accountability Through Conferring

All writers, even this one, live with deadlines. I am not referring to accountability as just the timely completion of a piece, however. A deadline is something much greater; it connotes expectations of progress for writing as writers. Confer regularly with your young writers to communicate and establish these expectations.

PHOTO 16.2 Learning during a writing conference

For example, join me in a conference with Austin:

Sherry:	Hi, Austin. How's it going?
Austin:	Good.
Sherry:	What are you working on right now?
Austin:	I'm writing about a trip to the beach. I just started today, so this is my first draft.
Sherry:	Okay, so you're not worried about everything being perfect just yet.
Austin:	Nope. I'm just trying to get my ideas down.

From this brief exchange, I already know that Austin understands part of the writing process. He knows that the purpose of the first draft is to just get his ideas down on paper without worrying about grammar and the other conventions. He is focused on the story and the meaning that he is trying to communicate to his reader. He realizes that he will have an opportunity to revise and edit as needed during another portion of the writing process.

Sherry:	Good thinking. Where did you get your original idea for the story?
Austin:	I found a page in my Writer's Notebook about stuff I did last summer. My family went to the beach with my grandparents, my aunt and uncle, and my cousins. They are younger than me.
Sherry:	So you're not writing about the whole summer, just the trip to the beach?
Austin:	Uh-huh!

Now I have further insight about Austin as a writer. He knows how to use resources such as a Writer's Notebook for ideas. He also can choose to narrow his topic or focus on a smaller topic, a common practice of published authors.

Sherry:	Austin, that's great! You know many writers choose to focus on a smaller piece of time when they write. It makes their writing more interesting and pulls their readers into the story. It's like the book we shared in Interactive Read-Aloud, *Saturdays and Teacakes* by Lester Laminack. Mr. Laminack didn't tell us about the boy's whole life. He chose to tell us about one event in his life—going to his grandma's house on Saturday. Writers make a lot of choices. It sounds to me like this time you are making the same choice that Mr. Laminack made. You are planning to tell about a trip to the beach, not the whole summer vacation.

Austin:	Yep. I just want to tell that part.
Sherry:	Do you have any questions or concerns that you want to talk about as you start this piece?
Austin:	Well, I'm having trouble getting started.
Sherry:	A lot of writers struggle with that, including me. You said that you got your idea from your Writer's Notebook, right?
Austin:	Yes. I found it in a list of stuff I did last summer.

In this conference, Austin is able to recognize his need and communicate it well; he doesn't know how to generate or expand his idea. Even if students don't communicate as clearly as Austin, they will often give you an opening to support their learning if you listen carefully and notice their nonverbal cues. Based on Austin's comment about having trouble getting started, I chose to provide him with several options and let him decide which one he wanted to try out.

Sherry:	Okay. Well, let me give you some writer's advice. You could do several different things to help get your thoughts together. You could make another list, but this time your list would be just of things you did or saw at the beach. You could make a web with the beach vacation in its center, then connect your memories in other bubbles to the main idea in the center. (I modeled the web on paper.) You could make a sketch of how the beach or beach house looked to you. You could even talk to another writer about your trip to bring back important memories and get their reaction to what they think is interesting about your beach trip. Do you think one of these ideas might help you get started?
Austin:	Yes. I'd like to try talking to another writer and maybe sketching the place where we stayed.
Sherry:	Great! Why don't you get started on your sketch, and I'll see if Drew has some time today to listen to your thinking about your beach trip. You will want to keep your writing folder with you during your talk in case you get a great thought that you want to add to your piece or Drew gives you some feedback about what he thinks is really interesting as you tell him your story. I'll go ask him if he can spare a little time for you today. Maybe later you can do the same thing for him. How does that sound?
Austin:	Good!

Writing Assessment Notes	
Name: Austin	
Date: 9/21	
Conference Observations (What do I notice about this writer?)	**Teaching Points & Goals** (How can I help this writer?)
✔ Working on first draft ✔ Trip to beach ✔ Memoir ✔ Uses Writer's Notebook for topics ✔ Values narrowing topic ✔ Needs help getting started	✔ Offered suggestions for generating, expanding topic (list, web, confer w/partner, sketch); he chose to confer with Drew

FIGURE 16.6 Assessment notes

After this conference with Austin, I recorded some observations on a form (see Figure 16.6). For example, Austin needed support with generating and expanding his thinking around a topic. I also noted that he uses his Writer's Notebook to generate ideas for writing. This type of conversation informs the teacher of what she can reasonably hold her students accountable for in their writing, and it allows the teacher to provide clear expectations for the students' writing in the future.

Driving Instruction

We all have requirements that motivate us on some level to evaluate our writers' finished pieces and compare them to writing examples of various degrees of quality, as established by local and state expectations. This process of comparison helps us establish a common vision for writing that exemplifies quality and measures progress toward it; it is the heart of accountability. Assessment is also an essential part of instruction, however. Only through close observation and analysis can you make good decisions about what to teach and when and how to teach it. As you look at an individual writer's work, look for quality. Identify what the writer is doing effectively and move from these strengths to what the individual needs to do more effectively. Next, look for patterns across students, and then decide whether the needed instruction can best be provided in individual, small-group, or whole-group settings—or should it be presented in different ways in all three? Let's look at a few examples across different grade levels.

Lila is a kindergartner who has written a story about going to her grandma's house (see Figure 16.7). I read the writing several times and viewed the supporting picture. Then I began to analyze by asking a question. What do I know about Lila as a writer?

FIGURE 16.7 Lila's story

- She uses symbols to represent letters, words, and sounds.

- She understands the concept of directionality (shown by recording symbols in a left to right sequence).

- She attempts letter/sound correspondence (shown by writing *mi* for the word *my*).

- She knows that print should convey a message.

- She doesn't use spaces between words.

- She has some confusion about letter/sound correspondence. (She wrote *y* to represent /w/ as the beginning letter for *went*. Beginning writers commonly write the name of the letter that matches the sound they hear. She heard the name of the letter *y* as she began to say *went*.)

Based on this analysis, I ask myself another question: What's next for this writer? The answer to my question will determine my future instruction. My analysis has revealed her greatest needs, and I reconsider these, looking for priorities. Then, I select two areas or concepts to focus on. One concept that I would choose to teach this writer is the importance of spaces between words. I know that this will make her writing easier to read and help her communicate her message more clearly. It also will support her understanding of directionality within words as she learns that most words have a beginning, a middle, and an end. Controlling this information will enable her to later take on more complex knowledge about how words work. I would also choose to help expand her knowledge of letter-sound correspondence. It is apparent that she has some ability to match letters and sounds; however, extending her understanding in this area will help her generate more writing in the future. The instruction provided to Lila could easily take place in various settings. In this case, I provide instruction in a whole-class setting during a mini-lesson at the beginning of Writing Workshop, because Lila was not the only student who needed to learn the importance of using spaces between words and letter-sound correspondence at this early point in the school year. These same concepts were repeated during interactive writing sessions. I knew that most of my students would benefit from instruction in these two areas; therefore, whole-class instruction was the best setting.

Let's take a look at a first-grade writing example from Michael (see Figure 16.8). Again, I ask myself the same questions: What do I know about this student as a writer? (analysis) and What's next for this writer? (instructional decisions).

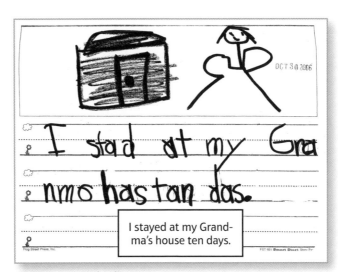

I stayed at my Grand-ma's house ten days.

FIGURE 16.8 Michael's story

Analysis:

- He uses left-to-right directionality and a return sweep for text that continues beyond the edge of the paper.
- He uses spaces between words consistently.
- He uses known words correctly, such as *I*, *at*, and *my*.
- He hears beginning and ending sounds in words and can make appropriate letter-sound correspondence
- For example, the /s/ and the /d/ in *stad* for the word *stayed*. He also recognized /t/ and /n/ in *tan* for the word *ten*.
- He hears and records blends, such as *stad* and *Granmo*.
- He uses vowels in words consistently.
- He uses punctuation properly.

Instructional decisions

Based on my observations of the writing, I believe that Michael is ready to expand his thinking about onset and rime and learn about word families. Examining the writing, I notice that he can manage the beginning blend /gr/ (onset) in *Granmo*. I would ask Michael to think of other words he knows that begin like *grandma*, and together we could list those words on chart paper. I could also draw his attention to the sounds at the middle and end of words (rime). After writing the word *ten* on a chart and showing him the part of the word that says -*en*, he and I could create a list of words that rhyme with *ten*. Being able to apply what he knows about a familiar word to another unknown word helps develop flexibility in the use of words and expands a writer's written vocabulary. This knowledge will support him in attempting to write words that may be a part of his spoken vocabulary but not his writing vocabulary.

This young writer had the same characteristics as two other advanced writers in our class. I believe that each writer makes progress when he is working at his own instructional level. Therefore, I chose to address Michael's instructional needs in a guided writing setting rather than a whole-class setting. So, I met with Michael and the other two advanced writers at my reading table. While the other students were working independently on their own pieces, I provided instruction similar to a whole-class mini-lesson to these three writers. The guided writing setting is brief (5–15 minutes) and allows me to focus my instruction on a small group of children with similar needs. In guided writing, I am able to use my time more efficiently by meeting with three or four students instead of just one. Writers in the group also have the benefit of seeing how the other writers apply the mini-lesson to their writing.

Lauren wanted to write about her vacation to Florida. During a writing conference, the teacher noticed that her original draft was more like an exhaustive list of activities and the events lacked details. Through their conversation, Lauren's teacher noticed that Lauren was giving interesting details about the portion of the trip when the family car broke down. The teacher took this opportunity to share examples of ways to make a piece more interesting for the reader, such as descriptive words, voice, and dialogue. Together, they located parts of the writing where these strategies could be used. As a result of this conference, Lauren decided to narrow her focus for writing from a summer vacation to just the event of the car breaking down. The book that follows (see Figure 16.9) is a direct result of the conversation that Lauren and her teacher had about her writing. The rest of the panels from this book can be found at Scholastic.com/RLResources.

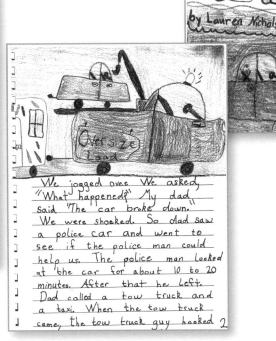

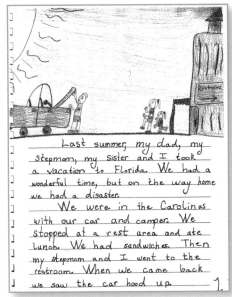

FIGURE 16.9 Lauren's book

As you continue conferring with students in your class, you may notice certain trends. Some areas may require additional instruction for the majority of students, some for only a small group. If many students are grappling with an area, instruction should take place in a whole-class setting, such as mini-lessons, a great way to address similar needs in a time-efficient manner. These brief lessons require about 10 minutes and provide opportunities for immediate application. Figure 16.10 is a basic plan for mini-lessons.

Basic Plan for Mini-lessons

1. Introduce the strategy or concept.

2. Explain why it is important for readers or writers.

3. Demonstrate the strategy or share examples of concept using a mentor text.

4. Explain the strategy or concept.

5. Engage the students in guided practice or conversation about the idea.

6. Summarize new learning.

7. Provide independent practice.

(Adapted from *Extending Our Reach: Teaching for Comprehension in Reading, Grades K–2*, Pinnell & Scharer, 2001, pp. 108–109)

FIGURE 16.10 Mini-lesson plan

You may discover that several students have similar instructional needs that are not shared by the majority of the class. In this case, the efficient approach is to gather those students and provide explicit instruction. This small-group setting is often referred to as guided writing (Fountas & Pinnell, 2001). It is useful because it addresses the instructional needs of these few students while allowing the rest of the students, who do not need this information, to work independently. To plan a guided writing lesson, follow the basic plan described above for providing a mini-lesson to the class; however, in this setting, you will provide each student with more individualized attention. As often as possible, you can use examples of students' writing or a previously shared text from an Interactive Read-Aloud to support this learning. It is extremely important that writers have examples from actual texts that illustrate the strategy or concept that is being developed.

Conclusion

It is often said that assessment and learning are two sides of the same coin—as we assess our writers, we are building a body of knowledge that will enable us to become instructional decision-makers. The decisions we make and goals that we set with our learners will ultimately determine their level of success as writers. Effective teachers learn from their students daily. Teachers should view assessment as a way of learning more about their students, and students should view assessment as a way of learning what they are doing well and what they need to work on to more effectively communicate their message. We should never forget why writers write—to communicate a message. Assessing only the craft or conventions of writing signals to writers that writing is only about the "bits and pieces." *Every* writer should know what her message is and who her audience will be in order to make good decisions about the use of craft and conventions.

It is important to communicate with our writers by providing them with feedback about their writing in a safe setting, which includes calling their attention to the progress they are making. Unfortunately, assessing is often confused with evaluating and is used only for determining a grade. We need to change our thinking about this. Most of us agree that a greater purpose is served when we follow the old adage of "teaching a boy to fish, rather than giving him one fish."

The same principle can be applied to assessing. Simply assigning a grade for writing will not have the far-reaching effect that conferring and assessing a piece of writing with a child will have. With a new perspective, assessment can be thought of as a fact-finding process that leads us to greater discoveries about our students' writing and to critical opportunities for us as teachers to help all our students to step into the role of a true writer.

Suggestions for Professional Development

1. Ask each teacher to bring a copy of one current writing sample each from a high-, a middle-, and a low-progress writer in his or her class. Have the teachers form grade-level groups, and then place some of the samples on roll paper to form a continuum from early to more sophisticated writing. (You may not need to use all the samples, but include those that represent a distinctive characteristic.) Write a specific description for each sample on 4-by-6-inch cards and tape each of these below the sample it describes. Think about the patterns of writing progress you notice from low- to high-progress writers. What patterns seem to emerge across grade levels over time? Share your findings with the whole group. (Later, the charts can be combined to form a school-wide continuum that can be used for reference and revised to reflect new learning.)

2. Using your state standards and school district writing assessments, rubrics, or guidelines, ask each grade-level group to generate a short list of benchmark writing behaviors/characteristics they would like to see in writers by the end of the year. Compare this list with the descriptors and samples analyzed in the last session. Have each grade discuss and chart the following:

   - Where are our students in their development as writers?
   - Where are the gaps?
   - What focus areas do we need to address in our teaching this year? (Keep your list short and prioritize the goals.)

   Share your end-of-year benchmarks and instructional focus goals with the whole group.

3. Have teachers work together by grade levels to develop an assessment tool that would support their collection of information about their writers. You could create an easy-to-use tool, such as a rubric or checklist, by reviewing state or local standards to clarify grade-level expectations and to use as guidelines. This tool could be used to note progress over time, as well as assist in decision-making about future instruction.

CHAPTER 17

Developing Writers, K–2: Navigating the Writer's Journey

Jenny McFerin

"We need to create joyful, inviting, intentionally structured environments where children can learn how written language works while coming to understand the varied and critical roles written language plays in their lives.**"**

—Eileen Feldgus, Isabell Cardonick, and Richard Gentry

Writing is hard to teach. Indeed, teaching the writing process to young children can seem like an overwhelming challenge. Often I have heard teachers talk about "the writing process" in their classrooms and share their stories with sadness and stress. They are not sure what to teach; their students are disengaged; and the process is long and daunting. In this chapter, you'll discover how to honor the developmental process of young writers in ways that create an engaging writing experience for both you and your students. We will revisit the writing process, the stages of development that writers move through, and show how writing and reading connect by following the growth of one child, Abby, and her development as a writer. As you'll discover, some children, like Abby, can't wait to start writing!

Abby's Writing Process

In Photo 17.1 you can see that Abby has made a list to tell her mother all the things she needs to pick up from the grocery store. She knows that words have meaning; each word needs its own space; and some words are longer than others. This young writer knows a lot about the printed message and she produced this list quickly. She saw herself as a writer, thought about the items needed, wrote the first three, reread

PHOTO 17.1 Abby's grocery list

the list, added the last two, reread the list and said, "Okay, Mommy, that's all, now we can go to the store!"

Abby engaged in the writing process without realizing it because it was a natural part of her writing world just like driving is to us. According to Fountas and Pinnell (2017), the writing process includes the following: rehearsing and planning, drafting and revising, editing and proofreading, and publishing. Figure 17.1 describes Abby's writing process using these terms.

This example shows us that the writing process does not have to be a special event; it just has to be part of our daily work as writers. Marie Clay (1998) offers, "Writing can contribute to the building of almost every kind of inner control of literacy learning that is needed by the successful reader" (p. 130). You may be wondering why I started a writing chapter with a quote about readers. To teach writers, we need to be teaching reading alongside writing. A reader uses sentences, phrases, words, and letters to find meaning in a story. A writer uses letters, words, phrases, and sentences to communicate meaning to an audience. When a teacher provides an environment where students weave in and out of the role of reader and author in authentic ways, the teacher will have a class of readers and writers at the end of the year.

Writing Process Analysis of Abby's Grocery List	
Rehearsing and Planning	Abby and her mom needed to go to the store, so a list needed to be made. They talked about the food needed from the store.
Drafting and Revising	Abby wrote the first three items on the list, read them to her mom, and added the last two items.
Editing and Proofreading	Abby and her mom did not make any spelling or convention changes to the list.
Publishing	They took the list to the store and purchased the items on the list.

FIGURE 17.1 Analysis of Abby's writing

Stages of Writing Development

To understand how to teach writers, we need to learn how writers develop. When we know how writers change over time, we can adjust our teaching to meet their needs and move them ahead as writers. McCarrier, Fountas, and Pinnell (2000) describe writers along a continuum as emergent, early, transitional, and self-extending. In this section we will learn about each kind of writer and the instructional supports that will best guide them.

Emergent

Emergent writers are about the age of preschool and kindergarten. They have had varying kinds of exposure to print before coming to school and are learning the differences between a letter, a word, and a picture. "Emergent writers are learning that what they say and think can be expressed in written language. They are also beginning to understand that writing naturally accompanies human activity and can be used for different purposes" (McCarrier, Fountas & Pinnell, 2000, p. 204). Look at the writing Abby offers in Photo 17.2. Both pieces of writing have messages about important people and events

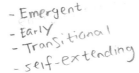

- Emergent
- Early
- Transitional
- self-extending

PHOTO 17.2 Abby's messages

Interactive writing

PHOTO 17.3
Using interactive writing to label and list

PHOTO 17.4 Abby's invitation

Invitation Analysis		
Word	**Abby's Attempt**	**Notes**
and	A	First letter
you	U	Sound that is heard
are	R	Sound that is heard
invited	EV	Sounds that are heard
to	T	First letter
birthday	BBy	Abby wrote 2 *bs* and the letter *y* and asked for help. I said, "What can you hear?" She crossed out the *y* and wrote the *b*. I wrote the rest of the word.

FIGURE 17.2 Analysis of Abby's writing

in her life. She knows that her experiences can be written down and communicated with others.

INSTRUCTIONAL SUPPORT FOR EMERGENT WRITERS

Emergent writers thrive in a classroom that is filled with engaging books and writing materials, where young writers are drawn into rich literary experiences. Shared reading and interactive writing are important for emergent writers. These high levels of teacher support show the emergent writer how writing works as the teachers and students create messages together. The writing should be purposeful and meet the needs of the writers. Consider the opportunities for interactive writing that different teachers have provided in Photo 17.3. Writers are learning how to make lists and label. Both of these kinds of writing are purposeful for emergent writers to do independently.

Early Writers

Early writers are different from emergent writers because they are using writing for a specific purpose. McCarrier, Fountas, and Pinnell (2000) state, "Early readers and writers are well aware of the print in the world around them and they seek to use it for many purposes. They have made the basic transition from beginning awareness and have become actual practitioners" (p. 208). Early writers make significant gains in this stage of development.

Consider the invitation that Abby wrote in Photo 17.4. She was having a birthday party and wanted to invite her friends. The words *Josh*, *Carley*, and *Wednesday* were in the kitchen where she was writing the invitation, so she could write those words on her own. She did not know these words: *and*, *you*, *are*, *invited*, or *to*. She said each of those words and made an attempt. When writers make an attempt at spelling words, it is called *invented spelling*. From scribbles to drawings to letters to words, when children write on paper, teachers are given a road map to learning what children already know about letters, sounds, and words. The invented

Invented spelling

spellings produced by writers help teachers understand what children know about words and where support is needed. Abby felt comfortable getting the message down without worrying if the words were spelled correctly. Figure 17.2 is an analysis of Abby's attempts at the words she did not know when writing the invitation.

Now look at the letter Abby wrote ten months later in Photo 17.5. She was writing a letter to her mom. It was a typical practice for Abby to leave sticky notes around the house with "I love you" messages. On this day, however, Abby had more to say to her mom. As she wrote the note, there was a faster pace to the writing

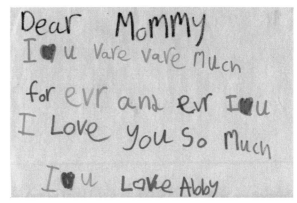

PHOTO 17.5 Abby's letter to mom

because more words like *dear, mommy, and, much, for, love,* and *so* were known. She now understands word boundaries and uses this concept consistently. The words *very* and *ever* were words she did not know. So, she said each of them slowly and wrote the sounds she heard.

INSTRUCTIONAL SUPPORT FOR EARLY WRITERS

Early writers need interactive writing every day. Each day these writers need to be part of a community of writers that engage in the writing process. This will build their knowledge of high-frequency words and conventions of print. More importantly, interactive writing will help

high-frequency words

early writers understand how to compose writing before putting pencil to paper. In Photo 17.6, first-grade teacher Amy Harrison helped her early writers understand stories, planning, and word solving using a book they loved, *Owl Babies* by Martin Waddell.

In addition to interactive writing, early writers also need Writer's Workshop. The teacher may launch Writer's Workshop with oral storytelling. As the

PHOTO 17.6 Retelling of *Owl Babies*

class engages in storytelling, the teacher is building a foundation of trust and expectation for her writers. Telling stories together helps writers remember the events they want to capture in drawings and words. Sharing with fellow writers also provides support for each other. Henry (2008) stated, "Young children take on oral storytelling and compose sentences, perhaps one at first, later a few that are connected, to communicate the images they hold as a life experience. We often prompt children to add a beginning, a middle, and an end to their personal narratives. Knowing how stories work may support students in writing about a vivid memory to turn it into a narrative that is interesting to readers" (p. 138).

After several weeks of storytelling, early writers are invited to draw and/or write their stories. The structure of Writer's Workshop provides a strong support for guiding writers to independence. The workshop begins with a five- to ten-minute mini-lesson, the children get their writing folders, then the teacher confers with writers in a small group or individually. Finally, Writer's Workshop concludes with sharing. Sharing allows the teacher to reinforce the mini-lesson so students can see an application of the lesson from their peers. The students also write while the teacher is working with guided reading groups.

From a high level of teacher support like interactive writing to independent practice, early writers learn best in an environment that supports their exploration of writing. These young writers thrive with opportunities to take risks in spelling words and trying a range of writing.

PHOTO 17.7 Abby's letter to her brother

Transitional Writers

Transitional writers have stories that are longer and more complex. Their stories will feature conversation, conventionally spelled words, and several episodes. Now Abby can express herself more clearly (see Photo 17.7). On this day, she needed to get some work done, so she hung this note on her door to ensure some uninterrupted time from her older brother, Connor.

INSTRUCTIONAL SUPPORT FOR TRANSITIONAL WRITERS

Even though transitional writers have many words they can write and they are able to solve many words they do not know, these writers still benefit from the support of interactive writing. The level of support for understanding how to compose and construct a more complex genre is exactly what a transitional writer needs. The kinds of writing will be more complex and the opportunity for sharing the pen even more strategic. Now the teacher will share the pen for words that are increasingly difficult.

Writer's Workshop also supports transitional writers. Writers need more options like paper with lines (either vertical or landscaped with a place for a picture). Mini-lessons will focus on writer's craft. The writer needs to learn how to organize the piece of writing, how to create beginnings or endings, how to use effective language, and how to improve the piece of writing over time. These writers need extended time to work on different genres while guided by a purposeful mini-lesson and supported by the teacher during writing conferences. In the pictures that follow, a first-grade class used interactive writing to showcase their study of Ezra Jack Keats. They produced an interactive mural of the story *A Letter to Amy* and synthesized their understandings of Keats using interactive writing. In the first scene (Photo 17.8) the students wrote directions for writing an invitation. Now anyone that came to this mural could learn about this part of the book and how to write an invitation. The mural even features a place for participants to get paper and "mail" their finished invitation. In Photo 17.9, the class recreated the party scene for the audience. Here, participants can guess the gift that is inside the presents. For every correct guess, a tally mark is written on the chart. Finally, in Photo 17.10, the class listed their understandings of Ezra Jack Keats as an author and illustrator. This in-depth author study helped these writers learn about writing craft.

PHOTOS 17.8 (top), **17.9** (middle), **17.10** (left)
Author study of Ezra Jack Keats

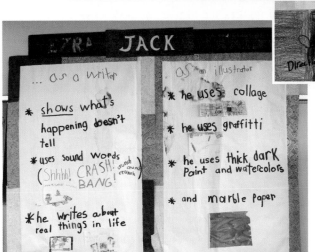

Self-Extending Writers

Self-extending writers are able to write a range of different genres with flexibility. McCarrier, Fountas, and Pinnell (2000) note that self-extending writers have become more automatic in engaging in the writing process. It is easier for them to compose messages, revise, and consider the overall message. When spelling, these writers use references and they are able to use what they know about words to spell new words. In Photo 17.11, Abby's writing has moved into this stage, and she is experimenting with writing

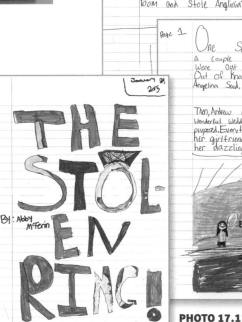

PHOTO 17.11 Abby's chapter book

chapter books. She uses elements of writer's craft that she has heard from stories that have been read to her and stories she has read in this piece of writing. Now, her story has characters, tension, resolution, and dialogue.

INSTRUCTIONAL SUPPORT FOR SELF-EXTENDING WRITERS

Interactive writing can still be a useful context for self-extending writers, especially while learning to edit and revise. Writer's Workshop is essential for self-extending writers. In Photo 17.12, Beth Cummings used a study on inventors to support her second-grade writers in a variety of writing opportunities. Writers were engaged in creating captions for the mural, writing directions for the invention, and engaging in an interactive edit (Photo 17.13). As writing becomes more complex for writers it is still important to purposefully plan instruction so writers know how to write across different genres of texts.

The second graders began their study looking closely at the characters in some of the books Beth had read aloud in class several times. In each of the books Beth selected to revisit, the class discovered that the main character had a problem that needed solving. Since they were studying inventors in science class, the students decided these characters would benefit from an invention to help them solve their problem. Through interactive writing, the class created a chart that compared the characters, their problems, and possible inventions.

After the initial chart was created, Beth divided the class into workgroups. From here, the groups decided on the invention and built and wrote about the invention. As each group finished their writing, Beth engaged the group in an

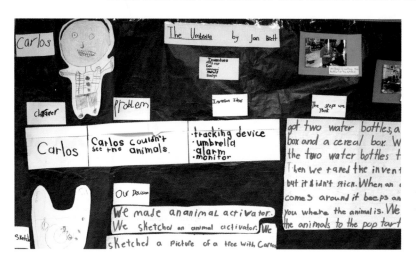

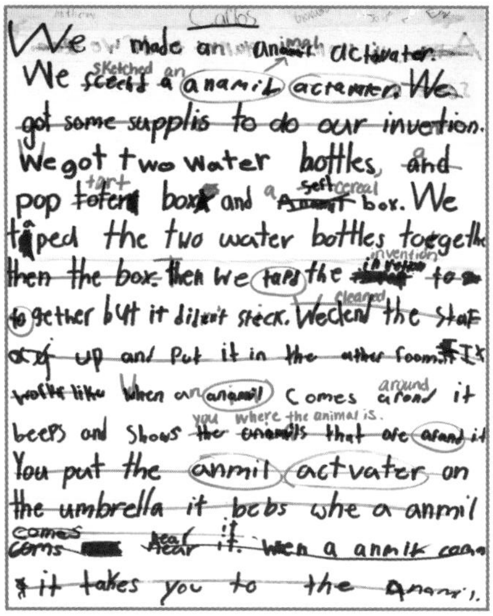

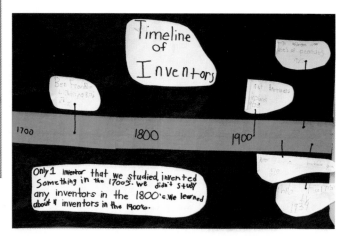

PHOTO 17.12 (top) Study on inventors

PHOTO 17.13 (middle)

PHOTO 17.14 (right)

interactive edit with the whole class (see Photo 17.13). The interactive edit provided an authentic opportunity for the class to talk about conventions and writer's craft. After the edit, the group could make their final edits and revisions before adding their final copy to the chart. Finally, Beth worked with one small group of students to create a timeline of inventors (see Photo 17.14).

Sometimes understanding something complex makes navigating the journey a little easier. Our voyage through the stages of writing may help you as you learn to teach writers. This foundation will guide your instruction as you take your writers to new and exciting places.

Suggestions for Professional Development

1. Create a writing continuum.
   - Have each teacher bring three writing samples. The samples should represent a range of development in your classroom, from a more developed writer to a writer who needs more support.
   - Look at all the writing samples. Determine the piece of writing that represents the earliest form of writing. Continue to examine the writing so that you create a developmental continuum that shows early writing through self-extending.
   - Consider these reflective questions: *How did you determine strength of writing (craft… conventions)? What did you learn about the writers in your classrooms? What are the implications for instruction?*

2. Analyze student writing.
   - Gather writing samples from your students. Using the descriptions about writing stages in this chapter, place the writing into the writing stages. You can put them into designated piles or write the student's names in a chart like the one seen in Figure 17.3.
   - Now think about the kinds of writing instruction you might provide for your writers based on your analysis.

WRITING STAGE	Interactive Writing	Writing Workshop
Emergent		
Early		
Transitional		
Self-extending		

FIGURE 17.3 Planning for instruction

3. Celebrate writing.
   - Work with colleagues in your grade level or across K–2. During your next professional meeting, bring samples of the writing you have been doing in your classroom (e.g., Writing Workshop, interactive writing, and/or writing from independent literacy centers).
   - Reflect on the writing: *What genres of writing are represented? What forms of writing are represented? What do we see as strengths in our writers? What do our writers need? What are the implications for instruction within a grade level and across grade levels?*

CHAPTER 18

Writing Workshop for Grades 3–6

Wendy Sheets

"Kids learn to write by writing about what matters to them, and by living in a community of writers."

—Ralph Fletcher

Writing Workshop is the time and space where students learn to live as writers. The workshop is designed to offer daily opportunities for learning, for meaningful application to writing pieces, for differentiated support for ongoing growth, and for interactions that develop writers within a literate community. It is within the Writing Workshop that intermediate writers gain momentum as they build a repertoire of tools and strategies through purposeful experiences with their own writing pieces and those written by others.

PHOTO 18.1 Every aspect of the Writing Workshop supports the development of each writer.

A Recipe for Writing: Moving From Planning and Rehearsing to Drafting and Revising

There's something extremely gratifying about creating a piece of writing. We can liken it, if you will, to creating a piece of artwork, or to cooking up something delicious. For instance, when I decide to prepare a dish, I face many decisions. Some are obvious before I even begin, and others prompt me to think in creative, flexible ways. When I have an idea, I begin working out a plan. I think about the purpose for the recipe and consider who my guests will be. Likewise, I consider the genre, purpose, and audience for my writing, deciding how my ideas may be best communicated. As I talk about it and mull it over, my process may adjust as I begin gathering ingredients through inquiry or research, and begin pouring thoughts onto the page. Even when I'm not sure how it's going to come together, I am confident in knowing I have a secret ingredient—a secret weapon—to begin what I consider the heart of writing: revision.

The Artist's Craft: Revision

Revising is to *re-see* our work, and it is here that we now become most intentional, most creative, and this is where the writing really gets good. As a writer, it is within the revision process that I make important choices by rereading and thinking about how I might improve the quality. I consider how I've organized the ingredients, or the ideas, in order to carry out my recipe, or writing, in a clear, logical manner that best communicates my message. I might bring out the full flavor or message by clarifying some ideas, or I may spice it up with some intentional work with language. I may add something that uniquely represents me as a writer, so that my voice comes through the piece. I may vary my sentence lengths and structures to add interest, or choose just the right word to convey meaning. In writing, I revisit texts as mentors so that I may learn from another writer's craft and try it out in my own writing.

There are endless choices I have as a writer. Because the process is complex, and is not linear, I may go back and pull in a completely new twist. It is exciting to know that there may be a dozen different directions I could take.

PHOTO 18.2 Writers engage in writing about topics of interest to them.

PHOTO 18.3 Writing instruction is differentiated for each learner within writing conferences.

Preparing the Product for Presentation: Editing

Proofreading and editing are opportunities to polish my work in order to make it most accessible to my readers. While revising is about improving the craft of writing, editing is focused on improving the conventions of writing (spelling, grammar and usage, punctuation, capitalization, etc.).

Sharing a Product: Publishing

Making sure everything looks its absolute best, I find great satisfaction in sharing my work. My own mother (who happens to be a superb cook and a talented writer) taught me that when we share a meal with guests, we bestow a gift unto them. We want them to savor the experience, noticing the balance between the presentation and the appeal to their taste buds. And when I share my writing, I also want my audience to savor it—enjoying the balance conveyed between the message, or meaning I've communicated—and the sound as they hear it in their ears (or minds). Like a great meal, my finished work should produce a sense of satisfaction that keeps my audience wanting more.

Developing Our Craft: Writing Workshop

Writing Workshop is the designated time and space within the literacy block for students to carry out their work as writers. Great recipes never come to fruition without getting into the kitchen, and great writing never gets produced without time to live as writers. Once a person takes on the identity of a writer, though, he or she is more willing to take risks that have the potential to produce something more magnificent. Your students may not see themselves as writers—*yet* (and oh, what power there is in that little word!). When they do, however, their lives as writers will be evident in various contexts in and out of school. The Writing Workshop will provide the supportive time and space in which they will find meaning and growth as writers.

From Oral Storytelling to Written Messages

Children learn copious lessons from the stories we read to them. And they love to tell their own stories! Ideas become spoken messages that may be written down, and we build on this notion from the early grades on. The drawings of preschoolers convey meaning and resound with stories. Young writers grow from experiences with interactive writing and shared writing as text is composed together in a guided process to communicate meaning. Within these contexts, teachers have an important role in simultaneously guiding instruction based on the range of behaviors students currently control and the needs they have. Children learn to construct meaning with one another; their language and vocabulary is expanded; they develop a sense of audience and learn about story structures; they come to understand the craft and conventions of written language; and they become writers as they engage in the group writing process.

The Structure of Writing Workshop

Writing Workshop offers a supportive structure in which students develop in the way they view themselves as writers and grow their skills related to the writer's craft and conventions. Within the structure, we find opportunities for whole-group, small-group, and individualized instruction, all within the setting of a developing, literate community.

Here is an example (see Figure 18.1) of the structure of a Writing Workshop typically found in an intermediate classroom. Each component is discussed in the following pages.

WRITING WORKSHOP

6–10 min.
- Writer Talk
- Mini-lesson

40–50 min.
- Independent Writing
- Conferring

5–10 min.
- Group Share

FIGURE 18.1 The basic structure of Writing Workshop

Author (or Writer) Talks

Teachers may begin the Writing Workshop by talking with students about a published writer. An author talk (or writer talk) is a glimpse into the life of a writer. During an author talk, share information in which your young writers will see themselves, such as where or how the author gets ideas for writing, advice on writing, or even how a Writer's Notebook is used. Interesting multimedia clips of writers may be found on various websites. Viewing an author talking about his or her work is a great way to use technology to bring a writer to life. Though brief (1–2 minutes), writer talks are beneficial to help students learn about the writerly lives of others.

Writer's Notebooks

The Writer's Notebook is a powerful tool within and beyond the Writing Workshop. It is a place for writers (typically second grade and above) to record their thoughts, and also a place where writing generates further thinking. During the first weeks of school (perhaps a month), students have opportunities to record ideas in their Writer's Notebooks in a variety of ways. Ralph Fletcher (1996) calls this planting seeds, and relates it to the notion of actually placing seeds in the ground. When we do so, we often return to those seeds in order to nurture them—ensuring they receive sunlight and water—and ultimately, they grow into something bigger and better. Likewise, the Writer's Notebook is a place where a writer records ideas—thoughts, memories, wonderings, sketches, responses to other things, examples of interesting quotes or language, story ideas, poems, artifacts, etc. Those ideas don't just lie dormant, however; students may revisit and expand them so the ideas may grow into something larger and more beautiful.

PHOTO 18.4 A Writer's Notebook is a powerful tool in which writers plant seeds of thought.

PHOTO 18.5 A writer creates an entry within her Writer's Notebook.

By guiding students in the process of planting seeds within the Writer's Notebook every day during those initial weeks—sometimes creating two or three or four entries per day—they, too, begin to grow and to bloom as writers. Students who are reluctant to write find that the Writer's Notebook is almost risk-free. They may respond in authentic ways to a topic teachers initiate or to a topic of their choice. Teachers provide a variety of different general topics to promote thought, rather than providing prompts that constrain writing. For example, asking students to write about a time an alien visited their school would be difficult for many writers. They have had no experience with aliens visiting school, may be completely uninterested in such a topic, and may have had little experience writing a fantasy piece. Instead, perhaps prompting students to write about someone who visited their school, or someone they would enjoy having visit the school, would be more meaningful.

There is no one way to respond in the Writer's Notebook as each writer is unique and should have some choice in deciding what works for him. Typically, each entry is completed as a quick-write, taking five to 10 minutes to complete. Making space for sharing after time for each entry contributes to the building of a literate community (see Photo 18.6). Writing

PHOTO 18.6 Sharing Writer's Notebook entries contributes to purposeful meaning-making and builds agency within writers.

identities develop as student voices and ideas are acknowledged and sharing becomes more and more comfortable. Writers fill their notebooks so they have many possibilities to which they may return when they desire to nurture their seeds, growing them into something bigger and better. It is a place where ideas are planted at times, and incubate at other times. The Writer's Notebook is not a place where ideas lie dormant and die; instead, it is a garden of ideas that can take off and beautifully bloom!

Figure 18.2 is a list of possibilities for planting seeds in the Writer's Notebook. Any may be modified to suit the needs and interests of your writers. You may choose to use some of these ideas, and to continue to add your own. Additionally, add options that are generated by students and also times of complete choice. Once writers have engaged in multiple experiences planting seeds, they become more adept at continuing to add their own self-initiated entries as well.

Possible Ideas for Writer's Notebook Entries

- Draw a self-portrait.
- Write about your name and how you got it.
- Write memories related to a favorite object.
- Write about a special person.
- List favorite foods, movies, books, and quotes.
- Collect strong story leads.
- Make a map of your bedroom, house, or neighborhood.
- Write about a special time in your life.
- Sketch an observation in your yard or neighborhood.
- Respond to a poem or story, telling how it speaks to you.

- List places you love.
- Make a web of vacations and special moments.
- Glue in a photo and write about it.
- Glue in a letter from a special person and respond to it.
- Collect examples of powerful words, phrases, or snippets of dialogue.
- Sketch a home you've lived in and label areas indicating special memories.
- Glue in a fortune from a fortune cookie and respond to it.
- Tell about a time you laughed super hard.

- Make a web of things that make you angry.
- List 10 things you are able to do well.
- List the best things that have happened in your life.
- List the worst things that have happened in your life.
- Make a list of things you wonder about.
- List family stories or traditions that have been passed down.
- Sketch a scene from your favorite book.

FIGURE 18.2 Ideas for writing

Writing Mini-lessons

Writing Workshop shifts from solely planting seeds within Writer's Notebooks to the whole-group, daily practice of the writing mini-lesson to teach important principles. A writing mini-lesson, based on the work of Fountas and Pinnell (2001; 2017), is a time to learn a brief, explicit principle related to the writer's craft, elements of conventions, or management. The teacher decides based on the strengths and needs of the writers and the standards under which they are required to teach. Another useful tool is the *Literacy Continuum: A Tool for Assessment, Planning, and Teaching* (Fountas & Pinnell, 2017), which includes grade-level behaviors and understandings to notice, teach, and support. Whether leading students in writing within a particular genre or form, or making space for students to make that decision, be mindful that students need multiple opportunities to experience a particular genre before writing in that genre. Many teachers choose to lead students in writing specifically within a genre at various points throughout the school year, while offering free choice writing in between those periods. The Writing section of the *Literacy Continuum* (Fountas and Pinnell) is a useful tool for teachers to think through aspects of genre as well as what students need to do within each genre. In addition, there is untold power in student choice. Rather than limiting writers to specific topics or restricting their creativity by requiring formulaic writing, teachers strive to develop in students a lifelong love for writing. They do this by equipping writers with ongoing tools within a supportive community of writers and offering opportunities for choice wherever possible.

PHOTO 18.7 Quality literature serves as effective examples of mentors during Writing Workshop.

During the writing mini-lesson, teach a specific principle and draw upon mentor texts that have been shared with the class in order to illustrate a point with a specific example (see Photo 18.7). Once a text has been shared within Interactive Read-Aloud and students have had an opportunity to simply enjoy and construct

PHOTO 18.8 All learners may see and hear one another in a circle or horseshoe, and their voices are important in contributing to the meaning-making.

meaning around it as a whole, teachers may revisit just a portion of that text to examine the way the author has used craft for a particular purpose. Through mentor texts, we marinate our thinking in the writing of others. Ralph Fletcher (2015) shared, "The writing in a classroom can only be as strong as the literature that surrounds and supports and buoys it up" (p. 57). Whether teaching about the writer's craft or conventions, examples are highly meaningful when using a mentor text to demonstrate a principle.

In order to convey a specific, brief mini-lesson principle, write a statement that tells *what* it is that writers do, and *how* or *why* they do it. It can be expressed in a succinct statement that is written on an anchor chart (or displayed on a smart board). Teachers may include on the chart brief, specific pieces of text (from one or more mentor texts) that illustrate the principle (as shown in Photo 18.9). Then, invite students to try out the principle. This may be done with a piece of a teacher's own writing that is shared with students, or it could be done with a piece of student writing. With either choice, the principle is tried out in a meaningful way within the context of a larger message, rather than as an isolated skill.

For example, after fifth graders constructed meaning with Tony Johnston's book, *The Harmonica* (2004), it was used as a mentor text during a writing mini-lesson. *The Harmonica*

> Writers use language in figurative ways - with similes - to make interesting comparisons that connect with *like* or *as*.
>
> "Like a length of kindling, in one stroke, they split our family."
>
> "I cannot remember my father's face, or my mother's, but I remember their love, warm and enfolding as a song."
>
> —The Harmonica by Tony Johnston

PHOTO 18.9 A writing mini-lesson chart showing how writers use language in figurative ways— with similes—to make interesting comparisons that connect with *like* or *as*.

PHOTO 18.10 Students contribute to the meaning-making during a writing mini-lesson.

is a sophisticated picture book that tells the story of a young Jewish boy, torn from his home during World War II, whose harmonica offers hope during his interactions within a concentration camp. The mentor text (see Photo 18.9) provided an example of Johnston's use of the craft of similes to make interesting comparisons.

Mini-lessons may build on one another. For instance, I may teach how writers use a variety of leads to grab the reader's attention over a series of days, sharing examples of each from mentor texts. Students may try out various leads in their Writer's Notebooks before making a decision about which one works best for them. Or I may teach mini-lessons on how writers use voice to convey their unique style, feelings, or passion in a story. Because this is so broad, I could introduce different tools for doing this over several days, adding to the original mini-lesson. With clear, concise teaching, students have the opportunity to try it out each day in their own writing in meaningful ways and share their work, and they take on greater understandings. Over time, writers build a repertoire of understandings related to craft and conventions—a toolbox, if you will—upon which they may draw over time. The learning is generative, as it may be applied to future pieces of writing.

Photos 18.11 through 18.13 are additional examples of charts shared during writing mini-lessons that all relate to the writer's craft.

Craft mini-lessons, like those shown here, draw attention to aspects of writing that improve the ability to convey meaning in interesting ways. Often, craft is improved with intention during revision, although as writers, we utilize what we know about craft during drafting as well. By focusing on one piece of text to notice the way an author has crafted it, we help writers identify what the author specifically did, and we discuss what that does for us as readers. By closely examining the craft of mentor texts, we learn how to try it out ourselves in our own writing.

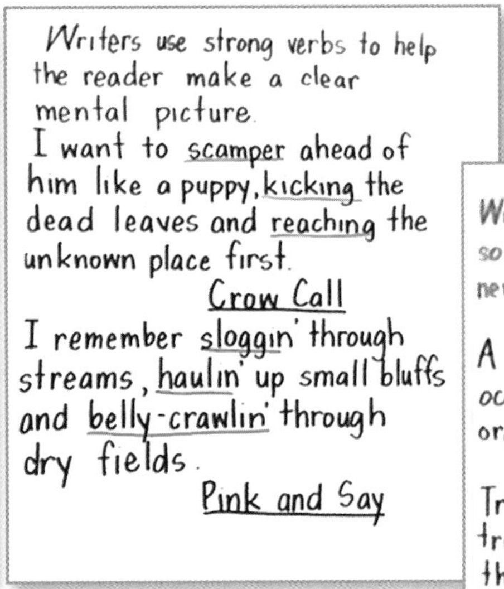

Writers use powerful language to create a picture in the reader's mind.

Gritch ran her bony finger with the long green nail down the list of ingredients. *Piggie Pie!*

There was thunder, the sky was black and the raindrops, big as bumblebees, hit the roof with a pir___d. *or the Love of Autumn*

Writers use strong verbs to help the reader make a clear mental picture.

I want to scamper ahead of him like a puppy, kicking the dead leaves and reaching the unknown place first. *Crow Call*

I remember sloggin' through streams, haulin' up small bluffs and belly-crawlin' through dry fields. *Pink and Say*

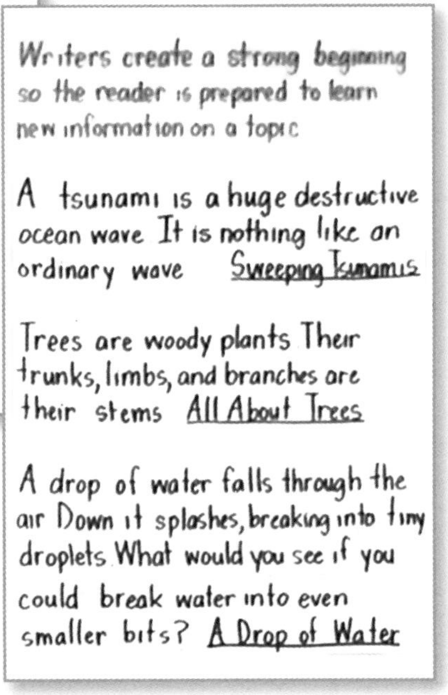

Writers create a strong beginning so the reader is prepared to learn new information on a topic.

A tsunami is a huge destructive ocean wave It is nothing like an ordinary wave *Sweeping Tsunamis*

Trees are woody plants Their trunks, limbs, and branches are their stems *All About Trees*

A drop of water falls through the air Down it splashes, breaking into tiny droplets What would you see if you could break water into even smaller bits? *A Drop of Water*

PHOTO 18.11 (left) A writing mini-lesson demonstrates the use of powerful language to create a picture in the reader's mind.

PHOTO 18.12 (center) A writing mini-lesson demonstrates how writers use strong verbs to help the reader make a clear mental picture. Examples from mentor texts are noted.

PHOTO 18.13 (right) This mini-lesson, specific to nonfiction text, demonstrates how writers create a strong beginning so the reader is prepared to learn new information on a topic.

Broad goals related to craft include organization, idea development, language use, word choice, and voice. Within each of these broad goals, there are many possible ways to improve writing.

- **Organization** includes the structure of a fiction or nonfiction text. Writers make decisions about the structural patterns they use to present their ideas according to their purpose and the genre that best conveys those ideas. Additionally, beginnings and endings, headings, and other text features are aspects of organization.

- **Idea development** includes decisions to introduce, develop, and conclude a story or topic in a logical way that effectively communicates a message. Clear, focused content is important to hold the reader's attention.

- **Language use** is a technique a writer uses to describe events, information, or actions through various sentences, phrases, and expressions. Borrowing and playing with memorable language makes meaning clear, shows and elicits feelings, creates sensory images, develops arguments, gives directions, provides examples, shares a point of view, creates mood, links ideas, and explains abstract ideas.

PHOTO 18.14 Using a mentor text to teach a specific writing principle during a mini-lesson

- **Word choice** is more specific than language use, as it focuses on choosing just the right vocabulary to convey meaning. Writers consider their purpose and audience and use a variety of techniques for selecting memorable words: description, dialogue, strong nouns and verbs, colorful modifiers, alternative words, and content or academic words.

- **Voice** is conveyed as the writer's unique style, feelings, or passion comes through in the writing. Specific examples of using voice might include the insertion of personal experiences; speaking directly to the reader; showing enthusiasm for the topic; using engaging titles and language; using narrative writing that is engaging and honest; revealing the writer's stance toward the topic; and reading the text aloud to think critically about the voice.

Developing craft through drafting and revising is where the quality of writing is improved, and the writing becomes exhilarating!

Conventions mini-lessons focus on aspects of the mechanics of writing. Even the best piece of writing is difficult to appreciate if the ideas are not communicated clearly. Equip writers to express ideas with substance, and to use the conventions of writing so that others value what they have to say as well. Broad goals related to conventions include text layout, grammar and usage, capitalization, punctuation, spelling, and handwriting and word-processing. Linda Hoyt's (2017) *Conventions and Craft* includes a year of lessons for lifting understandings related to conventions and writing craft.

Teach students (within mini-lessons) to use a variety of efficient strategies for revising (such as spider legs, sticky notes, inserting, using arrows, cutting and reorganizing text, etc.) and for editing (inserting, deleting,

> Writers tape "spider legs" onto a draft when extra space is needed for revision.

← spider legs →

PHOTO 18.15 This mini-lesson demonstrates a strategy for adding additional space when drafting or revising.

PHOTO 18.16 The class engages in a whole-group writing mini-lesson before trying out the learning in their individual writing pieces.

capitalizing, etc.). Photo 18.15 is an example of a writing mini-lesson on using the tool of spider legs for revision.

After engaging in a brief writing mini-lesson, invite students to return to their seats to try out the new learning in their own writing pieces. As writers try a revision technique, for instance, they understand that the purpose is to authentically improve their writing, not to simply complete a contrived task. Because of this, they may try it out in a few places, knowing the change doesn't have to be permanent if it doesn't convey their message more effectively.

Independent Writing and the Writing Process

Writers need opportunities to continue their important work each day. After the whole-group writing mini-lesson, students return to their own writing to continue their work, and try out the new understandings shared within the mini-lesson. Photo 18.18 is a brief look at the components of the writing process. Though a writer may move through the process in order, the process is often recursive, and writers may engage within any aspect of the process at any time. In addition, writers may confer with the teacher (or with a peer, if desired) at any time, as illustrated below.

PHOTO 18.17 Writers work independently on their writing pieces.

PHOTO 18.18
Conferring takes place at any time during the writing process.

Planning & Rehearsing
Make decisions, gather information, and try out ideas (orally, with drawing, reading, and writing) related to purpose, audience, inquiry, genre/form

Drafting & Revising
Often simultaneously, and then with intentional revision, focusing on craft (includes producing a draft, rereading, adding, deleting, reorganizing, and changing information, using tools and techniques, and understanding the process)

CONFERRING

Editing & Proofreading
Polish to prepare for publication by editing for conventions, using tools, and understanding the process

Publishing
As an option after a final draft is completed; may include cover graphics, typed or laid-out text, is shared with an audience and is celebrated

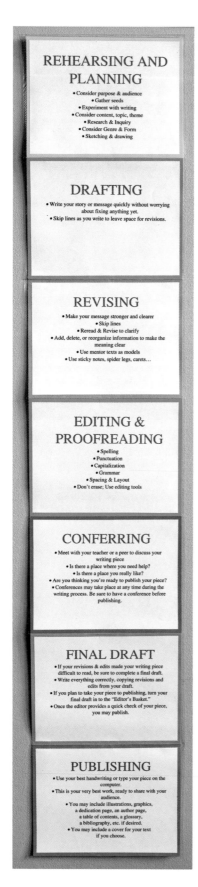

A writing process workboard (see Photo 18.19) is an effective tool that communicates each writer's place within the writing process. It is beneficial to writers as they develop an awareness of the work that is involved within each component. It also is beneficial to teachers as a management system that tells, at a glance, where students are within the process. Many teachers choose to include separate sections for drafting and revising to ensure writers employ intentional moves toward revising before beginning to edit. Students physically move clothespins on the board to reflect their work within the process. Writers learn that being able to continue to revise means they don't have to get things perfect the first time. The conferring section of the workboard also reflects which writers need to have a conference with the teacher. This prevents students from wasting valuable time waiting with hands raised or standing in a line. Instead, they may continue writing (within their current piece, in their Writer's Notebook, or may even begin creating a cover for publication or a new piece of writing) until they confer with the teacher.

Conferring With Writers

While students are independently writing, teachers have the opportunity to confer one-on-one with writers. A writing conference is a writer-to-writer conversation that allows for the differentiation of instruction while teaching the writer something generative. In other words, consider the current strengths and needs of the writer you sit beside, while focusing on teaching something he'll be able to build upon within other pieces or contexts. Over time, we want writers to take risks, to self-evaluate their writing, to articulate goals they have, to notice what makes their writing effective, and to notice what mentors do and try it out themselves.

PHOTO 18.19 (left) A writing process workboard communicates each writer's current work within the writing process.

PHOTO 18.20 (right) Conferring with a young writer

With every writing conference, be mindful of the following:

Writers are fragile. It doesn't matter how young or experienced writers are—they are sharing a piece of themselves that is often deeply personal. As the more expert other, you have the power to lift their identity as a writer or to squash it. For that reason, I *always* begin a writing conference by finding something positive to say. Even if I'm struggling to find any positive qualities about a piece of writing, I might simply smile and encourage with, "You've really been working on this piece of writing!"

PHOTO 18.21 A writing conference should be a positive experience.

Your goal is to lift the writer, not to fix the piece. While I could take over a child's writing with a red pen and spend a lengthy amount of time making it wonderful, I know that wouldn't benefit the writer. It's not my writing, and my goal isn't to fix the product. Whatever revision is done, it is ultimately the writer's decision based on the message he wishes to convey to his readers. Carl Anderson (2000) often begins writing conferences with the question, "How's it going?" This reflects the intended conversational nature of a conference, rather than the teacher doing all the talking. There are times you may ask a writer to discuss his piece and share how you may be of help. As you're looking over the writing, grasp an understanding of the whole while the writer is sharing. At other times, you may invite a writer to read the piece aloud. This provides him the opportunity to hear (and monitor) the *sound* of the text while helping you understand the intended meaning. Once you've experienced a taste of the piece, ask questions that help to get to the heart of the writer's needs. You might ask, "What is it that you really want your readers to understand?" or, "Tell me more about …" or, "Is there a part where you're needing some help?"

Teach something generative. While there may be a hundred different options for teaching a writer, strive to teach something that is within the writer's zone of proximal development and that is simple enough for him to take on, and will lift his skill as a writer. Attempting to teach several elements of writing will overwhelm a writer, and he will not take on the learning as his own. Instead, try to identify one, maybe two, goals to support. That may mean there is still much improvement to be made. Note that, and plan to teach accordingly during the next conference, a guided writing group, or a whole-class mini-lesson depending on other writers' needs.

For example, in a writing conference between a teacher and a fourth-grade student, the following conversation took place:

Teacher:	Hey, Shawn, how's your writing coming along?
Shawn:	Pretty good. I think I'm almost ready to publish.
Teacher:	Tell me a little bit about your piece. Is this the one about you going to a Buckeyes game? (The teacher recalls Shawn talking about this story with another writer during share time.)
Shawn:	Yeah. I wrote all about the football game.
Teacher:	Let's take a look.

The teacher notices the way Shawn has worked to develop particular details within the narrative. Additionally, she notices the writer has provided ample details about the day that may not have been relevant to his intended message.

| Teacher: | I see that here, on the third page, you tell what it was like to sit in the stadium, The Shoe. I appreciate the way you've described the setting here, making me almost feel like I'm there. You wrote, "We huddled together in the cold, but shot up like cannonballs when the team came onto the field. The band was playing and everyone was shouting and clapping. I screamed at the top of my lungs to cheer for my favorite team—the Buckeyes." Wow, Shawn, that sounds so exciting! You really appeal to my senses as a reader in this description. I can imagine how cold it must have been, and I can almost hear the band playing, along with the clapping and shouting and cheering. You've helped me to imagine that. |

By confirming what Shawn has done effectively as a writer, it is likely the craft will be reinforced, resulting in the craft being used effectively with other pieces.

Shawn:	Yeah, it was really cool. That stadium is huge, and everyone was on fire!
Teacher:	Sounds like you had a great time! I see you've also decided to describe some of the best plays of the game. Tell me about your decision as a writer to do that.
Shawn:	Yeah, I wanted people to hear about the plays that were the most exciting.
Teacher:	I agree that your description of the plays makes your piece very interesting.
Shawn:	Thanks.

Teacher:	What would you say your overall message is? What is it that you want your readers to take away from your piece?

The teacher wishes to coach the writer in articulating his overall message in order to help him notice for himself the way certain details don't enhance what he wants his readers to take away.

Shawn:	Just how cool the game was, and how much fun I had.
Teacher:	So, I hear you saying that you want your readers to understand and experience the game itself, and to know it was a lot of fun for you?
Shawn:	Yeah.
Teacher:	I think that's a cool message to share since the game was so meaningful to you. I'm wondering if you've included anything in your piece that might detract from that message…. Is there anything that you don't really need to include because it doesn't help convey your message?

The teacher continues to confirm Shawn's ideas, lifting his agency as a decision-maker about his piece of writing. Rather than telling him what changes he should make, she invites him to reflect on the writing in a specific way to better communicate his message.

Shawn:	Well…in the first few pages, I told a lot about what I did before I got to the game. Maybe I shouldn't include the parts about driving in the car and my sister being sick.
Teacher:	What are you thinking about those parts?
Shawn:	They don't really help my message. I guess it's not part of the focus of what I really want to tell about.
Teacher:	I can see how taking those parts out would help you to really hone in on what it is you want your readers to know. As a writer, that's often something we notice, and we can do some revision to take out the unnecessary information. The great thing is that getting our ideas written helps us to tell our stories, but as we reread and revise, we have options to make changes, to add information when needed, and to take out parts that aren't helpful. In this case, you've noticed that taking those parts out would make your message stronger and clearer. Do you have a plan for what parts you want to cross out of your draft then?

Building on the writer's noticing, the teacher reinforces the revision process and encourages the writer to articulate a clear plan.

Shawn:	Yeah, I definitely want to cross out these parts (points to much of the first few pages). I'll think about how I'll start it after I cross 'em out. Maybe I'll just jump right in to the scene at The Shoe.
Teacher:	Oh, that would be an exciting place to start. Sounds like you have a plan! Thanks for sharing your writing with me, Shawn. Go ahead and go jump into your revisions. I'll look forward to seeing what you've done to really focus your message after you finish.
Shawn:	Thank you.

Writing Goals

Organization	• text structure • strong beginning and ending • presentation of ideas: clear, uses time appropriately
Idea Development	• clearly communicate main points • engage reader by showing strong knowledge of topic • supporting details are accurate, relevant, helpful • clear, focused content
Language Use	• variety of sentence structures and lengths • show instead of telling • figurative language: alliteration, hyperbole, personification, onomatopoeia, simile, metaphor • uses dialogue • descriptive details (examples, anecdotes, facts) • create effect: convey mood, elicit feelings, repetition
Word Choice	• precise words reflect meaning • strong verbs, strong nouns, descriptive adjectives • figurative language • transitional words for time flow, vivid words
Voice	• voice: unique perspective, enthusiasm, inner dialogue • share thoughts, inner conflict, commitment, convictions • punctuation supports voice (e.g., :, …, or - :))
Conventions	• text layout: size, spacing, titles, headings, indenting • grammar: sentence structure, parts of speech, tense, paragraphs • capitalization, punctuation, spelling • handwriting or word processing

FIGURE 18.3 These goals support instructional decisions during a writing conference.

In this example, the teacher was able to confirm what Shawn had done effectively as a writer, and also lifted his thinking about revision. The work was generative, in that the writer will use what he learned to focus his message in future writing pieces. The tone of the conference was positive and encouraging, and the red pen was never waved! Instead, through a writer-to-writer conversation, Shawn was able to take on an important revision strategy and apply it in a meaningful way with his current writing piece.

While being mindful of the writer's concerns, along with needs that are evident, teachers may think about what element of craft or conventions will most benefit the writer at this time. Figure 18.3, based upon the *Literacy Continuum: A Tool for Assessment, Planning, and Teaching* (Fountas & Pinnell, 2017), may help to serve as a quick reference to guide thinking about a writer's strengths and needs. Jotting anecdotal notes will help establish writing goals for each writer.

Writing conferences will vary in terms of the length of time they take. Usually, they range from two to eight minutes, but will vary depending on the needs of the writer. You may choose to confer at a designated table in the classroom, allowing for an intimate side-by-side conversation without any distractions. Or you may choose to meet with writers at their seats by pulling up a chair beside them. Although other students may pause from their work to eavesdrop on your conference, that is fine—they may also benefit from what they hear.

Keeping anecdotal records reflecting students' strengths and needs is important as you continue to make instructional decisions. If most of your students have the same need, plan to teach within a whole-group mini-lesson. If only a few students have a particular need, you may address it during one-on-one conferences. When a handful of writers share a similar need, a guided writing group is an efficient way to work with them to meet their needs.

Guided Writing

There will be times when several students (perhaps three to six) have a similar need that may more efficiently be addressed within a small group. Guided writing is a temporary context in which a teacher works with a small group to teach something explicit or to shore up understandings related to something already taught. This takes place during independent writing time and may be more efficient than meeting with several students separately. For example, if a handful of students are having difficulty getting started with an opinion piece, a teacher may work with them together at a table to support the need. Or perhaps five writers would benefit from a mini-lesson on using variety in sentence structures; a guided writing group allows the flexibility to work specifically with the writers with a similar need.

Share Time

The Writing Workshop concludes with the class coming back together for a group share time. There are three main purposes for this valuable time:

PHOTO 18.22 A young writer shares his piece with his class.

1. As writers share their own work and hear from their peers, they help to build a literate community of writers.

2. Writers are held accountable for having tried out whatever was taught during that day's mini-lesson. In addition, they are able to gauge others' responses to their efforts, which propels their thinking about their own writing further. Hearing the ways other writers have incorporated the learning with their writing also furthers each student's understandings while building a collective identity of intelligence among writers.

3. Teachers collect valuable data. Noticing how effectively students take on the learning continually informs instructional decisions.

Students typically share just the place in their writing where they tried out the mini-lesson that day (with a partner, in small groups, or with the whole class). (See Photo 18.22.) By sharing in small groups first, every child's voice is articulated within the writing community.

PHOTO 18.23 Sharing written pieces is one piece of building a writerly community.

PHOTO 18.24 Writers have access to various tools for publishing.

(See Photo 18.23.) At times, invite specific writers to share with the whole group, and, with the help of a document camera, this might be projected for the whole class to see. In addition, as students publish pieces of writing, invite them to share their pieces with the group. Let this time be a celebration of each writer's growth.

Moving Toward Publication

It is helpful for students to have their own writing folders that include current drafts and some tools for writing (such as an editing checklist, a revision checklist, blank pages to record mini-lesson principles, a list of difficult-to-spell words, a list of finished or in-process writing pieces, a reflection of what has been learned as a writer from each piece, etc.). While prewriting may be completed in the Writer's Notebook, drafts should be written on separate draft paper while skipping lines to allow space for revising and editing.

A finished draft is often quite messy after revision and editing, so writers will typically need to produce a clean copy with their corrections in a final draft before publishing. Though conferring may have occurred at another time during the writing process, I prefer to also confer with writers a final time before they complete final drafts. As the classroom's final copy editor, you may have students turn their final drafts into an editor's basket. You then take a final look at the piece and make a few necessary corrections, if needed. If there are multiple issues with the final draft, confer again with the student so that he may make changes. After that, the student has the choice to publish the piece of writing.

Providing various tools for publishing, such as multiple types of paper, writing/coloring utensils, construction paper or tags for covers, or word-processing options makes publishing more enjoyable (see Photo 18.24). Writers make multiple decisions about their writing, and how they publish is one of the final choices they make. Once a draft is completed, place the stapled copies into a hanging file folder for each child. The drafts may be accessed later, if needed, and also serve to create a record of progress over time. Published pieces should be shared, celebrated, and displayed in the classroom for everyone to enjoy.

Conclusion

The Writing Workshop is an exciting, vital component of a comprehensive literacy framework. The structure allows for each valuable piece of teaching and learning to transpire smoothly. Once established, it flows beautifully because the work in which students are engaged is so purposeful and meaningful. It isn't a one-size-fits-all curriculum, because it allows for differentiated levels of support and for powerful instructional moves to continuously lift writers as they grow more productive and independent over time.

Whether I'm preparing a meal for guests or engaging in the art of writing, my work is meaningful, and it is my desire to share my flavorful message with my audience. In teaching students to savor the joy of writing, share your enthusiasm for the craft, along with your interest in their stories. Sharing your writing is akin to sharing a gift from your heart, and there's something extremely gratifying about that.

Suggestions for Professional Development

1. Invite teachers to analyze student writing pieces. Using the *Literacy Continuum* (Fountas & Pinnell, 2017), determine the strengths the writer already controls related to craft, conventions, genre understandings, and the writing process. Then, determine next steps for instruction for each writer based on needs.

PHOTO 18.25 The *Literacy Continuum* (Fountas & Pinnell, 2017) helps teachers determine writers' strengths relative to craft, conventions, genre understandings, and the writing process.

2. Invite teachers to analyze in-process drafts to look for evidence of ways students have applied understandings related to recent mini-lessons. For example, if a teacher recently taught a mini-lesson on using strong verbs to make the writing more interesting, that teacher may look for specific evidence of the writer having revised to use stronger verbs.

3. As teachers consider strengths and needs of the writers in their classrooms as a whole, have them plan a series of writing mini-lessons to address needs. Along with planning mini-lesson statements that include clear, concise language that conveys what writers do and how or why they do it, find examples within mentor texts to explicitly illustrate the principle. Teachers may also use their own writing as a mentor text to demonstrate decisions related to craft or conventions within mini-lessons.

PHOTO 18.26 A teacher and her literacy coach work together to analyze student writing.

4. Invite teachers to bring their anecdotal notes from writing conferences to share what they've learned about some of their writers. Then, have them plan next steps for instruction, along with the context (mini-lessons, writing conferences, or guided writing) in which to support student needs.

5. Encourage teachers to work together to create a unit of writing instruction based on required standards. Plan to include Interactive Read-Alouds that may serve as mentors during writing mini-lessons. A unit may begin with planting seeds within a Writer's Notebook, generating ideas over several days, to prepare students to begin thinking within a particular genre or form. Additional mini-lessons may be planned based on required understandings related to standards, but should also include lessons that support students in further developing as writers. Be sure to allow for the restructuring of plans in order to be responsive to students' needs during a unit of study.

6. Suggest teachers work in grade-level teams to create several writer's (or author's) talks. Having a repertoire of writer's talks will allow for more efficiency during Writing Workshop, and teachers may continue to add to their collection over time.

7. Ask teachers to watch a video of a writing conference between a teacher and a young writer, and then discuss what they notice—and what additional ways they see to support the writer. Providing a copy of the student's writing for each teacher to view will also be helpful.

8. Meet with teachers to reflect on the teaching and learning that resulted from a recent Writing Workshop. This may be done based on teacher records, or an analysis of videotaped lessons. Teachers may reflect upon a mini-lesson and group share within small groups to discuss the following:

   • Was my mini-lesson statement clear and concise?

   • Did my mini-lesson statement share what writers do and how or why they do it?

   • Did I share an example to illustrate the principle from at least one mentor text?

   • Did I clearly teach one principle that students could easily try out in their own writing?

   • What did I learn from students when we came back together to share at the end of the workshop? What evidence was there that students took on the new learning? What evidence was there that showed that additional teaching is needed?

9. Lead teachers to plant seeds within their own Writer's Notebooks. Have teachers create several entries, sharing in various ways after each one. Debrief by discussing the impact that the process had on teachers, along with the writerly community that has been developed. Encourage teachers to commit to additional entries to their own Writer's Notebooks. Begin each professional development session together with creating another entry, always sharing afterward. As teachers share their Writer's Notebooks with their students, young writers will be inspired as well.

SECTION FIVE:
BUILDING BLOCKS OF LANGUAGE

 Professional videos and downloadables are available at Scholastic.com/RLResources

CHAPTER 19

Phonics and Word Study: Assessment-Driven Instruction

Carla Steele, Patricia L. Scharer, and Denise Rowe

> "I wrestled with words again and again until, slowly, they became mine."
>
> **—Carmen Agra Deedy**

[handwritten note in margin: developmental word study]

Denise Rowe engages a small group of second graders in inquiry as she guides them in a word study mini-lesson. Down the hallway, name puzzles provide a scaffold for kindergartners to learn about letters and sounds, while sorting activities challenge fourth graders to compare, contrast, and categorize words. In a nearby middle school, students research the origin of root words in their ELA classrooms. What do all of these students have in common? They are active participants and have ownership in their journey to become successful, independent word solvers as readers and writers through developmental word study—an approach that looks very different than the traditional instruction many of us may have received.

How do I teach this way? What do I need to know? Where do I find the time? These are but a few of the questions commonly posed by teachers who want to implement—or continue to refine—effective word study in their classrooms. While a myriad of resources, articles, and approaches are readily available, navigating this sea of possibilities can be overwhelming and intimidating. The goal of this chapter is to address such questions and concerns—not as a "how-to" guide to word study, but as an opportunity to reflect on, consider, and examine key factors important when designing an instructional model for teaching and learning about how words work.

PHOTO 19.1 Denise leads a small-group word study mini-lesson.

What Is Word Study?

"Word study is aimed at developing children's spelling, vocabulary, and phonic-word recognition knowledge (as well as phonological awareness) through hands-on learning in ways that build on what students already know and that foster word consciousness—namely, appreciation and interest in word learning" (Ganske, 2014, p. 4). While Ganske's definition is one of many, there are common tenets that can be found across the work of scholars emphasizing that word study is a developmental approach that is:

PHOTO 19.2 Della works on her name puzzle.

- research-based,
- inquiry-based,
- student-centered,
- active,
- socially constructed,
- engaging,
- differentiated,
- process-driven,
- assessment-driven, and
- responsive to students' strengths and needs.

Bear, Invernizzi, Templeton, and Johnston (2016) agree that word study must match the needs of the child, arguing that it "…is not a one-size-fits-all program of instruction that begins in the same place for all students within a grade level. One unique quality of word study, as we describe it, lies in the critical role of differentiating instruction for different levels of word knowledge" (p. 10). It is through assessment-driven, intentional, and differentiated word study instruction

PHOTO 19.3 Word sort activity

that a shift in teaching and student learning is possible. Designed to build upon what children know and need to learn, a word study framework must afford students multiple opportunities to discover and practice how words work, across instructional contexts as well as within a systematic, organized, and daily block of time.

The ultimate goal of word study is to make word learning generative—that is, to support students in developing, "…powerful systems…as well as giving them many opportunities to use their word-study understandings in action while reading for meaning." (Fountas & Pinnell, 2017, p. 420). While it's important to provide systematic, intentional instruction in the principles, concepts, and word knowledge students need to know, the application of this knowledge goes well beyond spelling. Learning about how words work makes an important contribution to students as both readers and writers. The reciprocity between reading and writing includes word study; what is learned in each context influences the others. Quality word study offers an intentional link to reading and writing. It is no longer a stand-alone, isolated 20 to 30 minutes a day; rather, it is a key part of literacy instruction for all grades.

What Are the Theoretical Foundations of Word Study?

The origin, history, and application of word study can be found in volumes of work from researchers, psychologists, linguists, and educational professionals too numerous to detail in this chapter. While all are noteworthy, Charles Read, Carol Chomsky, and Edmund Henderson stand out as significant contributors in the 1970s and 1980s for returning spelling/word knowledge to the central role it plays in reading and writing.

Claire's Invented Spellings	Conventional Spellings
The girls Wun the tofe Mom sed les get A chet good girls.	The girls won the trophy. Mom said, "Let's get a treat, good girls."

Read's contribution stems from his work collecting and analyzing young children's attempts to write unknown words. He was able to identify and define characteristics that were common across children's invented spelling providing evidence of a consistency, a "… logic in the error patterns of children's early spelling and that this logic changed over time as their experience with modern English spelling broadened" (Henderson, 1990, p. 43). For example, Read found that young spellers often used the name of a letter to represent a sound (e.g., *mak* for make; *yat* for wait) and represented beginning affricates with combinations of letters that made sense to them (e.g., *hre* for /tr/ee and *jrv* for /dr/ive). While the way children organized and represented speech sounds differed from that of mature spellers, the logic behind their decision-making paved the way for understanding that word knowledge is a systematic developmental process that changes over time and with experience. Read's work continues to serve as a reminder that we should regard children's invented spellings as windows of opportunity, not errors to fix, as they provide valuable insight into children's varying levels of word knowledge.

PHOTO 19.4 Claire's writing illustrates an understanding of word knowledge typical of letter name spellers. She is able to write high-frequency words conventionally and her invented spellings are developmentally appropriate—as indicated in *tofe* for "trophy"; *les* for "let's"; and "*chet*" for treat. Interesting to note is her experimentation in how to represent the affricate sound /tr/—an indicator of her growing knowledge of how words work.

[handwritten: Invented spelling]

Invented spelling was also a focus for Carol Chomsky. In her article, "Write First, Read Later," Chomsky proposed that children could "…learn to read by creating their own spellings for familiar words as a beginning" (1971, p. 296). She asserted that if teachers supported the development of phonemic awareness, taught the sounds of some letters, and allowed children to trust their own judgment, children could begin to write words and, in turn, read. Chomsky advocated that writing should not only precede and support learning to read but that it should also become a daily practice within every classroom. Chomsky and Read both emphasized the need for educators to understand the characteristics inherent in children's invented spelling in order to better plan for and facilitate instruction responsive to each child's strengths and needs.

Henderson further advanced the study of spelling development by building on Read's work and expanded his studies to include older students as well. Among the major contributions of Henderson and his doctoral students was the identification of common error patterns children made as they progressed through what Henderson (1990) termed systematic stages of orthographic development. These sequential stages were defined by key understandings, characteristics, error patterns, and words children encountered as they journeyed, over time, to gain control of the English spelling system. Henderson's research resulted in the creation of a model of developmental word knowledge that remains a major influence in word study today— as evident in resources such as *Words Their Way: Word Study for Phonics, Vocabulary, and Spelling Instruction* (Bear, Invernizzi, Templeton & Johnston, 2016) and *Word Journeys* (Ganske, 2014).

[handwritten: spelling development]

[handwritten: systematic stages of orthographic development.]

Why Are Stages of Spelling Development Important?

Being able to discern a child's developmental stage of spelling development offers insight into the level of orthographic knowledge the student controls—is using, but confusing—and is ready to learn next. Assessment informs decision-making that supports differentiated instruction and ensures that instruction is appropriate and within a child's zone of proximal development. This is especially important as a child's strengths and needs may not always fall within just one stage of development. Even though stages and the key understandings and characteristics inherent in each are common to all children, the rate of progress within and through each stage can vary significantly from child to child. Ganske (2014) agreed with fellow scholars that "Orthographic knowledge is at the core of word study, and it is knowledge of the underlying sound (alphabetic), pattern, and meaning relationships in our English spelling system that enables children to become more fluent readers and writers" (p. 7).

[handwritten: ortographic knowledge]

Stages of Spelling Development

Adapted from *Word Journeys: Assessment-Guided Phonics, Spelling, and Vocabulary Instruction* (Ganske, 2014, pp. 30–51)

Stage	Definition	Characteristics/Features
Emergent	Time of emerging literacy in all areas of learning (ages: 1 to 5; approximate grade levels: preK–kindergarten)	Not yet reading; pretend writing with scribbles, marks, lines, waves; beginning awareness of environmental print
Prephonetic	Alphabetic principle not developed	No letter/sound correspondence between random letters, letter-like symbols, lines
Semiphonetic	Growing awareness of print, alphabetic principle, and concept of word	Some partial letter/sound correspondence; at first, initial/ final consonants represented; lack of spacing
Letter Name	Beginning readers; concept of word developed; writing begins to include beginning, middle, ending sounds with letters phonetically appropriate; invented spellings (ages: 4 to 9; approximate grade levels: 1–2)	Features include: initial/final consonants; initial consonant blends/digraphs; short vowels; affricates; final consonant blends/digraphs; omission of silent long vowel markers prevalent
Within Word Pattern	Beyond one-letter to one-sound correspondence; learning to attend to patterns and chunks in words; long vowel markers appear; sight word vocabularies build; silent reading increases (ages: 6 to 12; approximate grade levels: 2–4)	Features include: vowel-consonant-*e* patterns; *r*-controlled vowel patterns; other common long vowels; complex consonant patterns; abstract vowel patterns
Syllable Juncture	Polysyllabic words; more control and appropriate use of vowel patterns; compound words; inflectional endings; doubling; processing print proficiently (ages: 8 to 12; approximate grade levels: 3–8)	Features include: doubling and *e*-drop with -*ed* and -*ing* endings; other doubling at the syllable juncture; long vowel patterns in a stressed syllable; *r*-controlled vowels in a stressed syllable; vowel patterns in an unstressed syllable; learning that affixes are separate meaning units
Derivational Constancy	Continues through adulthood; mature readers and writers; constancy of some spelling patterns despite changes in sound; relationships of words with common root words; Latin and Greek roots (ages: 10+; approximate grade levels: 5–8+)	Features include: silent and sounded consonants; consonant changes (alternations); vowel changes (alternations); Latin-derived suffixes; assimilated prefixes

How Can the Level of a Child's Word Knowledge Be Determined?

The overall purpose of assessment is to improve student achievement, inform decision-making, and perfect teaching practices. Fountas and Pinnell (2004) suggest that "Within both formal and informal assessment contexts, we are always asking three questions:

- What do children know and control relative to letters, sounds, and words?
- What do children partially know?
- What do they not yet know?" (p. 4).

A multifaceted assessment plan that features an array of daily and periodic assessments is an effective way to gather the data needed to answer such questions.

Spelling inventories are an important element of such plans, as they not only aid in establishing a child's stage of orthographic or word knowledge development but also help uncover the child's control of the features within each. Other assessments, especially useful in interim progress monitoring, include classroom observations, running records/records of oral reading, and writing samples. When viewed in totality, the data from a combination of assessments make it possible to ascertain what children know, are using but confusing, and are ready to learn.

A word study approach relies on this type of sensitive, systematic, and intentional assessment of children to determine their progress in developing item knowledge as well as their use of word knowledge/word solving strategies in reading and writing continuous text. This continuous and multifaceted approach to assessment results in a wealth of data that can be mined to inform systematic and differentiated instructional decision-making throughout a child's educational journey.

PHOTO 19.5 A multifaceted assessment plan provides data and information important for instructional decision-making and progress monitoring.

How Do I "Do" Word Study?

While there is no one way to "do" word study, there is one valuable resource that is mandatory—the teacher. No one knows the strengths and needs of his or her students better. It is the teacher's knowledge, expertise, and professional judgment that guides decisions as he or she reviews and makes choices from the abundance of resources, approaches, and systems currently available.

Should I Plan Whole-Group or Small-Group Instruction?

A teacher's comfort level in organizing and managing differentiated word study is a major consideration. If the teacher does not have a lot of experience or is not yet comfortable in facilitating small-group word study, it may be better to begin with the whole group. However, the ultimate goal is to transition to small-group, differentiated instruction to better meet the diverse needs found in classrooms.

How Do I Start Planning for Instruction?

The first step is to study the data from a spelling inventory such as the Developmental Spelling Analysis/DSA (Ganske, 2014) or another assessment that can be used to determine students' stages of spelling or word knowledge. The analysis of these data will help you understand the level of control students exhibit of the features within each stage. When coupled with additional classroom data and information, you can decide on a starting point for instruction.

It's important to avoid focusing on what the student does not know. Look instead for what the student controls or is beginning to control. Initiating instruction from an area of strength allows both the teacher and student to build upon what is known. This helps a student gain confidence, become more willing to take a risk, and engage in inquiry and investigation. It also encourages the student to become strategic and generative in using what he or she knows. The *Literacy Continuum: A Tool for Assessment, Planning, and Teaching, PreK–8, Expanded Edition* (Fountas & Pinnell, 2017) and the *Comprehensive Phonics, Spelling, and Word Study Guide, PreK–8* (Fountas & Pinnell, 2017) are two examples of resources that can help target specific behaviors and understandings to notice, teach for, and support.

What Does Word Study Look Like in a Classroom?

Classroom curriculum must provide time for explicit word study that is inquiry-based, systematic, and intentionally addresses children's needs. It must also include time for embedded opportunities—across instructional contexts—for students to practice, extend, and deepen their understandings of how words work as they read and write continuous texts. It is not one or the other—it must be both. A comprehensive, balanced literacy framework makes this complex task achievable.

Explicit Word Study Block

Fountas and Pinnell (1998) suggest that the explicit word study block begin with a brief (5–10 minutes), intentional, and inquiry-based mini-lesson focused on a principle, concept, or aspect of word study that draws upon what students know and need to learn next. Assessment guides the decision-making as to the content and sequencing for these pre-planned mini-lessons—as well as monitoring and informing both the teacher and students throughout all phases of word study. An authentic, purposeful application activity follows, affording students numerous opportunities to practice and extend what is presented in the mini-lesson. Application tasks can take place during word study time, independent work time, or anytime during the day. The final step is a three-to-five-minute group share to provide time for students to express their thinking, reflect on new learning, encourage further inquiry, and check student understanding.

> **Explicit Word Study Block**
>
> - Component of language/word study block
> - Determine amount of time you can effectively fit into your daily schedule
> - Minimum time—20 minutes daily
> - Maximum time—30 minutes daily
> - Schedule when best for students

Elements of an Explicit Word Study Framework

(From *Word Matters*, Fountas & Pinnell, 1998, pp. 174–175)

Mini-lesson	Application Activity	Group Share
A brief, yet explicit word study lesson focused on a specific pattern, principle, strategy, or concept	An intentional and engaging activity or set of activities that afford students opportunities to extend, practice, and apply what they are learning in mini-lessons	A conclusion to word study each day; students are invited to share their learning, pose questions, and communicate their thinking
(whole or small groups)	(individuals, pairs, small groups)	(one to three students)

workboard

How Do I Manage This?

A workboard is important to establish the routines for the explicit word study block. It not only provides a schedule for students to follow, but also requires students to work independently and collaboratively with others as effective and successful members of a classroom community. Expected and predictable routines and behaviors are taught, demonstrated, and practiced so they become integral and organic components of daily learning—skills invaluable to students' lives inside and outside of the classroom.

Five-Day Schedule for Whole-Group Instruction				
DAY 1	**DAY 2**	**DAY 3**	**DAY 4**	**DAY 5**
Mini-lesson	Closed Sort & Write	Make Connections	Blind Sort	Monitoring Progress

The schedule above is an example of a workboard for whole-group word study instruction. This five-day cycle begins with a teacher-led, whole-group mini-lesson on an orthographic principle needed by the majority of the class. On subsequent days of the cycle, students engage in application activities designed to strengthen and expand their learning.

Closed Sort and Write For example, during a closed sort, students have a set of words and key words as headings to guide their sort such as *hat* for short *a* and *cake* for long *a*. The set may also include words like *weigh* to help students note exceptions. The students then write their words in columns in their Word Study Notebooks. An open sort is a little different— students are free to sort their words in any way they want to as long as they can identify how each set of words are connected. Students share their word lists from their Word Study Notebook, and the rest of the class can try to figure out the link between the words.

Making Connections Providing students opportunities to make connections between words is a powerful way to draw attention to specific letters, features, concepts, principles, or word structures being explored. It also challenges students to think about words in new ways and supports vocabulary building. Activities can include making connections between words or picture cards that have the same feature (*dad* is like *dog*, *day*, and *dish* because they all begin with the letter/consonant *d*); same or different patterns (*game* is like *rain*, *day*, and *came* because they all have patterns that result in a long *a* sound; *hat* is like *get*, *sit*, and *mop* because they all have a CVC/short vowel pattern); or by concept/word structure (an *apple* is like an *orange*, a *cherry*, or a *mango* because they are all fruits and are examples of two-syllable words). Investigation and monitoring for understanding—being able to articulate (orally or in writing) what was learned or noticed and why this is important— are at the heart of making connections.

The resources listed in the appendix offer many ideas for application activities and mini-lessons. They also serve as a collective springboard for further investigation of possibilities.

Monitoring Progress On days two to four, the teacher observes, monitors, and conferences with individuals and small groups of students; each day ends with a sharing session. The last day of the cycle can be used as an opportunity to assess student learning. Or, assessment could be every other week, and an additional activity can be added to the cycle. Students should have all materials for mini-lessons and application activities readily available so time can be used efficiently and effectively as they work individually, with partners, or in small groups. Differentiation and concerns for ELL and special needs learners must still be considered within whole-group instruction. Some small-group instruction could be planned while the rest of the class is engaged in application work.

Explicit word study takes 20–30 minutes each day. If you are worried about how to fit this time into your schedule, look closely at the amount of time spent on classroom activities with little instructional value, such as whole-class bathroom breaks, daily calendar, and taking children to and from special classes. Are there ways to shorten or delete activities to have enough time for a full two- or two-and-one-half-hour literacy block? Often, students can learn routines which maximize the amount of instructional time. For example, in a kindergarten class, children learned quickly how to hang up their coats and book bags, move their own attendance and lunch count markers, and begin the day with silent reading. In this classroom, they wasted no time so that instruction could begin right after the morning bell rang. Using similar routines, students in your classroom could learn how to begin their word study time as soon as the bell rings.

How Do I Teach Word Study in Small Groups?

The first step is to group students who have similar strengths and needs for instruction based on assessment data. Generally, three or four differentiated word study groups are manageable, depending on what is most effective for both the teacher and students. It is important that these groups remain fluid and flexible so that movement is possible between groups as students grow in their understandings and new learning needs arise.

A five-day study cycle is also possible during a 20- to 30-minute word study block; however, each group's focus of investigation and word lists are different due to student needs. No longer is the whole class studying the same feature, principle, concept, or strategy. Each group now meets with the teacher at least once a week, depending on the number of groups, and all can engage in the same application activities, with the only difference being the set of words assigned to each group. For example, on Monday, while one group is working with the teacher, the other groups are engaged in application activities such as a blind sort, making connections, or a closed sort and journal write. Word study application activities can also take place during independent literacy learning during the day. During this time, students continue to apply what they are learning—in authentic and purposeful experiences that build upon and extend the focus of mini-lessons from the word study block. There may be times when extended time is needed to study an area of focus in more detail. Planning a ten-day cycle, for example, provides more time for teaching and learning to unfold, as two explicit, teacher-guided mini-lessons and sets of accompanying application activities can be offered within that cycle.

PHOTO 19.6 Small-group word study

Explicit Word Study Block: Example of a Five- or Ten-Day Workboard for Small-Group, Differentiated Instruction

DAY	Student Names	Student Names	Student Names	Student Names
1	**Teacher-Led Mini-lesson**	Progress Monitor OR Assess	Blind Sort	Make Connections
2	Closed Sort and Write	**Teacher-Led Mini-lesson**	Progress Monitor OR Assess	Blind Sort
3	Make Connections	Closed Sort and Write	**Teacher-Led Mini-lesson**	Progress Monitor OR Assess
4	Blind Sort	Make Connections	Closed Sort and Write	**Teacher-Led Mini-lesson**
5	Progress Monitor OR Assess	Blind Sort	Make Connections	Closed Sort and Write
6	**Teacher-Led Mini-lesson**	Progress Monitor OR Assess	Blind Sort	Make Connections
7	Closed Sort and Write	**Teacher-Led Mini-lesson**	Progress Monitor OR Assess	Blind Sort
8	Make Connections	Closed Sort and Write	**Teacher-Led Mini-lesson**	Progress Monitor OR Assess
9	Blind Sort	Make Connections	Closed Sort and Write	**Teacher-Led Mini-lesson**
10	Progress Monitor OR Assess	Blind Sort	Make Connections	Closed Sort and Write

The characteristics of differentiated, small-group word study are:

- Each group begins its focus of study with a mini-lesson on an assigned day (word study does not have to begin on Monday and end on Friday).
- The teacher facilitates the mini-lesson, engaging students in inquiry, investigation, and social construction of knowledge.
- The teacher checks in with other groups as time permits.
- A group share ends the word study block each day.

Each group participates in a designated application activity (listed on the workboard) that extends and reinforces the mini-lesson; the teacher also checks in briefly with other groups, as time permits, to monitor and check for understanding. Application activities can include, but are not limited to: sorts (closed, open, blind, speed, picture, or concept), word hunts, word webs, making connections, word ladders, games, building words, name puzzles, and word origins. A day for progress monitoring can be included in each word study cycle to check for student understanding and inform instructional decision-making. A spelling test or other form of assessment can also be administered, if required by the school or district.

When first beginning small-group instruction, each group must await its first mini-lesson with the teacher due to staggered starts. During this time, students can engage in independent reading or writing, a word study activity, or any other learning experience the teacher designates.

The focus of each word study group can be displayed in a chart similar to the ones shown in Photo 19.7. These charts, each a different color, can be placed in the community area of the classroom as a reminder to the teacher and students to reinforce, make connections, and extend word study across other instructional contexts (Interactive Read-Aloud, shared reading, guided reading, independent reading, Writing Workshop, community writing, and independent writing). If the chart(s) are laminated, students can also hunt for words to write on them that represent the feature, principle, or pattern being studied.

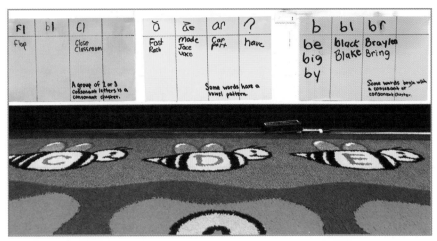

PHOTO 19.7 Visual reminders help teachers and students embed small-group word study throughout the day.

Embedded Word Study

Word study is woven throughout the literacy block. Interesting new words to talk about arise during Interactive Read-Aloud (see Photo 19.8). Exceptional spellings are noted during shared reading and added to charts in the classroom. A brief word study lesson is often part of guided reading based on the teacher's observations during the lesson (see Photo 19.9).

PHOTO 19.8 Encountering new and exciting words during Interactive Read-Aloud

PHOTO 19.9 Word work in guided reading

PHOTO 19.10 Word study during interactive writing

Word study also takes place as students read and write independently throughout the day. Primary grade students can also practice and extend what they are learning in mini-lessons from the word study block during independent literacy work (centers). Application activities could include word sorts and collecting interesting words like the student in Photo 19.10.

Word study is an essential element of interactive writing, as the teacher slows down the writing process to teach how words work. Nearly every chapter of this book includes an element of word study contributing to students' literacy learning. The many opportunities for embedded word study are shown in the chart below.

Embedded Opportunities for Word Study	
Teaching, Application, and Reinforcement of Phonics, Spelling, Vocabulary, and Learning About How Words Work	
Primary	**Intermediate–Middle Level**
• Interactive Read-Aloud • Shared Reading • Guided Reading (including 2–3 minutes of word work at end of lesson) • Independent Literacy Work • Independent Reading • Shared & Interactive Writing • Independent Writing • Writing Workshop	• Interactive Read-Aloud • Shared Reading • Guided Reading (including 2–3 minutes of word work at end of lesson) • Independent Reading • Shared Writing • Independent Writing • Writing Workshop

Selecting Words to Match Student Needs

Once the instructional stage of spelling development is established and the starting point for instruction is determined, the professional resources cited in the appendix will be helpful. Many include words and pictures cards that are grouped by categories either in lists appropriate for each lesson or sets of word cards for word sort lessons. While ready-made word lists are available, it is possible to create one that is customized. Most of the words on any list should comprise "core" words—words that represent the feature, principle, or pattern students are investigating. When choosing words, it is important to ensure they reflect the reading, writing, experience, and language of students at the time. Three to five words (or picture cards) should be selected for each category of study, keeping in mind the appropriateness for the grade level, and the strengths and needs of student(s). Because word sorts are a common application activity, it is important to have enough words to effectively compare, contrast, and categorize, and it is imperative that students are able to read each word or recognize each picture. It's also important to have a few "other" words that demonstrate exceptions. Once the "core" words are selected, two to four "personal" words can be added to student lists as well. These can be selected from high-frequency words, word wall words, or words students encounter in reading and writing that are developmentally appropriate and frequently used.

Classroom Resources Needed for Word Study

Primary classrooms are generally organized to include separate literacy centers that often include an ABC or Word Study Center. Intermediate and middle level classrooms, or primary classrooms with limited space, may not have separate center areas; however, an area should be made available to store word study materials and resources. Tubs, crates, or containers are often used as they can be easily transported to other areas of the room. No matter what grade level, materials and resources

Word Study Resources and Supplies

Primary–Intermediate–Middle Level
- word study workboard
- easel
- chart paper
- markers
- pocket charts
- magnetic letters
- blank index cards
- letter clusters—word tiles
- small magnetic whiteboards
- name charts
- word study notebooks
- word study folders
- word wall
- alphabet linking charts
- consonant cluster–digraph charts
- dictionaries and thesauruses
- other reference materials
- electronic spellers

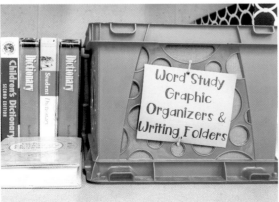

PHOTO 19.11 Word study resources and supplies should be organized and easily accessible to students.

need to be organized, labeled, and easily accessible in order for learning, inquiry, and exploration to occur.

Different sizes of envelopes, plastic baggies, rings, and file boxes can be used to store word/picture cards. Word cards can also be kept in the inside cover of students' Word Study Notebooks or in the pocket of word study folders. File boxes with ABC sections for each student make great word banks that students can use to create their own sorts or find words to support their writing.

PHOTO 19.12 Word study in action

Conclusion

A child's acquisition of word knowledge is a systematic, developmental process that grows and changes over time, at different rates for different children. Therefore, the instruction we offer our students must go far beyond the traditional, one-size-fits-all approach many of us may have received. This chapter is offered in support of such an endeavor so that we may reflect on, consider, and examine key factors important in selecting, designing, refining, and implementing an instructional model for teaching and learning about how words work.

A quality word study approach based on these factors generates excitement, encourages inquiry and critical thinking, and motivates active engagement and participation as students take ownership in their own learning as they journey to become proficient readers, writers, and language learners.

Suggestions for Professional Development

1. Individually, craft a definition of your current phonics, spelling, and vocabulary instruction. What implications or challenges does this chapter have for transitioning to, or refining, word study in your classroom? What further information or knowledge might you need?

   • Meet with your grade-level team and follow the same process. Ask each member to share his or her definition and chart similarities and differences. What did you notice? Are there consistencies within the grade level, common understandings, and shared beliefs? What implications or challenges does this have for students and for the team? What further information or knowledge might be needed?

   • Invite a colleague from each grade level in your building to meet with your building literacy team. Again, follow a similar process. What is noticed? Are there consistency, shared beliefs, and common understandings across grade levels? What implications or challenges does this have for students, for teachers, for the building? What further information or knowledge might be needed?

2. Form an inquiry group of interested colleagues to further study the theoretical and historical underpinnings of word study, using some of the professional resources listed in the back of the book. How and in what ways does research continue to impact and have implications for current teaching and learning of phonics, spelling, vocabulary, reading, and writing?

3. List your current word study assessments in the first column of the chart below.

   • Column 2: Record how often each assessment is administered or information is collected.

   • Column 3: Note if the assessment is formative or summative.

   • Column 4: Record the intentional purpose for the data/information gleaned from each assessment.

   Reflect on what you noticed and/or learned. What implications might this have for your word study assessment and instructional practices?

Assessment (Formal/Informal)	Frequency (Weekly, Twice a Year, Daily, etc.)	Formative or Summative	How and in What Ways Are Data/Information Used?

4. Select a spelling inventory from one of the resources listed in the appendix. Administer it to students in your classroom, score it, and analyze the data. In what ways are the data the same as or different from what you currently collect? How might this impact the teaching and learning in your classroom?

5. Take note of the word study resources and materials you have in your classroom. How are they organized? Are they labeled, accessible to students, and age/grade level appropriate? Do they support inquiry, investigation, social construction of knowledge, and a hands-on approach? Are anchor charts readily visible to students as they engage in word solving as readers and writers? Are self-reliance, accountability, and responsibility taught, modeled, and supported? Is there time allotted in the daily schedule for an explicit word study block? Are a myriad of opportunities available to embed what students are learning in word study throughout all elements of a comprehensive literacy framework? The answers to questions such as these will aid you in establishing the rich, inviting, and supportive environment that is needed for word study to take root and thrive in your classroom.

CHAPTER 20

Let's Talk About Words: Accelerating Vocabulary Development

Robert S. Drewry

> "The effective vocabulary teacher builds a word-rich environment in which students are immersed in words for both incidental and intentional learning and the development of 'word awareness.'"
>
> —Camille L. Z. Blachowicz and Peter J. Fisher

It seems so obvious that lively talk and conversation is important to language development from infancy through toddlerhood, yet it is easy to forget about the importance of talk once students reach school age. Research on the dynamics of classroom talk reveals that teachers often do most of the talking in their classrooms (Nystrand, Wu, Gamoran, Zeiser, & Long, 2003)—a lost opportunity to invite students to show us what they know and are learning by conversing with us. After all, when we speak with infants and toddlers, we allow response time for them to show what they know through their movement and verbalizations. If they are able to talk, then we can converse with them, extending and refining their verbal communication while helping them move toward a shared understanding. Talk is also an important driver of vocabulary development for children who are not yet in school.

Fast Mapping for Vocabulary Development Gap

Carey and Bartlett's (1978) concept of "fast mapping" can help us understand why talk is such a vital part of a child's early literacy development. According to this study, the conversations parents, caregivers, or teachers have with young children lead the children to quickly associate the meanings of words with objects in the immediate environment. As children begin this process of associating spoken words with environmental objects (or the concepts the objects refer to), they are deepening their knowledge of the words and of the world. Furthermore, parents' or caregivers' use of narrative-based conversations (i.e., talk that tells a story) can also improve the vocabulary of young children (Peterson, Jesso, & McCabe, 1999).

What Fast Mapping Means for Classrooms

Because K–12 students spend most of their waking hours at school interacting with teachers and not their parents or caregivers, it's clear that your students will benefit from more frequent and varied opportunities to converse in your classroom. Teachers' use of talk is even more important for those students who have not heard much talk in their homes prior to school entry. Although students arrive at school with a wide range of different vocabulary experiences, the conversations students engage in at school can help to increase the vocabulary sizes of all students. Clearly, students need access to frequent, complex, and supportive conversations both at home and at school. Students should discuss their learning opportunities with each other and the teacher as frequently as possible. Creating a language-rich classroom engages students and immerses them in more talk per day than they would encounter in a traditional classroom where the teacher controls the talking.

How Talk During Vocabulary Instruction Helps Accentuate Children's Existing Strengths

If students enter your classroom with limited vocabularies, then improving their vocabularies with vocabulary instruction is of paramount importance. There are multiple ways to accomplish your goal.

Select Vocabulary for Instruction Carefully

Beck, McKeown, and Kucan (2013) recommend that we select words of high utility, which they call "tier-two words." These tier-two words are important to use instructionally because they represent words that are not often found in oral language, that students are unlikely to have heard spoken before, but exist in multiple contexts (Beck et al., 2013). Because students are most likely going to encounter these words in the books they are reading, it is important to give them opportunities to talk about them and notice when authors use interesting, unconventional, or novel words. When you are selecting words for instruction from a specific text, keep these criteria in mind to enhance students' vocabulary development.

Tier One	Tier Two	Tier Three
Words that occur very frequently in everyday conversation and in texts students have already read.	Words that occur frequently in texts students are reading or will read (across a variety of genres and subjects), but that do not occur frequently in everyday conversation.	Words that occur in specific genres of text or particular subjects students are reading or will read, but that do not occur frequently in everyday conversation.
happy, catch, strength, walk, please, joke	*figure, table, conclusion, theme, batter, scene, inequality, document*	*metaphor, photosynthesis, fissure, divisor, parliament*

(Adapted from Beck, McKeown, & Kucan, 2013)

Use Interactive Read-Aloud to Introduce New Words

The easiest way to introduce new words from texts to students is through Interactive Read-Alouds with a large group of students. In these learning opportunities, teachers intentionally select texts that are above their students' current reading levels so that students will be exposed to more sophisticated narrative structures and vocabulary than they could access independently (Fountas & Pinnell, 2001). So, not only do students get to hear a multitude of new words in each text, but they also get to benefit from discussing some of these words with their teachers and peers during the reading of the text (see Photo 20.1).

PHOTO 20.1 An Interactive Read-Aloud is a perfect place to incorporate talk into vocabulary instruction.

To make Interactive Read-Alouds as powerful as possible, it is necessary to select vocabulary for instruction in advance of the reading. Although it may be tempting to save time by improvising when conducting an Interactive Read-Aloud, this practice does not ensure that your read-aloud, or the vocabulary instruction that is part of it, will be as effective as it can be. The time you save by not planning will need to be made up instructionally at some later point!

I recommend selecting between three and five words to discuss during an Interactive Read-Aloud. Reserve your in-depth discussion of these words for the second reading of the text. When students are listening to the book for the first time, they will want to follow the narrative or focus on conceptual information and may be frustrated with you for interrupting their comprehension of the book. During your first read, you might mention these words as you read aloud but discuss them in more detail once the read-aloud is over or during the second reading of the book.

Create Word Walls

Everyone from elementary to undergraduate students enjoys working with word walls. There are countless themes you can use to assemble your word wall. Although it is often easiest for younger students if you arrange your word wall by spelling patterns or sounds, I encourage you to start building students' vocabularies by focusing on word meanings in your word wall.

The simplest approach is to create a separate word wall for each unit of study in your classroom. The principal benefit of following this approach is that it deepens student knowledge of the concept underlying the unit of study. For example, one primary classroom studying feelings created the chart in Photo 20.2. If you are focusing on ecology, you will likely have words such as *biome*, *ecosystem*, *photosynthesis*, *predator*, and *cultivate* (see Photo 20.3). As these words are frequently used to discuss ecological concepts, students will create a mental network of the concepts and the words used to discuss them. It is important that you rearrange the words on your word wall as new concepts are added so that it reflects the genuine connections between the concepts. For example, the *ecosystem* entry could have examples of ecosystems listed under it, while the *photosynthesis* and *predator* entries should be kept physically distant from each other because one describes a concept related to plant life and the other animal life. These physical separations and relocations should, of course, be accompanied by talk about why they are placed where they are.

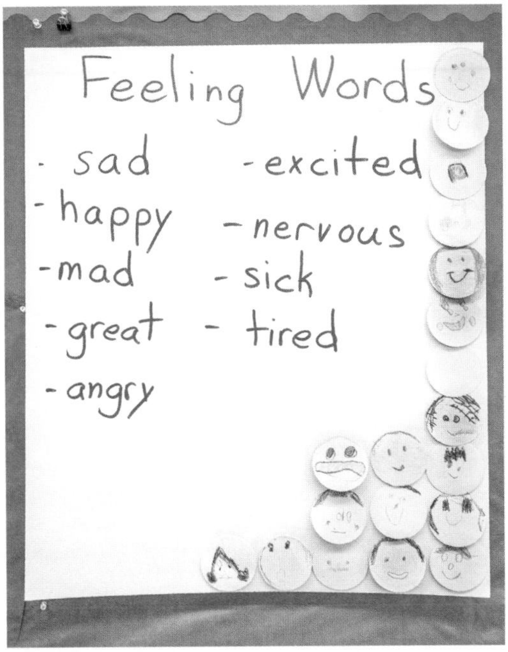

PHOTO 20.2 Word wall of feeling words

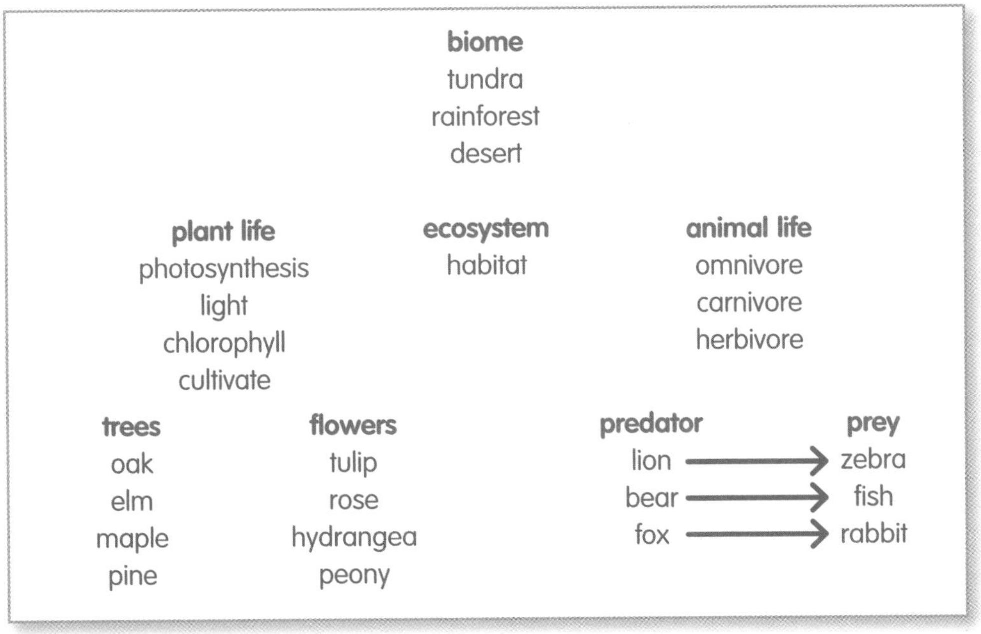

PHOTO 20.3 Ecology word wall

PHOTO 20.4 *The Giver* word wall

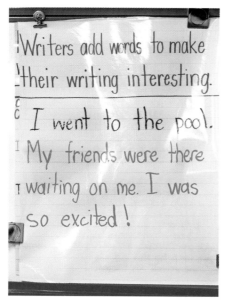

PHOTO 20.5 Anchor chart about using interesting words

When my students read *The Giver* by Lois Lowry (1993), they created a word wall using the vocabulary they were assigned to study (see Photo 20.4). As students posted each word, they also had the option of posting a teacher-provided synonym on the board. Each of these postings yielded an opportunity to deepen vocabulary knowledge by discussing the words' meanings and relationships with other words.

Vocabularify Your Routines

Building on Graves' (2016) recommendation to use rich language in the classroom, you can start teaching vocabulary immediately by "vocabularifying" your classroom routines. Make your everyday reminders to students more linguistically sophisticated. For example, compare "let's line up for lunch" to "Could you please assemble yourselves in an orderly fashion by the entrance to the corridor?" In the latter case, the vocabulary is likely to pique students' interests even though it describes a mundane task. If these words are unfamiliar to your students—even better! You have just created an opportunity for a discussion about word meanings in an authentic context—just the kind of experience that will make students more attuned to your language and more likely to use interesting words. Writing Workshop is another opportunity to talk about thoughtful, careful word selection. One class worked to make the sentence, "I went to the pool," more interesting and created the anchor chart in Photo 20.5 to remind them every day as they write.

As with selecting vocabulary for an Interactive Read-Aloud, you will want to plan ahead when vocabularifying your routines. The phrases you generate through careful planning will have more impact on your students' learning than a quickly improvised outburst. If you plan in advance, you will also have a better chance of remembering what you actually said and will thus be better able to discuss its meaning with students. The same may not be true for the ephemeral moment of genius that comes to you in the middle of a lesson.

Discuss Interesting Words With Students

I like each student in my classes to keep an individual word log (see Photo 20.6). When students learn, hear, or read a new word, they should add it to their log. In the word log, the first column has the word; the middle is where they found it or heard it; and the last is the meaning of the word. Graves and Watts-Taffe (2002) recommend helping students develop "word consciousness"; in other words, students benefit from becoming attuned to hearing interesting, clever, or novel uses of words (Graves, 2016).

In an ideal world, my students would keep sticky notes with them at all times so that their reading becomes a potential source of words to add to their lists. We review these logs at least once weekly for five to 10 minutes. This span of time gives them an opportunity to reflect on any interesting words they have learned recently as well as the time to clarify the meaning of a word with their teacher. When I ask students why they added a certain word to their list, the response is often, "I didn't know it." This response is helpful because it allows me to ask the student if they think they notice every word they do not know and, beyond that, how they know they know a word. These two questions ("Do you notice every word you don't know?" and "What does it mean to know a word?") are perfect ways to keep students word conscious as they continue to read.

In clarifying conversations, you can explore with students just how to use certain new words or where students will be likely to find them when reading. For example, elementary students might learn about *figure* in a math class and add it to their vocabulary log with an entry that says it is used to write or represent numbers. A discussion with a peer or teacher might reveal that *figure* can also be used in an artist's critique to describe how the artist depicted the human form in a painting, in a short story when one character uses *figure* as an informal substitute for *think* in conversation with another character, or how a repetitive set of images, or *figures*, can create a pattern. Students will enjoy discussing how to figure out all of the different meanings of a particular word they may use every day.

33.	lofty	Test	with a great height
34.	electrolytes	Water bottle	when melted is electronic
35.	Carbohydrate	Nutrition Facts	a food that contains Yeast
36.	Pier	Me	like a bridge
37.	Pupil	dictionary	a young peer in school
38.	Personification	Mrs. Stepen	giving an animal human form
39.	attire	word sort	clothing
40.	Obscure	word sort	to dim
41.	forwarn	Dr. Drewry	to tell ahead of time
42.	mature	word sort	to be well behaved
43.	Utopic	ELA	a good place to live
44.	Chatoyant	dictionary word of the day	changing in color or luster

PHOTO 20.6 Student word log

PHOTO 20.7 Independent reading books are a superb way for students to find words to add to a word log.

Conclusion

There are so many ways talking can improve your students' vocabulary development and develop their interest in discussing newly learned words with peers and teachers. When you are considering which words to select for a read-aloud or a class novel, reflect on Beck et al.'s (2013) three tiers of vocabulary. Take their recommendations a step further by talking with students about why you have chosen these words for your instruction. In this way, you can pique their interest as word-conscious learners (Graves & Watts-Taffe, 2002).

Suggestions for Professional Development

1. Meet with colleagues to discuss vocabulary selection.

   To get yourself and your colleagues better acquainted with talk about vocabulary and your reading selections, agree on a picture book to read independently. As you read the book, select vocabulary to use for instruction during an Interactive Read-Aloud. Once everyone has read the book and made their selections, discuss as a group the words you selected and why. Try to determine what criteria make a word worthy of instruction, and use these criteria to guide your planning in the future.

2. Read an article about vocabulary assessment.

   It can be difficult to measure vocabulary growth with traditional assessments. However, Stahl and Bravo (2010) describe two helpful, classroom-ready assessments: the Vocabulary Knowledge Scale (VKS) and Vocabulary Rating Tool (VRT). With the VKS, you assess students' depth of knowledge for specific words; with the VRT, you assess students' ability to categorize words conceptually. You can use these assessments for a simple pre-test/post-test experiment in your classroom to determine whether your students have learned the words found in a picture book, novel, or article.

CHAPTER 21

Learning About, From, and Through Handwriting

Lynda Hamilton Mudre & Gay Su Pinnell

"Handwriting is a complex skill engaging cognitive, perceptual, and motor skills simultaneously."

—**Richard Gentry**

At one time in our educational history, the curriculum area labeled "writing" was nearly synonymous with the term "handwriting." Students practiced long hours with copybooks. Children in kindergarten seldom wrote at all, and first graders copied, sometimes laboriously, from the chalkboard as part of their independent work (sometimes called "busy work"). Only after handwriting and spelling were mastered did children begin, as a special treat, to write their own stories.

Now, even kindergarten children are composing and producing their own pieces of writing, resulting in an amazing change in perception—young children could do far more in writing than previously thought. An unfortunate side effect of this productive new direction—along with the wide use of electronic devices in classrooms—has been a dramatic decrease in handwriting instruction. While we do not advocate a return to daily handwriting drills or to extensive copying, we believe that young children have much to learn from and through handwriting that will support them as writers and readers.

Effortless, legible handwriting is clearly related to the ability to engage in the writing process (Fisher & Terry, 1990). Laborious handwriting, on the other hand, may be so demanding that it constrains children's ability to compose, elaborate, plan, and revise. In fact, Berninger, Mizokawa, and Bragg (1991) suggest that difficulty in handwriting may lead children to avoid the act altogether or engage in it only when required. It makes sense that improvement in speed and legibility would contribute to a student's ability to compose texts. This claim is supported by researchers who studied first graders who had handwriting problems (Berninger et al., 1998). Graham et al. (1998) suggest that difficulty in getting language onto paper may cause a writer to switch attention in a way that will limit the capability of memory and interfere with the generation of content and recall of ideas.

Reciprocity Between Reading and Writing

For the last four decades, Marie Clay's research and theoretical works have directed educators to attend to the reciprocal relationship between early writing and reading—and this relationship includes the mechanics of producing letters and words. According to Clay (2001), when young children write, they search for "visual forms to represent the sounds in the messages they have composed. When they check visually by reading what they wrote, they find out whether it says what they intended to write" (p. 20).

Clay found that writing helps young children do the following:

- Attend closely to the distinctive features of letters (for example, the tall and short sticks, the tunnels and circles, the dots and tails)

- Become aware of the sounds within the words they are trying to write

- Begin to represent sounds with letters

- Build up a repertoire of known words that can be written with increasing speed and ease

- Develop a system for "learning how to learn" words

Clay's work (2005) places a greater emphasis on helping children, especially those who have reading difficulties, develop the ability to scan print left to right—not only lines of print, but also words and letters. This linear directional movement is very different from the kind of visual scanning most children have been required to do prior to school, and it is a huge advantage to young children to learn directional rules early. Directionality refers not only to the scanning of lines and words, left to right, but to the writing of letters.

Teaching Handwriting in the Early Years

As we observe young writers at work, we notice that much of their time is spent in the process of forming letters. After all, getting letters down on the page is an important task if you are going to relay a message to a reader. Some children seem to cope fairly well in figuring out how to transfer the form they are visualizing (or sometimes copying) to paper. Others are practicing—and habituating—inefficient and time-consuming actions. Some forget what they want to say because their attention is focused on letter formation. Some are even "drawing" letters in random ways.

> More automatic control would free them up to attend to one of the primary goals we have for them as writers—thinking about the message they are trying to communicate and writing it in a way that an audience can read and enjoy.

Letter formation can be frustrating and time-consuming for many students because they have not internalized where to start, which way to go, and how to make letters fluently in the easiest way. This confusion robs them of time they could be spending in thinking about what they want to say and how to say it. What if our students could write letters more easily and fluidly? More automatic control would free them up to attend to one of the primary goals we have for them as writers—thinking about the message they are trying to communicate and writing it in a way that an audience can read and enjoy. It seems logical to provide the kind of handwriting instruction that will not only result in fluent transcribing, but also facilitate the craft of writing.

When Children Are Learning Handwriting, What Are They Really Learning?

When children copy letters and words, they coordinate eye-scanning movements with hand movements. The visual analysis and motor response is a brain activity that must be developed through involving students actively in the process. The goal is that the child will be able to initiate and control smooth, consistent, and sequential movements automatically and independently (Clay, 1975).

Clay writes that "writing can contribute to the building of almost every kind of inner control of literacy learning that is needed by the successful reader" (1998, p. 130). If the act of writing is self-directed, the resulting "visual exploration behaviors" (Clay, 1975, p. 73) become a support system for learning to read. Writing slows the visual analysis process and encourages children to notice particular features of print—how certain forms are alike and different.

Writing, if concurrent with reading from the beginning, enhances children's ability to work on print resources in the books they are reading (Clay, 1998). Of course, *writing* is much more than handwriting. The formation of letters is only a part of the whole process of authorship. A writer uses multiple resources in flexible ways to produce message after message. Composition is the construction of meaning by the brain, mapped out in language and encoded in letters grouped into words and words arranged in grammatical patterns. This process sounds linear but, in fact, it is not. Everything is happening simultaneously.

> Teaching children how to form letters is part of becoming a writer because writers need efficient ways to encode their thoughts. And automatic eye-hand response frees them to compose.

The reciprocal benefits of teaching writing alongside reading are logical. All writers must undertake the activities that a reader does. They must use the words they have produced to guide the writing of the next word just as readers use the context of the sentence or story to decipher the words an author has written. Writers must often reread, check on their use of visual, semantic, or syntactic information, and sometimes correct it to fit the message being composed. Like readers, writers must keep meaning in their heads as the ultimate check on the composition. Teaching children how to form letters is part of becoming a writer because writers need efficient ways to encode their thoughts. Automatic eye-hand response frees them to compose.

How Can We Help Children Develop Efficient and Fluent Handwriting?

Our instructional goal is to help our students internalize the visual forms and directional movements necessary to produce letters. Using language to direct this movement helps. When the eyes, ears, mouth, and hands are involved together in performing a task, they can support and check one another. Seeing, hearing, saying, and moving concurrently is an especially effective way for our youngest writers to learn. For many children, this learning needs to occur before we expect them to use their eyes alone to act on print (Clay, 1975; 1998).

Your language can act as a scaffold for children until it becomes internalized by them, enabling them to self-direct their moves. How does this process work as we teach handwriting? Here is an example from a kindergarten lesson.

Formation of the Letter *h*	
Procedures	**Your Language**
Be sure you have your students' full attention. Show them how to hold a pencil or marker. Slowly demonstrate writing the letter in large, bold print.	*Let me see your eyes right up here. Watch very closely. I'm going to show you exactly how to make the letter h. Start at the top. Pull down, back up, over, and down: h.*
Use the same brief and specific language each time to guide your movement while you are producing a clear visual model. Name the letter.	*Down, up, over, and down: h.*
Ask students to watch your writing, use your language, and move in exactly the same ways you do. The children's writing of a letter is done in the air, then later on paper.	*Try it with me now in the air with your writing finger. Pull down, up, over, and down: h.* (Repeat several times, until the children are verbalizing the movements without your voice.)
Ask the children to try the writing on their own, and guide their attempts verbally and physically as necessary. Help children who are holding the pencil awkwardly or in their fist.	*Now, you try it. Say and make the moves. Show me how you can do it by yourselves. Good. Let me hear and see you again. Again, etc. Now trace it in the box with your finger and whisper. Again. Now use your pencil, and I'll come and watch—and I'll listen to your words.*
When you are satisfied that the movements are firmly established in a sequential, fluent pattern, create opportunities for the children to practice independently. Demonstrate each independent activity and involve students in guided practice before they do it on their own. Verbalizing is gradually discontinued.	*At the ABC Center, make the letter very slowly in each square and whisper the words that tell which way to go. Then check on yourself by finding a magnetic letter just like the one you made. Tell a friend the name of the letter you made.*
At the end of a handwriting session, have children underline or highlight the "best *h*" they made.	Children can develop self-evaluation concerning the readability of their handwriting.

Notice the gradual release of the teacher's support as the children take on the new behavior.

> Demonstration
>   Sharing the task
>   Guided practice
>   Independent practice
>   Self-evaluation

This lesson could be taught across a week, or a bit longer, in the beginning. As children gain control, you might demonstrate and practice several letters that are similar in shape and movement, such as *h*, *m*, and *n*. Be sure to name the letters after forming them. Independent work could be part of the ABC/Word Study Center, or each child could practice for a few minutes before moving on to other independent activities. After the formation for a group of letters has been learned, fluent writing of two- and three-letter high-frequency words containing those letters can be practiced, along with manipulation of magnetic letters to form the words. Teachers find it useful for children to have a personal handwriting book, which can just be pieces of paper stapled together or a bound composition book with a letter (upper- and lowercase) on each page, that serves as a model. This book helps children save a body of work so they can see improvement.

Instruction Changes Over Time and Across Grade Levels

How does this instruction change over time and across grade levels? The answer to this question is dependent on the teacher's knowledge of what students need. If children in a given class have had little formal instruction in letter formation, we suggest following a routine similar to the one above, and as students gain more experience, instruction can be less frequent and more self-directed. Of course, you will use language appropriate for the level of your students, and older students will need less time because they have had more experience with print. Some may need a little more practice to "relearn" efficient movements and overcome habits. Whatever you decide, you will want to keep lessons very short, about five minutes, because you are planning many other important learning opportunities throughout the literacy block.

Observation is key. How are the children forming letters? Is the movement fluent, choppy, confused, or too slow? Is getting letters down on paper interfering with meaning-making? How much support do they need? If many of your students are not forming letters in a smooth, efficient way, or if letter learning is new to students, whole-class lessons, beginning with demonstration, make good sense. Small-group and individual teaching will provide additional support for the children who need it. If students have had a consistent program for handwriting instruction, and you are satisfied with the result, handwriting might receive occasional practice. Be cautious about assuming that all students have internalized directional movement patterns. Identify those children who need more help as you observe writers, and review the language and movement for letters.

Lessons for More Experienced Learners	
Grade	**Procedures**
1	• Assess the class by observing students in the process of writing. • Decide the type of instruction that is needed. • Whole-group instruction might follow procedures similar to those suggested for kindergarten. The children might progress more quickly, because print features are more familiar. • When students are reaching fluency in formation of a particular group of single letters, teaching for fluency in writing high-frequency words containing those letters can be undertaken and practiced. • Attention to individual needs might mean adjusting both expectations and the type and amount of support you provide.
2	• Assess the class by observing students in the process of writing. • Decide the type of instruction that is needed. • Whole-group instruction might be a more rapid presentation of the language and movement for letter formation. Several letters formed in the same way might be presented at a time (for example, *a*, *g*, and *d*). • At first, you might provide practice pages with the written language for directional movement for each letter in the set. You will want to discontinue this support as students become independent. • Whole-group lessons will probably become less necessary and practice more occasional until cursive writing is introduced. • If cursive writing is introduced, we suggest you adapt the process presented previously as an example for kindergarten, because the learning is new. • In teaching cursive writing, it is important to demonstrate and practice how to connect one letter to another when writing words. Students will learn that cursive writing is more fluent and faster. • Teach letters in groups that are formed in similar ways and provide practice exercises for connections (for example, *h* and *n*).

What Guidelines Should I Keep in Mind as I Teach for Fluent Handwriting?

Begin With Children's Names

Writing their own names is a highly motivating activity for children, and it is a good place to start when teaching them about the features of letters. Make a name card for each student. For the mini-lesson, select one child's name card. Show one side of the card with the child's name written clearly. Emphasize the tall letters and how the letters are placed right next to each other in an exact order. Show the other side of the card. First with your finger and then with a dry-erase marker, trace each letter using efficient movements. Show the other side of the card with the name in dotted print. Trace each letter and use words to describe the action. You may want to say something like, "Your name is always written the same way, and you can write the letters in your name." Children can then use magnetic letters to make their names, using the fully written name on the card as a model. They can then trace the dotted outlines of the letters on the other side of the card, first with a finger and then with a marker or crayon.

Use Specific and Consistent Language

Figure 21.1 shows verbal paths for the formation of letters. This very specific use of language helps children form letters, especially if they learn to "talk their way through" a letter by saying the directions themselves. To teach this skill, you might say something like, "I'm going to make an *h*. To make a lowercase *h*, you pull down, up, over, and down." Have children make the letter slowly as you demonstrate on the board, a chart, or a Magna Doodle, and have them say the name of the letter with you. Teach children to use the verbal path every time they are practicing handwriting the letter. After efficient movements are learned, it will not be necessary to say the words (Fountas & Pinnell, 2017).

Lowercase Letter Formation

a	pull back, around, up, and down	**n**	pull down, up, over, and down
b	pull down, up, around	**o**	pull back and around
c	pull back and around	**p**	pull down, up, and around
d	pull back, around, up, and down	**q**	pull back around, up, and down
e	pull across, back, and around	**r**	pull down, up, and over
f	pull back, down, and cross	**s**	pull back, in, around, and back
g	pull back, around, up, down, and back	**t**	pull down and cross
h	pull down, up, over, and down	**u**	pull down, over, up, and down
i	pull down, dot	**v**	down, up
j	pull down, curve back, dot	**w**	down, up, down, up
k	pull down, pull in, pull out	**x**	down, down
l	pull down	**y**	pull in and down
m	pull down, up, over, down, up, over, and down	**z**	across, in, across

Uppercase Letter Formation

A	pull down, pull down, across	**N**	pull down, up, in, and up
B	pull down, up, around and in, back, and around	**O**	pull back and around
C	pull back and around	**P**	pull down, up, and around
D	pull down, up, around	**Q**	pull back and around, and cross
E	pull back, down, across and across	**R**	pull down, up, around, in, and down
F	pull down, across, across	**S**	pull back, in, around, down, and back
G	pull back, around, across	**T**	pull down, across
H	pull down, pull down, across	**U**	pull down, over, up, and down
I	pull down	**V**	down, up
J	pull down, curve back	**W**	down, up, down, up
K	pull down, pull in, pull out	**X**	down, down
L	pull down, across	**Y**	pull in, pull in, and down
M	pull down, pull in, pull up, pull down	**Z**	across, pull in, across

FIGURE 21.1 Verbal paths

Provide Opportunities for Guided and Independent Practice

Children can practice one letter at a time. They may trace sandpaper letters, trace letters on laminated letter cards, write the letter in salt or sand in a flat tray or box, or write the letter on paper with a crayon or marker. They may also want to make "rainbow letters" (see Photo 21.2). Write a letter in pencil on a large piece of chart paper and place dots and arrows on it with black marker to direct how to make the letter. First, the teacher shows how to make the letter using the arrows. Then, each child, while saying the verbal path, traces the letter on the newsprint using a different-colored crayon. At the end of the day, you will have a large letter written in many different colors. One child can take it home—perhaps someone whose name contains the letter.

In Photo 21.1, you see an independent writing activity. In the first column, the child makes a word using magnetic letters. This is easy to do once the model has been placed in the middle column by the teacher. Then, the child traces the letters in the word several times with different-colored crayons. Finally, in the third column, the child writes the word, using a verbal path to make each letter. The directions at the bottom are for the purpose of helping the parents understand the directions. Teach this task through a mini-lesson, and children can practice letters during independent work time.

PHOTO 21.1 Independent handwriting activity

Ask Children to Notice the Specific Features of Letters

Use magnetic letters to help children notice specific features of letters, including:

- Letters with tall sticks (*h, d, l, k, b*)
- Letters with short sticks (*r, n, m, a, u, r, i*)
- Letters with tunnels (*m, n, u*)
- Letters with dots (*j, i*)
- Letters with tails (*p, q, g, j*)
- Letters with a slant (*k, x, w*)

Children need some time finding and sorting letters by feature to notice these distinctions, but when they do, it will help them immensely. They can then write letters in different categories. See Figure 21.2 for letters formed in similar ways.

Letters Made in Similar Ways

c o a d g q
b h t i j k l p
n r m u
v x w y
f s
e z

FIGURE 21.2 Letters made in similar ways

Use Unlined and Lined Paper

Often, teachers face a dilemma as to whether to use lined or unlined paper. When young children have difficulty perceiving the distinctive features of letters (what makes a letter different from every other letter), then the lines on a page may be a source of difficulty. Some children may find it difficult to separate the lines on the page from the lines that make up the letter. Also, the task of making the letter with its distinctive features is a difficult enough motor task for some young children. Requiring them, at the same time, to make the letter a certain size and "sit" on a line actually makes the task even more difficult.

PHOTO 21.2 Rainbow letter

When children are just beginning to make letters, use plain white paper and dark markers or pencils. Erasing is unproductive because some children will simply dig holes in the paper. Teach them to cross out, rather than erase, when they want to do something over. If you want to provide some guidance for children's use of the space on the page, consider folding the paper into three to six long boxes. Children can use the folds as a general guide, and the folds help them to organize print on the page. As they gain control, you can demonstrate and teach how to make letters and at the same time touch lines. It will not take a long time to teach children to write on lined paper, but most will need explicit teaching and some concentrated practice.

Use a Handwriting Book

Give each child a notebook or stapled set of papers to use as their handwriting book. Select an easy letter that most children know and can make. Use the verbal path as you write the letter on a whiteboard, chart paper, or a Magna Doodle. Then, show children how to write the letter in their handwriting book. Demonstrate it several times, and then say, "Now I'm going to choose the best *c* that I have made. I'm going to highlight it in yellow (or underline it in red)." Then, close the book.

Give the children a letter to practice in their own handwriting books—perhaps one row of letters. Guide them to use the verbal path and say the name of the letter. Then, have students choose their best letter. Help them understand why this letter is "best." This self-evaluation will gradually become routine as children learn to evaluate their own handwriting. These handwriting books can be used several times a week, because it takes only a few minutes for children to write a row of letters and pick their best.

Look for Improvement

The improvement you are looking for is in the efficiency of the process and the control exhibited by the writer. Both will lead to greater legibility and writing fluency. It will be worthwhile to take a few minutes to walk around and notice the movements that children are using as they write. Also, you can examine the products for increasing control.

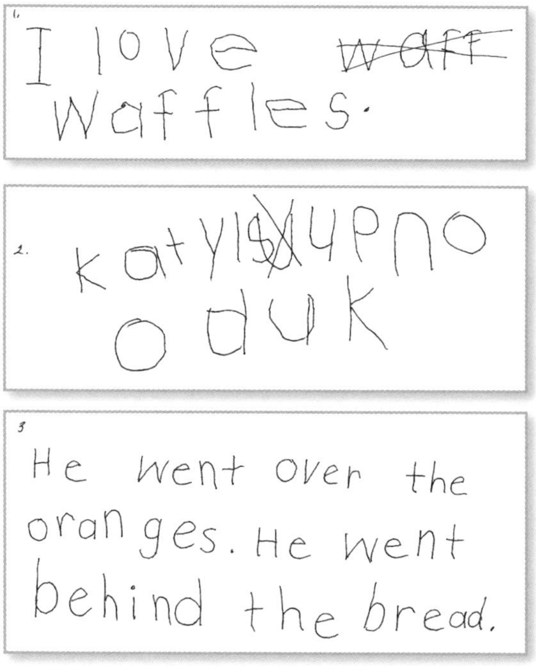

In Photo 21.3, you see three writing samples from Kyra. In Sample 1, she demonstrated good understanding of the distinctive features of letters, but her production was slow and a bit shaky. She took several strokes to make some of the letters, for example, *a* and *f*. It is almost as if she were "drawing" the letters. She showed that she knew that letters have to be together in a word, however, and her spacing was good.

In Sample 2, made about two weeks later, her spacing was not evident; however, she did self-correct the placement of the *u* over the *s*. She demonstrated some directional problems, and some letters were made with more strokes than necessary. About six weeks later (Sample 3), we can see considerable improvement in legibility, spacing, and the smooth production of letters. Most letters were made with efficient movement. In all three of the samples, Kyra was not necessarily practicing handwriting. In fact, she was writing about reading as part of a small-group lesson. But she was having handwriting instruction a couple of times a week for short periods. Her teacher had taught children to use a verbal path even during reading group instruction.

PHOTO 21.3 Changes in Kyra's writing

Photo 21.4 contains two writing samples from Ryan. In producing Sample 1, Ryan wrote quickly and fluently; some letters he made from bottom to top, others with a different motion. The problem here is that Ryan's print was not legible enough, and he was going so quickly that he ignored reversals, so his handwriting is hard to read. Within about five weeks, he was producing writing like that in Sample 2. He had not sacrificed fluency in writing but had incorporated more efficient movements, and the piece is much more legible. This more legible handwriting will make it easier for Ryan to proofread his work for spelling and punctuation.

At the beginning of first grade, Katie was already well underway as a writer. In the first sample in Photo 21.5, you see evidence that she could produce very accurate letters that clearly show the distinctive features. (She wrote this sentence to describe the results of a class survey.) Some of her letters, however, were produced with inconsistent motions, as if looking at a model and drawing them. Also, her control was a little shaky and she was still learning how to appropriately size letters and place them in relation to other letters within a word.

By January, as shown in Katie's list of "what to do to be a friend," her writing is much more mature. Her words are more clearly defined by space, and letters are consistent in size. More importantly, she has internalized efficient motions and gained a great deal of control. Her writing is clear and legible. It did not take a great deal of handwriting instruction to support Katie in this learning, but the help she received made her conscious of its importance. She is developing good habits that will help her write efficiently and legibly. As this becomes even more automatic, it will free her attention to composing the message.

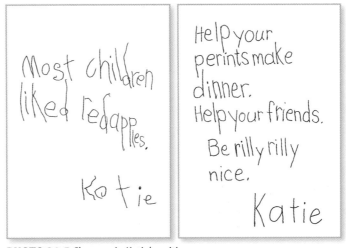

PHOTO 21.4 Changes in Ryan's writing

PHOTO 21.5 Changes in Katie's writing

Conclusion

Yes, we advocate specific teaching of handwriting in elementary classrooms. The ease and efficiency children can develop will free them to attend more to the goals you have for them as authors. Of course, you would never allow handwriting practice to consume hours of tedious copying over the year, taking the place of authentic literacy experiences. In fact, handwriting instruction takes only a few minutes a day or twice a week. Rather, instruction and practice must be designed based on student need with the goal of smooth, efficient handwriting.

We suggest the following:

- Provide brief lessons, perhaps twice a week, with very explicit demonstrations of the directionality of letter writing, at first using a simple, concise verbal path.
- Draw children's attention to efficient ways of forming letters and writing words across multiple contexts.
- Create opportunities for children to practice efficient directional movement for a few minutes daily.
- Link sounds to letters during the act of writing.
- Integrate letter formation with early letter learning. (Learning to write letters with fluent and consistent directional movement can help children learn the visual features of letters. Name the letter after you write it.)

You will find that investing in these brief, focused lessons has high payoff for helping young students attend to the features of print and develop ease in writing messages, informational pieces, and stories.

Suggestions for Professional Development

The following activities might be planned for one longer meeting or two shorter sessions with colleagues:

1. Ask each teacher to read this chapter before coming to the session. Ask the teachers to talk in pairs about the rationale for explicit lessons for teaching handwriting. How might such lessons benefit students? Find one or two quotes from the chapter that express the rationale. Next, explore several ways you might include handwriting instruction in your literacy block, and share your ideas and one of the quotes with the group.

2. Review the suggested language for teaching handwriting by demonstrating and engaging students in "a verbal path." Talk about why using a consistent method, language, and movement across classrooms is important. With a partner or in a small group, practice the movement you will use to accompany the language for each letter. Design/chart a handwriting lesson to include demonstration, guided practice, and independent practice during the week. Using the chart, share your ideas with the whole group.

3. Gather samples of students' writing by dictating two or three simple sentences. Provide a month of handwriting instruction and then dictate the same sentences. Analyze the "before and after" samples to plan future instruction.

SECTION SIX:
A LEARNING COMMUNITY:
Students, Teachers, Principals, and Families

▶ **Professional videos and downloadables** are available at Scholastic.com/RLResources

CHAPTER 22

Inquiry in the Classroom

Sherry Kinzel, Wendy Sheets, and Carla Steele

"Inquiry … is an active, lively classroom where children make choices and take responsibility for their learning. Inquiry is backed by research, and it promotes deep student engagement.**"**

—**Harvey "Smokey" Daniels**

As teachers, we open doors to learning and invite learners to enter, hoping to open their eyes to rich possibilities for learning and understanding in new ways. Therefore, we must create spaces that allow for the interrogation of ideas, for questioning in critical ways, and for understanding learning as something that is always in process. Patel (2015) writes, "We should see ourselves as stewards not of specific pieces of knowledge but rather of the productive and generative spaces that allow for finding knowledge" (p. 79). How might your pedagogical moves drive the instruction within your classroom, rather than allowing curriculum to drive it? How do you avoid being the classroom knowledge keeper, and instead invite your students to generate meaning from their own intellectually invigorating inquiry?

When students have opportunities to follow their own learning passions— their interests and questions—they engage much differently than when they are responding to an assigned task. Below, we look at instructional moves to engage learners in developing an inquiry stance—inquiry-based units of study and genre study appropriate for all grade levels.

Teaching for Understanding Through Inquiry-Based Units of Study

"Learners ask questions and search for information: they engage in inquiry… Our minds are never more active than when we are making discoveries—recognizing problems, formulating hypotheses, seeking data, analyzing and synthesizing information, posing tentative conclusions, and deciding on tentative actions. Inquiry is not an academic exercise; it's how we live our lives." Lyons and Pinnell (2001, p. 171).

Planning and implementing integrated units of study within a comprehensive literacy model is common practice for teachers Juakita Bowens and Amy Cox. They are skilled in facilitating teaching and learning opportunities that foster student engagement, support cross-curricular connections, and promote social construction of knowledge. As reflective practitioners, Amy and Juakita are committed to continuing their own learning in order to better support their students. Therefore, it was not unusual for them to accept a challenge that asked them to view their current practice from a different lens, a lens that brought into focus the powerful impact inquiry and an effective design model can have on teaching for understanding.

Setting the Stage for Inquiry

Wilhelm defines inquiry "…as the process of addressing problems expressed by guiding questions. Such big, underlying questions define and drive the activity of what cognitive scientists call 'communities of practice'" (2007, p. 10). He adds that "…inquiry-oriented classrooms cultivate motivation and engagement, deeper conceptual and strategic understanding, higher-level thinking, productive habits of mind, and positive attitudes toward future learning, no matter the subject area" (p. 16). It is about supporting students in learning how to learn.

PHOTO 22.1 Inquiry motivates and engages students.

Amy and Juakita were able to use their new learning and deeper understanding of the major tenets of inquiry-based teaching and learning to reflect on the effectiveness, strengths, and areas of need within their current practices. It also helped them determine if, and to what degree, their current practices were oriented to:

A results focus	vs.	A content or activities focus
uncovering the topic		covering the topic
deep, generative understanding		information transmission
strategic/critical thinking, problem solving, open-ended questioning		memorization, recall
teacher as co-collaborator, facilitator, reflective listener		teacher as lecturer, expert
student-directed inquiry, real-world application		teacher-led/directed
student as meaning-maker, decision-maker		student as receiver of information, follower
collaborative peer interaction, teamwork		limited interaction, individual work
assessment that is multi-faceted, authentic, formative, and summative		contrived, summative only

The observations and information gleaned from their analysis were reframed into questions for further investigation. How were students using what they were learning in other contexts? How might students become more engaged in decision-making and planning? Were the learning experiences offered to students geared toward hands-on learning, and in what ways? The interplay between the questions that surfaced and subsequent responses encouraged further inquiry, informed planning, and guided next steps—especially in how to facilitate the type of teaching and learning that an inquiry approach necessitates.

Planning for a Journey of Inquiry: Unit Design

Wiggins and McTighe suggest that "…what happens before the teacher gets in the classroom may be as or more important than the teaching that goes on inside the classroom" (2005, p. 341). Planning for intentional instruction, assessment, and learning is critical. While there are a variety of design models or frameworks to consider, Juakita and Amy followed the backward design approach detailed in *Understanding by Design* (2005).

What is "backward design," and how is it different from the process often used by educators? Wiggins and McTighe define backward design as an "…approach to designing a curriculum or unit that begins with the end in mind and designs toward that end" (2005, p. 338). Establishing, up front, what the results will be makes it possible to be more intentional and focused in teaching and selecting appropriate assessments that confirm these results are achieved. Teaching and learning are not left to chance or determined by a textbook. Teachers and students understand what is being taught and why.

One design model for planning inquiry-based units of study

Stages of Backward Design
From *Understanding for Design*, Wiggins & McTighe (2005, p. 18)

1. Identify desired results	2. Determine acceptable evidence	3. Plan learning experiences and instruction

Engaging in a Transformational Process

Juakita and Amy made the decision to start slowly with units of study that would be six to seven weeks in duration; however, they began their design process from different entry points. Amy chose to start with an existing second-grade topic, while Juakita took advantage of a challenge with which her second graders were grappling. What both approaches had in common was Amy and Juakita's commitment to engage students and themselves in inquiry—beginning with the end in mind—with the goal of teaching more deeply for deeper student understanding. The use of a balanced literacy framework, integration of curricular content areas, district/state standards, and backward design were also important considerations.

Responding to an Authentic Challenge

Juakita noticed her students had started to experience some challenges in behavior as they sought to forge friendships and settle conflicts. In order to address the issue, she believed it was an opportune time for the class to review, refine, and continue to acquire more effective ways to problem solve, settle disagreements, and work collaboratively. Being mindful of the power inherent in teachable moments, Juakita also decided to capitalize on this opportunity to engage her second-grade students in a powerful inquiry-based unit of study—one that empowered them to seek answers to guiding questions, establish enduring understandings, envision possibilities, and set goals for their own lives.

Design Plan Essential Question: *How have the actions of others changed our daily lives?*	Desired Results	• Develop a beginning understanding that the past influences the present. • Understand that personal actions can influence their futures. • Engage in goal setting. • Build awareness of the contributions each can make to their community and the world.
	Evidence	• Collaborative pre-assessment of current behavioral, social, and problem-solving challenges • Culminating Activity: Gallery Walk to showcase learning (oral presentations, murals, reports, book talks, writing in response to reading) • Progress Monitoring: reading and writing conferences, rubrics, observations, and anecdotal notes
	Learning Experiences and Instruction	• Responding to an Authentic Challenge • Slavery/Civil Rights • Famous Historical People • Current People of Influence

An abbreviated overview of the backward design plan that Juakita developed for her second-grade students.

Quality children's literature provided the foundation for the unit and gave it life. Well selected texts, as shown in Photo 22.2, provide students a mirror in which they can see themselves reflected—as well as a window in which they can view the lives and perspectives of others, and the world around them (Bishop, 1990).

Their journey began with carefully selected literature that Juakita shared during Interactive Read-Alouds. Her goal was to connect students with characters, situations, and experiences they could easily identify with as they sought understanding of and solutions for the challenges they were experiencing. She was also intentional in the order in which texts were shared to scaffold the new learning, understandings, and insights students would encounter.

PHOTO 22.2 Mentor texts connect students to characters and experiences they identify with.

PHOTO 22.3 Mentor texts that supported students' deeper understanding of more abstract concepts

Juakita chose to revisit *Enemy Pie* (Munson, 2000), a class favorite, to initiate a conversation about friendship, enemies, and the consequences of judgmental behavior. The topic of bullying and how bullying might be addressed were also discussed when students encountered Mean Jean from *The Recess Queen* (O'Neill, 2002). These texts afforded students opportunities to make connections to authentic experiences from their own lives and motivated them to become actively engaged in their learning.

The essential question—How have the actions of others changed our daily lives?—and those interjected by students and Juakita helped lay the foundation for enduring understandings that became common threads throughout the unit of study—understandings that addressed a number of cross-content standards and were easily reframed into questions that promoted further inquiry.

How might stories help us understand a central message, lesson, or moral? What can be learned from how characters in a story respond to major events or challenges? Questions such as these provided a natural bridge to issues raised in the text, *The Other Side* (Woodson, 2001). Students could now use what they knew and understood about personal accountability, responsible choices, empathy, and respect for others to begin to tackle more abstract topics—such as the issues that have and can create barriers among us.

The next series of mentor texts (see Photo 22.3) led the students and Juakita into further inquiry as they journeyed to make connections between how personal actions can impact others with a developing awareness and understanding of how the past influences the present. The lives, words, and actions of Harriet Tubman, Henry Brown, and Martin Luther King, Jr., not only provided a general overview, historical timeline, and perspective of slavery and civil rights, but the books also elicited student questioning and investigation. How is it possible to become an influential leader—make a difference—when one has been the recipient of unjust treatment oneself? In what ways are things better or worse than in the past? In what ways might we make a difference in our own lives and in others'? Questions such as these continued to move teaching and learning forward and afforded students opportunities to deepen their current understandings and grow new insights and learning. It also encouraged them to communicate their learning in innovative ways that could persuade others to engage in further inquiry as well (see Photo 22.4).

Thoroughly engaged in the inquiry process, students now wanted to learn about other influential people in history including Abraham Lincoln and George Washington. More recent and current individuals such as Amelia Earhart, LeBron James, and their teacher, Mrs. Bowens, were of interest. Every avenue of investigation encouraged students to further ponder the significance of their own actions and what contributions they might be able to offer. Mem Fox's *Whoever You Are* (2006) served as a reminder for students to celebrate both their similarities and differences—to exercise tolerance for one another—and, in so doing, make a significant contribution to humanity itself.

Throughout the unit of study, it is important to note that a second layer of inquiry was also underway. Juakita was actively teaching, demonstrating, and guiding her second graders in noticing and exploring the characteristics, structure, and features of the genre encountered during the many and varied reading and writing experiences afforded them. Coupled with the integration of curricular content areas across the elements of a balanced literacy framework, students were provided avenues to clarify, affirm, and grow new understandings that not only helped them achieve the overarching goals of the unit, but also supported their growth as literacy learners.

Reframing an Existing Unit of Study or Topic

Jeffrey Wilhelm, in consensus with other researchers, believes that "by recasting a curricular topic in terms of a guiding question, we set the stage for a model of teaching known as inquiry" (2007, p. 8). Such was the case for Amy when she decided to facilitate a unit of study focused on a topic often studied in second grade—habitats.

PHOTO 22.4 A student shares his knowledge at one of the reading/writing displays presented during the culminating Gallery Walk.

Design Plan	Desired Results	• An understanding of the reciprocal relationship that exists between an environment and the living things that inhabit it • A deeper understanding of the characteristics and importance of nonfiction reading and writing
Essential Question: • *How does the environment impact the way living things survive and thrive?* • *How do living things impact the environment they live in?*	Evidence	• K-W-L pre-assessment • Culminating Activity: iMovies of students' selected habitats in response to the essential questions and new/refined knowledge and understandings • Progress Monitoring: reading and writing conferences (individual/small group), observations, anecdotal notes, and rubrics
	Learning Experiences and Instruction	• Exploring the characteristics of non-fiction reading and writing • Whole-class investigation of an environment (desert) • Whole-class demonstration and mini-lessons for writing nonfiction texts • Small-group inquiry, reading, and writing of students' selected environments • iMovie presentations

An abbreviated design plan of Amy's science-based unit of study that encouraged inquiry across content areas using nonfiction reading and writing.

OWEN & MZEE
THE TRUE STORY OF A REMARKABLE FRIENDSHIP
GEORGE AND MARTHA
written and illustrated by
JAMES MARSHALL
THE RAIN CAME DOWN
David Shannon
SCHOLASTIC
WEATHER
SEYMOUR SIMON

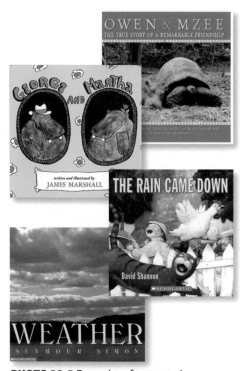

PHOTO 22.5 Examples of text sets Amy carefully selected to support students in noticing and understanding the characteristics and features inherent in nonfiction and fiction genres. These pairings also challenged students to question why an author might choose one genre over another to communicate his/her information, ideas, or feelings.

Amy set the stage for their journey by sharing a general overview of the unit plan, the essential questions, and the importance of the intended results. She explained they would be working collaboratively as a whole class and in small groups to uncover new knowledge and understandings, while becoming more adept at learning how to learn. She also emphasized that they would be encouraged to question, seek answers, and make connections from both a content perspective as well as readers and writers of nonfiction.

Since Amy's plan was to begin the unit with a whole-class investigation of deserts, she asked students to complete a K-W-L chart of what they already knew and had wonderings about. This initial information served as baseline data for Amy to further inform her instructional decision-making, monitor student growth over time, and ensure appropriate materials and resources were on hand to meet the varying strengths and needs of all her students. The same protocol followed when students formed small inquiry groups to learn about additional habitats.

Throughout the entire unit, Amy engaged students in whole-group investigation of some aspect of the desert environment and provided instruction in a particular aspect of reading and writing nonfiction texts prior to students breaking into small-group work. This process proved to be an effective way for Amy to check for evidence that she was teaching for transference and that what her students were learning had generative value.

Amy flooded the classroom with an abundance of carefully selected mentor texts and informational resources for both Reading and Writing Workshops. She was especially selective of the text sets shared and discussed during Interactive Read-Aloud (see Photo 22.5) as they were explicitly chosen to help students become more proficient in differentiating between realistic fiction and nonfiction—a confusion Amy noted in entries from her students' Reader's Notebooks. The accompanying anchor chart, crafted during shared writing, captured her students' growing understanding of the characteristics and features of these two genres; and was prominently displayed in the classroom as a visual mediator for further reference and discussion.

Fiction vs. Non-Fiction
"Story" Talk
(make believe)
•Read to ENJOY
•Must read in order
•Has a theme, moral, or lesson to learn
•Doesn't always give information directly (must infer/predict/draw conclusions)
•Not always based on real events
•Uses literary elements
-Plot: Beg., Middle, End
-Setting
-Characters
-Problem/Solution
-Talking Animals
-Make Believe Characters
"Fact" Talk
(true, real information)
•Read to LEARN
•Can read in any order
•Can inform the reader or teach "how to" do something
•The information is usually given straight to the reader
•Based on real information and events
•Uses text features:
-Table of Contents
-Index
-Glossary
-Real Photos
-Charts/Maps
-Labels
-Headings
Purpose: Entertain
Purpose: Inform

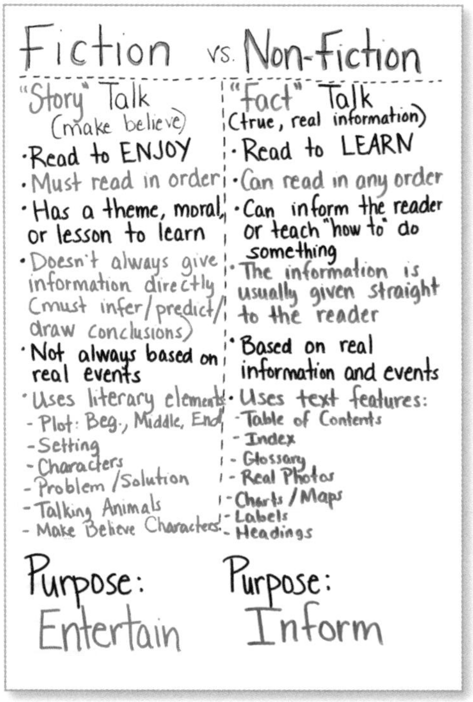

PHOTO 22.6 After reading fiction and nonfiction texts during Interactive Read-Aloud, Amy and her students discussed the differences between the two genres and created an anchor chart through shared writing. Students were encouraged to write a letter to Amy, in their Reader's Notebooks, about the nonfiction texts they were currently reading.

After reading and discussing books about the desert, students were asked to complete the last column on their K-W-L chart to share what they had learned. Time was then devoted for small groups to begin researching their designated environments from the collection of texts gathered specifically for their needs and in response to anticipated lines of inquiry. What students were learning was recorded on K-W-L charts, as well as questions/ investigations focused on the general characteristics of their habitat: its climate, why location is important, and the plants and

PHOTO 22.7 Collections of texts and big books were available to students for whole-class, small-group, and individual research and reading.

animals that inhabited this environment. What information is important to collect? How do I make this decision? How do I record the information I want to use? These types of guiding questions supported students in their investigations and in creating bulleted lists of facts to use for reference while crafting their individual nonfiction books.

Amy always started Writing Workshop with a mini-lesson that grew from and supported writers as they continued to work on their class book about deserts. She also challenged them to return to their own piece of writing and put their new learning into practice.

What type of structure will best present the information I want to convey to readers? How should I organize my information? Why is this important? In what way does the layout of my text make it easy or difficult for readers to follow? As students moved through the writing process, they began to show a deeper awareness and understanding of the reciprocity between reading and writing as the characteristics of nonfiction texts, investigated during Reading Workshop, were now coming into play in writing. Soon, bulleted lists were crafted into sentences, and sentences became paragraphs embedded within the growing pages of an informational book.

> Writers can move sentences around for better sequence and flow.
>
> ⓐTrees have deep roots so they can reach the water in the ground. The⓵re are not many plants in the desert since it is so dry⓶Cacti hold water in their stems⓷There are not many types of trees in the desert⓸Cacti are prickly.
>
> There are not many plants in the desert since it is dry. Cacti are prickly and hold water in their stems. There are not many trees in the desert. Trees have deep roots so that they can reach the water in the ground.

PHOTO 22.8 Anchor charts created during mini-lessons and displayed in the classroom serve as valuable student references.

> Writers can engage the reader with a strong lead sentence.
>
> Examples from Deserts:
>
> It is astonishing that any plants have learned to survive in desert conditions.
>
> * Opening sentence for Desert Plants section
>
> Hook your readers into each section!

> Writers can take out sentences that do not make sense or add to the meaning.
>
> The desert is very dryₓ ~~In the desert~~ becα̲u̲s̲e̲ it does not rain very much. There is a lot of sand in the desert.

Every decision these readers, writers, and researchers needed to make produced new questions to guide their inquiry and learning. Amy's keen awareness and sensitive observation of their strengths and needs continued to inform her instructional decision-making. Her responsiveness to the teaching and demonstration needed at the moment provided the scaffolding for students to realize the endless possibilities available to them as readers and writers. Transference of knowledge was evident in the culminating activities presented at the conclusion of the unit: sharing their published informational books and iMovies with parents and/or peers in other classrooms.

Taking an Inquiry Approach to Studying Genre

Teachers around the world are enthusiastically transitioning from traditional modes of delivering content information in the forms of lectures, readings with preplanned questions, and preplanned assignments or projects to using the elements of project-based learning to create opportunities for students to construct new understandings collaboratively and authentically. While project-based learning guides inquiry across the curriculum—in science, social studies, and math—taking an inquiry approach to the study of a genre is, surprisingly, a rather novel idea.

Consider the common tenets of project-based learning: significant content, 21st-century skills, in-depth inquiry, driving questions, a need to know, student voice and choice, public audience, and reflection and revision (http://www.educationworld.com/a_tech/key-elements-project-based-learning.shtml). Regardless of the current educational jargon, insightful educators know that these tenets are foundational to all authentic learning and, therefore, can encompass genre study as well.

In a true genre study, students take an inquiry stance. They seek to discover the characteristics of a particular literary genre organically by reading, thinking, and talking about the genre with other readers. Ultimately, each student should be able to create his or her own original, authentic writing piece using his or her new understandings of the genre.

PHOTO 22.9 Learning about and engaging in reading and writing experiences provide authentic and powerful opportunities for inquiry.

Think of the following as a recipe for genre study:

1. Collect examples of the genre.
2. Immerse readers in the genre.
3. Study the genre.
4. Define the genre.
5. Teach/reinforce elements of the genre.
6. Read and revise understandings.
7. Rehearse/plan original writing.
8. Draft an original piece of the genre.
9. Revise piece.
10. Publish the original piece of the genre.

PHOTO 22.10 Choosing an example of the genre

1. Collect examples of the genre.

Choose carefully the examples that you set before your learners; they will remember them. Consider the texts within a genre that you might share within various reading practices. The practices could include individual, small-group, and whole-class contexts.

For example, we highly recommend that you share picture book examples of the genre during Interactive Read-Alouds. Teachers often ask, "How many examples of a particular genre do readers need to experience in order to know a genre?" Of course, the answer really depends on the number of previous experiences students have had with the genre and the quality of those experiences. Many teachers underestimate the number and provide three to five examples. We recommend 10 to 12 rich, thoughtful whole-group experiences through Interactive Read-Alouds. You may not need this many examples for every genre.

You may also be able to provide additional experiences with a genre through small-group practices, like guided reading and book clubs. In these cases, you will need four to six copies of the same title for a small group of students to read. It isn't essential that students exploring a genre read that genre in guided reading, but it can offer an additional experience with that genre, which will only serve to strengthen student understandings. Of course, the book selected for guided reading must be high quality and at the instructional level for the group. Keep in mind that practices such as guided reading and book clubs are about teaching the reader, not the book.

In an inquiry approach to genre study, it is also valuable for a reader to be reading an example of the genre at his or her own independent reading level. Therefore, a teacher should consider the number and range of reading levels for a particular genre within his or her classroom library. If your classroom library is not currently organized by genre, you may not know how many examples or the range of reading levels you have per genre. Organizing your classroom library by genre is a great way to assess the resources you have and make genres more accessible to readers.

PHOTO 22.11 Reading examples of genre

PHOTO 22.12 Exploring examples of genre during guided reading

2. Immerse readers in the genre.

In order to take an inquiry stance in a genre study, a reader needs first to be immersed into the genre under investigation as much as possible. During an inquiry study, we highly recommend that students are reading their own examples at their independent reading levels. This reading can occur during an independent reading time within their instructional day or completed at home, after school. Reading their own examples of the genre gives them additional insights about the genre, opportunities to confirm their current understandings of the genre, and time to notice how another author uses the genre to craft his or her message.

Interactive Read-Alouds offer yet another way to immerse students in genre study. This whole-class teaching context allows readers to have a shared experience with multiple examples of a genre. Their collaborative conversations about the texts become the foundation for noticing characteristics of a genre and the variety of craft that multiple writers use to effectively convey their messages within a particular genre. Book Talks are brief "commercials" for texts by teachers and students, which ideally occur daily and encourage reading within a genre.

3. Study the genre.

Studying a genre requires a reader to experience a text and its message as a whole, and then examine it more closely to determine what is unique about that type of text. Many different texts may have similar traits, such as a narrative format or sequential organization, so the reader studying a genre must consider what traits are common and uncommon. Consider which traits consistently occur and which are frequently but not always occurring traits.

A great way to support students in this discovery is to share at least three texts using the Interactive Read-Aloud, and then to ask them what each of these three texts seem to have in common. Generate a list of what they are noticing. As you continue to engage readers in Interactive Read-Alouds and students read examples of the genre in their independent reading, return to the list of the class noticings. Add new ideas to the list and then confirm noticings. Cross out misconceptions. This is the essence of authentic learning—what students discover on their own and collectively as a class will impact their understanding of a genre far greater than handing them a list of characteristics. It also will set a precedent for how to study genres in the future.

4. Define the genre.

Defining the genre is a lot like creating a summary. Summarizing, though, is completely different from retelling. When readers summarize, they must weigh significance and then determine what is most important and what can be set aside for now. A class can create a definition for a genre as a whole group, or a class can break into small groups to generate possible definitions. Then each small group can share their definitions with the whole group prior to generating one class definition. Creating a class chart or individual documents that include the definition, a list of noticings, and a list of texts read in that genre is a powerful way to document the learning and make a wonderful resource for students (see Photo 22.13).

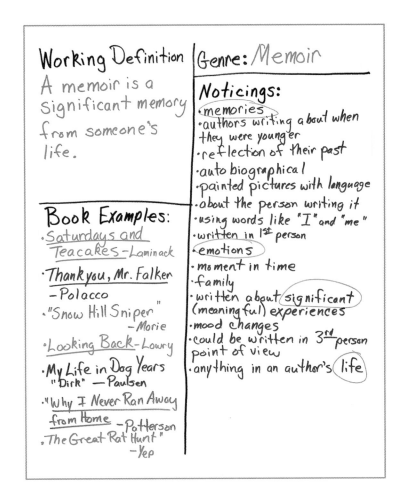

PHOTO 22.13 Charting what students are noticing about memoirs

5. Teach/reinforce elements of the genre.

At this point in the genre study, the teacher will consider what her students understand about the genre and decide what they need to know next. There may be elements of the genre that she believes need to be reinforced. She can provide a mini-lesson to develop that element, using previous texts from her Interactive Read-Alouds as mentor texts. Or, she may discover that there is a characteristic of the genre that students did not notice and decide to introduce that characteristic now that they have had more experience with the genre. Students should be given opportunities to notice any element that the teacher teaches or reinforces by applying that information to their own independent reading.

6. Read and revise understandings.

Continuing to read within a genre means that we have opportunities to continue to solidify our understandings. This also includes continuing to explore examples of the genre throughout the school year. Revisions can be made any time during a genre study and any time over the course of the school year. This sends the message that our learning is not stagnant, but constantly evolving.

7. Rehearse/plan original writing.

Now our students begin the process of creating their own authentic examples of the genre they studied. They go from thinking about the genre as a reader to thinking about the genre as a writer. As they make this transition, it is important that they do not lose sight of two critical concepts about writing: (1) Writers write because they have a message, and (2) Writers write for an audience. A writer who knows her message and knows her audience is thoughtful and passionate about her writing. She will also take the time and make the effort to select elements of craft that convey that message clearly. Again, we cannot stress enough: Start with the message.

Writers can scan through previous entries in their writer's notebooks for ideas or generate new entries. For example, if a writer is planning to write a memoir, she may select a previous entry about baking a chocolate cake with her grandmother and realize the message she wants to share is *it is important to take time to make positive memories*. She knows through her study of memoir that sharing the impact that a memory had on someone is a characteristic of memoir and a part of the class definition. Then, she begins planning her writing of this memoir. She may rehearse by verbally sharing the memory and its significance in her life with another writer. She could also use any previously learned writing strategies to plan her writing.

8. Draft an original piece of the genre.

Next, writers need to just get their thoughts down on paper. It's a draft. At this point, writers do not need to be concerned with grammar and spelling; these will be addressed during the editing portion of the writing process. Just let the ideas flow.

PHOTO 22.14 Teachers confer with writers to help them make their message clear and engaging.

9. Revise the piece.

During this writing phase, the teacher may provide a variety of mini-lessons based on writers' needs. Use the books previously read during Interactive Read-Alouds as mentor texts to illustrate the writing behavior you are addressing in the mini-lessons. These texts are already familiar, which allows writers to quickly focus on the writing behavior you are highlighting. It reduces your planning time since these mentor texts are readily available resources. During this time of revising, a teacher can confer with writers one-on-one or meet with a small group of writers who have a similar need in a guided writing lesson. Revising is work. It requires time, so it is important to dedicate several days to revision so that each writer's message is clear and powerful.

PHOTO 22.15 Revision is an exciting part of the writing process—especially when students are guided by mini-lessons that focus on the writing behaviors showcased in, investigated, and enjoyed in quality mentor texts.

10. Publish the original piece of the genre.

Publishing brings the learning process full circle for students. However, you should not feel as though every piece of writing that a child begins must be taken all the way to publishing. Often, a final draft, the writer's best effort, will suffice. However, when student writing is published, it should be shared and celebrated with an audience. This honors the work of writers and motivates them for future writing endeavors.

Learning With Your Students

Many teachers think that they must thoroughly research a genre before "teaching" their students this genre. They will spend valuable time skimming and scanning resources looking for the list of characteristics for a genre without realizing that a list alone doesn't create an understanding of the complexities on a genre. The list is actually the result of someone else's exploration and understanding of a genre. Therefore, teachers should give themselves permission to explore a genre alongside their students. Allow your students to view you as a learner. Let them see you ponder, question, and share revelations. Let genre study be an authentic learning experience for ALL learners in the classroom.

Conclusion

Students are eager to understand and to seek answers to the many questions and wonderings that fill their inquisitive minds. Designing and implementing inquiry-based units of study are exciting and powerful ways to draw upon their natural curiosity. Through authentic and purposeful literacy experiences embedded within a comprehensive literacy model, these units foster student engagement, support cross-curricular connections, and promote social construction of knowledge. They are initiated and driven by inquiry, problem-solving, critical thinking, and investigation as well as behaviors, understandings, and strategic actions students must know and be able to do. Teaching and learning are not focused on isolated, fragmented items of information but are guided by a process that naturally connects and integrates. It is through inquiry-based units of study that students can apply what they know, and learn in ways that support and encourage transference of knowledge.

Suggestions for Professional Development

1. Meet with your grade-level team and review one unit of study currently being facilitated in your classrooms using the following or similar criteria. Remember to view from an inquiry stance. Determine strengths and areas where improvements or refinements are needed.

A tool to review a unit of study from an inquiry lens				
To What Degree Is the Unit of Study Focused on...	**Or**	**To What Degree Is It...**	**Strengths**	**Ideas for Improvement from an Inquiry Stance**
Intended student learning; the end in mind (backward design)		Activities-based		
Student-directed inquiry; real-life application		Teacher-led or directed; contrived		
Uncovering the topic at a deeper level		Coverage of the topic at the surface level		
Integration and connections across content areas and across elements of a balanced literacy framework		Fragmented bits of information		
State and district standards, curriculum guides, maps to guide and support inquiry		State and district standards, curriculum guides, maps used as a checklist, in isolation		
Transference; generative value		Transfer of information		
Strategic, critical thinking; problem-solving		Memorization and recall		
Teacher and students as co-collaborators; decision-makers		Teacher as leader, the expert; students as followers, receivers of information		
Instructional decision-making through varied, authentic, and formative assessment practices		Assessment that is contrived and summative in nature		

Adapted from *The Curious Classroom* (Daniels, 2017, p. xxii) and *Understanding by Design* (Wiggings & McTighe, 2005, pp. 1–3, 5–7).

- What did you notice, and what are the implications for teaching, student learning, resources/materials, and further or additional unit development?

- Together, as a team, investigate or engage in a refresher of the backward design process, choose a template, and create a plan for the unit of study you reviewed.

- Introduce and facilitate this newly developed inquiry-based unit of study in your classrooms. Come together to discuss successes and challenges throughout its duration.

- Debrief at the conclusion of the unit. What did you notice that was similar or different from past units you facilitated? In what ways did a focus on inquiry-based teaching and learning shape the experience? What evidence do you have that what students were learning had generative value? What evidence do you have that you were teaching for transference? What are the implications for your teaching and learning and further refinement/development of inquiry-based units of study?

  - Continue the review, analysis, and planning of other existing units of study and/or plan a new one that grows from a classroom need or question.

2. Work with a group of colleagues to engage in your own genre study. Select a genre and follow the steps as outlined in this chapter. Create a chart to share what you are noticing through the examples, and create an original definition based on your noticings.

3. Meet with colleagues to discuss planning genre studies across the year. Decide which genres will be most productive for your students to study. Then begin making a list of titles of the genres that you want your readers to experience during the study.

CHAPTER 23

Creating School-to-Home Bridges Through Reading and Writing

John McCarrier and Gay Su Pinnell

> "A home with books as an integral part of the way of life encourages children to read for pleasure and encourages discussion among family members about what they have read, thereby providing children with information, vocabulary, imaginative richness, wide horizons, and skills for discovery and play."
>
> **—Mariah Evans, Jonathan Kelley, and Joanna Sikora**

One of the most effective ways to motivate young children to read and write is for them to see adults reading and writing. Ideally, every day, young children should enjoy being read multiple stories at school by their teachers and also at home with their family members, and they should see these adult readers engaged in their own reading as well.

The latter activity is especially valuable because hearing texts read aloud expands children's knowledge of the structure of written language. They also learn how stories and other texts are organized; the texts themselves become models for the young writer. Children see adults writing less often, except for the routine lists and forms that accompany daily life. Adults seldom share the writing process with children at home, and even at school, teachers are more willing to share the writing of authors of children's literature than they are their own written products. Yet, a powerful way to help young children become writers is to share our own writing with them and invite them into the process.

We in Literacy Collaborative (www.lcosu.org) at The Ohio State University kept this goal in mind as we developed KEEP BOOKS®, sets of small books designed to support readers from PreK to mid-grade 2. From children's first experiences at school, we wanted them to become engaged, *voluntary* readers who gain information from reading, collect books, find themselves in the texts they read, and experience the real joy of reading. To be readers and writers, children must do the following:

- Know the purpose of reading and writing
- Read with understanding and write to communicate
- Use reading and writing as tools for learning

The research is clear—the more children read, the better they get at reading (Anderson, Wilson, and Fielding, 1998). It is important for children to read successfully every day; it is just as important for them to read at home. All of this reading must be successful, interesting, enjoyable, and full of opportunities to learn more. Of course, most children cannot read when they enter kindergarten, and some are just beginning to read as they enter first grade; but with support and help, they quickly learn to read and enjoy very simple stories that usher them into the world of reading.

Since 1995, we have distributed more than 70 million KEEP BOOKS to schools, enabling millions of children to build home collections of books that they can read and read again. We have found that KEEP BOOKS raise children's interest and create greater confidence in reading (Gibson & Scharer, 2001). (For more information about KEEP BOOKS, visit www.keepbooks.org or see the appendix.) In this chapter, we describe a new way of using KEEP BOOKS, one that reveals to young children the process of becoming an author of a *real book*. Children develop knowledge of both the writing process and the structure of texts as they discuss the books with the authors and, what's more, try their hand at writing their own books. We explain the concept of KEEP BOOKS and then describe how one KEEP BOOK author invited children to become writers. Writing and sharing your own books is a process that you can use effectively in your own classroom; we guarantee that children will be delighted with it.

The Concept of KEEP BOOKS

We called our little books KEEP BOOKS because they are designed for children to read at school and then take home to keep. These 4¼-by-5½-inch books focus on everyday events that are familiar to children—such as eating pizza or catching a bug! Through experiences with KEEP BOOKS, children learn concepts such as these:

- You can get information from pictures, but you *read* the print. That's where the message is.
- Letters and sounds can help you figure out words.
- It helps to think about what would make sense.
- If you get stuck, it helps to start over and think what would sound right (and look right with the letters in the word).
- Punctuation helps you read better.

Seemingly simple ideas such as the ones above are only a part of the enormous amount of information that a young child has to acquire and coordinate in learning to read. During all of this learning, it's very important that the reading be fun and easy for the child. Without these qualities, learning will not be effective.

The Purposes of KEEP BOOKS

KEEP BOOKS serve a number of purposes, including the following:

- They provide a great deal of easy reading material, so children get lots of practice.
- They include many high-frequency words that children read again and again, so they build up word knowledge.
- They provide opportunities for children to notice how words "work" and learn phonics skills.
- They make it possible for children to read on their own, rather than always depending on adults.
- They motivate children to write.
- They build a ready store of books at home that children can access any time.
- They help children learn to store, care for, and retrieve books.
- They help children build confidence in themselves as readers.

KEEP BOOKS are not specifically designed for formal reading instruction. It is important to understand that a KEEP BOOK is a *different kind of book*. Children can write their names in these books, color the pictures, and keep them at home—this is different from how they should treat other books. KEEP BOOKS do not take the place of children's literature, which should be included in every classroom library. They do not replace the books that teachers read aloud to children or the leveled book collection that teachers use for small-group reading instruction. Instead, KEEP BOOKS are "extra" reading that begins in the classroom and moves to the home and community.

The Design of KEEP BOOKS

KEEP BOOKS are carefully designed to support readers as they progress in their ability to process texts. The very simplest KEEP BOOKS have characteristics such as these (see Photo 23.1):

- One or two lines of text
- Very easy high-frequency words
- Simple concepts
- Repeating patterns

Even the youngest readers, once they have heard the book or read it in a shared way, can process such simple texts independently. And, it is very good for them to read these texts over and over with family members. We would like for kindergarten and first-grade children to read a large number of these simple books while building knowledge of early understandings such as left-to-right directionality and word-by-word matching. As readers grow more sophisticated, they can progress to KEEP BOOKS such as the following (Photo 23.2).

PHOTO 23.1 *Trucks* (top) and *Look at Me!* (bottom)

PHOTO 23.2 *My Backpack* (left) and *Home Sick* (right)

As you can see, these texts are not so patterned; however, the language is natural and the topics are familiar. Also, there are easy high-frequency words, and readers are required to process simple dialogue. Even more challenging are KEEP BOOKS that present stories, such as the example below (Photo 23.3).

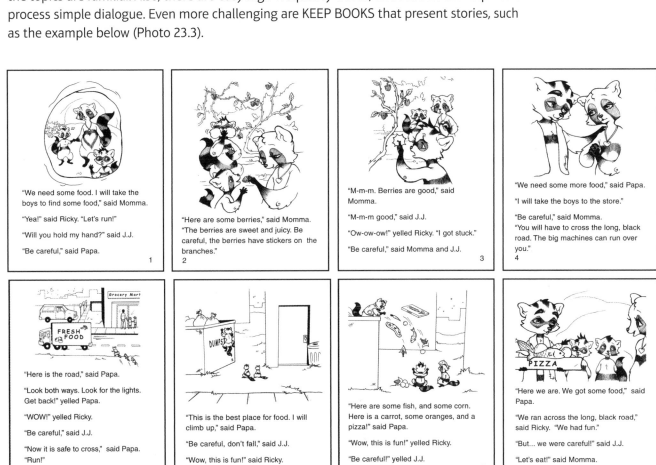

PHOTO 23.3 *Be Careful!*

These texts have the following features:

- Variety of dialogue
- Many lines of text
- "Pre-paragraphing" through spaces between lines
- A full range of punctuation
- More complex stories

At the most sophisticated level of KEEP BOOKS, you will find simple chapter books and fiction and nonfiction pairs (see Photo 23.4). These fact and fiction chapter books help children learn the characteristics of genre as well as conventions such as headings, graphics with additional information, and multiple paragraphs. They present the reader with extended dialogue, words in italics, complex sentences, and a variety of formats. If you examine the structure of KEEP BOOKS from the first very easy texts to the highest level (about mid-second-grade level), you can observe a gradual increase in complexity. Each level demands more of young readers, and children can gain an implicit knowledge not only of words, but also of the ways texts are organized. And, this knowledge can support them as writers.

Long ago, some people began to feed cats so that they would catch mice and other small animals that people did not want to have around their homes and farms.

Cats became working hunters!

Today, many farmers still keep cats in their barns to catch the mice.

3

Cats as Pets

After many years, people were comfortable having cats around and liked them so much that cats became pets.

After cats became pets, many cat owners did not want them to hunt little animals.

Today, many cats live in houses and apartments. They are good companions for their cat owners.

Did You Know?

- Cats spend 70 percent of their day sleeping or dozing off.
- A "cat nap" is said to describe a short nap.

PHOTO 23.4 Nonfiction *Cats Are Hunters* (top) and its fiction pair, *Mugs Indoors and Outdoors*

When Mugs saw the dog next door, everything twitched.

He hissed and yowled in a scary way. But Mugs was an indoor cat, so he couldn't go outdoors to hunt.

When Ann went outdoors, Mugs sometimes tried to go too. He made his body very slithery and tried to get out of the door.

But Ann always said, "No, Mugs, going outside is *not allowed*!"

When Ray went outdoors, Mugs sometimes tried to go, too. He made his body very thin and crept around the door.

But Ray always said, "No, Mugs, going outside is *not allowed*!"

5

So Mugs the indoor cat ate his kitty nibbles.

He sat in his red velvet chair by the window.

He watched squirrels, birds, and the big dog next door.

He hissed and yowled in a scary way.

Then Mugs the indoor cat went to sleep in the red velvet chair by the window.

6

PHOTO 23.5 Teaching a small group with a BIG KEEP BOOK

Of course, KEEP BOOKS are only a small part of a comprehensive literacy program that includes Interactive Read-Aloud, independent reading and writing, guided reading, and phonics and word study. In these classrooms, children are experiencing many texts each day, including those that the teacher reads to them as well as those they read for themselves. KEEP BOOKS provide clear examples, and if they are kept and shared and home with families, they add enormously to the school experience.

PHOTO 23.6 Children reading their own copy of the KEEP BOOK

The Literacy Collaborative has created several enlarged versions of KEEP BOOKS that correspond to many of the small versions. A BIG KEEP BOOK is 8½ by 11 inches, and its print has been redesigned so it is easy for children to see. These enlarged books are helpful in introducing books through shared reading. Then, children read the little books for themselves. My Own KEEP BOOKS, 8½-by-5½-inch blank books, were designed to encourage young authors to write their own stories. These tempting blank books led to an idea for engaging children in an author-to-author dialogue in the process of becoming authors themselves.

Author-to-Author—The KEEP BOOK Way

It is important for young children to understand the following:

- Adult writers follow the same process as beginners.

- Writing from personal experience is powerful.

- Perfection is not expected in writing, especially in a first draft.

- Other texts can be a good source of ideas for writing.

- The books they read in their classroom, as well as the books they take home, can be helpful as they do their own writing.

- Everyone can write an eight-page book and illustrate it.

Introducing the Mentor Texts

KEEP BOOKS were designed to be introduced at school (or in any other context that supports children's early literacy) and then to travel home with children. Teachers typically

- read the book to the child several times, inviting the child to "join in" as the story becomes familiar.

- read the book in a shared way (in unison, with the adult pointing to the words).

- encourage the child to read the book independently.

John uses a more personal approach. He begins by gathering the children on the carpet and showing them a mysterious box. He explains, "I am a writer visiting your school. I asked your teacher if she had any writers in her class that I could talk with. She said that you were all writers. Is that true? Oh, good—I love to talk with other writers about the stories that they are writing."

Then he asks the children to talk about their own writing. He asks questions about some of the pieces of interactive writing that are on the walls of the classroom and about individual pieces that are displayed. The children often talk about the writing that they keep in their writing folders and proudly show it to him. John then opens the box and shows the children a stack of KEEP BOOKS that he, his wife, Andrea McCarrier, and their daughter have written—16 books altogether. When talking with older children, John points out that writers write different things for different audiences. He illustrates this point by showing them books and articles that he and his wife have written for older children and adults. Students immediately become interested in knowing more about John as a writer. You, as their teacher, can use the same strategy—you can write your own KEEP BOOKS and make the same claim. You can read the children a letter to the editor that you

Sharing the Writing Process With Children

1. Introduce the book, showing the cover and indicating that you wrote it.

2. Read the book to the children.

3. Give each child a copy of the book and invite them to read it in a shared way.

4. Invite them to talk about the book by asking, for example, "What did this book make you think about?"

5. Tell why you wrote the book (personal experiences, something interesting).

6. Point out some of the decisions you made as a writer (as appropriate to the age group).

7. Ask children what they noticed about the writing.

are drafting or an article you contributed to your church newsletter. Your students will be fascinated to hear about all of the writing that you do.

Description of the Writing Process

John tells the children that the steps he and other adult writers go through in writing books are the same steps that they are learning right now. Children will be using the writing skills they are learning in school for their entire lives, even when they are grandparents—like him! He asks, "What's the first thing that you do when you sit down to write?" Children always say, "think." John responds, "That's just what I do!" Then he tells them that he does the following:

- Writes about things he really knows about
- Thinks of the people who might read what he writes
- Asks other writers to talk with him about what he has written
- Rereads his writing and changes it

Next, it is time to get specific about texts. John introduces several books, or mentor texts, to the class. The first one shows children, in concrete and simple terms, how a writer proceeds to produce a book.

Using Mentor Texts

Mentor texts can be a powerful influence on young writers, especially if teachers use them intentionally to foster writing abilities. John has selected four KEEP BOOKS as mentor texts that he uses with children in kindergarten and first grade. He has enlarged them to 8½ by 11 inches so the children can see the pictures and words as John and the children read them together.

MENTOR TEXT—*MY BROTHER'S MOTORCYCLE*

Of all the KEEP BOOKS John has written, *My Brother's Motorcycle* is his favorite because it

- captures the children's interest with a topic they like (motorcycles).
- leads to a discussion of a more important topic, sharing by members of a family.
- is told from a child's point of view.
- shows that a complete story with a beginning, a middle, and an end can be told in eight pages (see Photo 23.7).

John introduces the book by saying, "This book is called *My Brother's Motorcycle*. I wrote this book because I wanted to write a book about members of a family doing things together. I was a big brother and I had a motorcycle, so I decided to write about something I knew, an older brother with a motorcycle who was nice to his younger brother."

He then gets children talking about their families by asking, "How many of you have big brothers or sisters? How many of you are big brothers or big sisters?" This always leads to the students talking about their families and also volunteering that various family members and their friends own motorcycles, snowmobiles, all-terrain vehicles, dirt bikes, and so on. After reading the book, the class talks about their reactions to it: what they noticed about the writing, what they thought about the ending, how it made them feel. One child said the

My brother has a shiny motorcycle. It is red, black, and shiny silver.

1

He drives it to work every day. It makes a loud noise.

2

He keeps it under a cover every night. I help him put on the cover.

3

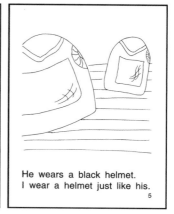

He washes it every Saturday. I help him shine the silver.

4

He wears a black helmet. I wear a helmet just like his.

5

Sometimes he lets me ride behind him.

6

When I see my friends, I wave to them.

7

My big brother is cool. All my friends wish they had a big brother just like mine.

8

PHOTO 23.7 *My Brother's Motorcycle*

ending made him feel jealous because his older brother was not like the one in the book. A second-grade girl at a school in Minnesota declared, "I have an older sister. She has a snowmobile. I think I'll write a story titled 'My Sister's Snowmobile.'"

Then John goes back into his box and takes out a stack of the blank My Own KEEP BOOKS described earlier. "I have all these blank books. What should I do with them?" Some children suggest that John use the blank books to write more stories, and when that suggestion arises, he says that he doesn't have time and points out that there are a lot of books. The children then decide that they can use the books to write KEEP BOOKS themselves. "You could give them to us! We can write our own KEEP BOOKS." John responds skeptically, "Are you sure?" "Yes!" the children reply. "We write all the time!" Finally, John gives everyone a blank book. But they do not begin to write just yet, because John says, "If you are going to write a book, you need to do a lot of thinking first. Let's look back at *My Brother's Motorcycle*."

John goes back through the mentor text, pointing out that it's really important to write about something you know. So, the children need to think hard about what they like, what's happening that they enjoy, and what they know about. He also points out that the pictures and words match and that he tried hard to make the ending interesting.

He finishes the mini-lesson by showing children a few examples of My Own KEEP BOOKS that other students have written, emphasizing that those children used their very best handwriting and spelling but that these books do not have to be perfect. He also asks the children to whom they are going to read their books when they are finished writing them. If the children mention only their teacher, then John asks them if they will be reading to many people—family members and friends. In this way, he helps them think about an expanded audience for their written pieces.

Works in Progress

Another approach John uses is to talk with students about a work in progress to illustrate the writing process.

KITCHEN BALLOON VOLLEYBALL

John introduces a story he wrote titled *Kitchen Balloon Volleyball* to demonstrate the craft of carefully choosing words and phrases to help readers create pictures in their minds as they read. He shows students a large photograph of two of his grandsons hitting balloons over a kitchen table to him. He explains that the photo was taken at a birthday party for the boys' grandmother. He asks students to listen carefully to the second sentence of the story to see if it helps them get a picture in their minds of the setting of the story. The sentence is: "The table was covered with dirty dishes, torn wrapping paper, and colored balloons." He asks what they can infer about the party from each phrase in the sentence and asks if he needs to add more details to help his readers form a picture in their minds. The students generally suggest that the sentence doesn't need anything added to it.

Then, he asked them about another sentence in the story that he is still working on. He missed one of the balloons that the boys hit to his side of the table but can't decide how to describe what happened next. Should he write that the balloon:

- hit the floor?
- fell to the floor?
- floated to the floor?
- floated to the floor like a piece of paper?

The students usually prefer "floated to the floor" because the feel of the sentence should focus on the action the balloon took to get to the floor rather than its final landing. They also feel that the word "floated" is more accurate than "fell," but they say that adding the comparison to a piece of paper is unnecessary and possibly confusing since, to them, a piece of paper flutters rather than floats as it falls.

CLICKETY-CLACK AND OUR FAVORITE SNOWMAN

John reads his enlarged versions of *Clickety-Clack* and *Our Favorite Snowman*, KEEP BOOKS written by his wife and daughter, respectively, and talks about them as models that are helping him to write another book (see Photos 23.8 and 23.9).

John shows the children a draft of the new book that he has written. He asks the children if they think he is finished with the story. They always say, "No!" Then he shows them two more drafts, and they discuss the additions, changes, and improvements on each draft. He emphasizes that being a writer is about making decisions, and among the decisions he talks about are the following:

"Here comes the train!" yelled Meggie Mack.
See those wheels roll down the track,
Four on this side, **four** on that.
Watch those wheels roll down the track.

1

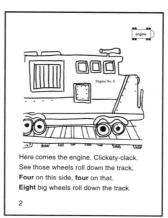

Here comes the engine. Clickety-clack.
See those wheels roll down the track,
Four on this side, **four** on that.
Eight big wheels roll down the track.

2

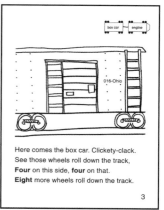

Here comes the box car. Clickety-clack.
See those wheels roll down the track,
Four on this side, **four** on that.
Eight more wheels roll down the track.

3

Here comes the tank car. Clickety-clack.
See those wheels roll down the track,
Four on this side, **four** on that.
Eight more wheels roll down the track.

4

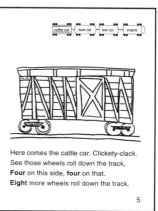

Here comes the cattle car. Clickety-clack.
See those wheels roll down the track,
Four on this side, **four** on that.
Eight more wheels roll down the track.

5

Here comes the coal car. Clickety-clack.
See those wheels roll down the track,
Four on this side, **four** on that.
Eight more wheels roll down the track.

6

Here comes the caboose. Clickety-clack.
See those wheels roll down the track,
Four on this side, **four** on that.
Eight more wheels roll down the track.

7

"How many wheels?" yelled Meggie Mack.
How many wheels rolled down the track?
Four on this side, **four** on that.
How many wheels rolled down the track?

$$8 + 8 + 8 + 8 + 8 + 8 = \underline{\hspace{2cm}}$$
$$8 \times 6 = \underline{\hspace{2cm}}$$

8

PHOTO 23.8 *Clickety-Clack*

- Making the book eight pages long
- Having four lines on each page
- Having a kind of rhythm or "beat" to the book
- Using simple words such as "big" and "plain" with hard consonant sounds to maintain the "beat"
- Using a repeating phrase, such as "clickety-clack"
- Using natural language with unconventional spelling for the repeated phrase "whadda ya know"

We made a snowman.

1

We found a scarf to put around his neck. Don't tell Mom we used her favorite scarf.

2

We found a hat to put on his head. Don't tell Dad we used his favorite hat.

4

We found a pipe to put in his mouth. Don't tell Grandpa we used his favorite pipe.

6

Doesn't he look nice? He is our favorite snowman!

8

PHOTO 23.9 *Our Favorite Snowman*

- Having a beginning, a middle, and an end

- Having a transition into the end on the next-to-last page

- Tying the end of the story back to the beginning by repeating the phrase "pile of snow"

Then, he shows the children the final story and reads it to them. He discusses some of the decisions that he made while writing it and also talks about the title, "The Snowman Rap." Below are pages 1, 2, 7, and 8 from the story, which illustrate these decisions. Pages 2 through 6 repeat the pattern of page 2 with different locations in the house and articles of clothing for the snowman.

> We built a big snowman, but I don't know.
> He looks too plain, just a pile of snow.
> He needs decoration, some style and flair.
> Let's look around the house and see what's there. (p. 1)

> We looked on the coat rack, and whadda ya know
> We found a fur hat. Now where should it go?
> On the top of his head. It sure looks fine.
> Let's keep on looking to see what we find. (p. 2)

> We looked in the hallway, and whadda ya know
> We found some old boots. Now where should they go?
> He doesn't have feet. What should we do?
> He looks pretty handsome. I guess that we're through. (p. 7)

> Our snowman is finished, and whadda ya know
> He looks really good, not a pile of snow.
> He looks warm and cozy in his borrowed clothes.
> He's all dressed up from his head to his toes. (p. 8)

Children's Writing

In this section we show some of the products that the author-to-author dialogue has inspired during many of John's writing workshop sessions with children. First, let's look at Aaron's book, *My Dad's Truck* (see Photo 23.10). Notice that Aaron stays on the topic of his dad's truck, describing important characteristics of it.

Here is another good example from John's "author-to-author" talk with children— Haley's story called *The Fat Dog* (Photo 23.11).

This text shows that Haley had internalized the idea of repeating patterns; yet, she includes a greater variety of sentences. Her informational book stays on the topic of the dog while providing a different piece of information on every page. She has numbered the pages, and several subtle characteristics indicate that she has learned a great deal from her experience with reading texts. For example, she begins page 1 calling her character "the fat dog," but she then uses a pronoun to refer to the dog on the rest of the pages. She begins her sentence on page 8 with the word *and*, creating a more literary feeling, and she has a conceptually satisfying ending.

PHOTO 23.10 *My Dad's Truck*

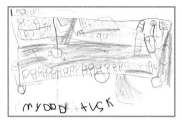  

My Dad's Truck	My dad's truck is red.	My dad's truck is red.

My dad's truck is from Russ N.	My dad's truck has big wheels.

It has a loud horn.	It has walkie talkies.	It has a bed.

PHOTO 23.11 *The Fat Dog*

The fat dog likes to lick you.	He likes to play.	He likes to bark.

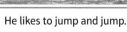

He likes to jump and jump.	He likes to bite.

He likes to jump in the snow.	He likes to be the king.	And he likes to be mine.

We are not implying that this is the only kind of writing we want Haley to do, nor will her writing continue only in this vein. She will be exposed to a wide range of texts during her first-grade year and will use many of them as models, thus internalizing a variety of ways for organizing her writing. Right now, she is learning how to produce an extended piece of text on a single topic.

Photo 23.12 shows Jacob's exciting account of *The Race*, which is dedicated to "My Mom."

PHOTO 23.12 Jacob's story, *The Race*

He's going.　　　　　　He's about to win.　　　　　　Go! Go! Go!

He's almost to the finish.　　　　　　Yeah! Yeah! Yeah!

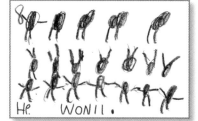

His car is red.　　　　　　It is the fastest.　　　　　　He won!

We love the way Jacob describes the action in an "it's happening now" kind of voice. It is obvious that all of these young children are making progress in the conventions of written text, for example:

- Using letter-sound relationships to spell words
- Using high-frequency words that they know well
- Using punctuation, such as ending marks
- Using parts of words they know to spell other words
- Beginning to use capitalization
- Writing from left to right
- Differentiating between text and pictures
- Numbering pages

Conclusion

These stories represent essential steps in beginning writing; but even more importantly, they allow children to learn some fundamental things that writers do, such as the following:

- Writing about things they know and/or are interested in
- Staying on a topic across a piece of writing
- Putting different and new information on each page (or in each section) of a text
- Creating a beginning, a series of events or categories of information, and an ending
- Making writing interesting by varying language

These young children are only beginning the long journey to becoming accomplished writers, but already, they show some important understandings. For them, the process is whole; they compose and think while engaging everything they know about conventions. They are supported by access to texts that are highly supportive, by talk, and by dialogue with other writers. John's experience with hundreds of young writers reveals the power of sharing the writing process. Every teacher can write simple texts and use the computer and/or individual artistry to "publish" them for the children in the class, thus providing a powerful model that can give children access to the joy of being an author.

Suggestions for Professional Development

1. Have teachers pair up and then tell a story to each other that they want to write. Then, have time for them to draft their story, share it with a colleague, revise, and publish it using a My Own KEEP BOOK. Ask individuals to share their stories and also their thoughts about the writing process while working. Then, have each teacher share her story and the process she went through to write her story with her students as part of a mini-lesson on the writing process. Share student responses to the lesson at a future meeting.

2. Help your colleagues find their voices as writers through a 10-minute write. First, read aloud one of the following books or start with one of the activities below. Then, model by telling and/or writing your own story. Finally, have teachers write their own personal narratives.

   - Introduce *Wilfrid Gordon McDonald Partridge* by Mem Fox with a memory basket and jot a list of ideas for additional items to include. Tell why.
   - Using *The Memory String* by Eve Bunting, create a list of big topics, such as vacations and families. Brainstorm many small topics that might trigger a memory. What buttons (memories) might you put on a string? Why?
   - Write about a photo that is important to you. What story might come out of your relationship with the person in that photo? Record the details of your life for the last 24 hours. Then, jot down some questions about yourself and your world. Think about which detail carries a story and write about it. Share your stories and then discuss these questions: What was involved in this process that led you to write? What are the implications for writing instruction?

CHAPTER 24

Coaching and Professional Learning: The Role of Reflection

Marsha Levering

> "Professional development is not about workshops and courses; rather, it is at its heart the development and habits of learning that are far more likely to be powerful if they present themselves day after day."
>
> **—Michael Fullan**

In education, we keep bumping into the term "reflection." We hear it, see it in numerous educational articles and books, and regularly reference it in written goals and evaluations. But can we define it, and can we describe its importance in our work in literacy instruction? In this chapter, I offer thoughts on building reflective capacity within coaching and professional learning.

What Is Reflection, and How Do We Develop Reflective Capacity?

Reflection is a process we use to think about events and the deeper meaning surrounding these events. Fountas and Pinnell (2001) remind us that adult learners channel their insights, beliefs, observations, and assumptions into a knowledge base that helps them construct new understandings or refine previous understandings to gain meaning. Reflection requires linking an event to our past experiences and current knowledge, and realizing how the new knowledge will inform what we do in a similar situation.

As literacy leaders, we use reflection on a continual basis. We reflect on student and teacher needs to determine professional development structure and content, to refine classroom implementation, and to determine actions that ensure shifts in teaching and learning. Using reflection to promote growth and achievement should be a "way of life" for a literacy coach. Yet, at times, the ability to be reflective is elusive, and we can find ourselves immersed in stale and ineffective teaching and learning patterns.

Over time and in the right setting, literacy leaders develop their reflective capacity. It is dependent on several factors. The following chart highlights some of these factors (adapted from Gustafson, 2002).

A variety of factors impact reflective capacity at different times and at different levels of intensity. For example, when the knowledge base for a particular topic is at an early stage, less reflection is possible. A deeper grasp on content makes it possible to reflect more extensively on the how, why, and what of the topic. Similarly, if reflection always occurs in large-group settings, the opportunity to synthesize, share, reflect, and adjust thinking is different from opportunities found within small groups or pairs.

Of special note in the "Feedback from the Coach" section of the chart is the *quality* of feedback given by the coach during instructional interactions with teachers. Feedback occurs on a continuum from brief to substantial. An example of brief feedback is a quick exchange in the hallway when a coach gives a teacher a page number in a professional text that will support her instruction in writing workshop. A substantial level of feedback involves the coach and teacher sitting down to discuss their observations of a recent writing workshop, analyzing student work, studying the professional text together, and planning how to apply new insights to the next day's instruction during writing workshop.

A literacy coach discerns the amount of feedback needed for a situation, and uses content knowledge and interpersonal skills to move beyond comments about completion or quality of a lesson into expanding and elaborating on experiences, responses, and learning. Teachers are asked to share their observations and wonderings, and these conversations lead to further questions that guide the direction of the next lessons. A coach who supports a teacher in bringing learning moments into fine focus is able to foster deeper clarity for instructional decision-making.

Reflective capacity is also connected to school culture. As Williams and Hierck (2015) point out, "traditional school culture doesn't encourage staff members to engage in collective reflection" (p. 8). Therefore, steps must be taken to create space for wondering, trying out, and discussing together. When inquiry into assessment, instruction, and learning is an accepted and expected practice, reflective capacity develops. Literacy coaches who are visible learners themselves help to build a culture of trust, knowledge, and collaboration. As

Factors Supporting Reflection	
Factor	**Description**
Personality	• Open to suggestion • Learner-oriented • Internal motivation • Readiness to engage
Physical Environment	• Free of judgment • Non-rushed • Ideas and opinions are valued
Knowledge Base	• Theoretical understandings • Connections between current and past experiences • Develop from professional texts and expert others
Social Interactions	• Individual, small group, and larger group • Consistent space and time • Construction of deeper understandings
Feedback from the Coach	• Quality and frequency of interactions • Inquiry approach • View from various perspectives • Consider framework, theoretical basis, underlying rationale for behaviors, methods, techniques • Ask "what if…how…why?" • Consider consequences

PHOTO 24.1 Teacher and coach reflecting together

they work with teachers from an open and authentically inquisitive stance, the space for deep thinking and intentional action is created.

Fostering Reflection as a Literacy Coach

A literacy coach directly influences everyone who touches the academic life of a child. Coaching can look and sound like a simple process, but, in fact, effective coaching of teachers is demanding! It requires practice, persistence, synthesis, and reflection. It also takes a belief that children and teachers deserve access to highly crafted instruction, designed to stretch literacy understanding in multiple ways. Done well, coaching is complex and rewarding at the same time.

Literacy coaches face a long list of responsibilities: to develop and sustain a culture of collaboration; lead people; gather resources; support teachers; improve instruction; use assessment results purposefully; conduct professional development; and manage a variety of other tasks. Yet, the most important focus of all is on improving the literacy instruction and practice of those working closely with children. Where does this start? With conversations.

Collaborative conversations between coaches and teachers ground the work done in classrooms. A coach is careful to link conversations to recent specific learning events; embed them in learning new concepts; use them to describe teaching and learning actions; employ them to deepen reflection; and tie them to action plans to improve teaching (Lyons & Pinnell, 2001). And, with an element of trust firmly established between coach and teacher, reflection becomes a critical piece of professional learning. Figure 24.1 demonstrates a coach's attention to preparation and reflection, a necessity for creating an expectation of reflection for teachers.

How does a coach know when a teacher is being reflective? When a teacher considers instructional options, discusses observations about students and artifacts, and explores the deeper meaning in a given situation, she is engaged in active reflection. That teacher also

FIGURE 24.1 Reflective coaching cycle

plans specific goals and steps for the next lesson, invests time and energy in inquiry around the work, and schedules ongoing time with the coach to further refine understandings and instructional moves.

What are the opportunities for helping teachers develop reflective capacity? Just like the "before, during, and after" aspects of a guided reading lesson, we can think of reflection in terms of "before, during, and after" a coaching session. If we know that the "coach serves as a guide and mentor, but that essential insight comes from within the teacher" (Mraz, Algozzine, and Kissel, 2009, p. 18), how, then, can a coach help develop those essential insights within the teachers he or she mentors and guides?

PHOTO 24.2 Reflecting on a recent lesson

BEFORE

An effective coach devotes time for preparation even before entering the coaching arena. Reviewing knowledge about the teacher's experience and beliefs beforehand, in conjunction with considerations for new learning or deeper understandings to come in the lesson, sets the coach up to fully engage with the teacher in a lesson pre-conference. Here, the coach examines new insights gained from the conversation and begins to construct a theory about the understandings of the teacher for content, process, and student development. Listening purposefully and asking for clarification shows teachers the importance of thinking together, and opens up space for wondering about the lesson to come.

DURING

The coach listens, takes notes, and watches for links between what the teacher conveyed in the pre-conference and actual occurrences of the lesson. Noting what is said or done becomes information that helps a coach reflect and prepare for the post-conference. A coach may also identify one or two areas where questions linger, forming possibilities for reflection after the lesson.

AFTER

Finding out what the teacher noticed or wondered about the lesson often affords coaches a venue for meaningful interactions. It is important to hear the perspectives of the teacher during this time and to use open-ended questions and paraphrasing to summarize the learning. A coach must also support and expand the teacher's knowledge base through professional texts and connections to past experiences. Deeper knowledge makes deeper reflection available. The next chart includes possible coaching actions that support reflection during all phases of the coaching cycle.

Coaching Actions That Support Reflection

Coaching Cycle	Coaching Actions
Prepare for the pre-conference	• Find out ahead of time what you and the teacher will be discussing in the pre-conference. You can establish this when you schedule a time for the observation. Does the teacher want you to observe a guided reading group, interactive writing, or how conferencing is going during Writer's Workshop? • Use professional texts/PD notes to review important aspects of the content, noting the location of specific information to support the coaching conversations to come. • Review notes from previous coaching sessions as a reminder of past foci and learning of the teacher. • Determine a potential coaching idea or two regarding this teacher and this lesson.
Use the pre-conference to discuss the teacher's observations and questions about students/lessons	• Take notes to support conversations to come. • What does the teacher know about students' learning thus far? • What does the teacher hope to accomplish in the lesson? • What plans are in place to monitor learning and application? • How are safety nets structured for this lesson if students do not take on the learning?
Observe the lesson	• Take note of what is seen/heard/said between teacher and students. • Keep general aspects of teaching in mind, such as materials, pacing, and engagement. • Recognize teaching/classroom practices that might be problematic (over-reliance on teacher, high noise level, and so on).
Prepare for the post-conference	• Review collected data in light of the teacher's concerns and the coach's analysis of teaching and learning. What are one or two coaching points that would support the teacher? • What foundational texts and articles are available to support the post-conference conversation?
Conduct the post-conference	• Consider the needs of the teacher: time, place, experience level, capacity for insight, etc. • Use notes from the observation as a grounding basis for discussion. • Ask for the teacher's perspective of the lesson in accordance with ideas stated in the pre-conference. • Use open-ended questions, paraphrasing, and reflective pauses to reach deeper understandings. • Listen for and clarify shifts in learning. • Plan the next steps with the teacher—a follow-up observation, discussing an article, or providing some resources.
Reflect as a coach	• What shifts in understanding and application came from this coaching session? • What does the teacher need to know or do next? • What plan will be designed to support learning?

Next, let's take a look at a brief excerpt of parts of a coaching cycle showing how a teacher is reflective over two days of Interactive Read-Aloud. The teacher first read a biography called *Marvelous Cornelius* (Bildner, 2015) which began with a quote by Martin Luther King, Jr. As you will see, the teacher did not get the level of conversation and deep thinking she hoped for. We join this Day 1 pre-conference, already in progress:

DAY 1: PRE-CONFERENCE

Teacher:	What I really want students to do is focus on author's craft of using quotes and think about the Martin Luther King, Jr. quote, which means that no matter what you do in life, do it well and put your best foot forward. I want them to realize the importance and influence one person can have.
Coach:	It will be interesting to hear the students' language, to see if they can go deeper with your questioning and conversation.

DAY 1: POST-CONFERENCE

Coach:	Let's think back to your book introduction. Can you talk a little bit about how you set the book up for the students?
Teacher:	My book introduction really did have mostly to do with the quote by Dr. Martin Luther King at the beginning of the book. Originally, I thought I would support students with the quote and tell them what Dr. King meant by that and go from there, to open up the discussion. At the last minute, I decided to see what they thought was the meaning of the quote. I wish I would have just gone with the support and told them what he meant, and then maybe that would have deepened the conversation and led it into the book.
Teacher:	What I'm hearing you say is that it was worth it to see how the students made meaning by listening to the book. But they probably needed a little bit more support in the introduction?
Coach:	Yes, I think that would have allowed them to think more deeply….

DAY 2: PRE-CONFERENCE

Coach:	So, talk a little bit about what you'll be doing today and the text that you chose.
Teacher:	We're continuing with our biography theme, reading about Nelson Mandela today, a new person for them. So I'm going to provide more support like we talked about yesterday in post-conference. There is really a nice introduction to the book already, but I'm going to put it in a more kid-friendly language and make sure they know how Nelson….

DAY 2: POST-CONFERENCE

Coach:	Let's think back to your introduction today and what was different about it compared to yesterday.
Teacher:	Yesterday I don't think I really set up the book at all. After our post-conference, I knew I wanted to be more effective in that area, and I think I was. But even today, there were things I could have left out or shortened, like not spending so much time on his father who passed away when Nelson was nine. And I could have spent more time on his importance in the struggle for equality and freedom in South Africa.
Coach:	You're reflecting on your approach to Interactive Read-Alouds, seeing that appropriate support is necessary so that conversations can take place to expand meaning for everyone.…

This short excerpt shows how attention to one aspect of instruction (setting the stage for comprehending a read-aloud) can lift the teacher and students in a way that will support discussion and comprehension in future lessons. There are limited minutes in a school day. Conversations that happen between a teacher and coach must be highly purposeful, reflective, and directed toward promoting student learning.

Fostering Reflection as a Staff Developer

Some building coaches are also in charge of planning and presenting professional development for fellow teachers. Reflection of practice is critical to the learning of adults and must be a consistent part of professional learning. Schon's work (as cited in Lyons & Pinnell, 2001) suggests that a learner's understanding is clarified through reflection; further, that a learner's "growth and development depends on their ability to: reflect on their learning, adjust their behavior based on that reflection, and develop a theoretical framework and set of understandings based on their own experience" (pp. 138–139). Fostering reflection, then, is an important aspect of a staff developer's work. In our current educational state of urgency, cultivating reflective capacity in teachers is one of the most critical responsibilities undertaken by a literacy coach.

In *Transforming Professional Development into Student Results*, Doug Reeves (2010) explains that "high-impact professional learning has three essential characteristics: 1) a focus on student learning, 2) rigorous measurement of adult decisions, and 3) a focus on people and practices, not programs" (pp. 21–22). All three highlight the importance of reflection within professional development.

For example, in a professional development session, when teachers link evidence of growth to teaching strategies, the focus becomes student learning (Reeves, 2010). Evidence of growth can be seen in anecdotal notes; running records; writing samples; conversation from Interactive Read-Aloud, guided reading; writing conferences; student-created projects; and more. As teachers reflect on these data, they are able to make instructional decisions based on evidence of student learning.

Teachers engage in *rigorous measurement of adult decisions* (Reeves, 2010) when they analyze the instructional decisions of their practice as it pertains to student results. It requires them to search for causes of student results, not merely report the results. Fullan (2010) describes "decisional capital" as the ability to make decisions in times of uncertainty—when we may not have clear evidence of what is needed. Decisional capital is acquired through repeated experience, practice, and reflection. Bringing to light the results of instructional decisions allows us to measure and judge our effectiveness.

PHOTO 24.3 Analyzing data as an instructional team

Lastly, *focusing on people and practices rather than programs* (Reeves, 2010) leads to authentic reflection because people and practices do not run automatically. Teachers need support for their practice. They need leadership, space, and time for considering the degree of their effectiveness, and encouragement to make instructional changes as needed for students.

With these three areas in mind—student learning, measuring adult decisions, and focusing on teachers and their practice—a literacy coach plans for and conducts professional development. But it doesn't end there; a coach must also reflect on the learning takeaways. From body language to conversation to created artifacts, coaches note levels of engagement and understanding. The following chart shows a coach's reflections after leading professional development.

Reflecting on Professional Development

What I See	What I Say or Do
The group was very engaged during Interactive Read-Aloud, but not during the small-group discussion on strategic actions which followed.	Is this because I made a great book choice, or is it about relevance/understanding of the topic being discussed? I will check on understandings in my next round of coaching and revisit this topic as needed at next PD.
Teachers had trouble getting started on the small-group charts involving strategic actions—a couple stepped out, one went to get a snack.	They didn't have an example to follow! I must use a gradual release of responsibility model, and provide them support to get started.
At the end of PD, several questions were turned in on the survey slips.	After sorting, three questions were procedural and five told me there are still confusions on Thinking Beyond & About the Text. During grade-level meetings next week, I will briefly restate and follow up on procedural questions. In coaching sessions, I'll link student behaviors to strategic actions and dig deeper into, beyond, and about text.

Conclusion

At the end of the day, here is the most compelling wondering of our literacy work: How do coaches take conversations about practice to locations of deep reflection? This is tied to experience, self-awareness, support, and time (Lyons & Pinnell, 2001). When the conversations are grounded in observation, knowledge, and inquiry, reflective practice is born. It is up to the coach to create a safe yet urgent environment in which teachers become dedicated to their own professional growth and student achievement, and lean into reflection as a means to accomplish more.

Suggestions for Professional Development

1. Based on notes during the coaching cycle, determine where shifts in a teacher's understanding or implementation occurred. Track what led up to the shift, and determine the agentive force: exploring a text together, observation of student behavior or artifacts, comparing instruction from one day to the next, specific question or comment, etc. Join with other literacy coaches and explore your coaching notes from this inquiry: "What leads up to shifts in understanding and implementation?" Use these new insights to strengthen your coaching moves.

2. Arrange to meet with grade-level groups after a professional development session in which teachers were asked to try out a strategy or new practice. Gather data about successes, adjustments made, and continued challenges. Reflect on these areas in preparation for the next professional learning session and revisit the topic at the start of the session. Revisiting offers another opportunity to clarify and advance the teaching.

3. Ask yourself, "What proportion of your professional development calendar in the year ahead suggests a commitment to refinement, reinforcement, and deliberate practice of the professional practices most essential for your school" (Reeves, 2010, p. 53)? In the year ahead, focus on deep and consistent implementation of a few literacy aspects.

CHAPTER 25

Leading Your School to a Comprehensive Literacy Framework

David Hensinger

"Investing in the professional development of excellent teachers is the best preparation for our children's future.**"**

—Gay Su Pinnell

In this chapter we will begin thinking about the role of the building administrator in implementing a tier one shift to a Comprehensive Literacy Framework. Together, we will explore the important instructional practices and resources that a building needs to implement a Comprehensive Literacy Framework. We will also explore the role that professional development and teacher leadership play in creating a lasting shift to a Comprehensive Literacy Framework. The primary aim is to provide tools to help you identify the steps your school community needs to take in order to build a sustaining Comprehensive Literacy Framework.

Looking at Implementation

What evidence would you look for in your building to identify the implementation level of a Comprehensive Literacy Framework? What resources do you already have in your building to promote a Comprehensive Literacy Framework? How would you engage and inform your community about your shift to a Comprehensive Literacy Framework? To inform these questions, I will share six Comprehensive Literacy Framework Rubrics designed to help you:

- evaluate what practices your building already has that aligns with a Comprehensive Literacy Framework.
- determine where you need to focus your professional development.
- identify the key resources that are needed in your building.
- set goals and build a personalized strategic Comprehensive Literacy implementation plan.

The six Comprehensive Literacy Framework rubrics are not an exhaustive list of the different components involved in a shift to a Comprehensive Literacy Framework. However, they will support your work as you begin to shift the culture and instructional practices in your building.

Introducing the Comprehensive Literacy Framework Rubrics

The focus of the six Comprehensive Literacy Framework rubrics is to help an administrator implement a building-wide tier one shift to a Comprehensive Literacy Framework. Careful thought and planning went into determining each of the categories, key components, and evidence that make up each of the rubrics. The six rubric categories were designed to fit into two sections: Instructional Rubrics and Non-Instructional Rubrics.

The Instructional Rubrics focus on the building-wide instructional practices needed to implement a Comprehensive Literacy Framework in a K–8 building. These rubrics provide an administrator a broad view of the Comprehensive Literacy Instruction practices in the building. They are flexible enough to help an administrator understand and evaluate each of the key components that are critical in the three instructional contexts in a Comprehensive Literacy Framework.

Instructional Rubrics	Non-Instructional Rubrics
• Language and Word Study • Writing Workshop • Reading Workshop	• Resources and Environment • Community Engagement • Mission and Building Brand

Language and Word Study

	Basic Level	Ready for CLF Practices	Implementing CLF Practices	Reflective CLF Practices
Mini-lesson	Teachers need an introductory course on components.	Teachers provide daily mini-lessons. Teachers clearly state the learning goal of the lesson.	Teachers use data and student need to plan mini-lessons. Teacher provides an opportunity for students to do some examples during mini-lessons.	Teachers continue to evaluate student understandings and plan lessons based on student needs.
Small Group	Teachers need an introductory course on components. Teachers have all routines in place for a quick and efficient small-group meeting session.	Teachers meet with small groups of students based on student needs (i.e., Phonemic Awareness, Phonics, Fluency, or Vocabulary).	Teachers track small groups' needs and continue to adjust each group's learning path to best meet their needs.	Teachers share information and resources with each other in order to differentiate more effectively.
Independent Practice	Teachers have students working in small groups based on Phonemic Awareness, Phonics, Fluency, or Vocabulary needs. Teachers have needed independent word study supplies available for student usage.	Students know and follow classroom word study routines. Most students are engaged and demonstrating independent learning strategies.	Students set their own word study learning goals. Students are engaged and maximize their independent word learning time.	Teachers reflect on their students' independent learning and adjust learning groups as needed.
Interactive Read-Aloud	Teachers need an introductory course on components. Most teachers use read-alouds as time fillers or transition activities. Teachers have access to high-quality Interactive Read-Aloud texts (digital or print).	Some teachers plan intentional read-alouds, and clear and specific learning is happening. Most teachers select Interactive Read-Alouds based on student needs.	Teachers plan intentional read-alouds, and clear and specific learning is happening. Teachers select Interactive Read-Alouds based on student needs. Students are engaged and conversing during the Interactive Read-Aloud.	Teacher and students reflect on the learning that happened during the Interactive Read-Aloud. Teacher evaluates students' conversations to determine future Interactive Read-Alouds.

Writing Workshop

	Basic Level	Ready for CLF Practices	Implementing CLF Practices	Reflective CLF Practices
Mini-lessons	Teachers need an introductory course on components.	Most teachers read and analyze student work to determine what standards to present. Teachers clearly state the learning goal of the lesson.	All teachers use all types of data to select teaching points during mini-lessons. Teachers share the learning target and the reason why the students need this understanding.	Teachers help each other evaluate student data and learning to improve mini-lesson instruction.
Independent Writing	Teachers have students writing independently with appropriate stamina. Teachers have needed independent writing supplies available for student usage.	Students have their own Writer's Notebook. Students have options on where they can write. Teachers meet with smaller groups (or one-on-one) during this time.	Students understand how to mine for a writing seed and take a writing piece from idea to final work independently. There is evidence that most students are applying the daily mini-lesson to their writing.	Teachers review students' work in order to plan instruction, reflect on instruction and confer with other teachers.
Conferring	Teachers need an introductory course on conferring. Teachers share what students should have learned during the workshop time. Teachers meet with students during independent time.	Teachers provide specific teaching points to students based on their needs. Students transition from mini-lesson to independent writing quickly. Teachers track student work and conferencing topics digitally or in written format.	Student needs drive the size of small-group conferencing. Teacher provides mid-workshop corrections when needed. After each teacher conference the student leaves with a better understanding on how writers work.	Teachers reflect on their writing conferences with students and seek professional development based on their own needs.

Reading Workshop

	Basic Level	Ready for CLF Practices	Implementing CLF Practices	Reflective CLF Practices
Mini-lessons	Teachers need an introductory course on components. Teachers clearly state the learning goal of the lesson.	Most teachers understand how to use data to select mini-lessons.	All teachers use data to select teaching points during mini-lessons. Teachers share the learning target and the reason why the students need this understanding.	Teachers help each other evaluate student data and learning to improve mini-lesson instruction.
Guiding Reading/ Small-Group Instruction	Teachers need an introductory course on small-group instruction. Teachers' small-group instruction is a repeat of the mini-lesson.	Teachers have needed items for small-group instruction and understand the basic routines that allow effective teaching. Teachers plan small-group instruction based on group needs.	Teachers collect observation notes during small group. Teachers provide teaching points during the lesson and help grow readers. Teachers pick texts based on student needs.	Teachers continue to evaluate their teaching and refine their efforts.
Managed Independent Learning (MIL)	Students are all working on the same item alone with little to no differentiation. Teachers have routines in place that allow them to meet with smaller groups of students. Teachers are utilizing technology in their MIL groupings.	Students are working in heterogeneous groupings and are completing different tasks. A workboard is in place, and students understand how to use it. Students transition between tasks efficiently, and transitions are only led by the teacher.	Students are working in heterogeneous groupings, finishing tasks at their own pace. Students complete tasks that were selected specifically for their learning needs. Students have their own personal Reader's Notebook and utilize it to grow as a reader.	Teachers change their Managed Independent Learning activities to match their students' needs. Students are able to self-regulate their learning.
Conferring	Teachers share what students should have learned during the workshop time. Teachers meet with students during independent time.	Teachers allow students to share what they learned academically and behaviorally. Teachers grow readers with specific conferencing language.	Teachers use students' reflections to plan future lessons. Teachers track their conferencing conversations.	Teachers reflect on their reading conferences with students and seek professional development based on their own needs.

The Non-Instructional Rubrics referenced earlier allow an administrator to focus on essential but non-instructional factors to shift a building toward a Comprehensive Literacy Framework. These rubrics were designed to look at the marketing and resources needed to create a building and community culture that will allow and sustain a shift to a Comprehensive Literacy Framework.

Resources and Environment

	Basic Level	Ready for CLF Practices	Implementing CLF Practices	Reflective CLF Practices
Bookroom	No leveled bookroom. An area in the school is located for the bookroom. Staff need an introductory course on the importance of a bookroom.	Bookroom is established, but limited in texts and text types. A staff member is identified to manage the bookroom. Staff understand the importance of a bookroom.	Bookroom has many text levels and a comprehensive selection. Teachers use the bookroom for small-group instruction.	Yearly funds are put aside to grow the building bookroom. Teachers make book recommendations based on student needs and state standards.
Classrooms	Staff have a way to allow students to work in groups (e.g., move desks). Staff still teach with a traditional approach. Staff need an introductory course on classroom setup.	Teachers have a small-group instructional area. Teachers have a classroom library. Teachers have wall space for anchor charts.	Teachers have a classroom library that offers students many choices. Teachers have specific areas designed for independent learning opportunities.	Teachers know how and why to set their room up and can mentor new teachers.
Building Schedule	Schedule is set up for adults in the building. The building schedule does not allow large literacy blocks for any grade levels.	Schedule is designed to maximize student instructional time. The schedule creates large literacy blocks for most teachers.	The schedule creates large literacy blocks for all teachers. There are common grade level planning periods, if possible.	The building schedule is a model for other buildings to follow.
Technology	Some classrooms have an interactive projector. Students have access to independent digital devices.	Most classrooms have an interactive projector.	All classrooms have an interactive projector and document camera.	Students have their own personal learning devices, and the building has a plan to keep up with their technology demands.

Community Engagement

	Basic Level	Ready for CLF Practices	Implementing CLF Practices	Reflective CLF Practices
Community Steering Committee	At least one staff member plans the messages shared with the community.	A group of staff members are identified to be part of the Community Steering Committee. Members need an introductory course on CLF practices.	Community Steering Committee meets three or more times a year. Committee creates documents to share with families and post online.	Committee evaluates its practices and adjusts as needed.
Social Media	Social media accounts are set up. At least one staff member is in charge of creating online messaging.	Social media posts are made almost daily. Multiple staff members are identified to help share the building message online.	Social media posts are informative and are in line with building direction. Daily posts are made by multiple staff members.	A large portion of staff members contribute to the social media footprint.

Mission and Building Brand

	Basic Level	Ready for CLF Practices	Implementing CLF Practices	Reflective CLF Practices
Building Leadership Team	A leadership team is created. The leadership team meets regarding daily building issues.	Leadership team understands CLF practices and is able to evaluate learning programs and resources to ensure there is alignment.	Leadership team only allows programs and learning events that align with mission and vision.	Leadership team meets regularly and continues to evaluate resources and programs.
Building Brand	A building mission, vision, and logo are created.	The building mission, vision, and logo are in line with CLF.	Teachers and community members know and understanding the building's mission and vision.	The building continues to find new ways to push their brand to ensure there is a clear message on what they stand for.

Reading and Understanding the Comprehensive Literacy Framework Rubrics

Whenever you begin using a new tool, it's important to understand how the tool works, what its key functions are, and how it can help you perform a task more efficiently. Let's start by looking closely at the Resources and Environment rubric. We can explore this rubric closely to better understand all of the rubrics.

The Resources and Environment rubric has its key components broken down on the left side of the rubric: Bookroom, Classrooms, Building Schedule, and Technology. While all of the key components are always listed on the left side of each of the six rubrics, there are different numbers of key components on each of the rubrics. The components will help you determine where you need to focus your efforts and help you converse with your staff around important Comprehensive Literacy practices.

Across the top of the Resources and Environment rubric boxes are the Comprehensive Literacy Framework Implementation ratings: Basic Level, Ready for CLF Practices, Implementing CLF Practices and Reflective CLF Practices. All of the rubrics share this common language regarding the ratings. The ratings across the top of each of the rubrics will help you understand how deeply embedded your Comprehensive Literacy Framework practices are and point out areas of weakness and strength.

The middle portion of the Resources and Environment rubric is the evidence portion of the rubric. The evidence portion in all of the rubrics is used to determine the specific practices/resources that are already in place or not in place that align with a Comprehensive Literacy Framework. The evidence will help you determine specific actions that you can take to move closer to a Comprehensive Literacy Framework.

How Do You Determine a Rating?

Figure 25.1 is a sample evaluation of the Resources and Environment rubric to show how to evaluate your own building with the rubrics. The yellow lines indicate the evidence that the building in this example has in place. The red lines reveal the elements that the building does not yet have in place.

Start looking at the evidence in the Basic Level rating first. It's important to read all of the evidence and mark the evidence that you already have in place and mark or leave blank the evidence that you do not have in place. Then move to Ready for CLF Practices and complete the same process. Continue this process all the way across the rubric, working left to right. You do not need all of the evidence in one rating area in order to move on to the next rating area. It's entirely possible to have some Reflective CLF Practices and still be in the Ready for CLF Practices. In fact, in Figure 25.1, you can see that there is not a staff member identified to manage the bookroom, even though there are two other pieces of evidence that demonstrate that the building is implementing CLF practices. Just as students have instructional gaps that you need to identify and teach for, your building will have the same.

Resources and Environment

	Basic Level	Ready for CLF Practices	Implementing CLF Practices	Reflective CLF Practices
Bookroom	No leveled bookroom. An area in the school is located for the bookroom. Staff need an introductory course on the importance of a bookroom.	Bookroom is established, but limited in texts and text types. A staff member is identified to manage the bookroom. Staff understand the importance of a bookroom.	Bookroom has many text levels and a comprehensive selection. Teachers use the bookroom for small-group instruction.	Yearly funds are put aside to grow the building bookroom. Teachers make book recommendations based on student needs and state standards.
Classrooms	Staff have a way to allow students to work in groups (e.g., move desks). Staff still teach with a traditional approach. Staff need an introductory course on classroom setup.	Teachers have a small-group instructional area. Teachers have a classroom library. Teachers have wall space for anchor charts.	Teachers have a classroom library that offers students many choices. Teachers have specific areas designed for independent learning opportunities.	Teachers know how and why to set their room up and can mentor new teachers.
Building Schedule	Schedule is set up for adults in the building. The building schedule does not allow large literacy blocks for any grade levels.	Schedule is designed to maximize student instructional time. The schedule creates large literacy blocks for most teachers.	The schedule creates large literacy blocks for all teachers. There are common grade level planning periods, if possible.	The building schedule is a model for other buildings to follow.
Technology	Some classrooms have an interactive projector. Students have access to independent digital devices.	Most classrooms have an interactive projector.	All classrooms have an interactive projector and document camera.	Students have their own personal learning devices, and the building has a plan to keep up with their technology demands.

FIGURE 25.1 Example of a completed rubric

I've Evaluated My Building, Now What?

After you've reviewed all of the rubrics and have determined your building's implementation level of a Comprehensive Literacy Framework, you will then want to begin developing a plan to move toward more reflective Comprehensive Literacy Framework practices. When you get to this point, I suggest you consider the different professional development opportunities you have throughout the school year as your first step. In Figure 25.2, you see the nine different professional development opportunities that are available in my district.

Professional Development Opportunities		
Staff Meetings	Delay Start Professional Development	Professional Development Days
Community Steering Committee	Building Leadership Team	Social Media Team
Grade Level Meetings	Intervention Team	Budget/Building Items

FIGURE 25.2

The rubrics will help you to identify the strengths and weaknesses in your building regarding implementing a Comprehensive Literacy Framework. Now you can identify where you can provide the needed professional development in order to move toward Reflective CLF Practices.

Let's work through an example together. Take a moment and review Figure 25.3, which is a completed evaluation of the Reading Workshop rubric.

As I analyze this rubric, I quickly notice the overall evaluation grade of Basic Level. This tells me that Reading Workshop, in general, will need to be a part of my professional development plan with my staff.

Now, looking more closely at each of the components, I notice that teachers have a general understanding of what a mini-lesson is. However, they are unclear on how to use data available to them to determine the topics for which they should be providing mini-lessons. I also noticed that teachers have routines in place that allow them to meet with small groups, but their small-group meetings are simply a repeat demonstration of their mini-lessons. After looking closely at the Managed Independent Learning component, I notice that teachers have all the basic routines down and in place, but there are no differentiated learning groups, nor is there evidence of the teacher using a workboard to help students gain independence. Finally, after reviewing the Conferring component, I notice teachers are taking the lead on sharing what should have been learned instead of a more student-centered approach of letting students reflect on their learning.

Now that I've determined needs, I can look at professional development opportunities and formulate a plan to address the needs. Figure 25.4 is an example of how these Reading Workshop needs can be addressed and built into a strategic professional development plan.

Reading Workshop

	Basic Level	Ready for CLF Practices	Implementing CLF Practices	Reflective CLF Practices
Mini-lessons	Teachers need an introductory course on components. Teachers clearly state the learning goal of the lesson.	Most teachers understand how to use data to select mini-lessons.	All teachers use data to select teaching points during mini-lessons. Teachers share the learning target and the reason why the students need this understanding.	Teachers help each other evaluate student data and learning to improve mini-lesson instruction.
Guiding Reading/ Small-Group Instruction	Teachers need an introductory course on small-group instruction. Teachers' small-group instruction is a repeat of the mini-lesson.	Teachers have needed items for small-group instruction and understand the basic routines that allow effective teaching. Teachers plan small-group instruction based on group needs.	Teachers collect observation notes during small group. Teachers provide teaching points during the lesson and help grow readers. Teachers pick texts based on student needs.	Teachers continue to evaluate their teaching and refine their efforts.
Managed Independent Learning (MIL)	Students are all working on the same item alone with little to no differentiation. Teachers have routines in place that allow them to meet with smaller groups of students. Teachers are utilizing technology in their MIL groupings.	Students are working in heterogeneous groupings and are completing different tasks. A workboard is in place, and students understand how to use it. Students transition between tasks efficiently, and transitions are only led by the teacher.	Students are working in heterogeneous groupings, finishing tasks at their own pace. Students complete tasks that were selected specifically for their learning needs. Students have their own personal Reader's Notebook and utilize it to grow as a reader.	Teachers change their Managed Independent Learning activities to match their students' needs. Students are able to self-regulate their learning.
Conferring	Teachers share what students should have learned during the workshop time. Teachers meet with students during independent time.	Teachers allow students to share what they learned academically and behaviorally. Teachers grow readers with specific conferencing language.	Teachers use students' reflections to plan future lessons. Teachers track their conferencing conversations.	Teachers reflect on their reading conferences with students and seek professional development based on their own needs.

FIGURE 25.3 Completed Reading Workshop rubric

Professional Development Opportunities

Staff Meetings

- Book Study: *Guided Reading: Responsive Teaching Across the Grades* (Fountas & Pinnell, 2016) (Focus: Small-group instruction and managed independent learning)
- Book Study: *Guiding Readers and Writers: Teaching Comprehension, Genre, and Content Literacy* (Fountas & Pinnell, 2001) (Focus: Mini-lessons and comprehensive framework, 3–6)
- Minimal day-to-day information

Delay Start Professional Development

- Provide grade-level-specific CLF routines and management information
- Address different ways to encourage student-centered approaches, specifically during and after conferring
- Provide specific examples of how to provide mini-lessons on phonemic awareness, phonics, fluency, and vocabulary

Professional Development Days

- Provide a blended introductory course on Writer's Workshop in K–1, 2–4 groupings
- Provide a blended introductory course on Word Study
- Provide a blended introductory course on Interactive Read-Aloud

Community Steering Committee

- Identify members of the Steering Committee
- Develop community documents that share a rationale for the building shift to CLF
- Create community engagement events to inform the community (e.g., Literacy Night, Assessment Night)

Building Leadership Team

- Provide a CLF overview to the BLT
- Using the building mission, develop a building logo and ensure CLF alignment
- Review current programs and practices and weed out anything that does not align with our CLF shift

Social Media Team

- Identify members of the Social Media Team
- Provide objective of the group
- Teach members how to tweet and make specific daily posts

Grade-Level Meetings

- Review classroom assessments and demonstrate how to build mini-lessons based on student need
- Review classroom assessments and demonstrate how to develop data-driven small-group instruction

Intervention Team

- Review student data and prioritize students according to need
- Provide additional supports for those students who have need
- Ensure that interventions match student need

Budget/Building Items

- Create a building schedule that has large literacy blocks for grade levels
- Locate funds for classroom libraries
- Increase classroom technology
- Find funding for document cameras
- Identify a staff member to manage bookroom

FIGURE 25.4 Professional Development Opportunities

Conclusion

Implementing a tier-one shift to a Comprehensive Literacy Framework can be challenging for an administrator. It's important to acknowledge that while you may find yourself stuck in the here and now, you can't tell yourself, "I don't have time to lead that kind of change." Instead, you need to focus your inner voice and thoughts on what's best for kids. Being an administrator is more than just opening and closing the building doors each day. As an administrator you have the opportunity and obligation to create a building that students, staff, and community members are proud to call THEIR school.

Suggestions for Professional Development

1. Review the six different CLF rubrics with your building leadership team (BLT). Reflect and review each of the six rubrics one at a time. Make sure that there is clarity among the group and that everyone has a clear understanding of what the evidence is. After reviewing the rubrics together, have each member of your BLT evaluate their building on all six of the rubrics. Collect all of your BLT members' rubrics and compare to your own reflection on the rubrics. Use the collective knowledge of this group to gain a sound understanding of your building's implementation level of CLF practices.

2. After you have evaluated your building's implementation level on the CLF rubrics, use the rubrics to create your building work plan. Identify the areas that need your immediate attention, and use the evidence in the rubrics to help write actionable steps you can take to shift your building's understanding of specific components on the rubric.

3. Assess your building using the CLF rubrics three times in a school year. Your initial assessments should be completed before the school year (baseline); the second assessment should take place in December/January (corrections); and the third and final assessment should take place at the end of the school year (measure growth). Completing these three assessments will allow you to celebrate your building's successes, allow you to measure your building's growth, and ensure that all staff members are taking the journey with you and in the right direction.

CHAPTER 26

Teachers and Principals Creating a Culture for Learning Together

Jason Hillman and Patricia L. Scharer

"... achieve the best possible results for your students... [with] a leader who is a positive driver of change; surrounded by colleagues who are skilled; receive great instructional guidance and support; and [forge] very strong ties with the families and community members that your school serves.*"*

—**Karen L. Mapp**

Implementing quality, comprehensive literacy instruction is not just the responsibility of classroom teachers. The role of the administrator of a school is vital. A positive, supportive partnership across the staff led by the building administrator can create a collaborative school culture that expects, supports, and celebrates learning—not only for the students, but for every educator in the building as well. This chapter focuses on such collaborations and leans on Jason's reflections on his role as an administrator relative to student and teacher learning. There are sections specifically directed at administrators and others aimed at teachers. We hope that powerful conversations will occur when administrators and teachers come together to read this chapter and then create and implement a shared vision for their school.

Teachers as Facilitators of Adult Learning

Administrators around the country are constantly searching for quality staff development about literacy instruction. It is costly for their staff to attend conferences or to bring in outside experts for professional development sessions. In contrast, they can maximize learning more economically by creating the capacity to create a knowledge base within their own building. Experts in the field of education agree that one of the keys to school improvement is continuous adult learning (Dufour, Dufour, & Eaker, 2008). We believe that teachers can transition from being the educators of children to also becoming facilitators of learning for each other within a school community. If this change of mindset occurs, schools will experience great success due to the building of shared knowledge that will occur among adult learners. There is not a step-by-step checklist to make this occur, but there are definitely strategies and a mindset that will make it possible. Administrators should set the stage for meaningful leadership and change. But how?

Thoughts for Administrators: What's the Plan?

All too often schools embark on a journey of change without a clear plan or vision of what the change will look like, or more importantly, what the school will look like once the change is enacted. Administrators have to ask themselves, "What is the purpose of our school?" You have to have a clear definition of what it is you want to accomplish within this context. It makes sense that you cannot communicate an idea or plan if you haven't clearly defined it. Think in these terms. In order to lead people to a certain place, you have to know where you are going. Once the place is defined, you need to know why you are headed there. Then, you can involve others in collaboration about the best way to get there.

Schools need a guide that defines the purpose of the school. First, have you established a vision for your school? This is an important consideration when it comes to school leadership, or any leadership for that matter. Jason spent 12 years as an elementary school principal in Sheridan, Wyoming; creating a school vision was the turning point in transforming the school. It was the one thing that began the journey from a failing school to a National Blue Ribbon School, as honored by the United States Department of Education. Once the school faculty developed a true vision of where they wanted to go, the transformation happened quickly; recognition of their transformation came within a few years. Most importantly, the vision and the steps they followed changed the lives of students and staff.

Writing Your Vision Statement

Some resources for writing vision statements produce wordy, inauthentic statements. This can be avoided by using a couple of guidelines for decision-making. These guidelines hold true to many of the decisions we are required to make in leadership roles. The first is to define the purpose of what is being done. An outstanding Reading Recovery teacher taught Jason this early on in his career as a principal. He had asked her to observe him teaching a literacy block and then coach him to increase his understanding of quality literacy instruction so he could become better at supporting the teachers in his building. The first thing she said was, "Jason, what was the purpose of that?" She answered most of his questions with that same question. It drove him nuts at first, but it really made him think about why he was doing certain things. From that point, he learned to start with that question when planning.

— Building Community —
- Buddy classrooms
- Saying "hello" to everyone
- Corny and goofy stuff for everyone
- Bobcat Pride certificates
- Annual event before P.A.W.S.
    - reduce stress
    - class adoption during testing
- Schoolwide expectations equal for everyone
    - trust adult and students to choose the right
        - show, not tell
- end of year slide show
- Everyone's kids
- Staff get togethers

- Taking care of everyone
    - meals - hugs - smiles
- Open door policy to parents
- Sharing our goals and vertical alignment
    - announcement celebrations
- Awards assembly
    - dancing
- Random after school activities
    - Goose and beyond on bikes
- Bringing people in from outside
- "Checking in" within a large building
- Celebrating unique talents
    - staff and students

PHOTO 26.1 Defining how to accomplish the vision of building community

For instance, think about the reason or purpose for creating your school vision. It should be to guide the school community and define what the school is all about. If that is the case, then write it in such a way that it fulfills its purpose. Get down to the business of writing a vision statement that can actually be used and understood by the people who are tasked with carrying it out. This is a true team-building activity and can be the first step in creating a culture of ownership and pride within the school. It sure did that for Jason's school! They shaped their vision as they discussed the type of school they wanted to create: what instruction looks like, how to monitor learning, how to collaborate, and how to treat each other. These are the targets that they set and the vision they created.

The vision at Jason's school was simple and had three goals:

1. Building Community
2. Celebrate Learning
3. Respect Diversity

That was it! These were the three goals the school would aim for on a daily basis. Next, the staff worked on school missions—ways to move the vision from theory to practice. Your mission is defining the behaviors and commitments that are necessary to make the vision a reality. How will these goals be supported and carried out by stakeholders? How do you move from paper to action? How do you live it? The work everyone did in defining what each one of those meant to us was extremely important. First, they made a list of what each of those goals meant.

Then, they defined activities and teaching strategies that supported each area of the vision. Photo 26.1 is an example of how the staff would work to accomplish their vision of building community. They also got rid of behaviors that did not support their vision. From then on, the vision statement was referenced whenever decisions were being made. The staff also designed personal commitments that would help support their vision. They took the time to define what they wanted the school to become and created ways to help them get there. Photo 26.2 lists how everyone in the building would be respectful and kind. This is culture building, and it is the root of all success in any organization.

Theory and knowledge are not enough when it comes to school transformation. Practice, based on theory and knowledge, is what makes the difference. Take the time to define specific responsibilities and actions that need to occur to support your vision. Be deliberate and collaborative in this process so there is a common understanding of what the vision is and what needs to occur to support it. It's also important to investigate what occurs within the building that does not support your vision statement. Be crystal clear on what types of activities and behaviors do not support, or even contradict the vision. Being explicit during this process will create a common expectation and foster ownership among stakeholders, as they are the ones creating the mission to achieve your vision. For example, Jason's staff decided that everyone needed to be on time for professional development sessions. They also designed consequences for those who did not get to meetings on time, such as wearing a funny shirt. These social norms were jointly established, universally understood, and helped to create the respectful school environment conducive to learning.

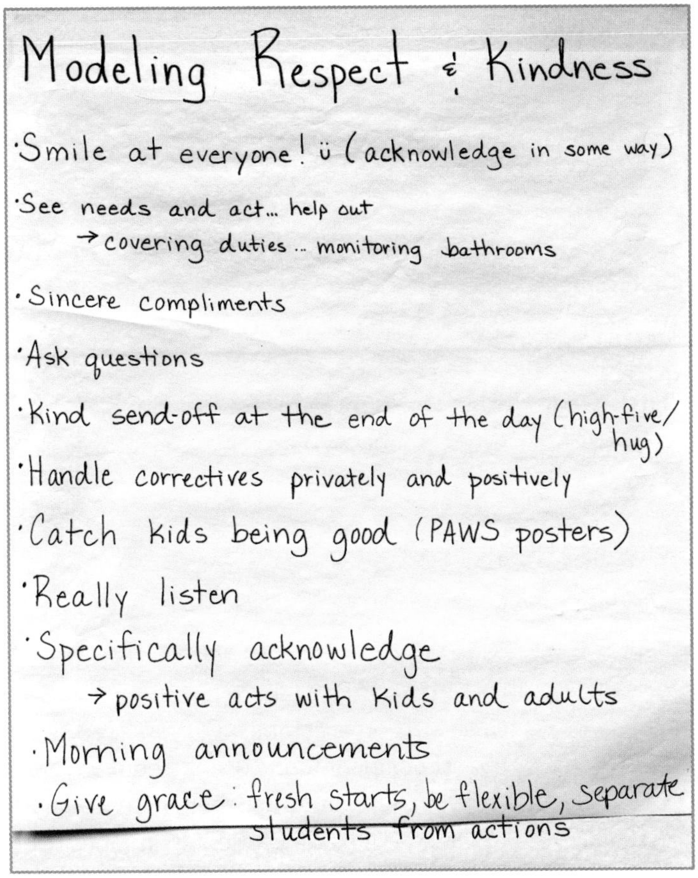

A good resource to help you get started is *Promising Literacy for Every Child: Reading Recovery and a Comprehensive Literacy System* (Askew, Pinnell, & Scharer, 2014). This inexpensive guide is available from the Reading Recovery Council of North America (www.readingrecovery.org) and offers tools to help you assess your school relative to six essential components of a comprehensive literacy approach and ways to establish goals, plus online forms you can write on to assess and plan.

Modeling Respect & Kindness

- Smile at everyone! ü (acknowledge in some way)
- See needs and act... help out
  → covering duties... monitoring bathrooms
- Sincere compliments
- Ask questions
- Kind send-off at the end of the day (high-five/ hug)
- Handle correctives privately and positively
- Catch kids being good (PAWS posters)
- Really listen
- Specifically acknowledge
  → positive acts with kids and adults
- Morning announcements
- Give grace: fresh starts, be flexible, separate students from actions

PHOTO 26.2 How to model respect and kindness

Changes in Writing Scores Over Five Years
Third-grade writing scores on the state assessment:
Pre: 41% proficient   Post: 100% proficient
Fourth-grade writing scores on the state assessment:
Pre: 59% proficient   Post: 95% proficient
Fifth-grade writing scores on the state assessment:
Pre: 51% proficient   Post: 98% proficient

FIGURE 26.1 Changes in Jason's school

Setting Goals

Writing was a real problem for students in Jason's school, so the staff chose that as their official school improvement goal. As they became a professional learning community studying writing instruction together, they created essential outcomes and interventions for struggling students. Students' ability to write proficiently increased. Teachers changed their daily practice, redefined what was being taught, and altered assessment methods. By promoting an environment that allowed the staff to work together to build shared knowledge in the area of writing, scores soared. Figure 26.1 is a comparison of how scores changed over five years in Jason's building.

Thoughts for Teachers: Mission Meets Vision

Once a vision is established, you need to think about what your personal mission is within the school community. Think about what you can contribute. Can you lead a study group? Can you invite other teachers in to watch a guided reading lesson and then work together to plan the next one based on student needs? Have a plan for how and what you will communicate with each other. Will there be grade-level meetings? Whole-staff meetings? Who leads the meetings? Who decides on the topics of learning, articles read, or books studied? Have some specific ideas when talking with your principal, and make sure you define the purpose of what you are proposing. These conversations are the beginning of an action plan to accomplish your vision!

When planning or formulating a goal, ask questions to put details into place. The following questions and answers can serve as a model as you create your vision and plan to communicate it.

Who Will Lead Professional Development?

Learning groups could be created in the form of grade-level teams consisting of teachers and ancillary staff members. Depending on the size of the school, the number of staff members will vary. Along with facilitating meetings, observation of teaching could be systematically scheduled when teachers observe one another and discuss their observations.

What Will the Focus of the Meetings Be?

Professional development based on student need/learning should be the general focus of team meetings. Who are experts in your building at analyzing student data to create learning goals for both students and adults? For example, the Reading Recovery teacher could provide coaching in the area of running records and running record analysis. This would help classroom teachers purposefully design instruction based on student data. A teacher returning from a conference could lead a discussion on professional readings discovered during a session. Teachers could take turns leading the discussion about a new professional book.

When Will Meetings Take Place?

These collaborative meetings could occur once a week during the school day if possible. The school schedule would need to be adjusted to accommodate the collaborative sessions.

Using these questions to design your mission gives you a starting point to discuss with your principal. Together, you can create a great opportunity to increase student and adult learning within the school and enact the change in the building.

PHOTO 26.3 Teachers plan together to lead professional development.

More Thoughts for Administrators: Communicate, Communicate, Communicate

So, you have created a vision statement and started to design ways to accomplish your vision within your school that work for you. This defines what you are about on a day-to-day basis, and you reference it in decision-making. Congratulations! You are on your way to creating a great school community. You, like every other quality administrator, are trying to think of ways to meet the needs of your school community. You want to help each student and staff member reach his or her potential as a learner. You know there is a gap between theory and practice, and you want to find a way to bridge that gap. Several of your teachers have expressed a willingness and passion for facilitating learning within the school. You have given input and checked it to make sure the vision fits your school, and now you are ready to put it into action.

Create a Plan to Communicate

Hold on! Having a clear vision is important, but that is not enough. Now, communication has to be done at the building level. The vision has to be effectively communicated and understood by all stakeholders. Purposefully create a plan to communicate; do not take for granted or assume that people will understand your plan without a thorough explanation. You know your vision is awesome; now is the time to help other people realize it is too. Dr. Anthony Muhammad, in his book *Transforming School Culture: How to Overcome Staff Division* (2009), writes that leaders make the mistake of thinking that others see things or understand things the same way they do, when in reality they may not. He argues that people will resist

Learning For All

- Collaboration
- Communication
  - → Develop and communicate learning targets
  - → Maintain and communicate high expectations
- Professional Texts
  - → Read, discuss and implement
- Unified Approaches
  - → See color coded writing sheets
- Re-evaluate expectations and adjust
- Share (honestly) successes and struggles in regards to learning
- Establish trust so all will take risks
  - Staff   Students

PHOTO 26.4 How the staff will support learning for all

change until they have a logical explanation for the change. Photo 26.4 is a chart the staff created to define how they will support learning for everyone in the building. Communication is key to accomplish this goal.

Learn to Collaborate

One way to support your conversation with staff is to have a book study of a text written about the effectiveness of collaboration and becoming a professional learning community. We suggest reading *Getting Started: Reculturing Schools to Become Professional Learning Communities* (2002) and *Whatever It Takes: How Professional Learning Communities Respond When Kids Don't Learn* (2004), both written by Richard and Rebecca Dufour along with Robert Eaker and Gayle Karhanek. These are great books that will help you understand the principles and concepts of collaboration and teamwork. But remember, it is your job to turn that theory into practice! Envision how you can create and foster the theory and examples given in the texts. Become an expert in the culture you are trying to create. Create learning activities for all your colleagues that help define what you want your school to become.

Lack of communication can kill an initiative; effective communication is key to effective change. This shared vision has to be communicated, and then collaboration has to occur in order to put the vision into action. Everyone must have a clear understanding and plan as to how each person will be utilized within the school. Be prepared to state the reason for this change and share data to support the initiative. Be creative in the sharing of data and keep it positive. If student performance is low, stress the plan to improve it. Be creative in your approach! Creativity is our trademark when working with children. Use it in communicating with adults also. Have fun, be inspirational, and use your sense of humor to show your passion for student and adult learning. Create a culture that can support teamwork and collaboration.

Jason's building had regularly scheduled celebrations to share their excitement for accomplishments, such as when students

- meet learning outcomes.
- complete Reading Recovery.
- demonstrate growth on assessments.
- carry out acts of kindness (we monitored and tracked these).
- read at grade level.

- demonstrate achievement on local and state assessments.
- meet goals—personal and academic.

The entire school would assemble in the gym and hoot and holler about their achievements. Every grade level was celebrated for something. All the grade level teachers would invite all of the school community to come and celebrate. It was commonly understood that if you come to the celebration… you had better bring your dancin' shoes! There was music, dancing, and fun! Jason would call kids up front to celebrate what they had done. There was also a slide show of student accomplishments that would continually run. And the staff celebrated their own accomplishments as well, especially those related to meeting their teaching goals.

> If you come to the celebration … you had better bring your dancin' shoes!

Conclusion

All schools face challenges in reaching their goals and encounter barriers to success. Leaders dedicated to promoting comprehensive literacy create opportunities, rethinking structures, strategies, and staffing in ways that build a culture of learning. Teachers become researchers in their own classrooms: observing, monitoring, and documenting their students' learning, collecting data, sharing and analyzing with colleagues, reflecting on their practice, and revising toward more effective instruction. The aim always is to work collaboratively to support the whole child—social and emotional well-being as well as academic success. All members of the school community work together to help all students thrive as readers, writers, thinkers, and learners.

And shared leadership is pivotal—promoting teacher agency, creating a climate of trust, enhancing adult learning, and building a school community that encompasses students' homes and families as well. Create your own vision, know where you are headed, and communicate with all members of your school community. Be creative and honest, reflective and proactive. Honor the cultural and linguistic riches of your school community, and lead. Take the opportunity! Be awesome!

Suggestions for Professional Development

1. Select one of the books recommended in this chapter and start a book club with the staff. Make it fun with refreshments and even some door prizes for those attending. Take turns leading the discussion, and set goals for the next meeting day. Be sure to keep a chart of implications for your school that you add to during each meeting.

2. Choose one aspect of your literacy program to assess and focus on, like Jason's staff focused on writing. It could be looking at the daily schedule to see how much time students have to read continuous text, the quality of the book collections in each room, or one of the instructional components described in this book. Determine where you are now and where you want to go. Then, set goals and identify how you will reach those goals.

LITERACY COLLABORATIVE®

Overview

Literacy Collaborative is a comprehensive school reform project designed to improve the reading, writing, and language skills of K–8 children. The cornerstone of this project is dynamic, long-term professional development. School-based literacy coaches are trained in research-based methods; provided with ongoing professional development as they continually implement research-based approaches in their own classrooms; and supported as they provide on-site training for the teachers in their schools. The goal of this comprehensive effort is to significantly raise the level of achievement for all students.

"Reading is a message-getting, problem-solving activity, which increases in power and flexibility the more it is practiced."

—Marie M. Clay

Literacy Collaborative incorporates all of the elements of effective schools to support improved literacy instruction and student achievement through:

- providing a research-based instructional model that is language-based, student-centered, process-oriented, and outcome-based;

- creating in-school and in-district leadership through the training and support of school-based literacy leadership teams, administrators, and literacy coaches;

- establishing long-term, site-based professional development for every member of the school's literacy faculty;

- aligning instruction with the Common Core State Standards for English Language Arts; and

- helping schools monitor the progress of every student through systematized assessment, data collection, and analysis.

"Investing in the development of excellent teachers is the best preparation for our children's future."

Gay Su Pinnell

Dr. Gay Su Pinnell, Ph.D.
Professor Emerita, The Ohio State University

"Because of the Literacy Collaborative's exciting and innovative blended learning design, coaches are away from their schools and families less during their initial training year and have greater contact with their trainers each month."

Patricia L. Scharer

Dr. Patricia L. Scharer, Ph.D.
Professor, The Ohio State University

Literacy Collaborative Project Components

- Research- and Theory-Based Practices
- Continuous Assessment to Inform and Support Instruction
- Comprehensive Instructional Framework
- Flexible Heterogeneous and Homogeneous Student Groupings
- Safety Nets for Struggling Readers and Writers
- School-Based Literacy Team Support
- Home-School Connections
- Professional Books, Children's Literature, and Leveled Reading Library

Professional Development Components

A trained literacy coach works with a school-selected literacy team to implement a plan to support professional development within the school.

- **Staff Development** Teachers participate in ongoing professional development that integrates theory and practice and is conducted by a specially trained literacy coach who is based in the school.
- **Staff Support** Literacy coaches offer ongoing support to the staff through study groups, in-class demonstration lessons, and coaching.
- **Professional Development of Literacy Coaches** Literacy coaches in-training participate in a yearlong course provided through a "blended learning" model. This model is a combination of computer technology and internet components with traditional face-to-face teaching.

Assessment and Research

- **Reflective Practice** Teachers continually reflect on the effectiveness of their teaching through discussions, videotaped analysis, and systematic observation of students' progress.
- **Systematic Assessment** Both formal and informal measures are used to monitor student progress. In the primary grades, these measures include tasks found in An Observation Survey of Early Literacy Achievement (Clay, 1993), running records of text reading, and standardized tests. Intermediate grade teachers base instruction on formal measures, such as Six Traits Writing Rubric, Benchmark Reading Assessment, and state/federal standardized tests, and informal measures such as individual reading & writing conferences and small-group reading observations.
- **Progress Monitoring** Schools monitor their progress by collecting and analyzing their data. A summary of their findings are forwarded to The Ohio State University. Literacy Collaborative conducts multi-year studies to answer research questions regarding issues of implementation.

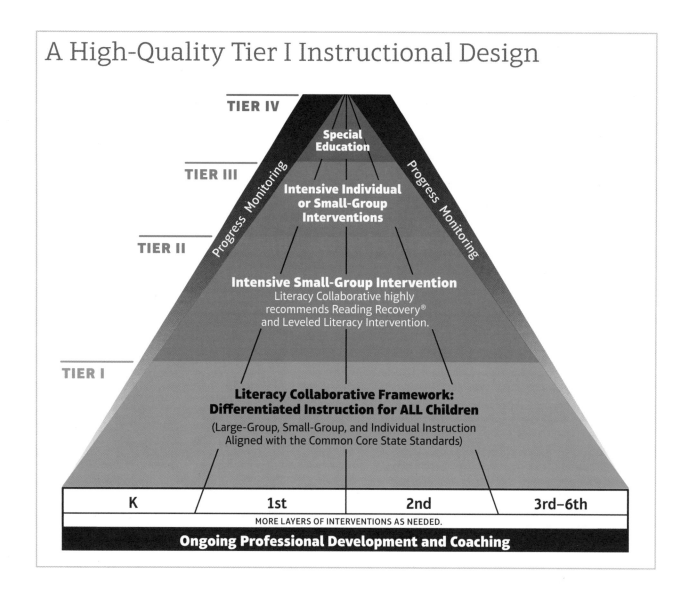

A High-Quality Tier I Instructional Design

TIER IV

Progress Monitoring

Special Education

TIER III

Intensive Individual or Small-Group Interventions

TIER II

Intensive Small-Group Intervention
Literacy Collaborative highly recommends Reading Recovery® and Leveled Literacy Intervention.

TIER I

**Literacy Collaborative Framework:
Differentiated Instruction for ALL Children**

(Large-Group, Small-Group, and Individual Instruction Aligned with the Common Core State Standards)

| K | 1st | 2nd | 3rd–6th |

MORE LAYERS OF INTERVENTIONS AS NEEDED.

Ongoing Professional Development and Coaching

Implementation and Training

Participation in Literacy Collaborative represents ongoing commitment to reshaping literacy education in a school district. Implementation takes place in four phases. For each phase, local planning and decision-making is required. The Literacy Collaborative staff development model builds school capacity by training primary, intermediate, and/or middle-level literacy coaches to work with teachers at their respective grade levels.

The following phases outline the implementation of Literacy Collaborative:

Phase 1: Awareness & Planning

- Participate in professional development designed to achieve broad ownership and understanding of the Literacy Collaborative project. Opportunities include Principals' Academy and Team Planning. (See lcosu.org for offerings.)
- Develop a school plan.
- Submit an application to train a literacy coach.

Phase 2: Literacy Coach Training & Start-Up

- Literacy Coaches are trained at The Ohio State University while simultaneously implementing the Literacy Collaborative framework in their classrooms.
- Create a school-based literacy team made up of stakeholders including the literacy coach, classroom teachers, intervention teachers, and principal who will collaborate to provide leadership for the project.
- Stakeholders begin to build a school book collection.

Phase 3: School-Level Implementation

- Literacy Coach provides a yearlong professional development course for primary, intermediate, or middle level teachers in one school.
- Literacy Coach supports and collaborates with classroom teachers through coaching in classrooms.

- Literacy Coach continues teaching students in a primary, intermediate, or middle-level classroom for the literacy block.
- Literacy Coach attends all ongoing professional development provided by Literacy Collaborative.
- Stakeholders continue to build a school book collection.
- Stakeholders begin a home outreach program such as KEEP BOOKS. (See keepbooks.org for details.)
- Stakeholders collect and analyze data.

Phase 4: Refinement

- Literacy Coach provides continued professional development and classroom coaching for teachers.
- Literacy Coach continues teaching students in a primary, intermediate, or middle-level classroom for the literacy block.
- Literacy Coach attends all ongoing professional development provided by Literacy Collaborative at Ohio State.
- Stakeholders continue to build a school book collection.
- Stakeholders continue a home outreach program such as KEEP BOOKS. (See keepbooks.org for details.)
- Stakeholders collect and analyze data.

Blended Learning Training Design

Mortera-Gutierrez (2006) defines blended learning as "a combination of computer technology and internet components with traditional face-to-face teaching forms." Businesses and educational institutions design learning experiences based on the needs of their students and the type of content to be delivered. The Literacy Collaborative trainers designed the blended training model to have nearly equal hours of face-to-face and online experiences.

The following are the components of Blended Learning:

Face-to-Face Learning
- Classroom Observations
- Behind-the-Glass Demonstrations
- Teaching and Coaching Experiences

Online Interactive Learning
- Interactive Presentations
- Video Sharing
- Large- and Small-Group Activities and Discussion

Self-Paced Learning & Blogging
- Reflection and Analysis of Teaching and Learning
- Application of Learning
- Evaluation and Creation of Lessons

Literacy Collaborative's Effects on Teaching and Student Learning: A Federally Funded Value-Added Study

Dr. Anthony Bryk, President of the Carnegie Foundation for the Advancement of Teaching, and his research team, including researchers from Stanford University, University of Chicago, Northwestern University, Lesley University, and The Ohio State University, conducted a four-year study of the value-added effects of Literacy Collaborative on student learning and achievement in grades K–2. The project was also designed to study growth in teacher expertise and changes in professional communication networks in Literacy Collaborative schools. The primary findings were:

- Students' average rates of learning increased by 16% in the first implementation year, 28% in the second implementation year, and 32% in the third implementation year.

- Teacher expertise increased substantially, and the rate of improvement was predicted by the amount of coaching a teacher received.

- Professional communication among teachers in the schools increased over the three years of implementation, and the literacy coach became more central in the schools' communication networks.

The complete study can be found at lcosu.org.

More information about Literacy Collaborative can be found at online at literacycollaborative.org or by contacting Literacy Collaborative at The Ohio State University or at Lesley University.

Literacy Collaborative®
The Ohio State University

Marsha Levering, Executive Director
614-688-4977 • levering.1@osu.edu
College of Education and Human Ecology
Department of Teaching and Learning
1100 Kinnear Road, Columbus, OH 43212
800-678-6486 • 614-292-7893 • lcosu.org

Literacy Collaborative®
Lesley University

Melissa Fasten
617-349-8424 • litcol@lesley.edu
Center for Reading Recovery and Literacy Collaborative
29 Everett Street, Cambridge, MA 02138
lesley.edu/center-for-reading-recovery-and-literacy-collaborative/literacy-collaborative-model • 617-349-8424

RESOURCES FOR INTERACTIVE READ-ALOUDS

Prolific Writers for Interactive Read-Aloud

Mac Barnett
Jen Bryant
Eve Bunting
Nicola Davies
Ame Dyckman

Michaël Escoffier
Bob Graham
Elise Gravel
Emily Gravett
Kevin Henkes

Oliver Jeffers
Jon Klassen
Patrick McDonnell
Andrea Davis
  Pinkney

Patricia Polacco
Doreen Rappaport
Dan Santat
Bob Shea
William Steig

David Ezra Stein
Melissa Sweet
Chris Van Allsburg
Mélanie Watt
David Wiesner

Mo Willems
Jonah Winter
Jacqueline
  Woodson

Fiction Picture Books: Younger Readers

Atteberry, K. (2015). *Bunnies!!!* New York: HarperCollins.

Bagley, J. (2015). *Boats for Papa.* New York: Roaring Brook Press.

Barnett, M. (2009). *Billy Twitters and his blue whale problem.* Illus. A. Rex. New York: Disney-Hyperion.

Barnett, M. (2012). *Chloe and the lion.* Illus. A. Rex. New York: Disney-Hyperion.

Barnett, M. (2014). *Sam and Dave dig a hole.* Illus. J. Klassen. Somerville, MA: Candlewick.

Boelts, M. (2009). *Those shoes.* Illus. N. Z. Jones. Somerville, MA: Candlewick.

Boelts, M. (2016). *A bike like Sergio's.* Illus. N. Z. Jones. Somerville, MA: Candlewick.

Cummins, L. R. (2016). *A hungry lion, or a dwindling assortment of animals.* New York: Atheneum.

Dormer, F. W. (2016). *The sword in the stove.* New York: Atheneum.

Dubuc, M. (2014). *The lion and the bird.* Brooklyn, NY: Enchanted Lion Books.

Dyckman, A. (2013). *Tea party rules.* Illus. K. G. Campbell. New York: Scholastic.

Dyckman, A. (2015). *Wolfie the bunny.* Illus. Z. OHora. New York: Little, Brown.

Dyckman, A. (2016). *Horrible bear!* Illus. Z. OHora. New York: Little, Brown.

Escoffier, M. (2013). *Brief thief.* Illus. K. Di Giacomo. Brooklyn, NY: Enchanted Lion Books.

Feiffer, J. (1999). *Bark, George.* New York: HarperCollins.

Fergus, M. (2015). *Buddy and Earl.* Illus. C. Sookocheff. Toronto, Canada: Groundwood Books.

Friend, C. (2007). *The perfect nest.* Illus. J. Manders. Somerville, MA: Candlewick.

Graham, B. (2003). *"Let's get a pup!" said Kate.* Somerville, MA: Candlewick.

Gravett, E. (2006). *Wolves.* New York: Simon & Schuster Books.

Hall, M. (2015). *Red: A crayon's story.* New York: Greenwillow Books.

Henkes, K. (2006). *Lilly's purple plastic purse.* New York: Greenwillow Books.

Higgins, R. T. (2015). *Mother Bruce.* New York: Disney-Hyperion.

Jeffers, O. (2011). *Stuck.* New York. Philomel Books.

John, J. (2016). *Penguin problems.* Illus. L. Smith. New York: Random House.

Judge, L. (2015). *Good morning to me!* New York: Atheneum.

Klassen, J. (2011). *I want my hat back.* Somerville, MA: Candlewick.

Klassen, J. (2012). *This is not my hat.* Somerville, MA: Candlewick.

Klise, K. (2017). *Stay: A girl, a dog, a bucket list.* Illus. M. S. Klise. New York: Feiwel & Friends.

Knudsen, M. (2006). *Library lion.* Illus. K. Hawkes. Somerville, MA: Candlewick.

Lindström, E. (2017). *My dog Mouse.* Wellington, New Zealand: Gecko Press.

MacGregor, R. (2014). *The highest number in the world.* Illus. G. Després. Toronto, Canada: Tundra Books.

McDonnell, P. (2011). *Me…Jane.* New York: Little, Brown and Company.

Morris, R. T. (2014). *This is a moose.* Illus. T. Lichtenheld. New York: Little, Brown Books.

Rabinowitz, A. (2014). *A boy and a jaguar.* Illus. C. Chien. New York: HMH Books.

Rathman, P. (1995). *Officer Buckle and Gloria.* New York: Penguin Group.

Rex, A. (2016). *School's first day of school.* Illus. C. Robinson. New York: Roaring Brook Press.

Roberton, F. (2010). *Wanted: The perfect pet.* New York: G. P. Putnam's Sons Books.

Polacco, P. (2005). *Emma Kate.* New York: Philomel Books.

Santat, D. (2014). *The adventures of Beekle: The unimaginary friend.* New York: Little, Brown Books.

Sarcone-Roach, J. (2015). *The bear ate your sandwich.* New York: Alfred A. Knopf.

Saudo, C. (2012). *My dad is big and strong BUT… A bedtime story.* Brooklyn, NY: Enchanted Lion Books.

Shea, B. (2015). *Ballet cat: The totally secret secret.* New York: Disney-Hyperion.

Steig, W. (1986). *Brave Irene.* New York: Farrar, Straus and Giroux.

Stein, D. E. (2010). *Interrupting chicken.* Somerville, MA: Candlewick.

Vere, E. (2015). *Max the brave.* Naperville, IL: Sourcebooks Jabberwocky.

Watt, M. (2006). *Scaredy squirrel.* Toronto, Canada: Kids Can Press.

Watt, M. (2007). *Chester.* New York: Scholastic.

Wiesner, D. (2001). *The three pigs.* Boston, MA: Clarion Books.

Willems, M. (2010). *City dog, country frog.* Illus. J. J. Muth. New York: Disney-Hyperion.

Woodson, J. (2012). *Each kindness.* Illus. E. B. Lewis. New York: Nancy Paulsen Books.

Yum, H. (2012). *Mom, it's my first day of kindergarten!* New York: Farrar, Straus and Giroux.

Fiction Picture Books: Older Readers

Beaty, D. (2013). *Knock, knock: My dad's dream for me*. Illus. B. Collier. New York: Little, Brown Books.

Bee, W. (2008). *Beware of the frog*. Somerville, MA: Candlewick.

Bildner, P. (2014). *The soccer fence: A story of friendship, hope, and apartheid in South Africa*. Illus. J. J. Watson. New York: G.P. Putnam's Sons Books.

Bunting, E. (1993). *Fly away home*. New York: HMH Books.

Cox, L. (2014). *Elizabeth, queen of the seas*. New York: Schwartz & Wade.

Daly, C. (2014). *Emily's blue period*. Illus. L. Brown. New York: Roaring Brook Press.

Deedy, C. A. (2009). *14 cows for America*. Illus. T. Gonzalez. Atlanta, GA: Peachtree.

Davies, N. (2017). *The promise*. Illus. L. Carlin. Somerville, MA: Candlewick.

Elliott, Z. (2008). *Bird*. Illus. S. Strickland. New York: Lee & Low Books.

Fraustino, L. R. (2001). *The hickory chair*. Illus. B. Andrews. New York: Arthur A. Levine Books.

Fleischman, P. (2013). *The matchbox diary*. Illus. B. Ibatoulline. Somerville, MA: Candlewick.

Henson, H. (2008). *That book woman*. New York: Atheneum.

Howe, J. (2012). *Otter and Odder: A love story*. Illus. C. Raschka. Somerville, MA: Candlewick.

Hughes, L. (2009). *The Negro speaks of rivers*. Illus. E. B. Lewis. New York: Disney.

Meyer, S. L. (2016). *New shoes*. Illus. E. Velasquez. New York: Holiday House.

Neeman, S. (2013). *Something big*. Illus. I. Godon. Brooklyn, NY: Enchanted Lion Books.

Nelson, V. M. (2015). *The book itch: Freedom, truth & Harlem's greatest bookstore*. Illus. R. G. Christie. Minneapolis, MN: Carolrhoda Books.

Tan, S. (2000). *The red tree*. Victoria, Australia: Lothian Books.

Van Allsburg, C. (1991). *The wretched stone*. New York: HMH Books.

Informational Picture Books: Biographies

Andrews, T. (2015). *Trombone Shorty*. Bryan Collier. New York: Abrams Books.

Berne, J. (2013). *On a beam of light: A story of Albert Einstein*. Illus. V. Radunsky. San Francisco, CA: Chronicle Books.

Bryant, J. (2014). *The right word: Roget and his thesaurus*. Illus. M. Sweet. Grand Rapids, MI: Eerdmans Books.

Burgess, M. (2015). *Enormous smallness: A story of e. e. cummings*. Illus. K. Di Giacomo. Brooklyn, NY: Enchanted Lion books.

Mahin, M. (2017). *Muddy: The story of blues legend Muddy Waters*. Illus. E. Turk. New York: Atheneum.

Malaspina, A. (2011). *Touch the sky: Alice Coachman, Olympic high jumper*. Illus. E. Velasquez. Park Ridge, IL: Albert Whitman & Company.

Nelson, K. (2013). *Nelson Mandela*. New York: HarperCollins.

Pinkney, A. D. (2016). *A poem for Peter: The story of Ezra Jack Keats and the creation of The Snowy Day*. Illus. S. Johnson and L. Fancher. New York: Viking Books.

Prévot, F. (2015). *Wangari Maathai: The woman who planted millions of trees*. Illus. A. Fronty. Watertown, MA: Charlesbridge.

Rappaport, D. (2009). *Eleanor, quiet no more*. Illus. G. Kelley. New York: Disney-Hyperion.

Rinker, S. D. (2017). *Big machines: The story of Virginia Lee Burton*. Illus. J. Rocco. New York: HMH Books.

Robinson, F. (2016). *Ada's ideas: The story of Ada Lovelace, the world's first computer programmer*. New York: Abrams Books.

Rosenstock, B. (2016). *Dorothea's eyes: Dorothea Lange photographs the truth*. Illus. G. DuBois. Honesdale, PA: Calkins Creek.

Schubert, L. (2012). *Monsieur Marceau*. Illus. G. Dubois. New York: Roaring Brook Press.

Snyder, L. (2015). *Swan: The life and dance of Anna Pavlova*. Illus. J. Morstad. San Francisco, CA. Chronicle Books.

Steptoe, J. (2016). *Radiant child: The story of young artist Jean-Michel Basquiat*. New York: Little, Brown Books.

Sweet, M. (2011). *Balloons over Broadway: The true story of the puppeteer of Macy's parade*. New York: HMH.

Sweet, M. (2016). *Some writer! The story of E. B. White*. New York: HMH Books.

Weatherford, C. B. (2017). *Dorothea Lange: The photographer who found the faces of the Depression*. Park Ridge, IL: Albert Whitman & Company.

Winter, J. (2002). *Frida*. Illus. A. Juan. New York: Arthur A. Levine Books.

Informational Picture Books: Science

Cox, L. (2014). *Elizabeth, queen of the seas*. Illus. B. Floca. New York: Schwartz & Wade.

Davies, N. (2015). *I (don't) like snakes*. Luciano Lozano. Somerville, MA: Candlewick.

Desmond, J. (2015). *The blue whale*. Brooklyn, NY: Enchanted Lion Books.

Desmond, J. (2016). *The polar bear*. Brooklyn, NY: Enchanted Lion Books.

Fleming, C. (2016). *Giant squid*. Illus. E. Rohmann. New York: Roaring Brook Press.

Gravel, E. The disgusting critters series. Toronto, Canada: Tundra Books.

Guiberson, B. Z. (2015). *The most amazing creature in the sea*. Illus. G. Spirin. New York: Henry Holt.

Guiberson, B. Z. (2016). *The deadliest creature in the world*. Illus. G. Spirin. New York: Henry Holt.

Huber, R. (2015). *Flight of the honey bee*. Illus. B. Lovelock. Somerville, MA: Candlewick.

Jenkins, M. (2011). *Can we save the tiger?* Illus. V. White. Somerville, MA: Candlewick.

Judge, L. (2014). *Born in the wild: Baby mammals and their parents*. New York: Roaring Brook Press.

Markle, S. The case of the vanishing _____ series. Minneapolis, MN: Millbrook Press.

Paul, M. (2015). *Water is water: A book about the water cycle*. Illus. J. Chin. New York: Roaring Brook Press.

Saxby, C. (2015). *Big red kangaroo*. Illus. G. Byrne. Somerville, MA: Candlewick.

Saxby, C. (2015). *Emu*. Illus. G. Byrne. Somerville, MA: Candlewick.

Shingu, S. (2015). *Wandering whale sharks*. Ontario, Canada: Owlkids Books.

PROFESSIONAL RESOURCES FOR WORD STUDY

Bear, D. R., Invernizzi, M. R., Johnston, F., & Templeton, S. (2010). *Words their way: Letter and picture sorts for emergent spellers, 2nd edition*. Upper Saddle River, NJ: Pearson.

Dahl, K. L., Scharer, P. L., Lawson, L. L., & Grogan, P. R. (2001). *Rethinking phonics: Making the best teaching decisions*. Portsmouth, NH: Heinemann.

Fountas, I. C., & Pinnell, G. S. (Eds.). (1999). *Voices on word matters: Learning about phonics and spelling in the literacy classroom*. Portsmouth, NH: Heinemann.

Fountas, I. C., & Pinnell, G. S. (2001). *Guiding readers and writers: Teaching comprehension, genre, and content literacy, grades 2+/3–6*. Portsmouth, NH: Heinemann.

Fountas, I. C., & Pinnell, G. S. (2005). *Word study: Phonics and spelling lessons/buddy study system [DVD video collection]*. Portsmouth, NH: Heinemann.

Fountas, I. C., & Pinnell, G. S. (2006). *Teaching for comprehending and fluency: Thinking, talking, and writing about reading, K–8*. Portsmouth, NH: Heinemann.

Fountas, I. C., & Pinnell, G. S. (2017). *Sing a song of poetry: A teaching resource for phonemic awareness, phonics and fluency, grade K, 2nd edition*. Portsmouth, NH: Heinemann.

Fountas, I. C., & Pinnell, G. S. (2017). *Sing a song of poetry: A teaching resource for phonemic awareness, phonics and fluency, grade 1, 2nd edition*. Portsmouth, NH: Heinemann.

Ganske, K. (2006). *Word sorts and more: Sound, pattern, and meaning explorations K–3*. New York: Guilford Press.

Ganske, K. (2008). *Mindful of words: Spelling and vocabulary explorations 4–8*. New York: Guilford Press.

Helman, L., Bear, D. R., Invernizzi, M. R., Templeton, S., & Johnston, F. (2009). *Emergent sorts for Spanish-speaking English learners*. Upper Saddle River, NJ: Pearson.

Helman, L., Bear, D. R., Invernizzi, M. R., Templeton, S., & Johnston, F. (2009). *Words their way: Letter-name alphabetic sorts for Spanish-speaking English learners*. Upper Saddle River, NJ: Pearson.

Helman, L., Bear, D. R., Templeton, S., Invernizzi, M. R., & Johnston, F. (2012). *Words their way with English learners: Word study for phonics, vocabulary, and spelling, 2nd edition*. Upper Saddle River, NJ: Pearson.

Helman, L., Bear, D. R., Invernizzi, M. R., Templeton, S., & Johnston, F. (2014). *Within word pattern sorts for Spanish-speaking English learners*. Upper Saddle River, NJ: Pearson.

Johnston, F., Invernizzi, M. R., Helman, L., Bear, D. R., Templeton, S. (2015). *Words their way for preK–K*. Upper Saddle River, NJ: Pearson.

Johnston, F., Invernizzi, M. R., Bear, D. R., & Templeton, S. (2018). *Words their way: Word sorts for letter name – alphabetic spellers, 3rd edition*. Upper Saddle River, NJ: Pearson.

Johnston, F., Invernizzi, M. R., Bear, D. R., & Templeton, S. (2018). *Words their way: Word sorts for syllables and affixes spellers, 3rd edition*. Upper Saddle River, NJ: Pearson.

Pinnell, G. S., & Fountas, I. C. (2003). *Sing a song of poetry: A teaching resource for phonics, word study, and fluency, grade 2*. Portsmouth, NH: Heinemann.

Rasinski, T., & Zutell, J. (2010). *Essential strategies for word study: Effective methods for improving decoding, spelling, and vocabulary*. New York: Scholastic.

Templeton, S., Johnston, F., Bear, D. R., & Invernizzi, M. R. (2009). *Words their way: Word sorts for derivational relations spellers, 3rd edition*. Upper Saddle River, NJ: Pearson.

Templeton, S., Bear, D. R., Invernizzi, M. R., Johnston, F., Flanigan, K., Townsend, D. R., Helman, L., & Hayes, L. (2015). *Vocabulary their way: Word study with middle and secondary students, 2nd edition*. Upper Saddle River, NJ: Pearson.

SUPPORTING WORD STUDY THROUGH CHILDREN'S LITERATURE *Patricia L. Scharer & Lisa Pinkerton*

Alliteration

Edwards, P. D. (1997). *Dinorella: A prehistoric fairy tale*. Illus. H. Cole. New York: Hyperion.

Edwards, P. D. (1996). *Some smug slug*. Illus. H. Cole. New York: HarperCollins.

Edwards, P. D. (1995). *Four famished foxes and Fosdyke*. Illus. H. Cole. New York: HarperCollins.

Enderle, J. & Tessler, S. (1997). *Six sandy sheep*. Illus. J. O'Brien. Honesdale, PA: Boyds Mills.

Jonas, A. (1997). *Watch William walk*. New York: Greenwillow.

Lindbergh, R. (1997). *The awful aardvarks go to school*. Illus. T. C. Pearson. New York: Penguin Putnam.

Most, B. (1998). *A pair of protoceratops*. San Diego, CA: Harcourt Brace.

Most, B. (1998). *A trio of triceratops*. San Diego, CA: Harcourt Brace.

Alphabet Fun

Arnosky, J. (1999). *Mouse letters: A very first alphabet book*. New York: Clarion.

Barrett, J. (2016). *An excessive alphabet: Avalanches of As to zillions of Zs*. Illus. R. Barrett. New York: Simon & Schuster.

Bingham, K. (2012). *Z is for moose*. Illus. P.O. Zelinsky. New York: Greenwillow Books.

Cabatingan, E. (2012). *A is for musk ox*. Illus. M. Myers. New York: Roaring Brook Press.

Cahoon, H. (1999). *Word play ABC*. New York: Walker and Company.

Chandra, D. (1999). *A is for Amos*. Illus. K. Narahashi. New York: Farrar, Straus, & Giroux.

Cohen, I. (1997). *ABC discovery! An alphabet book of picture puzzles.* New York: Dial Books.

Cox, P. (1997). *Abstract alphabet: A book of animals.* San Francisco: Chronicle Books.

Darling, K. (1998). *ABC cats.* New York: Walker.

Delacre, L. (2016). *Olinguito, from A to Z!: Unveiling the cloud forest.* New York: Lee & Low.

Edwards, P. D. (1999). *The wacky wedding: A book of alphabet antics.* Illus. H. Cole. New York: Hyperion.

Gerstein, M. (1999). *The absolutely awful alphabet.* San Diego, CA: Harcourt Brace.

Horenstein, H. (1999). *A is for…? A photographer's alphabet of animals.* San Diego, CA: Harcourt Brace.

Lester, A. (1998). *Alice and Aldo.* Boston, MA: Houghton Mifflin.

Rosenthal, A. K. (2011). *Al pha's bet.* Illus. D. Durand. New York: G.P. Putnam's Sons Books for Young Readers.

Schwartz, D. M. (1998). *G is for googol.* Illus. Marissa Moss. Berkeley, CA: Tricycle.

Tobias, T. (1998). *A world of words: An ABC of quotations.* Illus. P. Malone. New York: Lothrup, Lee & Shepard.

Twohy, M. (2016). *Oops pounce quick run! An alphabet caper.* New York: Blazer + Bray.

Viorst, J. (1994). *The alphabet from Z to A (with much confusion on the way).* Illus. R. Hull. New York: Atheneum.

Voiland, A. (2017). *ABCs from space.* New York: Simon & Schuster.

Walton, R. (1998). *So many bunnies: A bedtime ABC and counting book.* Illus. P. Miglio. New York: Lothrop, Lee & Shepard.

Wilbur, R. (1998). *The disappearing alphabet.* Illus. D. Diaz. San Diego, CA: Harcourt Brace.

Wood, A. (2001). *Alphabet adventure.* Illus. B. Wood. New York: The Blue Sky Press

Nouns, Verbs, and Palindromes, Oh My!

Agee, J. (1994). *So many dynamos! And other Palindromes.* New York: Farrar, Straus, & Giroux.

Agee, J. (1999). *Sit on a potato pan, Otis! More palindromes.* New York: Farrar, Straus, & Giroux.

Cleary, B. (2013). *Sparrow, eagle, penguin, and seagull: What is a bird?* Illus. M. Goneau. Minneapolis, MN: Millbrook Press.

Cleary, B. (2012). *Madam and nun and 1001: What is a palindrome?* Illus. B. Gable. Minneapolis, MN: Millbrook Press.

Cleary, B. (2012). *Feet and puppies, thieves and guppies: What are irregular plurals?* Illus. B. Gable. Minneapolis, MN: Millbrook Press.

Cleary, B. (2010). *I'm and won't, they're and don't: What's a contraction?* Illus. B. Gable. Minneapolis, MN: Millbrook Press.

Cleary, B. (2010). *But and for, yet and nor: What's a conjunction?* Illus. B. Gable. Minneapolis, MN: Millbrook Press.

Cleary, B. (2008). *Stroll and walk, babble and talk: More about synonyms.* Illus. B. Gable. Minneapolis, MN: Millbrook Press.

Cleary, B. (2002). *Under, over, by the clover: What is a preposition?* Illus. B. Gable. Minneapolis, MN: Carolrhoda.

Cleary, B. (2001). *To root. to toot, to parachute: What is a verb?* Illus. J. Prosmitsky. Minneapolis, MN: Carolrhoda.

Cleary, B. (2000). *Hairy, scary, ordinary: What is an adjective?* Illus. J. Prosmitsky. Minneapolis, MN: Carolrhoda.

Cleary, B. (1999). *A mink, a fink, a skating rink: What is a noun?* Illus. J. Prosmitsky. Minneapolis, MN: Carolrhoda.

Hanson, J. (1972). *Synonyms: Words that mean the same thing.* Minneapolis, MN: Lerner Publications.

Heller, R. (1997). *Mine, all mine: A book about pronouns.* New York: Grosset & Dunlap.

Heller, R. (1991). *Up, up and away: A book about adverbs.* New York: Grosset & Dunlap.

Heller, R. (1990). *Merry-go-round: A book about nouns.* New York: Scholastic.

Heller, R. (1989). *A cache of jewels: And other collective nouns.* New York: Scholastic.

Heller, R. (1989). *Many luscious lollipops: A book about adjectives.* New York: Scholastic.

Heller, R. (1988). *Kites sail high: A book about verbs.* New York: Scholastic.

Shulman, M. (2006). *Mom and dad are plaindromes.* Illus. A. McCauley. San Francisco, CA: Chronicle Books.

Always Time for Poetry

Brown, C. (1998). *Polka bats and octopus slacks.* Boston MA: Houghton Mifflin.

Brown, S. (2016). *Slickety quick: Poems about sharks.* Illus. B. Kolar. Somerville, MA: Candlewick Press.

Church, C. J. (2002). *Do your ears hang low?* New York: Scholastic.

Dominguez, A. (2016). *How do you say? Cómo se dice?* New York: Henry Holt & Company.

Florian, D. (1999). *Laugh-eteria.* San Diego, CA Harcourt Brace.

Florian, D. (1998). *Insectopedia.* San Diego, CA: Harcourt Brace.

Florian, D. (1997). *In the swim.* New York: Harcourt Brace.

Fogliano, J. (2016). *When green becomes tomatoes: Poems for all seasons.* Illus. J. Morstad. New York: Roaring Brook Press.

Goldstone, B. (1998). *The beastly feast.* Illus. B. Lent. New York: Henry Holt.

Harris, P. (1997). *Mouse creeps.* Illus. R. Cartwright. New York: Dial.

Harrison, D. (2016). *Now you see them, now you don't: Poems about creatures that hide.* Illus. G. Laroche. Watertown, MA: Charlesbridge.

Hopkins, L. B. (2015). *Jumping off library shelves: A book of poems.* Illus. J. Manning. Honesdale, PA: Boyds Mills Press.

Hopkins, L. B. (2012). *Nasty bugs.* Illus. W. Terry. New York: Puffin Books.

Janeczko, P. (1998). *That sweet diamond.* Illus. P. Carole Katchen. New York: Simon & Schuster.

Lewis, J. P. (2017). *Make the earth your companion.* Illus. A Balbusso & E. Balbusso. Mankato, MN: Creative Editionsl

Lewis, J. P. (2014). *Everything is a poem: The best of J. Patrick Lewis*. Illus. M.C. Pritelli. Mankato, MN: Creative Editions.

Lewis, J. P. (1998). *The little buggers*. New York: Dial.

Lewis, J. P. (1998). *Doodle dandies: Poems that take shape*. Illus. L. Desimini. New York: Simon & Schuster.

McKissack, P. (2017). *Let's clap, jump, sing, and shout*. Illus. B. Pinkney. New York: Penguin Random House.

Nichol, B. (1997). *Biscuits in the cupboard*. Toronto: Stoddart Kids.

Paschkis, J. (2015). *Flutter & hum: Animal poems/Aleteo y zumbido: Poemas de animals*. New York: Henry Holt & Company.

Raczka, B. (2016). *Wet cement: A mix of concrete poems*. New York: Roaring Brook Press.

Root, P. (1998). *One duck stuck: A mucky ducky counting book*. Illus. Jane Chapman. Somerville, MA: Candlewick Press.

Sayre, A. P. (2017). *Full of fall*. New York: Simon & Schuster.

Sierra, J. (1998). *Antarctic antics*. Illus. J. Aruego & A. Dewey. San Diego, CA: Harcourt Brace.

Singer, M. (2016). *Echo echo: reverso poems about myths*. Illus. J. Masse. New York: Dial Books for Young Readers

Vardell, S., & Wong, J. (2016). *You just wait: A poetry Friday power book*. Princeton, NJ: Pomelo Books.

Viorst, J. (2016). *What are you glad about? What are you mad about?* Illus. L. White. New York: Simon & Schuster.

Word Play

Archer, D. (2013). *Urgency emergency! Big Bad Wolf*. Park Ridge, IL: Albert Whitman & Company.

Archer, D. (2013). *Urgency emergency! Itsy Bitsy Spider*. Park Ridge, IL: Albert Whitman & Company

Baker, K. (1999). *Quack and count*. San Diego, CA: Harcourt Brace.

Banks, K. (2011). *Max's castle*. Illus. B. Kulikov. New York: Farrar, Straus, & Giroux

Banks, K. (2006). *Max's words*. Illus. B. Kulikov. New York: Farrar, Straus, & Giroux

Barretta, G. (2010). *Dear deer: A book of homophones*. New York: Square Fish.

Bryan, S., & Murphy, T. (2011). *A boy and his bear*. New York: Arcade Publishing.

Bryan, S., & Murphy, T. (2011). *A boy and his bunny*. New York: Arcade Publishing.

Bryan, S., & Murphy, T. (2011). *A girl and her gator*. New York: Arcade Publishing.

Bynum, J. (1999). *Altoona Baboona*. San Diego, CA: Harcourt Brace.

Carr. J. (1999). *Frozen noses*. Illus. D. Donohue. New York: Holiday House.

Cleary, B. P. (2006). *Rhyme and PUNishment: Adventures in wordplay*. Illus. J.P. Sandy. Minneapolis, MN: Millbrook Press.

Clements, A. (1999). *Workshop*. Illus. D. Wisniewski. New York: Clarion.

Davey, O. (2012). *Knight night*. Somerville, MA: Templar Books.

Falwell, C. (1998). *Word wizard*. New York: Clarion.

Gwynne, F. (1976). *A chocolate moose for dinner*. New York: Simon & Schuster.

Gwynne, F. (1980). *The sixteen hand horse*. New York: Simon & Schuster.

Hepworth, C. (1998). *Bug off!* New York: Putnam.

Hoberman, M. A. (1998). *Miss Mary Mack*. Illus. N.B. Westcott. Boston, MA: Little, Brown.

Huck, C. (1998). *A creepy countdown*. Illus. J. A. Smith. New York: Greenwillow.

London, J. (1999). *Wiggle waggle*. Illus. M. Rex. San Diego, CA: Harcourt Brace.

Long, E. (2012). *Up! Tall! And high!* New York: G.P. Putnam's Sons Books for Young Readers.

Maestro, G. (1984). *What's a frank, Frank?: Tasty homograph riddles*. New York: Clarion Books.

Martin Jr., B. (1967). *Brown Bear, Brown Bear, What do you see?* Illus. E. Carle. New York: Henry Holt & Company.

Martin Jr., B. (2003). *Panda Bear, Panda Bear, What do you see?* Illus. E. Carle. New York: Henry Holt & Company.

Martin Jr., B. (1982). *Polar Bear, Polar Bear, What do you hear?* Illus. E. Carle. New York: Henry Holt & Company.

Most, B. (1999). *Z-Z-Zoink!* Orlando, FL: Harcourt Brace.

Park, L. S. (2016). *Yaks yak: Animal word pairs*. Illus. J.B. Reinhardt. New York: Clarion Books.

Rand, A., & Rand, P. (2006). *Sparkle and spin: A book about words*. San Francisco, CA: Chronicle Books.

Root, P. (1998). *One duck stuck: A mucky ducky counting book*. Illus. Jane Chapman. Somerville, MA: Candlewick Press.

Rosenthal, A. K. (2012). *Wumbers*. Illus. T. Lichtenheld. San Francisco, CA: Chronicle Books.

Rosenthal, A. K. (2012). *I scream! Ice cream! A book of wordles*. Illus. S. Bloch. San Francisco, CA: Chronicle Books.

Schotter, R. (2006). *The boy who loved words*. Illus. G. Potter. New York: Schwartz & Wade.

Stein, D. E. (2010). *Interrupting chicken*. Somerville, MA: Candlewick Press.

Terban, M. (1988). *The dove dove: Funny homograph riddles*. Illus. T. Huffman. New York: Clarion.

Terban, M. (1987). *Mad as a wet hen!: And other funny idioms*. Illus. G. Maestro. New York: Clarion.

Terban, M. (1986). *Your foot's on my feet! And other tricky nouns*. Illus. G. Maestro. New York: Clarion.

Terban, M. (1985). *Too hot to hoot: Funny palindrome riddles*. Illus. G. Maestro. New York: Clarion.

Terban, M. (1983). *In a pickle and other funny idioms*. Illus. G. Maestro. New York: Clarion.

Terban, M. (1982). *Eight ate: A feast of homonym riddles*. Illus. G. Maestro. New York: Clarion.

Thomas, J. (2009). *Rhyming Dust Bunnies*. New York: Beach Lane Books.

Thomas, S. M. (2011). *Good night, Good knight*. Illus. J. Plecas. New York: Penguin Young Readers.

Ziefert, H. (1997). *Baby buggy, buggy baby*. Illus. R. Brown. Boston: Houghton Mifflin.

KEEP BOOKS®

The Joy of Learning to Read!

KEEP BOOKS are designed as a school/home (PreK through grade 2) book program that addresses the need for inexpensive but appropriate books in the home. KEEP BOOKS:

- were developed and written by educators at The Ohio State University.
- are sold on a not-for-profit basis and help support literacy programs at The Ohio State University for twice the literacy impact.
- provide children with books to take home to read again and again.
- create positive communications with parents and caregivers.
- allow children to take ownership and develop their own library.
- enhance achievement because children are motivated and encouraged to read at home.
- are leveled for Guided Reading (Fountas & Pinnell) and Reading Recovery®.

What are KEEP BOOKS?

KEEP BOOKS are little books that children can take home to keep and read again and again. These little books support beginning readers by offering enjoyable stories and a chance to read with independence. The stories in KEEP BOOKS are about children's everyday lives, and they are simple but interesting and often amusing. They are illustrated with black-and-white line drawings and have colorful covers. Most KEEP BOOKS have eight pages and measure 5½" by 4¼"—just the right size for a child's hands. Children will enjoy writing their names in their books and coloring or adding to the pictures. KEEP BOOKS also offer a good model for children as they begin to write. They can write their own books using My Own KEEP BOOKS®.

What Is the Purpose of KEEP BOOKS?

KEEP BOOKS:

- provide a great deal of easy reading material so children get lots of practice.
- include many high-frequency words that children read again and again, thus building word knowledge.
- provide opportunities for children to notice how words "work" and learn phonics skills.
- make it possible for children to read on their own rather than always depending on adults.
- motivate children to write.
- build a library of books at home that children can access any time.
- help children learn to store, care for, and retrieve books.
- help children build confidence in themselves as readers.

Some KEEP BOOKS sets have special purposes. For example, the *Letters, Sounds, & Words* sets are designed to help children learn more about letters, sounds, and words. The *Nursery Rhymes and Rhymes & Songs 1* sets are designed to help children learn traditional rhymes and songs and connect them with written language. *Letters, Words, & Numbers* and *Letters, Words, & Numbers Caption Books* sets focus on math concepts, so children are learning to "read" and figure out the kinds of problems that require mathematical reasoning. The *Fact & Fiction 1* set contains eight paired books. Each fictional title offers an interesting story that is paired with a factual book on the same topic. All are designed to increase children's confidence and their value for reading.

Variety of Uses for KEEP BOOKS

Shared Reading

BIG KEEP BOOKS correspond to their smaller counterparts and are available for the *Caption Books, Emergent Reader 1, Nursery Rhymes, Rhymes & Songs 1, Spanish Caption Books, Spanish Emergent Reader 1*, and *Spanish Nursery Rhymes* sets. BIG KEEP BOOKS measure 8½" by 11", have laminated covers, and their print has been designed so that it is easy for children to see. You introduce the book through shared reading, and then children read the little books for themselves.

Small Group Reading

The *Raccoon Family Adventure 1* series is available in color for use with individual and small group reading lessons. The resource *Teaching Suggestions for a Reading Lesson* is included on the inside back cover for:

- Interactive introductions
- Word study
- Language/vocabulary study
- Comprehension/discussion questions
- Writing ideas to extend the story

Add the Small Group Reading set to your permanent classroom collection and/or school book room. The corresponding black & white version is for students to take home.

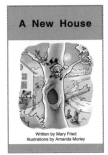
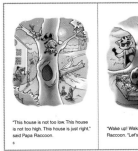

Self-Extending Reading

Relating fact to fiction can make learning fun for children. The *Fact & Fiction 1* KEEP BOOKS set features eight paired books focusing on fun topics like thunderstorms, the ocean, sunflower plants, and cats. Each fictional title offers an interesting story that is paired with a factual book on the same topic. These books are larger (5½" by 8½") and have 16 pages to challenge a self-extending reader.

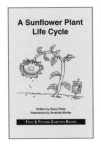
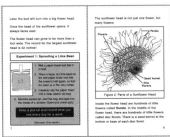

Story Writing

My Own KEEP BOOKS are blank books that can be used to reinforce a variety of lessons: reading, writing, drawing, and math! Many children enjoy writing their own KEEP BOOKS and are easily able to follow the format of their favorite story. My Own KEEP BOOKS can be purchased in individual and group quantities and also in large format (15 large 8½" by 11" books with 12 pages).

KEEP BOOKS®

The Ohio State University

Marsha Levering, Executive Director
614-688-4977 | keepbooks@osu.edu

College of Education and Human Ecology
Department of Teaching and Learning
1100 Kinnear Road | Columbus, OH 43212
800-678-6484 | 614-292-2869 | keepbooks.org

For more information on KEEP BOOKS including Spanish and Haitian versions, see Scholastic.com/RLResources.com. For ordering information, see keepbooks.org.

REFERENCES

Allington, R. L., & Johnston, P. H. (2002). *Reading to learn: Lessons from exemplar fourth-grade classrooms.* New York: Guilford Press.

Anderson, C. (2000). *How's it going? A practical guide to conferring with student writers.* Portsmouth, NH: Heinemann.

Anderson, R. C.,Wilson, P. T., & Fielding, L. C. (1998). Growth in reading and how children spend their time outside of school. *Reading Research Quarterly, 23*(3), 285–303.

Anyon, J. (1981). Social class and school knowledge. *Curriculum Inquiry,* 11, 1–42.

Askew, B., Pinnell, G. S., & Scharer, P. L. (2014). *Promising literacy for every child: Reading Recovery and a comprehensive literacy system.* Columbus, OH: Reading Recovery Council of North America.

Bagley, S. (1997). "How to build a baby's brain." *Newsweek, Special Edition,* spring/summer: 28–32.

Bakhtin, M. M. (1981). *The dialogic imagination,* trans. Holquist, M. and Emerson, C. Austin, TX: University of Texas Press.

Bear, D. R., Invernizzi, M. R., Templeton, S., & Johnston, F. (2016). *Words their way: Word study for phonics, vocabulary, and spelling instruction, 6th edition.* Upper Saddle River, NJ: Pearson.

Beaver, J. (2012). *Developmental reading assessment.* Parsippany, NJ: Pearson.

Beck, I. L., McKeown, M. G., & Kucan, L. (2013). *Bringing words to life: Robust vocabulary instruction* (2nd ed.). New York: Guilford Press.

Berninger, V., Mizokawa, D. T., & Bragg, R. (1991). Theory-based diagnosis and remediation of writing disabilities. *Journal of School Psychology,* 29, 57–79.

Bishop, R. S. (1990a). Keynote speech: "Windows and mirrors: Children's books and parallel cultures." San Bernardino, CA: California State University, Reading Conference.

Bishop, R. S. (1990b, Summer). Mirrors, windows, and sliding glass doors. *Perspectives: Choosing and Using Books for the Classroom, 6*(3), ix-xi.

Bishop, R. S. (Ed.). (1994). *Kaleidoscope: A multicultural booklist for grades K–8.* Urbana, IL: National Council of Teachers of English.

Bishop, R. S. (2012, Fall). Reflections on the development of African American children's literature. *Journal of Children's Literature, 38*(2), 5–13.

Bodrova, E., & Leong, D. (1995). *Tools of the mind: The Vygotskian approach to early childhood education.* Englewood Cliffs, NJ: Merrill.

Britton, J. (1970). *Language and Learning.* London: Penguin.

Bruner, J. S. (1983). *Child's talk: Learning to use language.* London: W.W. Norton & Co.

Carey, S., & Bartlett, E. (1978). Acquiring a single new word. Proceedings of the Stanford Child Language Conference, 15, 17–29.

Carter, R., Aldridge. S., Page. M., & Parker, S. (2014). The human brain book. New York: DK Publishing.

Chomsky, C. (1971). Write first, read later. *Childhood Education, 47*(6), 296–299.

Clay, M. M. (1975). *What did I write?: Beginning writing behaviour.* Portsmouth, NH: Heinemann.

Clay, M. M. (1991). *Becoming literate: The construction of inner control.* Portsmouth, NH: Heinemann.

Clay, M. M. (1991). Introducing a new storybook to young readers. *The Reading Teacher, 45*(4): 264–273.

Clay, M. M. (1993). *An observation survey of early literacy achievement.* Portsmouth, NH: Heinemann.

Clay, M. M. (1998). *By different paths to common outcomes.* York, ME: Stenhouse.

Clay, M. M. (2001). *Change over time in children's literacy development.* Portsmouth, NH: Heinemann.

Clay, M. M. (2004, Spring). Talking, reading, and writing. *Journal of Reading Recovery, 3*(2), 1–15.

Clay, M. M. (2005). *An observation survey of early literacy achievement.* Portsmouth, NH: Heinemann.

Clay, M. M. (2013). *An observation survey of early literacy achievement* (3rd ed.) Portsmouth, NH: Heinemann.

Clay, M. M. (2016). *Literacy lessons designed for individuals* (2nd ed.). Portsmouth, NH: Heinemann.

Coronel-Molina, S. (2003). Brian V. Street (Ed). Literacy and development: Ethnographic perspectives. *Language Policy,* 2, 3, 279–281.

Damasio, A. R. (1994). *Descartes' error: Emotion, reason and the human brain.* New York: Putnam's Sons.

Daniels, H. (2017). *The curious classroom.* Portsmouth, NH: Heinemann.

DeFord, D. (2002). Interactive read-aloud: Supporting and expanding strategies for comprehension (pp. 211–224). In G. S. Pinnell & P. L. Scharer (Eds.). *Teaching for comprehension in reading, grades K–2.* New York: Scholastic.

Delpit, L. (1988). The silenced dialogue: Power and pedagogy in educating other people's children. *Harvard Educational Review 58,* 3: 280–298.

Dewey, J. (1916/2009). *Democracy and education.* Hollywood, CA: Simon and Brown.

Diaz, R. M., C. J. Neal, & M. Amaya-Williams. (1990). "The Social Origins of Self-regulation." In *Vygotsky and education,* ed. L. C. Moll. New York: Cambridge University Press.

Dufour, R., Dufour, R., Eaker, R., & Karhanek, G. (2004). *Whatever it takes: How professional learning communities respond when kids don't learn,* Bloomington, IN: Solution Tree.

Dyson, A. H. (2003). *The brothers and sisters learn to write: Popular literacies in childhood and school cultures.* New York: Teachers College Press.

Dyson, A. H. (2008). Staying in the (curricular) lines: Practice constraints and possibilities in childhood writing. *Written Communication,* 25, 119–160.

Eaker, R., Dufour, R., & Dufour, R. (2002). *Getting started: Reculturing schools to become professional learning communities,* Bloomington, IN: Solution Tree.

Fisher, B., & Medvic, E. F. (2000). *Perspectives on shared reading: Planning and practice.* Portsmouth, NH: Heinemann.

Fisher, C. J., & Terry, C. A. (1990). *Children's language and the language arts.* Needham Heights, MA: Allyn & Bacon.

Fisher, D., Frey, N., & Lapp, D. (2008). Shared readings: Modeling comprehension, vocabulary, text structures, and text features for older readers. *The Reading Teacher, 61*(7), 548–556.

Fletcher, R. (1996). *Breathing in, breathing out: Keeping a writer's notebook.* Portsmouth, NH: Heinemann.

Fletcher, R. (2015). *Making nonfiction from scratch.* Portland, ME: Stenhouse Publishers.

Fletcher, R. (2017). *The writing teacher's companion: Embracing choice, voice, purpose, and play.* New York: Scholastic.

Fletcher, R., & Portalupi, J. (2001). *Writing workshop: The essential guide*. Portsmouth, NH: Heinemann.

Fountas, I. C., & Pinnell, G. S. (1996). *Guided reading: Good first teaching for all children*. Portsmouth, NH: Heinemann.

Fountas, I. C., & Pinnell, G. S. (1999). *Matching books to readers: Using leveled books in guided reading, K–3*. Portsmouth, NH: Heinemann.

Fountas, I. C., & Pinnell, G. S. (2001). *Guiding readers and writers (Grades 3–6): Teaching comprehension, genre, and content literacy*. Portsmouth, NH: Heinemann.

Fountas, I. C., & Pinnell, G. S. (2002). *Leveled books for readers grades 3–6: A companion volume to Guiding readers and writers*. Portsmouth, NH: Heinemann.

Fountas, I. C., & Pinnell, G. S. (2004). *Word study lessons: phonics, spelling, and vocabulary, grade 3*. Portsmouth, NH: Heinemann.

Fountas, I. C., & Pinnell, G. S. (2006). *Teaching for comprehending and fluency: Thinking, talking, and writing about reading, K–8*. Portsmouth, NH: Heinemann.

Fountas, I. C., & Pinnell, G. S. (2012a). *Genre study: Teaching with fiction & nonfiction books*. Portsmouth, NH: Heinemann.

Fountas, I. C., & Pinnell, G. S. (2012b). *Prompting Guide*. Portsmouth, NH: Heinemann.

Fountas, I. C., & Pinnell, G. S. (2016a). *Benchmark assessment system 1, 3rd edition, grades K–2, levels A–N*. Portsmouth, NH: Heinemann.

Fountas, I. C., & Pinnell, G. S. (2016b). *Benchmark assessment system 2, 3rd edition, grades 3–8, levels L–Z*. Portsmouth, NH: Heinemann.

Fountas, I. C., & Pinnell, G. S. (2016c). *The continuum of literacy learning: Grades PreK–8*. Portsmouth, NH: Heinemann.

Fountas, I. C., & Pinnell, G. S. (2016d). *Guided reading: Responsive teaching across the grades*. Portsmouth, NH. Heinemann.

Fountas, I. C., & Pinnell, G. S. (2017a). *Benchmark assessment system*. Portsmouth, NH: Heinemann.

Fountas, I. C., & Pinnell, G. S. (2017b). *Comprehensive phonics, spelling, and word study guide, preK–8*. Portsmouth, NH: Heinemann.

Fountas, I. C., & Pinnell, G. S. (2017c). *The Fountas and Pinnell literacy continuum, expanded edition: A tool for assessment, planning, and teaching PreK–8*. Portsmouth, NH: Heinemann.

Fountas, I. C., & Pinnell, G. S. (2017d). *Guided reading: Responsive teaching across the grades, 2d Ed*. Portsmouth, NH: Heinemann.

Fox, M. (2001). *Reading magic: Why reading aloud to our children will change their lives forever*. San Diego, CA: Harcourt.

Fox, M. (2013). What next in the read aloud battle? Win or lose. *The Reading Teacher, (67)*1, 4–8.

Frey, N., & Fisher, D. (2013). *Rigorous reading: 5 access points for comprehending complex texts*. Thousand Oaks, CA: Corwin Press.

Fullan, M. (2014). *The principal: Three keys to maximizing impact*, San Francisco, CA: Jossey-Bass.

Ganske, K. (2014). *Word journeys: Assessment-guided phonics, spelling, and vocabulary instruction* (2nd ed.). New York: Guilford Press.

Gibson, S. A., & Scharer, P. L. (2001). "She can read them by herself!": Parents and teachers respond to a kindergarten school-home literacy project. In J. V. Hoffman, D. L. Schallert, C. M. Fairbanks, J. Worthy, & B. Maloch (eds.), *50th Yearbook of the National Reading Conference* (pp. 238–247). Chicago, IL: National Reading Conference.

Goodwin, P. (Ed.). (2011). *The literate classroom*. New York: Routledge.

Gopnik, A. (2016). *Top of Form The gardener and the carpenter: What the new science of child development tells us about the relationship between parents and children*. New York: Farrar, Straus, and Giroux.

Gopnik, A., Meltzoff, A., & Kuhl, P. K. (1999). *The scientist in the crib*. New York: Morrow.

Graham, S., Berninger, V., Weintraub, N., & Schafer, W. (1998). Development of handwriting speed and legibility in grades 1–9. *Journal of Educational Research, 92*, 42–57.

Graves, M. (2016). *The vocabulary book*: *Learning and instruction* (2nd ed.). New York: Teachers College Press.

Graves, M. F., & Watts-Taffe, S. M. (2002). The place of word consciousness in a research-based vocabulary program. In A. E. Farstrup and S. J. Samuels (Eds.), *What research has to say about reading instruction* (pp. 140–165). Newark, DE: International Reading Association.

Greenspan, S. (1997). *The growth of the mind*. Reading, MA: Addison Wesley.

Gustafson, K., & Bennett, W. (1999). *Issues and difficulties in promoting learner reflection: Results from a three-year study*. Retrieved from http://it.coe.uga.edu/~kgustafs/document/promoting.html. June 1, 2016.

Hargreaves, A., & Fullan, M. (2012). *Professional capital: Transforming teaching in every school*. New York: Teachers College Press.

Harris, T. L., & Hodges, R. E. (Eds.). (1995). *The literacy dictionary: The vocabulary of reading and writing*. Newark, DE: International Reading Association.

Hart, B., & Risley, T. R. (1995). *Meaningful differences in the everyday experience of young American children*. Baltimore, MD: Paul H. Brookes.

Henderson, E. H. (1990). *Teaching spelling* (2nd ed.). Boston, MA: Houghton Mifflin.

Henry, T. (2008). Story structure as a support to meaning making. In Scharer, P., & Pinnell, G. S. *Guiding K–3 writers to independence: The new essentials* (pp. 132–140). Columbus, OH: The Ohio State University.

Holdaway, D. (1979). *The foundations of literacy*. Sydney: Ashton Scholastic.

Hoyt, L. (2017). *Conventions and craft, grade 3: A full year of literature-based micro-workshops to build essential understandings for grammar, sentence structure & word study*. New York: Scholastic Professional.

Jensen, E. (2009). *Teaching with poverty in mind. What being poor does to kids' brains and what schools can do about it*. Alexandria, VA: ASCD.

Johnston, P., Woodside-Jiron, H., & Day, J. (2001). Teaching and Learning Literate Epistemologies. *Journal of Educational Psychology, 93*, 1.

Johnston, P. (2004). *Choice words: How our language affects children's learning*. Portland, ME: Stenhouse Publishers.

Johnston, P. (2012). *Opening minds: Using language to change minds*. Portland, ME: Stenhouse Publishers.

Karolides, N. J. (1999, November). Theory and practice: An interview with Louise M. Rosenblatt. *Language Arts, 77*(2), 158–170.

Kiefer, B. (1982). The response of primary children to picture books. Unpublished doctoral dissertation, The Ohio State University, Columbus, OH.

Kiefer, B. Z., & Tyson, C. A. (2014). *Charlotte Huck's children's literature: A brief guide*. New York: McGraw-Hill.

LeDoux, J. (1996). *The emotional brain.* New York: Simon & Schuster.

LeDoux, J. (2015). *Anxious: Using the brain to understand and treat fear and anxiety.* New York: Viking.

Lewis, C. (2006). *Literary practices as social acts: Power, status, and cultural norms in the classroom.* New York: Routledge.

Lindfors, J. W. (1999). *Child's inquiry: Using language to make sense of the world.* New York: Teachers College Press.

Lyons, C. A., & Pinnell, G. S. (2001). *Systems for change in literacy education: A guide to professional development.* Portsmouth, NH: Heinemann.

Mann, K., Kaplan, J., Damasio, H., & Damasio, A. (2013). Neural convergence and divergence in the mammalian cerebral cortex: from experimental neuroanatomy to functional neuroimaging. *J Comp Neurol. Dec 15; 521*(18): 10.1002/cne.23408.

McCarrier, A., Pinnell, G. S., & Fountas, I. C. (2000). *Interactive writing: How language & literacy come together, K–2.* Portsmouth, NH: Heinemann.

McCarthey, S., & Moje, E. (2002). Conversations: Identity matters. *Reading Research Quarterly, 37*(2), pp. 228–237.

McTighe, J., & Wiggins, G. (2015). *Solving 25 problems in unit design: How do I refine my units to enhance student learning?* Alexandria, VA: Association for Supervision & Curriculum Development (ASCD).

Michaels, S., O'Connor, C., & Resnick, L. B. (2008). Deliberative discourse idealized and realized: Accountable talk in the classroom and in civic life. Published online: November 2007: Springer Science+Business Media.

Moje, E. B., & Luke, A. (2009). Literacy-and-identity: Examining the metaphors in history and contemporary research. *Reading Research Quarterly, 44*(4), pp. 415–437.

Mraz, M., Algozzine, B., & Kissel, B. (2009). *The literacy coach's companion preK–3.* Thousand Oaks, CA: Corwin Press.

Muhammad, A. (2009). *Transforming school culture: How to overcome staff division.* Bloomington, IN: Solution Tree.

Nystrand, M., Wu, L. L., Gamoran, A., Zeiser, S., & Long, D. A. (2003). Questions in time: Investigating the structure and dynamics of unfolding classroom discourse. *Discourse Processes, 35*(2): 135–200.

Peterson, C., Jesso, B., & McCabe, A. (1999). Encouraging narratives in preschoolers: An intervention study. *Journal of Child Language, 26*(1), 49–67.

Pinnell, G. S., & Fountas, I. C. (1998). *Word matters: Teaching phonics and spelling in the reading/writing classroom.* Portsmouth, NH: Heinemann.

Pinnell, G. S., & Fountas, I. C. (2003). *Phonics lessons: Letters, words, and how they work, grade K.* Portsmouth, NH: Heinemann.

Pinnell, G. S., & Fountas, I. C. (2003). *Phonics lessons: Letters, words, and how they work, grade 1.* Portsmouth, NH: Heinemann.

Pinnell, G. S., & Fountas, I. C. (2003). *Phonics lessons: Letters, words, and how they work, grade 2.* Portsmouth, NH: Heinemann.

Reeves, D. B. (2010). *Transforming professional development into student results.* Alexandria VA: ASCD.

Rogers, R., & Elias, M. (2012). Storied selves: A critical discourse analysis of young children's literate identifications. *Journal of Early Childhood Literacy 12*(3), 259–292.

Rosenblatt, L. M. (1978/1994). *The reader, the text, the poem: The transactional theory of the literary work.* Carbondale, IL: Southern Illinois University Press.

Rosenblatt, L. M. (1995). *Literature as exploration* (5th ed.). New York: Noble and Noble. (Original work published 1938).

Rosenblatt, L. M. (1998, Fall). Readers, texts, authors. *Transactions of the Charles S. Peirce Society, 34*(4), 885–921.

Sarris, G. (1993). Keeping slug woman alive: The challenge of reading in a reservation classroom. In J. Boyarin (Ed.). *The ethnography of reading* (pp. 257–271). Berkeley, CA: University of California Press.

Scharer, P. L., & Pinnell, G. S. (Eds.) (2008). *Guiding K–3 writers to independence: The new essentials.* New York: Scholastic.

Sipe, L. R. (1999, Summer). Children's response to literature: Author, text, reader, context. *Theory into Practice, 38*(3), 120–129.

Sipe, L. R. (2000). "Those two gingerbread boys could be brothers": How children use intertextual connections during storybook readalouds. *Children's Literature in Education, 31*(2), 73–90.

Sipe, L. R. (2008). *Storytime: Young children's literary understanding in the classroom.* New York: Teachers College Press.

Stahl, K. A. D., & Bravo, M. A. (2010). Contemporary classroom vocabulary assessment. *The Reading Teacher, 63*(7), 566–578.

Tharp, R. G., & Gallimore, R. (1988). *Rousing minds to life: Teaching, learning and schooling in social context.* Cambridge, UK: Cambridge University Press.

Trelease, J. (1989). *The new read aloud handbook.* New York: Penguin.

Trelease, J. (2013). *The read aloud handbook* (7th ed.). New York: Penguin Books.

Vygotsky, L. S. (1978). *Mind in society: The development of higher psychological processes.* Cambridge, MA: Harvard University Press.

Vygotsky, L. S. (1986). *Thought and language.* Cambridge, MA: MIT Press.

Vygotsky, L. S. (1987). Thinking and speech. In L. S. Vygotsky, *Collected works 1*, 39–285. http://blog.fountasandpinnell.com/post/a-level-is-a-teacher-s-tool-not-a-child-s-label.

Waters, K. C. (2014). Using shared reading and close reading to bridge intervention and the Common Core. *Connecticut Reading Association Journal, 2*(2), 9–22.

Wiggins, G., & McTighe, J. (2005). *Understanding by design, expanded* (2nd ed.) Alexandria, VA: Association for Supervision & Curriculum Development (ASCD).

Wilhelm, J. D. (2007). *Engaging readers & writers with inquiry: Promoting deep understandings in language arts & the content areas with guiding questions.* New York: Scholastic.

Williams, K. C., & Hierck, T. (2015). *Starting a movement: Building culture from the inside out in professional learning communities.* Bloomington: IN: Solution Tree.

Wood, D. (1988). *How children think and learn: The social contexts of cognitive development.* Cambridge, MA: Basil Blackwell, Inc.

Wood, D., Bruner, G. S., & Ross, G. (1976). The role of tutoring in problem-solving. *Journal of Child Psychology and Psychiatry* (pp. 89–100).

Woodside-Jiron, H., & Day, J. (2001). Teaching and Learning Literate Epistemologies. *Journal of Educational Psychology, 93*, 1.

CHILDREN'S BOOKS CITED

Adler, D. A. & Byrd, S. (1992). *A picture book of Harriet Tubman*. New York: Holiday House.

Agard, J. & Nichols, G. (1995). *No hickory no dickory no dock: Caribbean nursery rhymes*. Cambridge, MA: Candlewick.

Ahlberg, A. & Ahlberg, J. (1979). *Each peach pear plum*. New York: Viking.

Antony, S. (2016). *I'll wait, Mr. Panda*. New York: Scholastic.

Bandy, M.S. & Stein, E. (2015). *Granddaddy's turn: A journey to the ballot box*. Illus. J. E. Ransome. New York: Scholastic.

Bennett-Armistead, S. (2015). *Animals everywhere*. Los Angeles, CA: Hameray Publishing Group.

Bennett-Armistead, S. (2015). *Growing things*. Los Angeles, CA: Hameray Publishing Group.

Bergmann, A. (2017). *Starry the giraffe*. New York: Simon & Schuster.

Bildner, P. (2015). *Marvelous Cornelius: Hurricane Katrina and the spirit of New Orleans*. San Francisco, CA: Chronicle.

Brown, D. (2015). *Aaron and Alexander: The most famous duel in American history*. New York: Scholastic.

Brown, M.W. (2002). *Bonsoir lune/ Goodnight moon*. Illus. C. Hurd. New York: Harper.

Bunting, E. (1994). *Sunshine home*. New York: Clarion.

Bunting, E. (2000). Illus. T. Rand. *The memory string*. New York: Houghton Mifflin.

Byrne, R. (2015). *We're in the wrong book!* New York: Scholastic.

Cachemaille, C. (1996). *Sam's mask*. Wellington, NZ: Learning Media Limited.

Carle, E. (1969). *The very hungry caterpillar*. New York: Philomel.

Cowley, J. (1983). *Greedy cat*. New York: Richard C. Owen.

Cowley, J. (1997). *Greedy cat is hungry*. Wellington, NZ: Learning Media Limited.

Cowley, J. (1986). *The little red hen*. Auckland, NZ: Heinemann Education.

Cowley, J. (1986). *Splish splash!* Auckland, NZ: Heinemann Education.

Cowley, J. (2012). *Wishy-washy ice cream*. Illus. P. Webb. Los Angeles, CA: Hameray Publishing Group.

Cowley, J. (2012). *Wishy-washy sleep*. Illus. P. Webb. Los Angeles, CA: Hameray Publishing Group.

Clyne, M. & Griffiths, R. (1999). *Trash or treasure*. Littleton, MA: Sundance.

Cullinan, B.E. (Ed) (1996). *A jar of tiny stars: Poems by NCTE award-winning poets*. Honesdale, PA: Boyds Mills.

Cyrus, K. (2017). *Shake a leg, egg!* New York: Scholastic.

Davis, A. & Tarlton, J. (2001). *The lion and the mouse*. Aukland, NZ: Shortland Publications.

Dyckman, A. & Campbell, K. G. (2013). *Tea party rules*. New York: Viking Book.

Dyckman, A. & OHora, Z. (2015). *Wolfie the bunny*. New York: Little, Brown and Company.

Dyckman, A. & OHora, Z. (2016). *Horrible bear!* New York: Little, Brown and Company.

Dyckman, A. & Climo, L. (2017). *You don't want a unicorn!* New York: Little, Brown and Company.

Dyckman, A. & OHora, Z. (2017). *Read the book, lemmings!* New York: Little, Brown and Company.

Esbensen, B. J. (1986). *Words with wrinkled knees*. New York: Thomas Y. Crowell.

Fox, M. (1984). Illus. J. Vivas. *Wilfrid Gordon McDonald Partridge*. LaJolla, CA: Kane Miller.

Fox, M. & Staub, L. (2006). *Whoever you are*. Boston: HMH Books for Young Readers.

Francis, J. (1995). *A retold tale: The three little pigs*. Columbus, OH: The Ohio State University.

Fried, M.D. (1999). *Zoo animals*. Columbus, OH: The Ohio State University.

Fritz, J. (1992). *George Washington's mother*. New York: Grosset & Dunlap.

Fulton, K. (2017). *Long may she wave: The true story of Caroline Pickersgill and her star-spangled creation*. Illus. H. Berry. New York: Simon & Schuster.

Galdone, P. (1970). *The three little pigs*. New York: Houghton Mifflin.

Gibbons, G. (2002). *Tell me tree: All about trees for kids*. New York: Little, Brown.

GrandPré, M. (2016). *Cleonardo: The little inventor*. New York: Scholastic.

Hatkoff, C., Hatkoff, J., & Hatkoff, I. (2017). *Cecil's pride: The true story of a lion king*. New York: Scholastic.

Hatkoff, I., Hatkoff, C., Kahumbu, P., & Greste, P. (2006). *Owen & Mzee: The true story of a remarkable friendship*. New York: Scholastic.

Hayes, J. (2013). *Don't say a word, Mamá*. Illus. E.A. Valencia. New York: Scholastic.

Hoffman, M. (1991). *Amazing Grace*. New York: Dial.

Higgins, R. T. (2017). *Be quiet!* Los Angeles: Hyperion.

Hyman, T. (1983). *Little red riding hood*. New York: Holiday House.

Jamison, G. R. (2011). *My loose tooth*. Illus. A. Johns. Los Angeles, CA: Hameray Publishing Group.

Johnson, A. (1990). *Do like Kyla*. New York: Orchard.

Johnston, T. (2004). *The harmonica*. Watertown, MA: Charlesbridge

Keats, E. J. (1968). *A Letter to Amy*. New York: The Penguin Group.

Kimmel, E. (1988). *Anansi and the moss-covered rock*. New York: Holiday House.

Lê, M. (2016). *Let me finish!* Illus. I. Roxas. New York: Scholastic.

Levine, E. (2007). *Henry's freedom box: A true story of the Underground Railroad*. New York: Scholastic.

Lobel, A. (1970). *Frog and Toad are friends*. New York: HarperCollins.

Lowry, L. (2009). *Crow call*. New York: Scholastic.

Lowry, L. (1993). *The giver*. Boston, MA: Houghton Mifflin.

MacLachlan, P. (2017). *Someone like me*. Illus. C. Sheban. New York: Roaring Brook Press.

Marshall, J. (1974). *George and Martha*. Boston: HMH Books for Young Readers.

Martin, C. (1993). *My bike*. Willington, NZ: Learning Media Limited.

McCarrier, A. (1995). *Growing a pumpkin*. Columbus, OH: The Ohio State University.

Micklos, J. (2006). *No boys allowed: Poems about brothers and sisters*. Honesdale, PA: Boyds Mills.

Munson, D., & King, T. C. (2000). *Enemy pie*. San Francisco: Chronicle Books.

Naden, N. (1989). *Dad didn't mind at all*. Crystal Lake, IL: Rigby.

Numeroff, L. J. (1985). *If you give a mouse a cookie*. New York: HarperCollins.

O'Neill, A. & Huliska-Beith, L. (2002). *The recess queen*. New York: Scholastic.

Opie, I. (1999). *Here comes Mother Goose*. Cambridge, MA: Candlewick Press.

Palatini, M. (1997). *Piggie pie!* New York: HMH Books for Young Children.

Parker, J. (1989). *Emma's problem*. Crystal Lake, IL. Rigby.

Parkes, B. and Smith, J. (1986). *The enormous watermelon*. Crystal Lake, IL: Rigby.

Pinnell, G. S. (1996). *Mugs*. Columbus, OH: The Ohio State University.

Polacco, P. (2015). *An A from Miss Keller*. New York: Scholastic.

Polacco, P. (2008). *For the love of autumn*. New York: Philomel Books.

Polacco, P. (1994). *Pink and Say*. New York: Philomel Books.

Polacco, P. (2006). *Rotten Richie and the ultimate dare*. New York: Scholastic.

Raczka, B. (2016). *Wet cement: A mix of concrete poems*. New York: Roaring Book Press.

Randell, B. (1994). *The lion and the rabbit*. Crystal Lake, IL: Rigby.

Rappaport, D. & Collier, B. (2001). *Martin's big words: The life of Dr. Martin Luther King, Jr.* New York: Hyperion Books for Children.

Reynolds, A. (2017). *Nerdy birdy tweets*. Illus. M. Davies. New York: Roaring Brook Press.

Reynolds, P. H. (2016). *Playing from the heart*. New York: Scholastic.

Shannon, D. (2000). *The rain came down*. New York: Scholastic.

Shaw, C. (1947). *It looked like split milk*. New York: Harper & Row.

Sidman, J. (2011). *Swirl by swirl: Spirals in nature*. Illus. B. Krommes. Boston: Houghton Mifflin.

Simon, S. (2006). *Weather*. New York: HarperCollins Publishers.

Sookocheff, C. (2017). *Wet*. New York: Henry Holt and Company.

Spillsbury, L. & Spillsbury, R. (2010). *Sweeping tsunamis (Awesome forces of nature)*. Portsmouth, NH: Heinemann.

Sweet, M. (2016). *Some writer! The story of E.B. White*. New York: Houghton Mifflin Harcourt.

Van Allsburg, C. (1986). *The stranger*. Boston: HMH Books for Young Readers.

VanDerwater, A. L. (2016). *Every day birds*. Illus. D. Metrano. New York: Scholastic.

Waddell, M. (1992). *Owl babies*. Cambridge, MA: Candlewick Press.

Watts, J. (2016). *A piece of home*. Illus. H. Yum. New York: Scholastic.

Wick, W. (1997). *A drop of water: A book of science and wonder*. New York: Scholastic.

Willems, M. (2010). *City dog, country frog*. Illus. J. J. Muth. New York: Hyperion.

Woodson, J. & Lewis, E. B. (2001). *The other side*. New York: Putnam.

Yolen, J. (1987). *Owl moon*. New York: Philomel Books.

Yuly, T. (2017). *The jelly bean tree*. New York: Macmillan.

INDEX